Acclaim for Da

Shooting the Moon

The True Story of an American Manhunt Unlike Any Other, Ever

"One of the wilder and — until now — least-known stories in modern American history. . . . Like the best of thrillers, this is a tale of betrayal and murder, of drug-smuggling and arms-dealing, of a powerful international crime syndicate. . . . In this gripping book, David Harris brings us the behind-the-scenes account of what really happened, and why nothing like it may ever happen again." —*African Sun Times Review of Books*

"A gripping prosecutor procedural."
— Steve Weinberg, *Atlanta Journal-Constitution*

"Harris is terrific at chronicling the bizarre events that make up this story. . . . This exhaustively researched, brilliantly paced investigation is an indictment of what Harris believes is the U.S. government's quixotic, wasteful zeal in pursuing Noriega." — Connie Fletcher, *Booklist*

"An accessible, eye-opening account of one of the murkiest episodes in recent history. . . . The story is told colorfully, with lots of tough-guy cop-talk, scummy informers, and brief cutaways to beleaguered wives. It is unquestionably readable." —*Kirkus Reviews*

"A fascinating and highly readable book."
— Karen Sandlin Silverman, *Library Journal*

"A smartly rendered, admirably detailed exploration of the bizarre, violent road from Iran-Contra to the prosecution of Panamanian General Manuel Noriega. . . . Harris persuasively argues that the dictator's cartel business overlapped with CIA incursions, primarily against the Nicaraguan Sandinista government. . . . Harris's investigative epic of government malfeasance and retribution reads like an international thriller." —*Publishers Weekly*

Also by David Harris

Our War

The Last Stand

The League

Dreams Die Hard

The Last Scam

I Shoulda Been Home Yesterday

Goliath

SHOOTING THE MOON

THE TRUE STORY OF AN AMERICAN MANHUNT UNLIKE ANY OTHER, EVER

DAVID HARRIS

LITTLE, BROWN AND COMPANY
BOSTON NEW YORK LONDON

Originally published in hardcover by Little, Brown and Company, April 2001
First Back Bay paperback edition, June 2002

Library of Congress Cataloging-in-Publication Data

Harris, David.
Shooting the moon : the true story of an American manhunt unlike any other, ever / by David Harris.—1st ed.
p. cm.
Includes index.
ISBN 0-316-34080-4 (hc) / 0-316-15480-6 (pb)
1. Noriega, Manuel Antonio, 1934– 2. Narcotics dealers—Panama—Biography. 3. Drug traffic—Investigation—United States—Case studies. 4. Arrest—Panama. 5. Prosecution—United States—Case studies. 6. Panama—Foreign relations—United States. 7. United States—Foreign relations—Panama. I. Title
HV8079.N3 H37 2001
972.8705'3'092—dc21
[B]
00-065498

10 9 8 7 6 5 4 3 2 1

Q-FF

Designed by Fearn Cutler de Vicq

Printed in the United States of America

CONTENTS

PART ONE

THE PRELUDE

CHAPTER I

THE GENERAL IN MIAMI, 2000

— 1 —

One of a kind, this story begins at its end, in the here and now of Miami, where the afternoon rain sizzles off the pavement and cruise ships dock for weekends on Biscayne Bay, flags limp, smothered in warmth on all but the very worst of days, the air heavy with the breath of swamps long since paved over; Miami, jumping-off place for America's hemispheric underbelly, where all directions point south, the evenings end with breakfast, and the fast lane runs bumper-to-bumper from the beach to the jungle and back; Miami, no holds barred, where if it weren't for "under the table," there would be no table at all; Miami, nose open and packing heat, where twenty-dollar bills are moved around town by the suitcaseful and almost anything goes as far as it is able and not much farther. Miami, where this story started and finished and without which, of course, this would be no story at all.

Here, south and west of Miami International Airport, the Orange Bowl, Coconut Grove, and the Policemen's Hall of Fame, inland, right next door to the Metropolitan Zoo, General Manuel Antonio Noriega, sixty-five years old, former commander in chief of the Panama Defense Force, identified on his Interpol arrest warrant as "de facto ruler of Panama," is confined in the Miami Federal Correctional Institution, separated from the nearest public thoroughfare by a dozen locked doors, a double Cyclone fence, and several rows of impenetrable razor wire. Rarely visible even to the other inmates, the General lives in a single-story building adjacent to the prison hospital, in his own private suite of four converted cells, with its own private fifteen-foot-square patio where he grows vegetables in a pot and takes the morning sun, sweat running into his collar, sometimes wearing his uniform, sometimes not.

General Manuel Antonio Noriega is the only officially recognized prisoner of war currently held by the United States of America under the rules of the Geneva Convention on Prisoners of War and the only such military prisoner ever to serve simultaneously a prison sentence meted out and administered according to the strictures of American civilian law. The General's unique status entitles him to living conditions comparable to the quarters provided a soldier of his rank in the United States Army, as well as the right to dress in his Panama Defense Force regalia, including his general's shoulder boards, even though the Panama Defense Force has long since ceased to exist. It also entitles him to regular visits from the International Red Cross and to a monthly stipend of some sixty dollars from the government of the United States, which crushed the Panama Defense Force and captured him in the first place.

There is no other prisoner in the federal prison system treated quite the same way.

Nonetheless, the General's story ends as all prisoners' stories do, over and over again, day in and day out, always the same way — his fate long since decided, even though the General himself was little more than a bystander to much of what eventually brought him to this place.

And, of course, by the end of this once crowded story, he is the only one left in it, a famously ugly little bastard from the hardscrabble dead end of the Panama City slums — with a face that looks like somebody lit it on fire and then extinguished the blaze with an ice pick — now an American icon, anointed by combat, forcibly transplanted, and stuck in time, off the tourist track, just a left turn going south on the 15000 block of South West 137th Avenue, virtually invisible to the America that once put a million-dollar bounty on his head and hunted him down because he was, in the words of the commander of the 20,000-man army sent to arrest him, "a truly evil man" who wore red underwear "to ward off the evil eye."

The General's eventual sentence for violating nine counts of the United States Criminal Code and the Racketeer Influenced and Corrupt Organizations Act was reduced on appeal in 1999 from its original forty years to thirty and, so far, he has finished almost a decade of those thirty here in his private cell block next to the prison hospital, watching his television, riding his stationary bicycle, and taking escorted walks on the correctional institution's grounds when the rest of the inmate population is locked down and can get no closer than a distant view of him out a few barred windows, his shortness almost lost in the heat ripples and muggy sightlines, flanked by whatever jailers have been assigned to keep him under close watch. Back in his private cell block, the General has his own phone, on which he can only call out, and the guards listen to all his calls except those to his attorneys. He talks mostly with his wife and his three daughters, as well as his girlfriend and her family, often patching through to Panama or the Dominican Republic on his attorneys' switchboard to get a little privacy. He occasionally signs notes with his initials, MAN, and the designation, "POW 0001."

None of this is expected to change soon.

— 2 —

The General did, however, leave the Miami Federal Correctional Institution briefly in August of 1992, during Hurricane Andrew, when he had been imprisoned just two and a half years. Hurricane Andrew, eventually judged the single most damaging natural disaster in American history, was headed straight for greater Miami, so the Bureau of Prisons temporarily evacuated the correctional institution as part of its emergency preparedness plan, moving its Miami prisoners out of the storm's path and on to safer institutions.

At the time, the General was driven to the federal penitentiary in Atlanta, alone in a Jeep Wagoneer with two United States marshals. The three of them rode north, the General in the backseat, making occasional stops for fast food, and, along the way, became momentary chums. The General had an easy presence and proved a pleasant traveling companion. His halting English was just enough to get along in a very rudimentary way, though he understood more than he was able to say.

Eventually, the conversation shifted to an incident in late 1989, some three weeks before the General's arrest, when he'd been filmed by American television crews at a rally in Panama City, taunting the gringos, pounding his chest, and brandishing a machete. One of the marshals asked flat out what in the world had possessed the General to do such a crazy-ass thing as that?

The General assumed a sheepish expression. "I guess I fucked up," he said.

By all accounts, General Manuel Antonio Noriega remains a proud man, despite his circumstances.

Proud that, having started with nothing on Panama City's meanest streets, he came to own five houses in his homeland, an apartment in Paris, and another house in Tel Aviv, not to mention a fleet of cars and more than a few airplanes, as well as dozens of Panamanian businesses. And, while proud that he rose so far to own so much, the General is equally proud that he was so hard to pry loose from his perch when that time came; proud to have done all the things he did for the United States, even if they refused to credit his help, yet proud also to have ended his military career as the gringos' worst nightmare, if only for those last two years before his imprisonment; proud that it took so many of them finally to run him to the ground.

And he is proud, above all else, for having ended up one of a kind.

In the latter, at least, he is correct. Of all the thousands of rulers, potentates, strongmen, juntas, and warlords the Americans have dealt with in all corners of the world, General Manuel Antonio Noriega is the only one the Americans came after like this. Just once in its 225 years of formal national existence has the United States ever invaded another country and carried its ruler back to the United States to face trial and imprisonment for violations of American law committed on that ruler's own native foreign turf.

And the General, of course, is that once.

The General has always believed that the reason for all that befell him was the Panama Canal and the United States' reluctance to hand it over to Panama as the treaty between the two nations required. However accurate that accusation may be, it doesn't go very far toward explaining what actually transpired to reduce the General from "de facto ruler of Panama," highest man on the totem pole, to MAN, POW 0001, growing vegetables in a jailhouse pot and sometimes watching Spanish-language soaps when he gets bored.

In truth, the General is most likely still a little unsure himself. He never did have much understanding of how the gringos work and, though this is his story, it is just his luck that it finally turned out to be a story far more about the Americans who brought him down and how they did something never done before or since, than it would be a story about the General himself.

And now, as such, it can finally be told.

CHAPTER 2

THE FIRST PRECONDITION

— 1 —

There were three essential preconditions to *United States v. Manuel Antonio Noriega,* the legal construction which would eventually yield the General's one-of-a-kind capture and imprisonment. And each of those three was indispensable to this case ever being undertaken.

The first precondition, of course, was that *the law had to be on the General's trail already.*

Which is how this story commenced, during the summer of 1985, in a suburban office park out among the Wal-Mart fringes of Greater Miami, between the Palmetto Expressway and the Doral Country Club, where the Drug Enforcement Administration maintained its Miami Divisional Office, covering the federal law-enforcement jurisdiction known as the Southern District of Florida, by then the hottest battleground in America's War on Drugs. A trafficking hub and wholesale distribution center, Miami was what the narcs called "Elephant Country," where all the big boys in the business roamed, making money hand over fist.

And in the summer of 1985, the long-ballyhooed war against these traffickers was accelerating toward a geometric escalation. President of the United States Ronald Reagan was about to issue a secret national security directive instructing his government to consider drug-trafficking a threat to the survival of the republic, opening the federal vaults to elevate total governmental expenditures for its suppression to more than ten billion dollars a year. Even then the DEA would be hard pressed to simply keep pace with the white powder flowing north, much less turn the tide. In 1980, perhaps forty metric tons of cocaine entered the United States. Four years later, that total had tripled. And four more years after that, it would almost triple again — an explosion of consumption that signified a new industrial age of cocaine, in which huge batches of the chemical were manufactured in Colombia, then moved to the United States in quantities that, at least for a moment, boggled even Miami's imagination. Where once the narcs crowed over seizing a kilo, now hundred-kilo confiscations were run-of-the-mill. During only fifteen days in January 1985, total cocaine seizures in the Southern District and the rest of the Florida jurisdictions overseen by the Miami Divisional Office equaled the entire amount seized in those same jurisdictions throughout all three hundred sixty-five days of 1981.

It was in the midst of this illicit tidal wave that the name of General Manuel Antonio Noriega first surfaced as a possible candidate for nine counts' worth of the United States Criminal Code and the Racketeer Influenced and Corrupt Organizations (RICO) statutes.

Though that was, in retrospect, a portentous moment, the shift of suspicion in the General's direction was the next closest thing to random when it actually happened. The General, of course, still professes to believe otherwise, convinced that what finally befell him was an enterprise hatched with full intention among the highest gringo echelons, but, in fact, there were no directives from on high which set this legal process under way.

In the summer of 1985, General Manuel Antonio Noriega was just one of hundreds of potential suspects identified at the ground level in the daily combat in the drug war raging around Miami, down where the DEA's rubber met the road. No one had been looking for the General until then. His extraordinarily singular outcome germinated from nothing more than standard investigative procedure, pursuing a thin lead stumbled upon in just one investigation among the dozens inherited by DEA Assistant Special Agent in Charge Kenny Kennedy when he transferred down to Elephant Country from headquarters in Washington, D.C.

— 2 —

Kenny Kennedy, forty-two, was on a roll at the time, still fifteen years from mandatory retirement but already a GS-15, last bureaucratic stop on the ladder before the Drug Enforcement Administration's executive "super grades." Kennedy had first "popped his cherry" as a street agent in

New York City for the old Federal Bureau of Narcotics, in which he'd enlisted after working his way through Seton Hall University at night. Kennedy was New Jersey to his core, a self-described "half mick, half polack," born on Saint Patrick's Day, raised in Jersey City, and now some five-and-a-half-feet worth of lumpy-looking white bread, except for his face, which was various shades of blotchy red and pink spreading outward from a meaty nose. And he knew as soon as he first touched down in the steamy Miami morning that he "wasn't gonna miss my fuckin' snow tires, not one fuckin' bit. This place was like fuckin' paradise."

In an organization bulging with egos sized XXL, Kennedy had always succeeded by making friends and keeping his edges soft, and he assumed when he arrived in Miami that he'd be doing somewhere between three and five years here before making his next promotion jump, the big one into executive status. He couldn't even imagine how wrong about his future he would turn out to be.

Kennedy settled easily into his role as one of the War on Drugs' major south Florida players, quick to laugh, quick to back the guys who worked for him. At the Miami office in those days, there were no other bureaucratic plateaus between the Assistant Special Agent in Charge and the Special Agent in Charge who ran the whole regional show, and there were only two ASACs altogether, one for administration and the other for enforcement operations. Kennedy now ran all of the latter, some five groups of special agents, his "boys" in narc shorthand, all four dozen or so on the loose in Elephant Country, looking for tracks.

The lead that first raised a mention of General Manuel Antonio Noriega was generated by Special Agent Danny Moritz, a former army commando who'd used an introduction from an undercover informant to infiltrate a nest of smugglers who hung around DIACSA, an aircraft brokerage and parts supply referred to conversationally as "die-a-kassa" and located in a warehouse on NW 12th Street near Miami International. One of DIACSA's frequent visitors was a Panamanian national named Floyd Carlton, who owned a flying service in Panama City and used his planes and pilots to fly coke to the United States out of Colombia, via Costa Rica, and to fly money back to Panama on the return trip, millions of dollars per load. The word among the hangers-on at the warehouse was that Floyd was connected in Panama "all the way to the top."

The big break in that summer's investigation of Carlton came when Danny Moritiz's snitch at DIACSA was offered a job off-loading four hundred kilos of cocaine that were to be flown north in a two-engine

Cessna driven by a jockey-sized pilot who had once been employed by the Panamanian air force and was now one of several airplane drivers who did loads for Floyd. Moritz managed to secure the Cessna's tail numbers in advance, so on the morning of September 23, 1985, U.S. Customs stalked the tiny pilot's flight with a wing of its own planes operating in tandem, only revealing themselves in the early light over Miami itself.

The way Kenny Kennedy told the story, it was at this point that this case dropped on him out of the sky, quite literally. "Right out of the fuckin' sky," in the middle of I-75 during his morning commute through Broward County. The boys he'd used to hang with back at Washington headquarters had actually predicted this kind of thing to Kenny while making fun on the eve of his departure for Miami, most of them talking out of the side of their heads over one beer or another. Cases just fell out of the air down there, they'd said, and Kennedy had laughed at them.

But then this one actually did, up between Miramar and Alligator Alley, "no bullshit, right out of the fuckin' sky. First," Kenny remembered, "I heard a call for assistance on the DEA radio band. One of the air group that had joined the hunt was a DEA helicopter that was ready to jump on the smuggler whenever he landed, but the chase had been goin' on for so long that the fuckin' chopper was running out of gas and had to break off to refuel. Then I heard this two-engine Cessna, right over my head, cruising low, looking for a place to put down quick. The rest was just like the fuckin' movies."

The tiny pilot was desperate to escape and made for a stretch of I-75 that crossed a sawgrass slough and was still under construction, thus free of ground traffic. Kenny slapped the flashing blue light onto the roof of his unmarked Oldsmobile and came barreling, pedal to the metal, toward the construction site where the Cessna was landing. That unfinished segment of interstate was blocked by steel drums and Do Not Cross barriers, but, Kenny recounted, "I sucked wind, kept my light flashing, and busted through. I was just praying that there was pavement on the other side and not some fuckin' sinkhole."

When Kennedy reached the Cessna — first law man on the scene — the plane's propellers were still turning and the pilot had disappeared out its open hatch and into the nearby swamp, leaving Floyd Carlton's airplane and four hundred kilos of cocaine parked in the middle of the unfinished freeway.

Kennedy plunged into the muck, hoping to follow the pilot's trail, but only managed to soak himself up to his armpits, stumble over a snake, and lose one of his shoes, sucked off by the ooze. The rest of the narcs arrived and organized a more complete search, but the tiny pilot eluded them by submerging and breathing through hollow reeds.

When Kennedy was finally back at the Miami office that afternoon, filing a form to cover his lost shoe, the fugitive pilot emerged from the swamp, hailed a bus to Miami International, and caught the next flight back to Panama City.

The Cessna's pilot didn't stay gone for long.

As 1986 began, the fugitive Panamanian was apprehended at a Customs post in the Los Angeles airport, trying to enter the United States, traveling tourist class on a commercial jet. Customs shipped their captive to Miami, where Kennedy and Moritz were waiting. The pilot was eager to cooperate and become a government witness, in exchange for a little help with his eventual prison sentence — the first of dozens of such deals cut in the course of the General's story.

This initial snitch said everybody in Panama who was involved in "the business" knew that Floyd Carlton and General Manuel Antonio Noriega were tight. He used to see them hanging around together all the time, out by the hanger Carlton kept at Paitilla airfield. He also said the General was a player in "the business" in his own right. The pilot claimed to have once flown several million dollars from the Medellín cocaine cartel in Colombia to Panama, stashed in sealed cartons that he was told were destined for the General, though he never gave them to the General in person.

It wasn't much to go on, but Kenny Kennedy now began using every opportunity that presented itself to bring this slim lead on the General to the attention of Dick Gregorie, the First Assistant United States Attorney for the Southern District of Florida and the second-highest-ranking prosecutor in the district. The two of them were old buddies from their days together on a New Jersey Organized Crime Strike Force more than a decade ago and Kennedy figured that this was a case perhaps only Dick Gregorie would be willing to make.

When the manhunt for General Manuel Antonio Noriega reached its final denouement some four years later — with smoke drifting off smoldering patches of Panama City and the early morning air full of helicopter clatter and the sounds of live ammo going off in the distance — six members of the American invasion force would kick in the door of one of the General's offices, hoping to place him under arrest. The General, of course, had long since fled, but the soldiers found $120,000 cash still on the premises, two decorated Christmas trees, assorted pornographic materials and sex toys, a collection of porcelain frogs, a framed picture of Adolf Hitler, a closet full of uniforms, a walk-in cigar humidor, and 110 pounds of tamale flour, which the invasion command would mistakenly identify to the international press as cocaine. The Americans would also discover an altar for black magic Santería worship upon which candles had been burned and animal entrails arrayed in hopes of bringing ill fortune to several people listed on an attached piece of paper.

Close to the top of this voodoo list was the name of Dick Gregorie, First Assistant United States Attorney for the Southern District of Florida.

From the time he joined the Miami United States Attorney's Office in 1982, Dick Gregorie, then thirty-five, had treated the War on Drugs as a personal jihad, living with his cases to the exclusion of just about anything else. The nation was at stake, he was fond of pointing out, and if they didn't turn the tide in Miami, chaos for the whole country wouldn't be far behind. In Gregorie's reckoning, his job was all about enforcing the social contract upon which the mass of Americans depended for the quality of their lives and defending it against those who sought to make the law for themselves. While he got on easily with his colleagues, "working for Dick," one of the assistant U.S. attorneys under him remembered, "you felt like you were on a mission from God."

Great-grandson of an Italian policeman whose son had immigrated to Boston and shortened the family name from "Giangregorio," the law was like a religion to Gregorie and he was like a priest toward it. Still single, Dick Gregorie was married to his calling. He even looked the part of a relentless champion of the penal code — still as fit as he'd been in his days as the Most Valuable Player on the Georgetown University baseball varsity, with a head that was bald and square and a jaw covered by a full beard, dark and cut close, he had the features of a cartoon guard dog. "Relentless" was the least that could be said about Gregorie. A lifelong diabetic, he routinely ignored his plummeting blood sugar levels and approaching hypoglycemia while transfixed by his own prosecutorial frenzy, and those who worked with him often carried pieces of candy with which to rescue him from possible physical collapse.

The strike force in New Jersey where he and Kenny Kennedy met had been Gregorie's first job with the Justice Department, fresh from Georgetown Law School. After Newark, Justice had assigned the driven young prosecutor to pursue organized crime in his hometown of Boston and then on to Connecticut for three years overseeing another strike force, where he sent more major mobsters off to prison than were convicted in any other federal district. Gregorie's work against the Mafia caught the eye of the new United States attorney for the Southern District of Florida, who recruited him to move south and serve as the district's chief of narcotics prosecution. Intrigued, Gregorie reported to the Southern District's offices at 155 S. Miami Avenue, in the heart of Miami's crumbling downtown overrun with dime stores, bodegas, and burrito parlors, for a job interview.

At that first meeting, Dick warned his future boss that, while he was long on zeal, he was not good at sweet-talking politicians or pulling his punches and said he would take the job only on the condition that he report directly to the U.S. Attorney himself and that he be given free reign to make whatever cases he deemed appropriate.

To Dick's surprise, the new United States Attorney agreed to all his terms. Even after that boss left to become a judge, his successor would renew his predecessor's pledge of independence and promote Gregorie from chief of narcotics to First Assistant United States Attorney, supervising all criminal prosecutions in the Southern District. As always, Gregorie's marching orders remained the same, first framed when he was hired in 1982.

At that point, the new United States Attorney told Gregorie that he didn't want the Southern District of Florida to keep making drug cases the way it had been — randomly, seizure by seizure. This dope business was ruining the country, and the previous approach would no longer do. It was not enough simply to run around confiscating as much cocaine as they could stumble across. He wanted his new chief of narcotics to find out where these drugs were coming from and identify the organizational structure upstream from Miami that was spawning all this traffic. Then he wanted Gregorie to follow the trail wherever it went and prosecute the hell out of whoever he found there.

Dick Gregorie told his new boss that he was just the man for the job.

And he was, of course, right.

— 3 —

Dick Gregorie's weapon of choice in this mission was the Racketeer Influenced and Corrupt Organization statutes in the Federal Code, known around grand juries as RICO. This body of law had originally been written to attack the Italian organized crime families whose upper echelons had historically managed to insulate themselves from personal involvement in the actual commission of crimes, while still maintaining control of the larger criminal syndicate those crimes served. Gregorie had arrived in Miami already adept at using RICO and his grand jury powers to chase the Mafia around the Northeast and wanted to do the same to the drug thugs who had overrun the Southern District of Florida.

To convict under RICO, a prosecutor had to prove that an interstate criminal enterprise existed, in whose conduct the defendant participated, and that the defendant had committed at least two offenses in a pattern that furthered that criminal enterprise. With this burden of proof satisfied, anyone who even facilitated a cocaine ring's movement of drugs along the pipeline from Colombia to Miami could be held personally responsible for the totality of the ring's activities, not just their own particular personal role.

It was on this point of law that Dick Gregorie would eventually impale General Manuel Antonio Noriega.

No one in the history of the Justice Department had ever attempted to attach such offshore criminal responsibility to anyone of the General's stature, but Dick Gregorie had already made it clear he was willing to prosecute foreigners of rank if he had the goods. Over his first three years at 155 S. Miami Avenue, Gregorie made cases charging the Cuban ambassador to "Columbier"— as Colombia was mangled in Gregorie's Massachusetts pronunciation — as well as a vice admiral in the Cuban navy, the chief adviser to the prime minister of the Bahamas, and the prime minister himself of the Turcs and Caicos Islands, a British West Indian dependency. All of them had tapped into the cocaine pipeline, and all of them, Gregorie argued, ought to be made to pay.

"These guys thought they could just sit outside our borders and never be held responsible for what they were doing here," Dick explained, "and we weren't going to allow it."

Given that attitude, the de facto ruler of Panama was just the kind of target Gregorie would be eager to chase if his DEA investigators could give him enough evidence to take to a grand jury.

And Kenny Kennedy, of course, knew it.

Otherwise, however, Kenny only had a sketchy idea at best of who General Manuel Antonio Noriega was.

And, as a consequence, there was a lot more at stake in this investigation than he realized when he first began talking it up to Dick Gregorie.

Unbeknownst to the assistant special agent in charge of the Miami Divisional Office, *United States v. Manuel Antonio Noriega* was not a case that the Drug Enforcement Administration was looking to make.

Far from it, in fact. The General had been quick to enlist in the gringos' War on Drugs and, in Washington, over Kennedy's head, he was appreciated for it. From the time he assumed his general's stars in 1983, Manuel Antonio Noriega had facilitated two major DEA secret operations against the Colombian cocaine traffic, had almost eradicated the domestic Panamanian marijuana crop, and had given the United States Coast Guard blanket permission to search all ships of Panamanian registry, a significant portion of the world's civilian fleet. The latter alone had already generated more than two hundred seizures of some thirty-one tons of cocaine, trumpeted by the U.S. Coast Guard commandant as "a milestone in high seas law enforcement."

The DEA was also at that moment hip deep in another major secret operation, code name Pisces, which it eventually described as "the largest and most successful undercover investigation in federal drug law enforcement history," and needed the General's help to pull it off. Targeted against laundered cocaine profits, the heart of the operation involved accessing information from the books of the Panamanian international banking industry — access which the Panamanian Defense Force allowed the American narcs despite the prohibitions against it explicitly written into Panamanian banking laws. Pisces would eventually net 115 arrests and seizures of more than $50 million. All, of course, thanks to the General.

Upon Pisces' completion, the administrator of the DEA wrote General Noriega, officially praising him for his "personal commitment" to the operation, which had been "essential" to its accomplishments. "DEA has long welcomed our close association," the administrator pointed out.

Such letters were known inside the DEA as *attaboys,* designed to stroke the big-ticket people who did the DEA favors and cheer them on, as in the exhortation, "'at a boy." In this case, the *attaboy* was genuine. The

Drug Enforcement Administration's director of intelligence at the agency's Washington headquarters described the General as "the best goddamn friend the DEA has in all of Latin America" and, at the time Kennedy began chatting up Moritz's slim lead with Gregorie, there was already an institutional attachment to General Manuel Antonio Noriega among the Drug Enforcement Administration's upper ranks. And Kenny Kennedy, GS-15, hadn't a clue it was waiting out there, like a land mine in the path of his heretofore charmed career.

Years later, Kenny sat amid the final wreckage of his possibilities and speculated that it wouldn't have been much different even if he had known. Kennedy was the offspring of a post office worker and a machine tool operator, someone who had worked all his life, starting with shining shoes in Jersey City as a kid, then setting pins in a bowling alley, followed by distributing barroom displays for a local brewing company. He'd always wanted to be a cop because of his uncle, a mounted policeman, and Kennedy's blue-collar approach was as obvious as the veins on his face.

"The taxpayers hired me to put fuckin' dope peddlers in jail," he explained, "and that's what I do. No sweetheart deals and that kinda bullshit."

— 4 —

For Dick Gregorie, the case wasn't even about General Manuel Antonio Noriega when it started. It was about the Medellín Cartel. Pursuing these Colombian cocaine barons was the obsession that ruled Dick Gregorie's life more than any other. And what hooked Gregorie when Kennedy first came to him was the story told by Floyd Carlton's tiny Cessna-driver-turned-snitch about hauling boxes of dollars to the General from those very same Colombians. As far as Dick was concerned, the Medellín Cartel was the single most important target in the entire War on Drugs.

Of which Kenny, needless to say, was again well aware. Indeed, one of the bonds between the First Assistant and the ASAC was that Kennedy had been instrumental in helping Dick make his very first case against these Medellín traffickers.

Kenny had done so when he was still in Washington, a GS-14, doing operational support and representing the Drug Enforcement Administration on several interagency task forces, including Vice President

George Bush's South Florida Task Force in the War on Drugs. In early 1984, a three-hundred-pound former airline pilot with a checkered past that included some apparent contract work for the Central Intelligence Agency and a lot of smuggling of all types was brought to Kennedy's attention by one of the task force's military reps. The fat pilot had been arrested trying to fly a plane full of contraband Quaaludes into Louisiana, was facing a lifetime's worth of state charges, and had been trying desperately to find some agency to whom he could trade evidence for leniency.

The fat pilot was in Washington at the time and Kennedy agreed to meet with him. When he did, the pilot talked knowingly for several hours about a lot of names Kennedy didn't recognize but whom the prospective snitch identified as the kingpins of the Colombian cocaine trade. Kennedy decided to take a flyer on the fat man and connected him to a DEA agent working out of Miami.

That agent then approached Dick Gregorie with a proposal. He wanted to let the fat pilot fly back down to Colombia to make contact with the people he had been talking about and then use him on a leash, the Southern District of Florida's own private observer inside the highest reaches of the Colombian cocaine business. The agent also called Kennedy and asked him to put in a good word with his old strike force buddy on the plan's behalf.

"Jesus, Kenny," Dick complained, "this guy's a convicted smuggler facing major time with every reason in the world to just take a hike as soon as his plane touches down."

"You got to know the guy," Kennedy answered. "This fat man don't want to live in fuckin' South America. He's not gonna turn rabbit. He'll turn tricks for you first." The Miami office was already telling Kennedy that the fat pilot was connected enough "to do some real fuckin' good."

On Kennedy's say-so, Gregorie agreed.

That may have been the smartest thing Dick ever did.

The fat pilot was a character, whose girth made just getting in behind an airplane's controls a challenge, but, once there, he could make anything from a Cessna to a C-123 dance and stand on its tail. He never had phone conversations on anything but pay phones for which he hauled an enormous stash of quarters with him at all times, and he invariably drove Cadillacs if one was available. Whenever the subject of the CIA came up, the fat pilot just chuckled. Nonetheless, he was even better connected than he had claimed and his transformation into a government informant was a landmark in American drug investigation, providing an unprecedented window into the cocaine business.

It was the fat pilot who first informed Gregorie that there even was a Medellín Cartel. Early in his debriefing, he claimed that all the major cocaine exporters operating out of Medellín, Colombia, had banded together a couple years earlier into a loose association to manage the trade in their product in an almost industrial model that included joint factories, joint smuggling ventures, and joint marketing, so risks were shared. Rather than control the entire process, in the fashion of La Cosa Nostra, these smugglers used hired subcontractors to supply them with raw materials and to move and distribute most of their goods. In the case of pilots like Dick's new fat snitch, the Colombians often held open auctions at which freelance fliers bid on contracts for carrying various loads.

The news galvanized Gregorie and, while the pilot continued to deal with the Colombians, Dick and a squad of assistant United States attorneys lived at 155 S. Miami Avenue off and on for weeks, fashioning the information that the fat pilot was providing into something that the Southern District of Florida could eventually take in front of a grand jury. The most memorable breakthrough in the process came when one of the younger assistants named the enterprise they were trying to decipher.

These Colombians worked more like the old Standard Oil cartel than a Mafia family, he pointed out.

That remark stuck. Henceforth, the Colombians were collectively referenced as the Medellín Cartel, a name that would soon become legendary once Gregorie went public with the indictment.

Along the way, the pilot also provided a few scraps of information about General Manuel Antonio Noriega. He reported after one trip south in 1984 that most of the cartel's principle members had temporarily left Colombia because of internal police pressure following their assassination of the country's justice minister and had moved to Panama, paying several million dollars to the General for the privilege. The fat pilot himself, however, had no dealings with the General face to face.

In his renewed, now undercover, career, the cartel had the pilot moving planeloads of cocaine through various transshipment points. Gregorie and DEA agents from the Miami office tracked his smuggling, often bending over backward to keep the fat man's true mission a secret. On one occasion, the fat pilot flew into Nicaragua, picked up 300 kilos the cartel had moved there from Colombia, and flew the load back into greater Miami. Gregorie and the other investigators were bound by law not to allow the coke to move onto the open market, so they arranged a ruse on the Miami end of the smuggle. The 300 kilos were to be hauled away from the landing strip in a motor home, so Gregorie's team of DEA agents had the vehicle sabotaged and, as planned, it broke down shortly after the rendezvous. At that point, a uniformed cop who was in on the operation cruised up to inspect, leaving the motor home driver, who was not in on the secret, just enough room to run off, which he, predictably, did.

If the driver had been arrested, the rules of discovery at any trial would have forced Gregorie to disclose the fat pilot's existence, so Gregorie elected to give the small fry a walk. The maneuver almost failed, however, when the driver, having escaped the cop, was chased down by a passing civilian who, spotting what was going on, tackled the fleeing suspect and held him for the law. Gregorie was forced to retrieve the situation by dropping charges because the cop's search of the motor home was "illegal," thereby preserving the fat pilot for bigger game.

As hard as he tried, however, Dick's secret informant would not stay secret long and, once unveiled, would be of little further use. And the process in which that secrecy was breached framed an issue that dogged Gregorie for the rest of his days as First Assistant United States Attorney. A decade and a half later, the now former first assistant was still repeating the mantra that consumed him.

"If this is really a War on Drugs," he argued, "then the rest of the government ought to damn well behave like it is too."

The source of Gregorie's upset arose from the considerable interest in national security circles over the fat pilot's ventures into Nicaragua, where unseating the Marxist Sandinista government had become the Reagan administration's holy grail. On one of the fat man's flights, the CIA rigged the C-123 transport he was flying with an automatic camera with which to photograph the Sandinistas assisting in the cocaine's transshipment. That high-tech camera failed to operate but the fat pilot, ever resourceful, managed to use his own hand-held tourist model to get the picture anyway.

A copy of that photo somehow made its way to the attention of one Lieutenant Colonel Oliver North, a marine seconded to the staff of the National Security Council in the White House, "specializing" in Nicaraguan policy. And, at the point the photo reached North, the fat pilot's days of usefulness were numbered.

A crucial vote in Congress on aid to the rebel contra guerrillas being promoted against the ruling Sandinistas by the Reagan administration was coming up in Congress, and North contacted the DEA seeking help in making the public point that the Sandinistas were dope-traffickers. At the time, North revealed himself as someone considerably in the know. Despite never having been informed by anyone in Gregorie's investigation with authority to do so, North was aware that the fat pilot was about to be dispatched back to Nicaragua by the cartel to carry a $1.5 million bribe from the Colombians. North had an audacious proposal: Instead of taking the money to the Sandinistas, he wanted the fat pilot to fly it to the contras' guerrilla base and, as part of a coordinated public announcement in Washington and in Central America, hijack the cash and deliver it to the contras for use in their struggle.

The DEA declined. North also wanted the fat pilot's photo of the Nicaraguan unloading released, and that request was declined as well.

Shortly after North's unsuccessful approach, word that definitive concrete proof of Sandinista complicity in cocaine traffic existed was announced by the United States military's Southern Command, based in the Panama Canal Zone, apparently after being tipped off to the fact by the CIA. That was then followed quickly by a leak to the press of a photo, provided by an unnamed Washington source — which the DEA ultimately concluded was Oliver North — reportedly showing a Nicaraguan Ministry of Interior official offloading bundles of cocaine.

The fat pilot was never mentioned when his photo was leaked, but Dick assumed it wouldn't take the cartel long to figure out who must have taken it. His snitch was actually on his way to Colombia at the time the photo ran and the Southern District of Florida had to have him radioed while over the Caribbean and ordered to turn back, for fear he would be executed when he set down in Medellín.

The fat pilot's ongoing exposure of the cartel was now over and Gregorie's hand was forced. Not long after the picture was leaked, a federal grand jury for the Southern District of Florida met in their ground-floor chambers in the new annex to the old Miami courthouse down the block from 155 S. Miami Avenue and returned an indictment titled *United States v. Jorge Ochoa, et al.*

According to his own accounting, this was the first of what would eventually be three cases against the cartel that Dick Gregorie would make. The third would be *United States v. Manuel Antonio Noriega.*

The original indictment named the entire cartel as a criminal enterprise under the standards set by RICO, primarily on the testimony provided by the three-hundred-pound flyer that Kennedy had sent to Miami. The fat pilot was, of course, mentioned by name in the court papers, and Gregorie's fury at the turn of events that had forced his hand never quite dissipated.

"Some war," Dick later pointed out. "They take our best weapon out of our hands before we get to really use it."

The fat pilot himself was actually willing to keep working, pointing out that the cartel knew him only under an assumed trade name, not his given one listed in the grand jury documents, but Gregorie thought the risk would be far too great. He did use the fat man on a couple of unrelated cases until early 1986, when the informant was required to start serving a reduced sentence for his original conviction back in Louisiana at a state-run halfway house. He was offered enrollment in the Federal Witness Protection program instead, but he was unwilling to restrict himself to a life of hiding so he refused. At least this way he could continue to circulate. He was aware that the cartel had figured out who he was and had contracts out on him, but he still thought he was safer in his own hands.

Shortly after he began his sentence, the three-hundred-pound pilot was sitting in his white Cadillac outside his Louisiana halfway house when a person or persons then unknown approached and cut loose on him with a MAC 10 machine pistol, firing a thirty-two-shot clip on full automatic. The local police found the fat man wedged in behind the wheel, dead as a pork roast and leaking out from under the door on the driver's side.

On January 23, 1986, a little more than a month before the fat pilot's assassination, the next step in the chain of evidence that would eventually become *United States v. Manuel Antonio Noriega* was taken by the Southern District of Florida. After one of Gregorie's assistants secured a secret grand jury indictment based on Danny Moritz's testimony, the Miami DEA office finally took down DIACSA out on NW 12th Street by the airport, as well as private residences in Coral Gables and Tamarac, and just about everyone who had been hanging around the warehouse talking shit and making loads was hauled downtown to the federal lockup — except for the biggest fish of all, Floyd Carlton, who was nowhere to be found.

Once the dust settled, Kenny Kennedy let Dick Gregorie know that they were now on Floyd's trail.

In the meantime, Dick Gregorie's desire to chase General Manuel Antonio Noriega only multiplied, egged on by two specific incidents involving the cartel.

The first of these two commenced almost as soon as the first indictment against the cartel cleared the grand jury. Dick Gregorie had not intended his indictment of the Colombians to be a publicity stunt, he meant actually to get these guys back to the Southern District to stand trial, so he quickly began to focus on extraditing the Colombians from wherever in the world they stayed long enough to be cornered. The Republic of Colombia itself seemed a hopeless case on that front, such was the cartel's influence there, but almost immediately, a more realistic opportunity to capture an indicted cartel member had dropped into Gregorie's lap. In this instance, the Spanish police had arrested one of the cartel's kingpins after he had been living in Spain under an assumed name for some six months, having entered the country on a flight from Nicaragua, traveling on a Panamanian passport that had been personally arranged for him by General Manuel Antonio Noriega.

All of the ensuing extradition fight in Spanish courts was handled by the United States State Department. Gregorie was never consulted in the process — informed only if he insisted on it — and, then, told as little as could be managed. He made two short trips to Spain to see some of the court action first hand and, when he did, it was obvious that he and the extradition he was seeking were something of a hot potato as far as the American embassy was concerned. Gregorie never secured a meeting with the American ambassador despite his requests, and the only one who would let him know what was going on was an embassy secretary who, taking pity on his ignorance, pointed out that this whole extradition controversy was a very delicate situation. The Spanish were worried about defending their sovereignty and the Americans were in the midst of negotiating new leases on their Spanish air bases and were very worried about causing any undue offense while that process was ongoing. From Dick Gregorie's point of view, the combination was deadly.

In the absence of any American arm twisting on the Spanish government, this extradition fight worked its way through twelve separate judicial hearings involving a total of twenty-eight different Spanish judges. Eventually all of the cartel man's legal arguments foundered and for a brief moment it appeared as though he would actually be sent back to

Miami for trial. Then, however, the Republic of Colombia filed a competing extradition request and the whole thing went back to court to see who would get the cartel man first. Colombia's request was on a charge of illegally exporting several prize breeding bulls but, when the Spanish courts ruled that the American claim had primacy because of the greater severity of the alleged crimes, Colombia filed a second extradition request. This one was essentially a rewritten version of the indictment Gregorie had pushed through the grand jury for the Southern District of Florida, and it carried the day.

As the spring of 1986 was turning to summer, the cartel man was extradited to Colombia instead of to Miami and, after a six-week grace period, he then escaped from police custody under mysterious circumstances, and the best chance Gregorie ever had to imprison one of the indicted cartel disappeared with him.

"The bottom line was that the American government cared more about a couple airfields than it did about busting one of the biggest dope dealers on the planet," Gregorie complained. "Some goddamn War on Drugs that is."

Gregorie had little time that spring to indulge his anger, profound as it was. The assassination of the fat pilot had left the most important investigation in his office without a witness and, had the Spaniards actually given up their cartel prisoner, the United States Attorney's Office for the Southern District of Florida might not have been able to try him for want of evidence.

At this juncture, however, fortune again smiled on Dick Gregorie, in the form of a new witness. This one was a native of Brooklyn, who was married to a woman from Colombia and in federal custody in San Diego facing enough Continuing Criminal Enterprise charges to consume the rest of this life and the better part of his next. When the Brooklyn man informed his captors that Miami would be interested in what he had to say, Gregorie flew to California and personally arranged for him to be shipped to the custody of the Southern District of Florida, where, dressed in cowboy boots and pants that couldn't quite contain his gut, the man sat in a high-security cell and more than replaced the fat pilot. The new witness had been trained as an engineer, was brilliant, boasting an IQ of 160, and seemed to have no moral compass. He had worked as a Mr. Fix-It for the cartel since its early days, setting up stateside importation and distribution networks and flying to Colombia regularly to meet with the cartel members — including the one who had just slipped through Gregorie's hands in Spain.

To prove his bona fides once in Miami, Gregorie's new snitch told Gregorie just what had happened to his last cartel witness.

The man from Brooklyn said he had been at a private home in North Miami used by one of the cartel members when the fat pilot was discussed. The upshot was that Brooklyn was given a contract to do something about the snitch once and for all. The cartel preferred the pilot be kidnapped, so they could kill him themselves, and said they would pay $1 million if he was. If that wasn't possible, the cartel would pay $500,000 for the fat pilot dead. The man from Brooklyn was told he had been selected because he was an American and would therefore attract less attention, but he claimed under interrogation that he had the distinct impression that if he didn't accept the contract, he would have been killed himself.

In any case, Brooklyn explained, he was left with a problem. Though cold-blooded, he wasn't much of a killer, was ambivalent about pulling off the hit, and only made desultory efforts to get the fat pilot in his sights. Finally, the cartel sent a hit man known as The Chin up to the States to let Brooklyn know the cartel was impatient to have this done and then, the message delivered, The Chin offered to take the contract off Brooklyn's hands and Brooklyn didn't hesitate to accept. Brooklyn told Gregorie that The Chin didn't have much luck himself until the fat pilot checked into the halfway house. Then the snitch became a sitting duck.

When one of the agents mentioned that the job had been done with a MAC 10 machine pistol, which the cops had found abandoned near the crime scene, Brooklyn said he knew the weapon. The Chin had come by Brooklyn's house in Golden Beach, Florida, just up the road from Miami, with the MAC 10, saying he had just bought the piece and needed to test-fire it. Brooklyn had then taken the Colombian to a back room, where he set up several phone books in front of a bucket of water, and The Chin blasted away. According to Brooklyn, several rounds from the MAC 10 had gone through the phone books and the bucket and buried themselves in the room's baseboard. Gregorie immediately dispatched a squad of DEA agents out to Golden Beach, where they entered Brooklyn's old house and dug five slugs out of the baseboard, just where he said they'd be. All five matched those the Louisiana coroner had removed from the fat pilot's corpse.

From that point on, Dick Gregorie had no doubts that the man from Brooklyn was the real deal. Dick spent much of the first half of the summer of 1986 picking his new informant's brain and eventually developed enough information not only to cover for the fat pilot's absence but also to write a second indictment against the cartel.

Like the failed extradition, the response to this second indictment multiplied Dick's resentment about how the War on Drugs was not being fought, stoking his normal relentlessness with an extra dose of outrage. And, when the time came, that only made him want to nail the General all the more.

Dick Gregorie's decision to seek a second cartel indictment that summer was inspired by what he thought was another prime opportunity to lay his hands on some or all of the fugitives from Medellín. While still debriefing the man from Brooklyn, Gregorie was contacted by several Colombian journalists. According to them, the Spanish extradition episode had created a political furor in Colombia, and the government was now facing rising pressure to stand up to the drug lords. The Colombians implored Gregorie to act against the cartel again soon before the window of opportunity disappeared. They thought another American indictment would get huge play in the current atmosphere and that might very well be enough at least to secure the extradition of the cartel man Gregorie had missed in Spain.

Gregorie thought it was worth the effort and, after sorting the new information provided by Brooklyn as well as information that had surfaced in other cases, he went to the grand jury with a second, larger, and more sweeping rendition of *United States v. Jorge Ochoa, et al.* A press conference was scheduled to follow immediately after Gregorie obtained the grand jury's approval, but he never got that far. Instead, he was interrupted in front of the grand jury by one of his assistants.

The press conference was off, the assistant said.

What?

It's been canceled, the assistant repeated. Washington had just called. The indictment was to be sealed and remain secret.

Secret? Gregorie railed. Secret? The whole point was for this to be public so the Colombian government could be pressured into flushing these sons-of-bitches out of Colombia.

The assistant said Washington was sending someone down to Miami to explain.

The man they sent was a Department of Justice hack known as the National Security liaison. He had a reputation as a jellyfish among Justice's lifers, who believed the man's sole function was to deliver bad news and absorb the ensuing abuse.

This jellyfish told Gregorie that Colombia was a country in a precarious state and that the Communist guerrillas in the countryside would take advantage of the crisis this indictment might well instigate. It was important to the security of the United States that these guerrillas not be given any more leverage. Therefore, the Southern District had to back off and keep the indictment secret.

Gregorie let the messenger from Washington know — at the top of his lungs — what he thought about doing so, but the seal stood and the indictment remained a secret to the world.

After the messenger returned to Washington, Dick Gregorie swore to himself that the next time he got a run at these guys, he was not going to let himself be stopped halfway.

5

That "next time" was, of course, *United States v. Manuel Antonio Noriega,* and the first of the case's preconditions was now in place.

Shortly before his boys actually located Floyd Carlton that summer, Kenny Kennedy saw Gregorie at a retirement party for one of the Miami Divisional Office's agents who, having reached the mandatory age limit of fifty-seven, was on his way out of the DEA to live on his pension and whatever work he might scare up as a private investigator. Most of the crowd were narcs for whom this gathering reflected their own, often dreaded, future, fraught with boredom — so there was a lot of small talk about exploits and how lucky they all were to carry a badge that let them have them.

Held on a Friday afternoon at a country club in Broward County, the party was the kind of event that constituted just about the entirety of the socializing prosecutors and agents did together, a de rigueur appearance for both the ASAC and the First Assistant. Outside, south Florida was cooking along at its usual pace, asphalt bubbling, an unbroken flatness saturated in a glare so stiff it transformed every unshaded surface into polished metal. Inside, the air conditioning kept the hospitality room pleasant, a notch under seventy degrees. The bittersweet character of the parting they had gathered to celebrate touched Kennedy a little more than Gregorie and the ASAC would work his way through several "brewskis." Gregorie would nurse one beer through the whole show.

The two old strike force buddies stood off to the side together for a while and, as it did just about every time they met these days, the subject of the lead they had on the General came up. By then, Danny Moritz, the case agent chasing Floyd Carlton, had made it a practice to do the same thing every time he bumped into Gregorie in the hallways of 155 S. Miami Avenue. Moritz always told Dick he was going to give him Noriega to prosecute and thus make Dick famous.

Kenny weighed in on the same theme. It was both agents' experience that if you didn't toot a case's horn, the prosecutors wouldn't notice it.

Gregorie was familiar with the drill.

Talk's cheap, he pointed out. Get some evidence and then they wouldn't have to just talk.

"Look, Kenny," Dick repeated. "You get me the goods and I'll indict the son-of-a-bitch. I don't care who he is."

CHAPTER 3

THE SECOND PRECONDITION

— 1 —

The second precondition essential to making *United States v. Manuel Antonio Noriega* was that *the General's friends were in no position to prevent it.*

All these "friends" who might have counted when the time came could be found in Washington, D.C., where the chains of command looming over Dick Gregorie and Kenny Kennedy reached their apex. Washington, where agendas are stacked in holding patterns all over town, and those who don't have one are busy looking for someone else's to which to attach themselves; where only juice really matters, and those without it are left for road kill; where the prize for first place is getting to stay there, and the prize for second place doesn't exist; and where, at the time this story began, the General figured mightily in the plans of some very important people — which is, of course, about as close to friendship as Washington gets.

Making powerful "friends" and being "useful" to them had been the dominant discipline of the General's life, the thing he did best of all, and it accounted in large part for his rise from nothing, not to mention for his fortune. When the Americans had asked him for help, he had helped, like any close "friend" would, expecting to be helped in return. For the General, such exchanges ordered the universe and grounded his sense of self and the prospect that his "friendship" with the gringos could fail him was no doubt a severe blow when he had to face it.

Just as unimaginable and even worse — not only did that "friendship" prove insufficient, but, in the General's case, those "friends" for whom he had been so "useful" eventually became either enemies or weapons in his enemies' hands, preventing whatever protectors he had left from doing what they might have otherwise done on his behalf. And he, with more than enough sins to defend in his own right, would eventually have to take the fall for some of theirs as well.

In the end, the agenda of the General's "friends" collapsed into the gringos' scandal of the decade and sent much of Washington running for cover, while the rest of the town poured fire onto the wreckage. And the General's "usefulness" vanished in that conflagration, leaving him stripped of cover just as *United States v. Manuel Antonio Noriega* was about to get under way and Dick Gregorie's sights came to bear.

And then, when the General really needed it, there was no one who mattered in Washington to whom he could call out for help.

— 2 —

The best of General Manuel Antonio Noriega's Washington "friends" in September 1985 was William J. Casey.

And, on the Washington ladder, you couldn't get much higher than Bill Casey, Director of Central Intelligence and President Ronald Reagan's campaign manager in the 1980 election. The director kept a formal office at CIA headquarters out in Langley, Virginia, and a less formal one in the Executive Office Building, just a stroll through an underground tunnel from the White House, where he was a regular sight, hunched at the juncture of his neck and shoulders, hairless on top, jowls folded into a double chin, with a posture that made him seem to be squatting even when standing up.

A Wall Street attorney who had amassed a considerable personal fortune, Casey, seventy-two, was credited with having invented the tax shelter while practicing law in New York. For the duration of World War II, he had served in the old OSS, the CIA's precursor, and ever since had been a militant Cold Warrior, chafing at the Americans' failure to roll back communism and making himself a major player in the Republican Party in the process. And now, having crafted a Republican victory late in his life, he was going to take his own run at that holy mission.

Almost as soon as he assumed his post at the CIA in 1981, Casey's eyes turned to Central America with that in mind.

At the time, General Manuel Antonio Noriega was still a colonel, heading the Panama Defense Force's G-2 — the military intelligence command that included responsibility for acting as Panama's institutional liaison with the CIA — and Casey summoned him to their first meeting within three months of becoming director.

"The car pulled off the parkway after less than an hour's drive [from Washington]," the General remembered in his ghostwritten memoirs.

> Then I was driven into the CIA grounds, directly to the imposing administration building. I recall crossing the threshold, looking in passing at the globe of the world inlaid in the floor . . . and the stars on the wall, representing the CIA agents killed in duty. . . . There was a lone receptionist seated in the large foyer. . . . I was [eventually] ushered into the office of William Casey. He was not exactly an imposing man, standing there, hunched over and handling himself like any other American businessman, but with the appearance of a kindly old grandfather. Still, I was impressed with him. He seemed to be a classic, old style intelligence officer and I found a great kinship in that; here was a man [like me] who had been consumed by the process and the art of intelligence gathering. . . .
>
> [In talking] with Casey, my knowledge of English did little good. He cocked his head as he spoke from a turned lip with words that tripped out in ways I couldn't understand at all. And yet, with the help of translation, our chat, extending two hours or so . . . was animated. . . . Central America, he said, was on the verge of being overrun by Communism. Panama was uniquely situated to observe events in Central America because our doors were open to all sides. The United States knew this and welcomed our openness and our help. . . . He said that the United States would take all possible steps, including covert action and mounting guerrilla insurgencies, to . . . eliminate Marxist-Leninist insurgencies wherever they found them and especially to repel and terminate any involvement, communication, or dependence on Fidel Castro anywhere in Latin America. . . . Casey told me, . . . "We need [your] help."

Some two decades after that first meeting, when attorneys representing Noriega asked the United States Court for the Southern District of Florida to reduce his forty-year sentence, a former American ambassador to Panama testified on the General's behalf, describing him as Bill Casey's "protégé."

Certainly, the colonel-soon-to-be-general had a lot to offer to the new man at the CIA. Once, when Fidel Castro was praised for his knowledge of what was going on Latin America, Castro pointed out that Noriega knew more about that subject that anybody, north or south, including Fidel himself. The General, it seemed, was connected to everybody who mattered, whichever side they happened to be on.

And, of course, he was prepared to use that connection for his "friends."

When the Reagan administration needed someone to get a message to the Cubans in advance of the United States' 1983 invasion of Grenada, it was Noriega, still G-2, to whom Casey turned. By 1984, when Noriega was now the general and commander in chief of the PDF, Casey got off the plane in Panama City when he visited the Isthmus and greeted the local CIA station chief with "Where's my boy? Where's Noriega?" When the General visited Washington, the two met alone at Casey's home.

Seeking to explain the obvious attraction between them, a colleague of the director later theorized that there was something in the General's tawdriness, a kind of primordial upsurge of the illicit that captivated Bill Casey's own uglier side.

Whatever their bond, shortly after the first threads of legal suspicion about the General surfaced in Broward County, Bill Casey made it abundantly clear that the General's "usefulness" was reciprocal and that the Director of Central Intelligence intended to protect his Panamanian protégé, by whatever means necessary.

The centerpiece of that demonstration was a visit the General made in response to a Casey summons, on November 1, 1985.

At the time, the General's act was flapping a bit in the Washington breeze, at least at the State Department. The General had just forced Panama's civilian president to resign, after the president began talking about staging an inquiry into the unsolved assassination of Hugo Spadafora, a local Panamanian hero who had become Noriega's most visible public critic. The forced resignation effectively stripped away the veneer of democracy erected when the General had allowed rigged presidential elections the year before. And the State Department was also picking up rumors that the General was dabbling in drug traffic. None of this behavior was considered "acceptable" by State's standards and they wanted Casey to summon his Panamanian protégé and read him the riot act.

Bill Casey could not stand the State Department, as a rule, but agreed to schedule a meeting with the General anyway.

On the appointed day, General Manuel Antonio Noriega was once again driven out to Virginia from his hotel in Washington, and cleared through the agency's security perimeter to visit the administration building. There he again crossed the cavernous lobby that he would remember as giving "no outward projection of the espionage and intrigue one could imagine going on throughout the premises," past the lonely receptionist, and up to the director's office.

Others there that day sensed the General's trepidation. He already knew the State Department wanted him dragged on the carpet and was at least a little unsure of what his gringo mentor would do. This would be the first time their "friendship" had been put to any kind of significant test.

Bill Casey did not disappoint. The two men sat down together in the director's office and proceeded to have a conversation remarkable for all that was not said. Casey didn't mention the presidential firing in which the General had put the lie to his own claims of Panamanian democracy; he didn't mention the dead Spadafora, who had been beheaded by his anonymous killers after what appeared to have been a particularly grisly torture session; nor did he mention the smuggling rumors, the Medellín Cartel, or any of the other behaviors and alliances that eventually left the General taking escorted walks in the heavy Miami glare, a guard on each arm and razor wire in every direction he looked.

The only thing the director complained about on November 1, 1985, was that the General was allowing the Cubans to use Panamanian front companies to bypass the American economic blockade. The issue was an old saw between them. And that was it.

In his after action report on the encounter, Casey noted that he had hoped to reassure Noriega of American backing and he didn't care what the State Department thought about it.

To that end, he engaged the General, hail-fellow-well-met, towering over him and harrumping in what passed for a laugh. They each had a scotch, one of the General's favorite bonding rituals, then Casey's underlings reinforced the message afterward by taking the General out to a very expensive lunch full of more scotch, along with half-drunken toasts, and macho strokes at every turn.

When the General returned to Panama City the next day, he must have noted with a mixture of bravado and relief that the gringos had brought him all the way to Washington just so they could kiss his ass.

A decade and a half later, General Manuel Antonio Noriega remained convinced that if Bill Casey had survived, none of what befell the General would ever have come to pass.

The agenda for which the General proved by far the most useful was the one closest to Bill Casey's heart.

The director had meant what he had said the first time they met about "rolling back" the Cuban-Soviet tide, and the place Casey intended to do so was Nicaragua, where, after leading a popular revolution against a longtime dictator, the avowedly Marxist-Leninist Sandinista party had assumed power in the late 1970s. Almost as soon as he took over the agency's reins, Bill Casey began hatching a strategy for rooting the Sandinistas out. As far as he was concerned, no Communist governments would be allowed in Central America, no exceptions. The director of Central Intelligence called his approach "the Reagan Doctrine."

Casey was at his most passionate when speaking of it, though, given his ever-present mumble, simply the word "Nicaragua" was hard for him to enunciate. At his best, it still came out "Nickawoggwha." Sometimes, the headquarters wags would get the director to say it just for the fun of hearing his verbal gyrations. Nobody, however, laughed in his presence. Nickawoggwha was by far the most serious subject in what little remained of Bill Casey's life.

The heart of the director's strategy lay with what he called "the democratic resistance" but to whom most referred as "the contras." A scraggly guerrilla army reportedly several hundred strong, raiding Nicaraguan territory from camps in Honduras and Costa Rica, this force had been raised by Casey's CIA and included agency operatives out in the field. But, in order to maintain the contras' credibility and appearance of independence, Casey did not want their CIA backbone to show, and Noriega proved very useful in providing camouflage that let the contras' exile leadership claim they were doing it all on their own.

The General allowed Panama to be used as a secret staging base for the guerrillas' supply line, even though doing so was a violation of the Panama Canal treaties negotiated before Casey came to power. Utilizing his close connections to the Israelis, the General acted as a middleman when the CIA funneled weapons to Israel, which dispatched them to Panama, and from there on to the contra camps in Honduras. He helped the gringos find bush pilots to fly their loads into Nicaragua from Panama and from another staging area in Costa Rica, utilizing many of the same fliers and planes used by the Medellín Cartel in their ongoing transshipment enterprises. He even made a personal contribution of several hundred thousand dollars to the contra cause.

But General Manuel Antonio Noriega's real "usefulness" to the director of Central Intelligence and his war in Nicawoggwha emerged after that strategy came under heavy attack around Washington, D.C. In 1984, the Democrat majority in Congress, upset that the CIA campaign had gone so far as to mine Nicaragua's harbors — a recognized act of war between nations about which Congress had never even been consulted — passed legislation prohibiting any American support of any sort for the contras. That left Bill Casey with two options: he could either cease his campaign or he could wage his own private war against the Sandinistas outside the framework of constitutional government, concealing the administration's ongoing involvement in it altogether, even from the rest of the United States government.

In an extraordinarily fateful decision, a year or so before the capture of Floyd Carlton's Cessna out on I-75, Bill Casey chose the latter option.

And, not surprisingly, General Manuel Antonio Noriega played a not inconsiderable role in the director's attempt to pull it off.

Noriega was well aware of the value of being in on someone else's secret — he had been collecting them on whomever he could for more than a decade at the helm of G-2 before coming to power himself. So, when Casey asked for the General's help in carrying out his transgression, the General had to have figured that sharing as sensitive a secret as this one would likely earn him protection for life, at least at the CIA, which the General thought of as the most powerful force in the American government, just as his G-2 was in Panama. He also apparently assumed that Bill Casey could pull off his gambit.

The General, as it turned out, was wrong on all counts.

— 3 —

Most of the General's participation in the now-underground Nicaragua enterprise was orchestrated through an intermediary, since Casey himself, against whom the congressional prohibition had been directed, had to keep his distance.

The intermediary was Lieutenant Colonel Oliver North, United States Marine Corps, seconded to the National Security Council in the White House, forty-two years old, a former gung ho jarhead platoon leader in Vietnam turned gung ho jarhead national security staffer. North had been chosen for his role in part because the director's reading of the congressional legislation concluded that while it certainly banned agencies, like the CIA, from providing assistance, the bill was worded in such a way that it technically failed to exclude the White House itself. As a consequence, the National Security Council, part of that White House apparatus, was not restrained from involvement. So North was enlisted as Casey's cut out, managing the extralegal Nicaragua enterprise on the director's behalf.

The marine's office in the Executive Office Building, Room 302, was just a couple of hallways from Casey's, Room 345. "I came to know [Casey] well," North later recounted in his own ghostwritten memoirs. "Our relationship was close and yet, it wasn't especially personal. We often spoke on the secure telephone and we met regularly at one of his offices, or occasionally at his house. . . . I admired him and he knew it [but] we were not buddies. . . . Yet we were more than colleagues. He was someone I could turn to and say, 'What's going on here?' . . . I often asked him for advice. . . . He was incredibly bright and knowledgeable."

The way one CIA hand remembered the two of them, "Bill'd say 'shit' and Ollie'd be squatting as soon as the word left his lips."

Among Ollie North's responsibilities was servicing the director's "friendship" with General Manuel Antonio Noriega, and, of course, being serviced by it. For his part, the General was being "useful," as usual. He had his own personal attorney draw up the papers for a group of Panama City front companies so the neophyte operative North could conduct his subterfuge in Panamanian obscurity, under the cover of Udall Corporation, Energy Resources International, Dolmy Business, Inc. and their like. Next, in early 1985, when the contras were in desperate need of some kind of public victory about which to brag, the General loaned North the use of a PDF saboteur who, working under the supervision of a British mercenary hired by North, planted a series of explosive devices in Managua, capital of Nicaragua, using information gathered by Noriega's intelligence agents. The blasts ignited an ammunition dump and mangled a military headquarters structure. Citing the attack, for which the contras claimed responsibility, North then circulated around Washington maintaining that "the democratic resistance" was obviously strong enough to strike anywhere they had a mind to, even if the Americans weren't helping them.

About the time this story began, the General was meeting face to face with Ollie North for the second time, on a yacht the marine lieutenant colonel had chartered to cruise Balboa Harbor off the Pacific entrance to the Panama Canal.

Suffocating heat shortened the horizon, cooking the harbor into a hazy vapor, but, under way, the yacht managed to generate enough of a breeze for the passengers to feel reasonably cool. North had two attractive women with him, one an interpreter. Though dead set on making a Central American revolution, North spoke no Spanish.

The General brought along a short, bespectacled, prematurely gray political operative named Jose Blandon, who eventually played a major supporting role in this story himself. That day on Balboa Harbor, the General used Blandon, Panama's leading Marxist intellectual and one of Noriega's most trusted advisers, to engage North in conversation, thus allowing the General himself to watch a lot and say little.

The General, who had met North face-to-face only once before, was struck by what a loudmouth the marine was. Ollie North, for his part, thought that the General — his face a solid mask of acne scars so pitted and bumpy his detractors called him "the pineapple"— was perhaps the ugliest-looking human he'd ever laid eyes on.

North began the conversation by talking about how strong the contras were. He bragged that his own intelligence indicated that they would be operating on the outskirts of Managua "within six months." The gringo then complained that he had two thousand new volunteers willing to join "the democratic resistance," but he had no place to train them. He wanted the General to set up camps for their use in Panama. Once they had been trained, North said he would launch the two thousand on a series of attacks along the so-called Southern Front, where, at the moment, a small group of contra guerrillas was operating out of enclaves in Costa Rica. If his cause got lucky, North pointed out, the Sandinistas might then counterattack across the border into demilitarized Costa Rica, outraging international opinion. North also pointed out that "the democratic resistance" was desperate to escape its current diplomatic isolation. He wanted Panama's civilian president, titular head of the Isthmus's government, to receive a delegation of their leaders.

Jose Blandon, sharp edged and more than a little skeptical, played devil's advocate to North's presentation. Blandon offered that it all sounded great, but, with all due respect, this talk of two thousand volunteers was bullshit. North didn't have the bodies to back up his talk, and what soldiers he did have didn't fight. Blandon pointed out that the General knew all about the Southern Front that North kept talking up, and all the contras there did was fuck whores, smuggle dope, and shoot randomly into the treeline. As far as the claims of contra success, North was just hearing what he wanted to hear from a lot of people who either had no idea what was really going on or who just wanted to peddle their story for North's dollars. Blandon told the visiting American that the contras would be in Managua about the time icebergs floated into Balboa Harbor.

At that point, the General stepped in. No need to bicker, he said. Whatever reservations he might have about Colonel North's plan were of little consequence. The General would help the contras simply because the United States had asked.

Before North's rented yacht docked, Noriega had promised the contras use of two jungle training bases, though the details weren't yet arranged. Two weeks after that, the president of Panama officially received a delegation of contra leaders.

In his memoirs, the General described Ollie North as "the greatest of true believers, [for whom] I was no different from . . . mere operatives who did his dirty work. North was a user of men [who] wanted to be an American hero. He would . . . find friends of convenience . . . and discard them when their work was done."

The American the General counted on wasn't North, but Casey. And, true to form, Bill Casey pursued his commitment to the General by moving to widen Noriega's circle of "friends" to include one more member, this time from, of all places, the State Department with whom Casey was usually in a state of perpetual feud.

The director's candidate was Elliott Abrams, thirty-seven, Assistant Secretary of State for Inter-American Affairs, with whom Casey got along better than he did with anyone else in the department. Their affinity was all the more unexpected given that Abrams was the protégé of the

Secretary of State, whom Casey detested and openly referred to as an incompetent traitor. Abrams, however, had a fervor about all the same things Casey did and was in a position to do something about them.

Elliott Abrams grew up in New York City's upper-middle-class Hollis Hills neighborhood in Queens, eventually married into the neoconservative intellectual circle, and after spending the seventies as a congressional aide to right-wing Democrats, switched to the Republican Party just in time for the election of Ronald Reagan. His combination of intellectual credentials and Washington connections made him a natural for the Reaganauts who swept into the State Department in the transference of power. Abrams was a right-wing boy wonder — Harvard '69, masters in international relations from the London School of Economics, Harvard Law '73 — and started his diplomatic career as Assistant Secretary of State for International Organizations, the youngest ever to reach the assistant secretary rank. He then did a tour as Assistant Secretary for Human Rights before the secretary of state tapped him for the inter-American job in 1985. Henceforth, the secretary referred to Abrams privately as "the King of Latin America."

Elliott Abrams was certainly arrogant enough for such a title; just about anyone who knew him would testify to that. One of the assistant secretary's friends from high school remembered the adolescent Elliott staring out the window of his father's law office high over Fifth Avenue and saying, "Look at all the tiny people down there. Someday, I'll have control over them all." Confident in his own destiny, Abrams struck many on first contact as an overbearing know-it-all. Typically, when a colleague inside the administration who later became one of Abrams's closer friends initially approached the new assistant secretary with a document to read, Abrams brushed him aside, explaining that he worked on the political level and didn't waste his time digesting paper. The assistant secretary's future friend took him for a first-rate creep.

Personalities aside, what mattered to Bill Casey was that Abrams was, in the words of the chairman of the Joint Chiefs of Staff, "a very dedicated fanatic," particularly on the subject of Nicaragua. Like the director of Central Intelligence, Abrams believed he was part of a vanguard called forth to roll back the Communist menace and cleanse the hemisphere in decisive battle — a development that, upon completion, would prove a pivotal moment in the history of the twentieth century.

Whatever the approach, Abrams's new post as King of Latin America was a hairy beat to cover. In Guatemala, the United States was backing a military government waging a war of extermination against indigenous guerrillas that would eventually claim 200,000 lives, mostly by summary execution; in El Salvador, the United States was backing a collection of rightist military men and death squad leaders in another war against leftist insurgents whose bloody tally would also approach six figures; in Nicaragua, the leftists held power and the United States was backing a collection of former army officers from the previous dictatorship and upper-class exiles — up to and including, of course, Bill Casey's war on their behalf in which hundreds more would be killed; Costa Rica and Honduras were front line staging areas for all the other wars, both identifiable chips in the Americans' game; and, in Panama, there was the General, overseeing a kind of combination of Casablanca and Switzerland, where all the various sides mingled and kept bank accounts.

The sharp-tongued Elliott Abrams's most visible role was as the Reagan administration's point man handling the issue of aid for the contras. On this front, his greatest early success in Congress was the passage of a revision of the previous prohibition legislation, this time authorizing limited "humanitarian" assistance, to the tune of some $27 million earmarked for refugee relief and the like. Abrams also assumed the chairmanship of the Restricted Interagency Group that coordinated Central American policy. The National Security Council representative to the RIG was Lieutenant Colonel Oliver North, who immediately lobbied the new chairman to hire several members of North's clandestine network with funds from the "humanitarian" aid package when it passed.

Shortly after this first encounter with North in the fall of 1985, Abrams approached one of his underlings in the intelligence section at State for more information. "In front of someone who didn't have any business hearing," the intelligence section official remembered, "Abrams asked if I knew or if the CIA knew what North was doing to help the contras. I didn't and told him so and explained that senior people in CIA had made plain they wanted to stay away from North's doings."

Abrams also discussed the subject with the secretary of state and warned him that North was a "loose cannon." The secretary instructed Abrams to keep track of North and report back.

Over the length of this story leading up to the General's exile, more than a few participants changed their tunes. Among them, however, only Elliott Abrams changed his tune twice.

Abrams's starting point in this process was framed when Noriega forced out Panama's civilian president, shortly after Abrams's elevation to the inter-American affairs desk. Abrams phoned the General to browbeat him into rescinding his action but the General wouldn't even accept the assistant secretary's call. Not surprisingly, Abrams emerged from that incident in a fighting mood and, in December 1985, became one of the leading voices on a delegation dispatched to Panama City and tasked with, among other things, "correcting" the impression left by Casey's November ass-kissing. Abrams described that December encounter in Panama as the "first serious message to Noriega" about the dangers inherent in the corruption of the Panama Defense Force in general and its one and only General in particular and, by the time he returned to Washington, Abrams was well established as one of the General's stiffest critics inside the administration.

But not for long. Between that December and his appearance before the Senate International Relations Committee's Subcommittee on Western Hemisphere Affairs on April 21, 1986, to testify about the state of affairs in Panama, Elliott Abrams's approach to Panama "evolved." And, though he never went on record explaining this unexpected transformation, whatever epiphany had visited him over those four months was sufficient to earn him what had heretofore seemed a highly unlikely membership in the small circle of "friends" Bill Casey had organized on the General's behalf.

This induction of Elliott Abrams into the ranks of Noriega's protectors was a landmark moment, though, at the time, it drew little notice. The assistant secretary was simply his usual self that day, as Washington had come to know him over the administration's first five years — a hot right-wing property whose self-assurance was still enough to make him credible, delivering his message with a slight curl on his lip that might have been a sneer had it only curled a bit more: as though Abrams expected to be believed simply because it was obvious that he was the smartest son-of-a-bitch in the room.

On April 21, 1986, however, the message Abrams delivered about Panama was different from anything that anyone had heard from him on the subject before. His railings at the General behind closed doors during the previous fall about Noriega's control of Panama were now nowhere in evidence, and Abrams's testimony bore no resemblance at all to the dressing down he claimed to have personally delivered to Noriega barely four months earlier.

Instead, Elliott Abrams told the subcommittee that the Panama Defense Force was a "commanding" institution with a "unique character"—part police, part army, part private holding company that funded itself largely through commercial enterprises it controlled — but described the Panamanian system of government as

> not straight-out military control, such that the Panamanian Defense Force runs the government. But they intervene [in] a lot of the affairs of the government and [that] is inconsistent with the kind of control by an elected government that you would have to have, I think, before you would be willing to call it a democracy. . . . [On the other hand,] we have never lacked a sympathetic hearing for our views from Panama's government. . . . There has been no dispute concerning U.S. military forces in Panama. In a region where we have too many problems, [the] virtual absence of difficulty about our most significant military bases [in Latin America] is notable and beneficial to us. . . .
>
> We have our tactical differences [and Panama's] behavior has not always coincided with what we might like most, but its objectives . . . are compatible with ours. It wants to protect the peace of the region and preserve territorial integrity and democratic political independence for itself and its neighbors. Its people do not want a foreign-dominated, anti-democratic state such as Nicaragua fomenting armed conflict in the region.

Perhaps the most remarkable aspect of the assistant secretary's April 21 testimony was that Elliott Abrams spent more than an hour in front of the subcommittee testifying about the state of affairs in Panama without ever once mentioning General Manuel Antonio Noriega, the country's de facto ruler.

Looking to bolster his new "friend," Abrams, in effect, simply pretended for public consumption that the General did not exist.

While that opening gambit on the General's behalf came off without a hitch, Elliott Abrams would never be able simply not to mention the General again. Ignoring him had worked because, in April, the General was still largely invisible around Washington. But that invisibility was about to end forever and, when it did, Abrams would have to turn his defense of the General from the passive to the active.

To be exact, General Manuel Antonio Noriega's notoriety began being assured forever on June 12, 1986. That morning, the *New York Times,* the American newspaper of record, focused in on him with two front-page columns of print and a somber portrait of the General himself above the fold, plus a jump page inside, all headed "Panama Strongman Said to Trade in Drugs and Illicit Money." With the *Times* exposé, written by a Pulitzer Prize–winning reporter considered the best investigator in the business, the General, previously a cipher to virtually all of the gringo public, began entering the American lexicon, eventually to become a cultural icon roughly synonymous with "lowlife scumbag warlord son-of-a-bitch." No one could know as much that morning, but from there, it was only a short leap further to thirty years just off SW 137th Avenue.

The *Times* alleged, among other things, that the General had successfully spied on the United States when he ran the PDF's G-2 during the 1970s; that he maintained "tight control of drug and money laundering activities" in Panama; that he was a secret partner in a number of Panamanian businesses; that he shared intelligence with both the United States and with Cuba; that he had told associates he wanted the local hero Hugo Spadafora's head and that U.S. intelligence organizations had proof that it was the PDF who actually cut Spadafora's head off; and, finally, that, according to an unnamed White House source, "the most significant drug running in Panama was directed by General Noriega." The *Times* followed with more details in a shorter piece the next day as well.

When the first story ran, the General was in Washington, D.C., on another of his heretofore publicly invisible visits. This time, the Department of Defense had invited him to deliver an invitation-only speech at the biennial meeting of the Inter American Defense Board convened at the army's nearby Fort McNair. The General had originally planned to hang around for a few days afterward, but, as it turned out, June 21, 1986, was the last day General Manuel Antonio Noriega spent in the United States until January 4, 1990 — when he would return dressed in a DEA jumpsuit and manacles.

The General learned of the *Times* article when it was featured on that morning's television broadcast of *Good Morning America.* He was traveling with an entourage of several PDF colonels and had made plans to meet after his speech with his personal banker from Washington's branch of the Bank of Credit and Commerce International, with whom he maintained a steady balance, often in the millions. But the General's plans changed.

General Noriega delivered his address to the Inter American Defense Board as scheduled, making no mention of the *Times* charges, even though he was suddenly an object of considerable curiosity to the audience. Then he dropped the rest of his schedule and immediately flew home to Panama City.

— 4 —

At Fort McNair, the General confined his remarks almost exclusively to the need to stop the Sandinistas, hinting strongly that he would support a full-scale war in the region to get rid of them once and for all. To those in the know, his speech sounded almost like a signal to his "friends" that he was holding up his end of the deal and expected them to hold up theirs.

Elliott Abrams apparently caught the signal. Fallout from the exposé quickly began reaching the assistant secretary of state and he dealt with it accordingly. On June 13, when the *Times* ran their follow-up article, the Restricted Interagency Group, of which Abrams was the chair, met in a special session. Oliver North was not in attendance, but someone else from the NSC was, along with a number of representatives from State, the CIA, and the Department of Defense. The White House e-mail that summoned them advertised the agenda as, "to discuss Panama: our press line, what we say in Congressional hearings, and where our policy stands."

The starting point for the RIG was a review of the charges against Noriega, including a presentation by the State Department's Bureau of Intelligence and Research. As one State Department participant later summarized that review, the Bureau of Intelligence and Research "said in effect that Noriega runs Panama and Noriega is corrupt. We know for certain PDF officials are involved in the cocaine trade but don't have that evidence on Noriega. But not a sparrow falls without him taking a feather. Noriega has to know and is getting a share."

After considerable and sometimes testy discussion, according to the after-action report filed by the man from the NSC sitting in for Oliver North, the RIG "decided: That we cannot say there is no evidence to support [the *Times*'s] charges; that would be untrue and [such a] defense of Noriega would undermine our Central American policy. [It was decided] that at Congressional hearings . . . CIA will give a factual presentation . . .

State will draw up a list of very specific items which we will insist require action . . . CIA and Defense will take a careful look at the PDF to identify some leadership alternatives. . . . Finally, when Abrams is summoned for hearings, he will seek to educate Congress on the complexity of the situation: yes, it's rotten, but we cannot solve the Panamanians' problem and any precipitate action would make things worse."

A second meeting, internal to the State Department, followed the RIG. Here, the issue of the longer-term American policy toward the General was again engaged. State partisans of a change hoped to alter Abrams's born-again stance on Noriega and carried a certain optimism over from the RIG discussion. In it, Abrams almost seemed to be having second thoughts, as though he might consider pulling back from Casey's efforts to defend the General.

Accordingly, much the same points made at the RIG were made again at this internal State discussion: Now was the time to start looking for options; the issues the General posed were not going away, particularly since his transgressions involved dope; the United States needed to find out whether, as one of the meeting participants put it, "there were senior officers in the PDF who were clean enough and smart enough to understand that Panama's future (and the future of the PDF) rested on the transition to democratic rule"— and, should the answer turn out to be yes, they should dump Noriega as soon as possible.

Whatever hope these advocates had for changing Abrams's mind was quashed when the assistant secretary finally spoke up.

The issue of what to do about the General had to be shelved until after a final contra victory in Nicaragua, he said. In the meantime, the General was simply too important to dump. Period.

End of discussion.

While Abrams's efforts were helpful, it is likely that if events had worked out the way the General had expected, Oliver North would have been the actual mechanic called out to dispatch *United States v. Manuel Antonio Noriega* when that time came.

Once the Washington spotlight suddenly focused on this heretofore clandestine "loose cannon" over at the National Security Council, most of the attention was on Oliver North's international activities and on the fact that he sold sophisticated weapons from American stockpiles through the Israelis to the Iranians, despite an American legal embargo against all such arms trading, and then used the profits from those sales to support the contras, who, of course, the law prohibited the United States from helping. Almost lost in the clamor was the "fixer" role North played along the way — looking after Bill Casey's "friends" on the American domestic front — when, in fact, such fixing actually consumed no small amount of North's energies. Senate investigators would later identify at least seven different criminal investigations in which the lieutenant colonel had involved himself, attempting to influence their disposition and outcomes, and usually succeeding in one form or another. By his own account, in the summer of 1986, alone, Casey's fixer succeeded in getting a Miami criminal investigation into contra gunrunning slowed to a crawl and a congressional inquiry into contra drug smuggling derailed indefinitely.

Typical of Ollie North's approach to such tasks was the case of the Honduran colonel, another one of the Casey strategy's Central American "friends." The colonel had been instrumental in securing base camps and staging areas for the contras on Honduran territory abutting the Sandinistas' border. North's assistance was called for after the FBI apprehended the colonel in a failed attempt to smuggle some seven hundred pounds of cocaine into the Southern District of Florida, the proceeds from which were intended to finance the assassination of the elected president of Honduras and the installation of a general in his place who was sympathetic to Casey's underground enterprise. North, worried that the colonel might, in North's words, "sing songs we don't want to hear," mobilized a campaign to ease the law's sting. In total, some eight high-ranking officers from the United States Army's Southern Command, the Defense Department, the Central Intelligence Agency, and the State Department contacted the court to urge leniency on the Honduran colonel's behalf. All the subordinate staff at State wanted the department to refuse to participate in that process, but Elliott Abrams overruled the opposition and added himself to the list.

In the end, the Honduran was sentenced to two concurrent five-year terms, to be served in a minimum security prison, and he would be allowed to stay in the United States when he was released.

North filed a short hand report with the NSC on the affair by e-mail. The "objective [was] to keep [the colonel] from . . . spilling the beans," he wrote. As it was, the colonel "was convicted of conspiracy under RICO, which would normally have gotten him 25–30 years. He was also convicted of conspiracy to do harm/assault a friendly head of state . . . with a sentence up to life . . . [but] he was 'awarded' two concurrent five year terms [instead]. The judge is on our side."

The highest priority request for such fixing from a "friend" to come North's way in the summer of 1986 was from General Manuel Antonio Noriega.

The General and Ollie were not, of course, actually friends. "Noriega was probably the single most despicable human being I ever had to deal with," North later claimed. "After a meeting with him, you just wanted to go home and take a shower."

And the dislike was mutual. The General had asked his political adviser, Jose Blandon, to analyze the *Times* exposé with an eye to figuring out who all the unnamed administration sources were, and Blandon had concluded that most threads led back to North. In addition to considering him duplicitous, the General and his adviser also thought the gringo was incompetent and gullible. "Even when he's listening to you," Blandon pointed out, "he's not paying attention."

Nonetheless, Noriega and North managed to care for their mutual business reasonably well. The General knew North had Casey's backing, and the General was convinced Casey could deliver. North, for his part, may very well have shared Casey's fascination with the General's perceived wickedness. More than that, and despite his denials to the contrary, he knew he needed what the General could deliver. Indeed, Lieutenant Colonel Oliver North even bragged on their connection.

"Over the years," North e-mailed his boss at the NSC that summer, "Manuel Noriega in Panama and I have developed a fairly good relationship."

During the summer of 1986, in what turned out to be the last major run of contacts between the two of them, the General got in touch and asked North for some help "improving his image." Since, to the General's way of thinking, North had played a key role in his image's destruction by the *New York Times,* the NSC loudmouth seemed the logical place to go to put it right.

North, demonstrating virtually no feeling at all for where his "friend" was coming from, simply referred him to a public relations firm that North had used for his own contra fund-raising efforts.

The General figured their shared PR force made for a convenient backdoor means of communication and persisted in his quest. During the third week of August 1986, word arrived to North over that public relations back channel that the General had a proposal to make and was sending his emissary, a Cuban American with connections to the PR firm, up to Washington to relay it in person.

The Cuban American "flew in this morning," Oliver North reported in an August 23 e-mail,

> and he outlined Noriega's proposal: In exchange for a promise from us to "help clean up his (Noriega's) image" . . . [Noriega] would undertake to "take care of" the Sandinista leadership for us. I told the messenger that such [assassinations] were forbidden by our law and so [instead I] countered that Noriega had numerous assets in place in Nicaragua that could accomplish many [other] things that wd be essential and that after all, Noriega had helped us with the operation last year that resulted in the . . . arsenal explosion and fire in Managua and that w/o many more of these kinds of actions, a contra victory was out of the question. I thanked the emissary for his message and told him that we wd get back.

Oliver North was mightily tempted by the opportunity.

> My sense is [he advised his immediate superior, the national security adviser] that this is a potentially very useful avenue, but one which wd have to be very carefully handled. A meeting w/ Noriega could not be held on his turf — the potential for recording the meeting is too great. . . . Noriega travels frequently to Europe this time of year and a meeting could be arranged to coincide w/ one of my other trips. My sense is that this offer is sincere, that Noriega does indeed have the capabilities proffered . . . [and might provide] a very effective, a very secure means of doing some of the things which must be done if the Nicaragua project is going to succeed.

Five days later, North brought up the subject of meeting with the General at the regularly scheduled RIG meeting. The group's usual chairman, Elliott Abrams, was absent, but the rest of the members were in a jubilant mood. While the contras were down to their last supplies, barely holding on to their Northern Front and in a state of open collapse on their Southern one, relief was in sight. The assistant secretary had just skillfully lobbied Congress into resuming official support of the contras by the end of October, which would allow the whole Nicaragua enterprise to come in out of the cold. The first order of business before the RIG was North's presentation of a list of activities he had engaged in on the contras' behalf. Which, he asked the room, did it want him to continue until the congressional money was actually in hand? After securing a chorus of approvals for every item on his list, he brought up the subject of the approach he had received from the General.

North told the RIG that, among other things, Noriega was willing to commit sabotage inside Nicaragua for a straight payment of $1 million cash. North thought that, all in all, it would be an effective way to get the contras on the political map again quickly.

The RIG went on record as being leery of the proposal, but that did little to slow North down.

On the morning of September 22, 1986, General Manuel Antonio Noriega and Lieutenant Colonel Oliver North met in the lobby of London's Victoria Gardens Hotel, in an alcove toward the back where coffee was often served. The General's ghostwriter later described it as "an isolated and private spot where you feel you're in a room by yourself." Unbeknownst to either, this would be the last time each would lay eyes on the other.

North was accompanied by two retired American military officers who worked in his Nicaragua enterprise, the General by a young man from the Panamanian embassy and a translator. The Americans arrived looking every inch as though they had just flown through the night from Washington, as they indeed had, grabbing a couple of hours of sleep curled up in business class. They were all rumpled and North smelled as though he had been drinking at some point in the night as well. The General had been briefed by his contacts in the Israeli Mossad about some of what North was up to on his incessant runs around the world, so the gringo's weary appearance was not unexpected.

This time, North began the conversation by being frank about the troubles his contras were having. He also said it was the appropriate moment for Panama to play a major role in pulling them out of their nadir.

As the General recounted the conversation, next North dangled the payoff in front of him.

In return for the General's assistance, the gringo offered, "there will be a clean slate; we'll forget about all the bad stuff we've heard [about you]. We'll just forget about it."

That was, of course, about as clean a slate as anybody could offer and might very well involve no small amount of fixing on North's part to actually pull off.

What the contras needed, North continued, were "a few spectacular acts of sabotage." He then pulled out a notebook and ran through a list of targets that included an oil refinery and an airport. He also mentioned setting up a training facility for his contras, something Noriega had promised long ago and had yet to deliver. This time, North also wanted to include some guerrillas from Afghanistan in the training.

The General claimed he was blunt about the contras in his response. He said they were, quite simply, a lost cause. The contras had missed their moment, if indeed they ever really had one. His own intelligence indicated that the Sandinistas had learned counterinsurgent warfare quickly, using Soviet strategies, and the contras would continue to get nowhere against them.

Rather than dispute the point, North instead asked the General if he would write up an analysis of the military situation inside Nicaragua that North could show to President Reagan.

In his memoirs, the General maintained that he took the request as a gesture designed to stroke his ego and responded with a promise to send the paper along shortly, and that was the only promise with which Oliver North left the Victoria Gardens on September 22, 1986.

If so, this London meeting was the first and only time either of the two of them ever left the other's presence empty-handed.

The strongest evidence contradicting the General's disclaimer was the gringos' behavior once the London encounter was done.

Certainly there was no slackening in his "friendship" with Bill Casey. Almost simultaneously with the Victoria Gardens meeting between the General and North, the director of Central Intelligence called a Republican member of the Senate Foreign Relations Committee. The senator was sponsoring an amendment to the Senate's Intelligence Authorization Bill that would require the CIA to investigate the General's drug-trafficking, his money-laundering, and his involvement in the murder of the local hero Hugo Spadafora, then report back to the congressional intelligence committees.

When Bill Casey reached the senator on the phone, Casey was so angry he was sputtering into the receiver, making him even more difficult than usual to decipher.

"You don't understand," Casey insisted. "You are destroying our policy. There are some things you don't know about, things Noriega is doing for the United States."

The senator invited the director to come up to the Hill and tell them all about those things, maybe change a few minds.

Casey responded with more sputter, saying that it was "demeaning" to force the CIA to take inquiries like this amendment seriously. Then he slammed down his receiver.

For his part, Oliver North returned from London acting very much like a fixer with a slate to clean.

Some two weeks after Casey's call to the senator, North phoned the Administrator of the Drug Enforcement Administration, the DEA's top officer. North had heard rumors of some investigation going on in the Southern District of Florida, looking into drug allegations against the General, and he wanted to enlist the administrator in helping him cover the General's flank.

The administrator declined the offer, mostly out of distrust of North, whom he remembered from his outing of the fat pilot.

Had Ollie North then proceeded true to form, he would have, with Casey's backing, recruited some additional leverage from around the administration and, once reinforced, returned to the DEA to twist the administrator's arm with far more force. This technique of North's had a strong track record and, had his usual success then followed, *United States v. Manuel Antonio Noriega* might very well have died before it was born.

But that never happened. Despite their intentions, the General's "friends" would never get the chance.

— 5 —

The collapse of the Nicaraguan enterprise being run by the General's "friends" was, in Washington time, extraordinarily rapid. And, like most such relatively instant implosions, the consequences soon dwarfed the occurrence that set the collapse in motion. In this instance, the precipitating event was an otherwise unremarkable plane crash in southern Nicaragua on October 5, 1986.

The aircraft involved was the exact same C-123 that the CIA had rigged with a malfunctioning camera almost two years earlier for the late fat-pilot-turned-informant's cocaine flight into the same area. This time, minus the camera, the cargo plane was carrying one of Ollie North's extralegal contra supply shipments for an air drop to one of their few remaining bands operating inside Sandinista territory and, as the pilot prepared for the run toward a pre-set drop zone, a Sandinista military patrol riddled the C-123 with small arms fire. The shot-up airplane flew straight into a hillside, killing the American pilot and copilot along with an unidentified Latin crew member.

The only survivor was the cargo kicker, an American national who managed to parachute out before the old C-123 nosed in. Captured by the Sandinistas and paraded before the world press several days later, he explained that the flight had left an airfield in El Salvador, from which it had been operating regularly under the protection of the American client government there. He had flown out of El Salvador on nine previous air-drop missions over Nicaragua, he said. The plane was maintained by Southern Air Transport, long identified as the CIA's airline, and its flights were overseen by the CIA's man on the ground at the Salvadoran air base.

After the cargo kicker's revelations began working their way along Washington's political food chain, all the secrets that Lieutenant Colonel Oliver North had managed to keep in suspension for the previous two years started falling out of the air, one by one, most of them seemingly well outside the bounds of the law. It was called the Iran-contra scandal and it was clear early on that Oliver North had been running his own war out of the White House in total contravention of congressional controls, even raising money from foreign governments to help finance his activities. The largest such foreign donation was eventually pegged at some $10 million personally coaxed out of the sultan of Brunei by Elliott Abrams. As the news was first breaking, Ollie North tried to lay low and Bill Casey commenced damage control, arguing that the administration ought to stonewall all attempts to investigate the situation. Casey even went so far as to recommend in writing that the president fire his "traitor" of a secretary of state when the secretary argued for full and immediate disclosure.

At the same time, the General's other "friend," Elliott Abrams, assistant secretary of state for inter-American affairs, became the administration's initial point man in managing the affair.

Abrams convened the Restricted Interagency Group on the subject three days after the C-123 crash. Ollie North was due back later from a foreign trip and was not in attendance. Abrams himself hadn't spoken to North about the crash, but when they did speak, Abrams wouldn't inquire whether or not the plane was one of North's because, as North would later explain to a Senate committee, "he didn't have to ask me." North would simply assure Abrams that the families of the dead pilots would be looked after by their employer and leave it at that.

In North's absence, the RIG discussed demanding access to the cargo kicker being held by the Sandinistas in order to get him to shut up. They also discussed making sure the Salvadoran government would deny having given any contra support as well. To that end, the CIA's representative reported that contra supply flights had already been shifted from El Salvador into Honduras. The CIA was particularly worried about the Southern Air Transport connection being exposed. It was decided that Elliott Abrams would call North as soon as he got back and make sure that North had the contra organization claim independent responsibility for all such flights and deny having been helped in any way by the United States government.

Two days later, Abrams appeared before the Senate Foreign Relations Committee in a closed session.

> I think I can say [he told the senators] that while I have been an Assistant Secretary . . . we have not received a dime from a foreign government [for the contras], not a dime. . . . [The contra supply system that sponsored the crashed flight into Nicaragua] is not part of our supply system. It is one that grew up after we were forbidden from supplying [the contras], and we have been kind of careful not to get closely involved with it and to stay away from it. . . . The notion that we are generally in favor of people helping the Contras is correct. [But] we do not encourage people to do this. We don't [recruit] people . . . we don't have conversations [with the contra supply network], we don't tell them to do this, we don't ask them to do this. . . . [They act] without any encouragement or coordination from us.

The day after that testimony, Elliott Abrams taped a talk show for CNN. The host asked Abrams straight out if he could give "categorical assurance" that this crashed C-123 was not "under the control, the guidance, the direction or what have you of anybody connected with the American government."

"Absolutely," Abrams responded without hesitation. "That would be illegal. We are barred from doing that and we are not doing it. This was in no sense a U.S. government operation."

Two days after the television show aired, Elliott Abrams told a secret session of the House Intelligence Committee that he had no idea who had organized and paid for the crashed C-123. The day after that, Abrams told a public hearing of a House Foreign Affairs subcommittee that not only did he have no idea, but he doubted that anybody in the entire government had such knowledge. "We don't track this kind of activity," the assistant secretary of state explained with a straight face.

It was a bravura performance, but the State Department's boy wonder was pissing into the wind.

In a matter of several weeks, Bill Casey realized that the moment had come to prepare for disaster. The director of Central Intelligence called his acolyte, Oliver North, and told him that the whole thing was about to come unraveled and he should start covering their trail as best he could.

The following weekend, Ollie North and several NSC staffers stayed at the White House for what he later referred to as a "shredding party" at which stacks of potentially incriminating documents were destroyed and a number of others altered in order to conceal information. Among the former was a paper recently arrived from General Manuel Antonio Noriega evaluating the military situation inside Nicaragua, an evaluation the General had promised North in London.

Five days after the shredding began, the White House announced that Lieutenant Colonel Oliver North had been relieved of his duties and his office at the National Security Council was being sealed by the attorney general. North would spend the next three years testifying to congressional committees and defending himself against criminal charges.

Bill Casey struggled on without North — obfuscating as best he could, his mumble often at its thickest, confining himself to curt, almost unintelligible responses when he testified about what North had been up to and what he knew of it.

The director's public bobbing and weaving lasted until December 15, 1986. That morning, while in Room 345, his Executive Office Building headquarters, preparing for further testimony before yet another Senate committee, the director suffered a seizure and was rushed to the hospital. There, surgeons identified a cancerous tumor on the underside of his left brain. Casey remained hospitalized, not quite comatose, but virtually unable to speak, for six more months. He died without ever reappearing for public examination again.

And that was it.

Barely two months after Oliver North first approached the Drug Enforcement Administration for help with his "friend" the General's potential legal vulnerabilities, the entire superstructure of General Manuel Antonio Noriega's high-grade Washington support system had collapsed:

Casey was done for, North was out of power and in disgrace, and Abrams, though still an assistant secretary, was on the run, looking for someone to throw to the congressional wolves now dogging his heels.

The second precondition essential to the making of *United States v. Manuel Antonio Noriega* was now a fact.

The ranks of the General's Washington "friends" were decimated, and when he needed the fix to be in, it wouldn't be, neither then nor later.

CHAPTER 4

THE THIRD PRECONDITION

— 1 —

Despite the police on the General's trail and the inability of his "friends" to "help," *United States v. Manuel Antonio Noriega* would never have even been attempted without a third and final precondition:

Someone close to the General had to be prepared to betray him.

That is, of course, the way almost all such cases are made. Soliciting betrayal is a standard practice among narcotics agents, and nine out of ten charges arraigned in the War on Drugs germinate from the same moment — sometimes in an interrogation room, sometimes a holding cell, sometimes standing handcuffed in front of a pile of dope — when a prisoner, slack-jawed and frozen like a deer in the onrushing headlights of a long stretch in the penitentiary, gets in touch with just how screwed he now is and how helpless he is to prevent it. Many break into tears at that point and those who don't, feel like it. Narcotics officers are trained to attempt what is colloquially known as "nutting" in such moments of maximum emotional vulnerability. Reciting the various laws that have been violated and how much time in prison his captive has coming, the narc typically points out that the only choice the scumbag has left is either to do all that time or to help the narc bust someone else and receive some consideration from the judge as a consequence. Once the prisoner jumps for the deal, he is considered "nutted" and now turned to the purposes of his captors.

In the chase after the General, of course, such nuttings ran rampant. All told, over the entire course of this story until its end, the United States of America reduced a total of five potential life sentences and 1,435 years' worth of other alleged violations on the part of some fifteen different informants to a total of just 81 years, 6 months, and 21 days in prison, split between them — not to mention allowing the fifteen to keep property valued in the tens of millions of dollars as well as receive witness protection services and legal American residency, all in exchange for information and testimony leading to General Manuel Antonio Noriega's conviction and eventual sentence of thirty years.

Among all those betrayals, however, Floyd Carlton's was by far the most pivotal. Floyd, the thirty-seven-year-old Panamanian whose Cessna had been ditched in September 1985 on Interstate 75 with some four hundred kilos of cocaine on board, was the right man at the right time with all the right things to say. And, without turning Floyd when the Southern District of Florida did, there never would have been a case for any of the other snitches to bolster. Floyd Carlton was the pathfinder.

Fittingly, Floyd's relationship with the General was of longer standing than any of the bonds violated by the others who eventually sold their betrayal to the Southern District of Florida.

Floyd and the General went all the way back to Panama's Chiriqui Province in 1966. They met in the city of David there, out near the Costa Rican border, when Floyd was just seventeen and the General was a thirty-two-year-old lieutenant. Floyd — whose father, an American sailor stationed for a while in the Canal Zone, had given him little but his name was a high school dropout who had a clerk's job with the municipal court but was looking to advance himself. He harbored dreams of going off to flight school in Panama City someday and becoming a bush pilot. The lieutenant was stationed at the local National Guard garrison, a graduate of a Peruvian military academy, remarkably ugly-looking, with cheeks like an alligator's back and something of a reputation for beating up prostitutes. That said, he was nonetheless a soldier on the rise who had already lifted himself from far more desperate circumstances than Floyd was facing in Chiriqui — a likely candidate, Floyd thought, to give a young clerk in David the boost he needed. Their "friendship" was a "use" relationship for both from the get-go.

Not surprisingly, Floyd jumped at the opportunity to do the future General a favor. The possibility arose when Lieutenant Noriega, in a moment of drunken recreation, ventured into a pasture and shot a farmer's horse with his National Guard pistol. The farmer then sued the lieutenant in the David court in which Floyd clerked. In response, the lieutenant approached Floyd, who, in turn, arranged for the whole affair to be thrown out of court and dismissed.

Afterward, Floyd and Lieutenant Noriega became drinking buddies, with Floyd escorting him over to the house of Floyd's best friend, César Rodríguez, where the three of them sat around getting bombed on the homemade liquor that César's father made from mangoes. The trio's carousing continued after Floyd was laid off from his clerk's post and held successive jobs repossessing cars and then managing his in-laws' ranch. Along the way, the lieutenant repaid Floyd's earlier favor and got charges of public drunkenness against Floyd dismissed and Floyd released from jail.

By all accounts, the three of them — the older Noriega, and the younger Floyd, and César — would remain "tight" after they all left David, Noriega to run the G-2 and Floyd and César to flight school in Panama City. And his ongoing connection to General Manuel Antonio Noriega would eventually make Floyd Carlton a very rich man. He owed his drinking buddy from the old days a lot, Floyd liked to point out, but not that much. And when suddenly faced with the prospect of never leaving prison for the rest of his life and losing everything he had accumulated since he'd left Chiriqui, Floyd Carlton squirmed, swallowed hard, and then told all he knew about his old friend the General, trying to get as good a deal from Dick Gregorie and the Southern District of Florida as he could get.

And when he made that deal, Floyd opened the door through which *United States v. Manuel Antonio Noriega* entered this one of a kind story, seemingly out of nowhere, stage left.

2

Floyd Carlton's journey into betrayal began in the fall of 1985, with Floyd in the middle of a long run of very bad luck.

In addition to the 400 kilos of cocaine that ended up parked on I-75, another 538 kilos Carlton was shipping for some minor cartel members had disappeared at some point after leaving Medellín and before reaching a Costa Rican airstrip, where the plane was to be refueled on the way to the United States. No trace of either the plane or the pilot was ever found. After investigating, Carlton concluded that the Costa Rican ground crew, the leader of whom was active in supplying the contra guerrillas next door in Nicaragua, had killed the pilot and taken the load to another airstrip owned by an American working with the contras, where Carlton believed his plane and the cocaine — worth some $25 million on delivery in Miami — had been sold to benefit the contra cause.

The cartel members who owned the cocaine didn't buy that explanation, however, and, assuming Carlton had stolen the load for himself, dispatched several hit men to Panama to blow him away. While searching unsuccessfully for their target, the hit men kidnapped and tortured Floyd's cousin, then took a motorized backhoe to the front lawn of Floyd's ranch in Chiriqui to see if he'd buried the missing coke there. Carlton, fearing for his life, called his friends at the DENI, the Panama Defense Force's investigative police, and had his stalkers arrested.

Unfortunately for Floyd, word of the whole affair leaked to the opposition press in Panama and, that fall, front pages began appearing with stories about how two pilots known to work with the General were suspected of involvement in drug smuggling. The articles mentioned Carlton and his closest friend, César Rodríguez, by name, alleging that both had long associations with the *comandante* of the PDF, and cited the General's protection of Carlton from his recent pursuers.

To halt the clamor, the DENI were called in again during October, 1985, this time to arrest Floyd. In explaining his later behavior, Floyd Carlton quite accurately pointed out that it was the General who had changed the footing of their relationship first, not he.

At DENI headquarters in Panama City that October, Floyd — small, disheveled, and submissive — sat in a hard-backed chair while he was interrogated for some five hours by the head of the narcotics bureau, the head of DENI itself, and the chief Panamanian liaison with the American DEA, all members of the General's inner PDF circle. The opening rounds of the interrogation were spent trying to cajole Carlton into telling them where the missing 538 kilos of cocaine were hidden.

When that was unsuccessful, the interrogation moved on to the subject of General Manuel Antonio Noriega himself. During the arrest, DENI had searched Carlton's homes and office and seized any materials they found implicating the General, including a notebook in which Floyd had recorded all of their mutual financial transactions, going back to the days when he and César had started on their road to the big time, flying loads of weapons to the guerrillas in El Salvador at the General's behest.

The General was upset, the chief of narcotics pointed out. When Floyd fucks up, the press connects it right back to the General and the General didn't need to give his enemies those kinds of weapons. At the time, the beheading of the local hero, Hugo Spadafora, and the dismissal of the civilian president were both still topics of intense controversy all over the Republic of Panama. The narcotics chief assured his prisoner that the General had a lot better things to do than clean up after a half-wit fuckup like Floyd.

Then Carlton's interrogators began soliciting an official statement:

Floyd owned two houses in Panama City, a house in David, a villa at the beach, a sports car collection, a ranch in Chiriqui, two condos in Miami, plus several airplanes and boats, was that right?

It was.

How did Floyd get the money to afford all that?

Floyd answered by telling them they should ask the General; he would know the answer to their question.

Did Floyd get the money from the Colombians? they persisted.

"Ask the General," Floyd answered again.

Was Floyd a cocaine smuggler?

"Ask the General," Floyd answered yet one more time.

Floyd Carlton's Panamanian interrogators reminded him that they were making an official record and the official record could not include any mention of the General, was that clear?

Carlton answered that it was and suggested that they write up whatever they wished said and he would sign it.

When that had been done, the head of DENI made a phone call from the room next door while Carlton listened to fragments of the conversation that drifted back to him. The party on the other end was never identified but received a report that included the information that Carlton claimed that the contras in Costa Rica had stolen the coke; maintained that he had no idea where the missing kilos were, even after they had offered to split the load with him fifty-fifty; and that Carlton had been very cooperative about making a statement. Then the DENI chief returned to Floyd.

The General wanted Carlton out of circulation for a while, the DENI chief said. That way neither the press nor the Colombians could get to him and the General could claim he had taken action. Floyd would have to do what looked like ninety days in jail, starting immediately. He was free to spend his nights at one of his Panama City houses, but he had to spend all his daylight hours in one of DENI's cell blocks.

As he always had where the General was concerned, Floyd submitted and served his ninety days, emerging from custody in January 1986, but he had not missed the message embedded in his treatment. Just four years earlier, when the General was still a colonel commanding the G-2, he and Floyd Carlton and César Rodríguez had been a regularly visible trio, hanging around together at Floyd and César's hangar on the tarmac at Paitilla Airport in Panama City. They had a flight service then, and César's C.A.R. Corporation was a silent partnership in which the G-2 commander held a major invisible interest. In those days, Floyd had carried a PDF identification card with a handwritten note on it from the colonel that pretty much gave him the run of the airfield. But those days were obviously now history. The rules had been changed from *all for one, one for all* to *every man for himself.*

Floyd, of course, was prepared to behave accordingly. As much was obvious almost immediately after his release by the DENI, shortly before the DIACSA roundup in Miami turned him into a fugitive from American justice.

At that point, Floyd solicited a meeting with the chief of the Drug Enforcement Administration's Panama country office. The DEA chief and two other agents picked Carlton up at the Panama City Holiday Inn and drove around while they talked.

First, Floyd wanted to know if the narcs had heard his name before.

The agents answered that they had.

Floyd then made it clear how upset he was that the intermediaries he had earlier dispatched to the narcs had been rudely treated. Every time he had tried to make contact with the DEA, Floyd complained, they had told his representatives that they had nothing to talk to him about. Floyd informed the agents that any such conclusion about him was bullshit. The fact was, he, Floyd Carlton, had a lot of things he could tell the DEA about what was going on in Panama and could prove everything.

Like what? the agents asked.

Like money laundering, Floyd began, like drugs, like weapons, like corruption, like assassinations. Floyd declared that he could also tell them a whole lot about General Manuel Antonio Noriega himself.

Immediately upon Carlton's mention of the General, the DEA chief and his two assistants became visibly upset. The Panama station was at that moment hip deep in Operation Pisces, "the largest and most successful undercover investigation in federal drug law enforcement history," functioning courtesy of that very same General. It was obvious that they didn't want to hear what Floyd had to say.

Floyd Carlton read the gringos' reaction and suddenly got very nervous himself. It occurred to him that this overture he was making might not be such a good idea after all, and he immediately began backtracking, ended the conversation, and had the agents drop him off at the Holiday Inn.

For their part, the DEA's Panama country office would never follow up on what Carlton had revealed, nor would they report the incident to their DEA counterparts in Miami, who would shortly be looking to place Floyd under arrest.

For his part, Floyd Carlton concluded that the DEA was simply too close to the General to risk any more encounters and made no moves to resume the contact.

In any case, the first opportunity to "nut" Floyd Carlton and initiate his betrayal had been blown outright, and it was the better part of a year before another such opportunity arose.

Besides the General's rejection, the most important element adding momentum to the betrayal building inside Floyd Carlton was the fate of Floyd's best friend, César Rodríguez — for which Floyd Carlton would ultimately hold the General responsible.

Floyd Carlton was visited in one of his Panama City houses by César Rodríguez shortly after Floyd's release from custody, and they talked about their mutual patron.

To start with, César wanted to know what had happened with the DENI and wasn't particularly surprised by what he learned.

Things were very different, César told his old friend. The General was now a leopard trying to change his spots. According to César's theory, the General wanted to be president, so his power would be legitimate — he had admitted as much to César several times — and was planning to run in the next election in 1989. Now, the General was trying to clean up his act in preparation for such a candidacy. And that meant distancing himself from the two of them. César railed about how the General had recently insisted that César sell his own house down the street from the General's mansion, a palace that occupied an entire block of the exclusive Altos del Golf neighborhood. And sell it immediately, even if he lost money. It wouldn't do for the General to be living down the street from his old friend the cocaine smuggler — it would only remind people of their connection — so César had to move.

Just the memory of the snub still pissed César Rodríguez off. They should all get ready to protect themselves, César warned, Floyd included.

The two old friends next saw each other a few days later at a meeting in the Panama City Holiday Inn. César came over from the top floor of the Bank of Boston tower, where he kept offices and ran a very fashionable nightclub.

Wearing his dark glasses, a mustache, and gold neck chains, César looked like the player he was. Floyd, on the other hand, looked like the municipal court clerk he'd once been, whatever he wore. They were joined at the Holiday Inn by two brothers they both knew. The brothers and César were putting together a smuggling deal and the conversation was all business. César wanted to know if Floyd could arrange some alternate landing strips for him, either in Costa Rica or the Panama border regions nearby. He was setting up a structure for moving a number of loads of cocaine, he said, and he would also need airplane gas eventually. At the immediate moment, he was putting together a smuggling operation using a private yacht to ferry a load to Florida straight from Colombia. César told his old buddy that he was off to the border between Colombia and Venezuela to arrange the coke next week. It was a safe bet. The General's G-2 chief was handling the security on his trip out to the Venezuelan border and the General was taking a piece of the action on the smuggling itself.

Floyd told César he didn't want to know anything more about it and wanted no part of the deal. He had enough shit falling on his head without signing on for more.

Floyd Carlton saw his old friend for the very last time several days after that, when César called and asked Carlton to come by his new house.

There, they began talking about the local hero Hugo Spadafora, whom both men had known when he led a unit of Panamanian volunteers in the Sandinistas' revolution in Nicaragua. The two pilots had run guns to Spadafora then and had kept in touch, even after he became the General's stiffest Panamanian critic. The local hero's headless body had been found floating just across the border inside Costa Rica a month before Floyd had been arrested by DENI. César told his old friend that he had no intention of ending up like Hugo.

To make his point further, César Rodríguez fetched a pile of audio cassettes and put one in his machine. He needed insurance, he explained to Floyd, so he had been taping the General's phone calls. The passage César then played began in the middle of an exchange:

. . . The General wanted to know what the message was that César wanted to give him. He didn't want César to send him any more messages through some fucking second-class officer.

César responded on the tape by pointing out that he had the balls to tell him anything he wanted face-to-face. Why didn't the General pay César what he owed him? Stop fucking with him and pay up.

The General wanted to know what the hell César thought he was owed.

César then demanded cash for a Learjet and part of a hangar, some $4 million. He told the General to pay him his money and to stop sending him messages, threatening that César was sitting on a time bomb.

The General answered that he would pay César what he owned him, but first César had to sell his fucking house. They also needed to talk face-to-face . . .

César then switched off the tape deck. He told Floyd that he had been taping the General for quite a while and, in a moment of macho bombast, had recently told the General point-blank that he had the tapes and that if anything ever happened to him, the tapes would be made public. César was convinced that he had the General by the short hairs and, because of that, was safe.

Floyd Carlton couldn't help but think that his old friend was balancing on a very thin wire stretched over a very deep gorge.

The next thing Floyd heard about César was a call from César's secretary in early March, several days after their last meeting. She wanted to know if Floyd had seen her boss.

Floyd told her not to worry. César had told him he was going out near Venezuela on business.

The secretary said no, César wasn't out near Venezuela. He was in Medellín and he was supposed to have returned yesterday at the latest. He was traveling with one of the brothers and the brother was missing too.

Floyd immediately had a very bad feeling about what had happened. And his feeling proved accurate.

The next thing Floyd heard about his best friend was that the Colombian national police had discovered the bodies of César Rodríguez and two companions outside Medellín, all three executed at close range by gunfire and dumped in the bush.

Floyd Carlton concluded after a brief reflection that the General must've had César murdered and used his G-2 to cover up the execution.

Shortly thereafter, Carlton, scared shitless, fled Panama City for San José, Costa Rica, hoping to hole up until his options improved.

— 3 —

Before Floyd Carlton could betray the General, of course, he had to be betrayed himself.

In Floyd's case, the turncoat's role was played by the Cuban exile proprietor of DIACSA, the aircraft brokerage out by Miami International that served as the south Florida nerve center for Floyd's off-loading and money-laundering operations. The DIACSA proprietor had flown air cover for the ill-fated Bay of Pigs invasion back in 1961 and was known around Miami as a successful businessman who had remained loyal to a "free Cuba" and active in the anti-Communist community. When the Sandinistas took over in Nicaragua, the Cuban exile had again rallied to the cause. One of his money-laundering clients was Oliver North's "democratic resistance" and one of his coventures with Floyd Carlton had reportedly been to fly arms and ammo into Costa Rica for the contras before flying cocaine back in the opposite direction. Even when out on bail, facing some twelve counts of money-laundering and conspiracy to smuggle narcotics — including the cocaine captured out on I-75 — the DIACSA proprietor was awarded a contract by the "humanitarian aid" program that Elliott Abrams had shepherded through Congress.

This Cuban exile turned out to be relatively easy to nut. It had taken only the short time he spent in the Miami Correctional Center waiting to be bailed to realize that he couldn't handle a serious prison sentence. Shortly thereafter, he indentured himself to DEA Special Agent Danny Moritz, in exchange for what turned out to be five years' probation.

At that point, the only one left for the Cuban to give up was Floyd Carlton. The ambush that netted Floyd began being set in early July 1986, when Floyd called the Cuban exile from his own exile in Costa Rica. Floyd, of course, had no idea his former *compadre* had been nutted, was working for the narcs, and was under the specific guidance of Danny Moritz throughout their conversation. All Floyd knew was that the Cuban had been busted for their mutual enterprise and was out on bail.

Floyd confessed to the DIACSA proprietor that he was short on information about the bust and wanted to know what all the charges were and what the gringos knew about him.

The Cuban exile answered that he didn't want to get into details over the phone — who knows who might be listening? — but he had legal papers that his lawyers had pried out of the prosecutors that he was willing to share. And since the DIACSA proprietor also held the Cessna franchise for Costa Rica, he told Floyd he would be coming his way soon to do business, assuming his lawyers could get him permission to travel from the court. Why didn't they get together and talk?

Floyd liked the idea and mentioned that he had a plane he wished to sell and maybe they could discuss that as well. The two made a date to connect in San José, Costa Rica, during the last week of July.

To set the trap, one of the assistant United States attorneys from Dick Gregorie's office had to secure the Costa Rican police's agreement to serve the American arrest warrant. Even then, the attorney warned Moritz, when the Costa Ricans arrested Carlton, he would be held in Costa Rican custody while he went through a lengthy extradition process, and that process would have to be completed before Moritz could even conduct an interrogation. Moritz said he would take whatever he could get at this point, but ground his teeth at the prospect of more delays.

As a special agent in the Miami Divisional Office, Moritz's clock was ticking. In 1986, DEA policy still dictated that field agents' duty stations had to be rotated every four years, without exception. For Moritz, that requirement meant that when the Cuban received his call from Floyd, Moritz had less than a year left in which to make this case.

After that, he would be transferred somewhere else to do something different.

On July 30, 1986, some ten months after Floyd Carlton's Cessna had been abandoned on I-75, Danny Moritz was finally able to lay his hands on Floyd, at least briefly.

The Cuban exile DIACSA proprietor took a suite in the exclusive Cariari Hotel in San José, Costa Rica, and, when Floyd Carlton arrived there to meet his old business associate, Danny Moritz, dressed up like a room service waiter, was across the hall in a room with the Costa Rican police.

The Cuban and Floyd sat in the suite and the Cuban dialed room service for drinks. Ten minutes later, Moritz knocked on the door in his waiter's outfit, carrying a tray of concoctions from the bar. When the Cuban answered his knock, Danny stepped inside, followed by a swarm of Costa Rican policemen who jostled his tray and spilled the drinks all over the floor.

Floyd Carlton surrendered without a struggle.

Realizing this was his only chance until the extradition was done with, Special Agent Danny Moritz talked to Floyd as he was sitting handcuffed in the Cuban's hotel suite. Moritz hoped to at least begin nutting Carlton before the Costa Ricans took him away.

Look, the agent said in Spanish, Floyd had better face facts. His canoe was up shit creek without a paddle. Check the numbers, scumbag: importation of cocaine, three counts at twenty years apiece; possession of cocaine with intent to distribute, four counts at twenty years apiece; illegal use of an interstate facility, five years; and running a continuing criminal enterprise, life in prison without parole. Add it up, Floyd, life plus a hundred and forty-five. Carlton had better start looking after himself before it was too fuckin' late.

Danny wanted to lock eyes with Floyd Carlton, but Floyd, trussed up like a chicken and stunned at the seeming bottomlessness of the pit into which his life had just fallen, never looked back and never said a thing. Then the Costa Ricans took Floyd off to jail.

Floyd Carlton had a lot of time to think about betraying the General before he actually committed himself to that course.

At first, his reaction was a kind of psychological denial. Having backtracked from his earlier offer to the DEA's Panama station, he now resisted being nutted, worried about whether the DEA could really be trusted where the subject of General Manuel Antonio Noriega was concerned, and also feeling an almost superstitious bond with the General, his old Chiriqui homeboy. It was as though Floyd believed he could make everything he had just lost reappear, if only he behaved as though his bond with the General still existed the way it once had.

To that end, Floyd spent much of his first few weeks in the San José, Costa Rica, prison remembering "the good old days," when their possibilities had seemed endless and things were still *all for one, one for all* among the three of them.

By 1978, Floyd and César Rodríguez had become bush pilots, operating out of Paitilla Airfield in Panama City and their golden age was about to begin. They were making $600 a month from a flying service run by a former Panamanian diplomat when their old drinking buddy began turning them into rich men. The G-2 was facilitating the supply of insurgent Sandinista troops in Nicaragua, and Noriega, who was then a colonel, recruited his old cronies to fly arms shipments from Costa Rica to the Panamanian expatriot volunteers led inside Nicaragua by Hugo Spadafora. Shortly after that, Noriega went into the arms business on his own and expanded his operations into El Salvador, so Floyd and César began flying arms to the guerrillas there as well.

Eventually, they were pulling in some $35,000 apiece per load and operating out of their own hangar at Paitilla, right next to the National Guard hangar where Noriega kept one of his offices as well. The cards both Floyd and César carried included a note from the colonel advising whomever it might concern that the bearer was "a personal friend" and requesting "all cooperation be afforded him that he might require."

Of the dozens of gunrunning flights they made in those days, the only serious scrape from which Colonel Noriega ever had to extricate his two Chiriqui homeboys involved a 1980 arms transaction for El Salvador that began when César was approached by two Salvadorans of the guerrilla persuasion with a laundry list of weapons they wanted filled. César said he would get back to them and took their list to the then colonel, who sent him on to the colonel's front man for arms dealing. A deal was soon made for the Salvadorans to buy their weapons and for Floyd and César to fly them into El Salvador from a field in Costa Rica, but things never went quite right.

Floyd was flying a Piper Seneca belonging to the charter company owned jointly by the two pilots and the former diplomat who fronted for the colonel's interests. César was flying an Aerocommander supplied by the colonel that was officially the property of the Panamanian Air Force. The enterprise's first mistake was not painting over the Aerocommander's tail numbers, and the mistakes only snowballed from there. Next, the Salvadorans had a brief encounter with the Costa Rican National Guard on the way to the airfield and consequently rushed their loading. The cargo included a lot of AK-47 infantry assault rifles and 7.62mm ammunition, boxed in containers labeled as the property of the Venezuelan Army.

Floyd took off first in the twin-engine Piper and barely made it into the air. César's single-engine Aerocommander was even more seriously overloaded and clipped its landing gear on the fence at the end of the runway before slowly climbing to join Floyd's Piper. The two pilots flew in formation out over the Pacific to avoid Nicaraguan air space and then ducked into El Salvador in the dead of night. The airstrip was lit by guerrillas holding flashlights and torches. Floyd went in first, unloaded, and took off to circle. Then César followed suit, only to discover when he touched down that the fence he'd clipped on takeoff had severed the hydraulic lines feeding his brakes. Unable to stop, César Rodríguez and the Panamanian Air Force Aerocommander plowed into the forest at the end of the runway.

Floyd quickly landed a second time and found the Aerocommander smashed. He had to kick in the cockpit windshield to extricate César, who had broken both legs and was in severe pain. Carlton had the guerrillas carry his best friend to the Piper, then, after instructing them to burn the crashed plane, he took off.

That was yet another mistake. The guerrillas fled without setting the fire and a Salvadoran Army helicopter soon landed on the scene and captured the wrecked Aerocommander intact, including not only 20,000 rounds of Venezuelan ammunition but the official papers that listed the plane's owner as the air force of Panama.

Floyd knew nothing of the Salvadoran Army seizure as he headed off in the Piper with César to Chiriqui, where César's relatives checked him into the hospital. Floyd then called G-2 and reported what had happened. The colonel wanted to know if they had burned the Aerocommander and Floyd, assuming the guerrillas had done what they'd been told, said he had. The colonel said he'd be in touch.

Half an hour later, an army officer located Carlton in the city of David and ordered him to phone a jeweler in Panama City who was another of the colonel's front men. When Floyd phoned, the jeweler told him that the Aerocommander had been found intact and now, thanks to César and Floyd's fuckup, there was an international incident going on. Fortunately, the colonel had been assigned the task of defusing the affair. Floyd was instructed to go immediately to Panama City to be interviewed by the Panamanian attorney general. The jeweler also explained what Floyd was to say.

Floyd, as usual, did as he was told and the incident blew over. He and César and the eventual General were back in business shortly.

In Floyd Carlton's memories, sorted again and again while staring out the Costa Ricans' barred windows, the General assumed an almost mystical power to fix anything he had a mind to. In "the old days," Floyd was convinced, the General would never have let him waste away in a Costa Rican jail.

But that, Floyd also knew, was "the old days."

Six years was a long time, and if Floyd Carlton needed to remind himself of how different things were now, he only had to close his eyes and picture the late César Rodríguez on his knees in the Colombian jungle catching a 9mm round that made a neat hole on the way in and splattered brain matter all over the back side of his head on the way out.

While his Costa Rican attorney contested the United States' claim for extradition, Floyd Carlton's urge to betrayal ripened as his denial and initial resistance waned. Floyd was a brave flier but a soft man, and incarceration quickly reduced him to his emotional roots. And the further he eroded, the more Danny Moritz's parting admonition to look out for himself resonated in a way it simply hadn't before.

At first, Floyd tried to deal with his circumstance on his own and offered a million American dollars to the warden of the facility in which the Costa Ricans had incarcerated him, all for a little assistance in escaping. But the effort blew up in Floyd's face. An informant passed word of the bribe to higher Costa Rican authorities, and the only result of Floyd's offer was a transfer to an even heavier security facility from which escape would be virtually impossible. There, all he had to entertain himself was an electronic game called Donkey Kong, his menthol cigarettes, and his memories.

Eventually, Floyd felt desperate enough to turn to his former Chiriqui drinking buddy and patron, even though he knew the General had already imprisoned him once and had killed his best friend. In his jailhouse logic, however, Floyd began to figure that he had cut the General in on all of his deals for years to insure against just such a predicament as this. And the more jail rubbed, the more Floyd thought the General owed it to him to rescue his ass, the sooner the better. This was a service he had already paid for and Floyd was not going to accept simply being abandoned. The General had certainly fixed a lot worse things than Floyd's low-grade mess in the past, and Floyd saw no reason he couldn't do so again now.

Floyd made contact with the General by writing to another old friend from Chiriqui who was now married to the PDF colonel who served as the General's chief of security. Her husband ferried Floyd's messages to his boss.

In total, Floyd sent the General four letters from his Costa Rican jail cell by this back channel. The first was jokingly referred to as "the grovel letter" by Carlton's eventual interrogators, such was its obsequiousness. Floyd addressed the General in only the most reverential tones and quickly prostrated himself, begging for help and pledging his everlasting fealty. The best Carlton got back was the General's assurance that if his old Chiriqui buddy would just do five years for the Americans, by then the General would be able to secure his release as part of an international prisoner exchange.

That didn't satisfy Floyd, and each succeeding letter he sent became more threatening. There were people who wanted to know all about the General, and he had things he could tell them, Floyd warned.

The General's responses increased their belligerency in step with Floyd's threats, alluding regularly to just how vulnerable Floyd was.

As Christmas approached, Floyd Carlton became sick of writing letters and concluded that the General would do nothing for him, whatever approach he took. And that was the last straw.

Fuck him, Floyd finally told himself, just like he was gonna fuck me.

Carlton notified his Costa Rican attorney that he no longer wanted to contest his extradition to the United States, and the Costa Ricans then called the Southern District of Florida with the news.

On a Friday in January 1987, Kenny Kennedy and Danny Moritz arrived in San José, Costa Rica, in a two-engine DEA plane flown by a DEA pilot, come to fetch their prisoner, some fifteen months after they had first busted his load out on I-75.

Kenny was happy to be able to finally deliver the witness he had promised his old strike force buddy, Dick Gregorie, and he was particularly happy that Danny Moritz was getting his prisoner before he had to be rotated off the case at the end of spring. Moritz would be moving on to Cleveland to work street dealers, and there was nothing Kenny could do to derail the transfer — it was policy, cut and dried. Kenny thought of his own presence on this errand as a statement that the Floyd Carlton investigation had a priority rating, whatever happened with Moritz. It was also just a chance to get out of Miami for a weekend in Costa Rica.

On Saturday morning, Kennedy and Moritz drove to the prison where Floyd Carlton was waiting nervously, playing Donkey Kong. Their small caravan of sedans had been organized by the DEA's Costa Rican country agent. The Americans presented their extradition papers to the warden, but the warden claimed he knew nothing about it and was not going to release the prisoner until he did. All of the DEA country agent's arguments were fruitless, so the caravan drove off to the home of one of the Costa Rican judges overseeing the extradition. The judge told Kennedy and Moritz that he would straighten the warden out, but that couldn't happen until the next day. This time, the Americans were instructed to wait at their plane and the Costa Ricans would deliver Floyd Carlton to them.

At the appointed Sunday hour, Kenny Kennedy and Danny Moritz watched the Costa Rican caravan approach, a handful of police vehicles surrounding what looked like an ice cream truck painted in military camouflage stripes and swirls. When the truck reached the tarmac, Floyd Carlton emerged in shackles.

Kenny's first impression was amazement at how small Floyd was. "I mean he was skinny and shorter than me," the ASAC remembered, "and I'm pretty fuckin' short."

The DEA agents and their prisoner were airborne within five minutes.

Kenny made Floyd as comfortable as he could, but the pilot of the DEA plane wouldn't allow anyone to smoke, so Floyd got a little twitchy as the flight progressed. For most of the journey, Carlton played Donkey Kong in silence with Kennedy, winning every game.

Danny Moritz read Floyd his Miranda rights in Spanish shortly after they lifted off.

Floyd listened politely and then got straight to business.

"What do you want?" he asked Moritz.

"I want the General," Moritz answered.

Floyd told him they would talk about that later.

— 4 —

The official nutting of Floyd Carlton by the Southern District of Florida took place over three days in February 1987, inside a high-security facility known as the Submarine, a windowless underground cell block guarded by teams of armed United States marshals twenty-four hours a day. The only light in the Submarine was generated by fluorescent tubes that hummed and flickered on the ceiling, thickening the air into a kind of antiseptic porridge with an almost white tint. The only breeze was from an air-conditioning vent in the ceiling. Eventually Floyd's prolonged stay here gave his skin a translucent cast, making him seem even more vapid than he was.

When Dick Gregorie, First Assistant United States Attorney for the Southern District of Florida, first saw his new star witness after only a couple of weeks underground, Floyd was already pale. He was also haggard, in a state of emotional exhaustion that occasionally drifted over into outright collapse, and given to fits of crying that often commenced without warning and lasted as long as fifteen minutes at a stretch.

On top of that, Floyd was a whiner, who started every conversation with a list of complaints: the food wasn't right; what about his cigarettes?; when would he get something in Spanish to read?; the fuckin' TV wouldn't get channel 8. Most of all, he complained about how much he missed his wife and kids and went to great lengths to describe the pain their absence caused him.

When Floyd was calm enough, he and Gregorie got down to business and the deal they struck was fairly standard for the genre. While Carlton was prepared to betray the General, whom he now regularly referred to as "the son-of-a-bitch who didn't do nothing to help me," Floyd insisted that he wouldn't testify against anyone else. He also wanted Witness Protection for himself and his family. Gregorie granted those requests and eventually agreed to drop all of the counts outstanding against Floyd except for one, so his total exposure was reduced from life plus 145 years to just a maximum of twenty. Sentencing would be delayed for at least six months so there would be an opportunity for the judge to see just how cooperative Floyd was going to be before determining how much of that twenty Floyd would have to do. Floyd would also be allowed to keep all his holdings in Panama without threat of confiscation.

Before any of that was set in stone, however, Gregorie insisted on hearing just what Floyd actually had to say about the General and warned that if his story wasn't up to the claims Floyd had made for it, the deal was off.

Like most informants, Floyd Carlton had to be educated to the task. In that first session with Dick Gregorie in the Submarine, wrapped in fluorescence, with the overhead lights humming and air vents rattling,

Floyd hemmed and hawed, puffed on his menthol cigarette, and wanted to talk in generalities, like how nothing happened in Panama without the General's say-so and just what a rotten *chingadera* motherfucker that "son-of-a-bitch who never did nothing to help me," General Manuel Antonio Noriega, really was.

Gregorie told Floyd that was all very nice but didn't amount to squat. He needed to hear about what specific acts were undertaken in what order on what day, by whom and where. That was evidence. The rest was gibberish.

Having challenged him, Gregorie saw a different Floyd from the whipped noodle who sniveled through the start of every day. Floyd Carlton was no dummy. Before he left the Submarine, he'd become fluent in English and was reading a dozen paperbacks a week. He also had a detailed memory. And, of course, a story to tell.

Gregorie and Danny Moritz extracted the high points in fits and starts, Moritz translating Floyd's Spanish, eight or nine hours a day, three days running.

According to Floyd Carlton, the transgressions that eventually became the backbone of *United States v. Manuel Antonio Noriega* began in the summer of 1982 when Floyd was approached by a flashy Colombian he'd encountered around the Paitilla hangars on several occasions. The Colombian said he had noticed that Floyd and his buddy César seemed to have "a special kind of access" around the airport and was also very loud about how he worked for "some of the richest men in Colombia"— men, he eventually indicated, who might like to make Floyd a business proposition. The nearest the flashy Colombian got to specifics was mentioning that these rich men from Colombia needed money transported to Panama from the United States. Floyd thought about it for a couple of months and then agreed to fly down to Colombia for further discussion. That flight from Panama City to Medellín took place, as best Floyd could remember without checking his logs, sometime in the month of October, four and a half years ago.

Two of the men Floyd met with there were listed among the RICOs laid out in both of Gregorie's cartel indictments. The cartel men were in a huge office in Medellín that Floyd described to his captors as looking "like something very very important." The immense room was also lined with sinister men carrying every variety and caliber of weapons. Floyd could see right away that he had walked into something "deep." Both cartel men greeted Floyd effusively. They pointed out that they had attempted to make contact with him on several previous occasions but that Floyd had ducked them.

Floyd admitted he had been very busy. Then, he said, when this flashy guy showed up with talk of some easy work, he decided to check it out.

The cartel men asked what the flashy guy had said.

Floyd responded that it was something about money-hauling.

Actually, the cartel men explained, they preferred to be more frank than the flashy man could afford to be. What they really wanted hauled was cocaine, between Colombia and the United States, through Panama.

Floyd said he didn't fly powder into the United States.

But, the two Colombians pointed out, Floyd was connected enough in Panama to get the dope into the country from Colombia if they had another way to move it from Panama to the United States. For that alone, they would pay him $400 a kilo.

Floyd said he couldn't do anything like that without "permission."

He never told the cartel men from whom he would seek such "permission" and, with his interrogators down in the Submarine, Floyd still took great pride in never having mentioned the General directly in any of his conversations with the Colombians. This was the way the General wanted things done and Floyd wanted the gringos to understand that the "son-of-a-bitch who didn't do nothing to help me" had always been well served.

In the immediate moment, though, not saying the General's name out loud had been a hollow fiction. The Colombians knew full well that Floyd was going to get permission from Noriega, then a colonel in command of the PDF's G-2. The cartel men pointed out to Floyd that they had dealt with this Noriega before. The last time, his troops had seized one of their fishing boats carrying a thousand kilos of cocaine and it had cost almost a million dollars to get the boat and their men returned. And the dope never came back. The cartel men laughed at Floyd's pretense of concealment and told him to go ahead and talk to the colonel.

Floyd then returned to Panama and, the following week, while flying Colonel Noriega from Panama City to Rio Hato and back, raised the subject.

The colonel almost tore Carlton's head off in response. He said that fucking Floyd had better thank God that the two of them had been friends for such a long time. Otherwise, he would be in the deepest kind of shit for even raising such a subject. The Colonel said he never wanted to hear about it again.

Then, perhaps a week later, Floyd was at his home when the colonel's front man, the jeweler, called and instructed Floyd to drive out to the colonel's beach house at La Playita, a place he used for discreet private socializing. This evening, the colonel was hosting a cocktail party, populated largely with PDF officers and foreign diplomats. The colonel gave Floyd a big hug when he arrived and took him into a side room, his arm around Floyd's shoulder until they were out of possible earshot from any of the other guests. Then Noriega asked how that business Floyd had mentioned on their trip to Rio Hato was going to be done.

Floyd, taking his cue from their previous conversation, said he didn't want to talk about it. That was a dead subject.

Noriega assured him that it was all right, he would like to hear more details.

Floyd said he didn't really have any, since he wouldn't think of doing anything without the colonel's OK and he thought their talk on the Rio Hato flight had been clear about it.

Noriega said Floyd ought to find out more about these Colombians' proposition and get back to him. Anything like this, of course, could not involve planes of Panamanian registry and would have to be something about which the colonel himself "knew nothing."

Floyd agreed. Then the two old Chiriqui homeboys shared a drink and told several stories to each other about women they claimed to be screwing.

Shortly after the colonel's party, Floyd called the flashy Colombian who had initially contacted him. The Colombian said his bosses would pay Floyd's "anonymous" source of "permission" $30,000 for each load.

When Floyd relayed those numbers to the colonel, Noriega acted as though he had been insulted. He said these fucking Colombians must think he was starving or something. This was impossible to do for anything less than $100,000, and he wanted the money in advance.

Floyd flew to Colombia and delivered the colonel's message in person to the two cartel men with whom he had visited on his previous trip. One of them began chuckling.

"Oh, Noriega, Noriega," he laughed.

Floyd, true to the colonel's instructions, asked what Noriega had to do with it?

"OK," the cartel man said, and, tipping an imaginary hat to Floyd's pretense, changed his chant to, "Oh, Floyd, Floyd."

Carlton delivered the cartel's money to Noriega through a PDF officer who was the colonel's principal gofer, all $100,000 cash in a cardboard box wrapped in plastic.

Then in mid-November 1982, Floyd landed a Piper Cheyenne of Colombian registry at the uncontrolled Calzada Larga strip in the Panamanian bush and unloaded a number of duffel bags that were whisked away by the cartel's Panama operatives in a pair of minivans. Afterward, the cartel men let Floyd know that there hadn't been any cocaine in the duffels, that they had used the haul as a test run, but paid him for three hundred kilos anyway.

The next load was four hundred kilos in the middle of December, essentially a repeat of the earlier practice run only for real. A third load followed in May 1983. For it, the colonel raised his price to $150,000, again in advance. The cartel messenger brought the money to Floyd's hangar at Paitilla wrapped in a plastic shopping bag from a downtown department store, and Floyd met the colonel personally to hand it over, this time in a parking lot.

Floyd set about arranging the fourth of his smugglings through Panama on the cartel's behalf in December 1983. Now, however, the colonel was the General, *comandante* of the Panama Defense Force, and there were complications. The Colombians had recently attempted a smuggle through Panama on their own without using Floyd or purchasing anyone's "permission," and the General's men had intercepted the operation down at Coronado Beach, costing the cartel another half million dollars to ransom their smugglers out of Panamanian custody. The General was pissed and when Floyd called, told him to come out to La Playita immediately. There, he brought up the cartel's failed smuggling attempt right away.

These Colombians must think Panama is just some fuckin' Indian tribe, the General complained. They think they can come and go and just do their business as they please. Well, fuck them.

This was the last time, the General told Floyd. No more flights after this one, and he wanted $250,000 for it, up front.

For this fourth smuggling venture, Floyd again delivered the General's money in a sealed box to the General's gofer, but it was not a smooth transaction. The gofer got back to Carlton right away and said the box was $50,000 short. Since all Floyd had done was pass on the cartel's sealed package, he had to return to the enormous office in Medellín to meet his two cartel contacts and report the problem. They treated it as not unexpected news and one of the cartel men began to mutter that he'd known they were going to have problems with "that ugly little son-of-a-bitch."

The General, however, was paid his "missing" $50,000 and the cartel's cocaine passed through on its way to the Southern District of Florida without a hitch.

And that, Floyd Carlton told his captors, was the last load of cocaine Floyd had personally arranged with the General for the cartel.

After their three days in the Submarine, Gregorie told Floyd Carlton that he'd passed the test. His deal with the Southern District of Florida was on and the betrayal of General Manuel Antonio Noriega by his old Chiriqui homeboy was now under way.

— 5 —

Its third and final precondition set, *United States v. Manuel Antonio Noriega* was now possible.

As much was apparent just in the way Dick Gregorie related to it once Floyd Carlton was in hand. For the first time, Dick now felt that he had direct evidence against the General that was credible enough to take to a grand jury. Floyd Carlton's interrogation was still a long way from an actual case, the First Assistant pointed out, nothing but a scumbag's story in dire need of corroboration and examination in detail, but Gregorie was already convinced "there was something there," and he wanted to run with it right away.

Unfortunately, however, Gregorie now lacked a case agent to do that running. Danny Moritz was headed for Cleveland on a mandatory rotation, and there was nothing Gregorie could do about it, no matter how much he bitched to his old strike force buddy, Kenny Kennedy. Kenny was helpless as well and was frank with Gregorie that it would take a while to find Moritz's replacement. Since the United States Attorney's Office was essentially stuck with whatever investigative resources the DEA provided for the office's dope cases, the First Assistant could do little but whine at Kenny, which he did whenever the opportunity arose.

More than ten years later, Dick Gregorie was still annoyed at the memory of what had happened. "They take my case agent, who is fluent in Spanish, knows Floyd, and is familiar with all the details," he griped, "and they send him up to Cleveland to buy nickel bags on street corners when he is in the middle of an investigation that could strike at the heart of the Medellín Cartel? This makes absolutely no sense at all. What kind of War on Drugs is that? I had to start all over again from scratch."

That spring in 1987, Kenny Kennedy just listened, shrugged. There was nothing either of them could do about it.

Danny Moritz's final role in this story involved writing up the internal paperwork on what Floyd had said over his three days in February. The first document Moritz produced was a teletype. This form of internal DEA communication was generally reserved for high-priority announcements, rarely running more than a page in length. Moritz's teletype ran fourteen pages — the bureaucratic equivalent of giving a speech over the public address system — in which he summarized all the goods Floyd Carlton had given up about the General. He also earmarked the teletype for the widest allowable circulation. Moritz's logic was apparently to draw as much attention as possible to this embryonic case in an appeal for further leads and, if nothing else, hopefully to ensure that nobody would silently sweep this under the rug.

If he was also hoping to make a big enough splash to be reprieved from Cleveland, that strategy failed. Moritz's last duty before leaving the Miami Divisional Office was to write up a standard DEA form 6 report on Carlton's interrogation, which he filed during April 1987. Having produced this documentary starting point, Danny Moritz's contribution to the General's thirty years behind the razor wire off SW 137th Avenue was now done.

And for the next two months, despite Dick Gregorie's chafing, *United States v. Manuel Antonio Noriega* sat in investigative limbo, just a file folder in Kenny Kennedy's office drawer filled with a one-of-a-kind case waiting to be made.

PART TWO

THE INDICTMENT

CHAPTER I

THE CASE AGENT

— 1 —

The wait ended during the second week of June 1987, when Kenny Kennedy sent instructions for Special Agent Steve Grilli to report to the ASAC's office in the front corner of the Miami office's second floor. Grilli was in the Group Five squad room right down the hall, so it didn't take long to get there once the message reached him. Kennedy stared out the window in the meantime.

That particular Miami day was nothing special, just the usual ozone smudge suspended in the distance by the glare that always abuses south Florida as July Fourth approaches, cooking jungle vapors out of the ground, every cloudburst followed by the hiss of evaporation. Nobody in their right mind spent any more time outside in weather like that than they had to, narcs included. So the Drug Enforcement Administration's Miami Divisional Office — an unmarked, unremarkable three-story commercial structure halfway between the Palmetto Expressway and the Doral Country Club, deep in the Kroger Executive Center office park — was buttoned up tight against the summer and pumped full of refrigerated air, 67 degrees Fahrenheit. Kenny Kennedy noticed a trickle of sweat inside his collar nonetheless.

The ASAC's nervous anticipation was understandable. At the time, his choice of Steve Grilli involved a certain amount of bureaucratic daring: though thirty-four years old, Grilli was only a GS-11, in the middle of just his third year as a DEA agent, at least two pay grades below what might have been expected for this assignment. Giving such a junior agent free rein to hunt up a case on "the de facto ruler of Panama" would prove controversial, to say the least — but not, of course, until the rest of the organization found out what Kennedy was up to, and that would take a while.

Despite the risk, Kenny still chose Grilli — because he believed Grilli might very well be the smartest agent he had and because Grilli was hot. Out of nowhere, this "big fuckin' Italian kid from Brooklyn" had chased down the Miami end of a case over in Group Five, known by its tracking number, 85-Z017 a.k.a. "85 Zulu One Seven." This was when he was still just a GS-9, having come straight to Elephant Country after graduating from the training academy, second in his class. Eighty-five Zulu One Seven ended up the most notorious heroin bust since "The French Connection" and was featured on the cover of *Newsweek* magazine.

On top of that, Grilli's smarts were certifiable — he even had a masters degree in history, earned in his previous life as a graduate student and public school teacher. Kenny raved to Gregorie that this "kid" was a natural talent, despite coming late to his calling. He had a brain like a fuckin' computer and the balls of a barracuda. And he worked like a fuckin' coolie. The whole time Grilli was making a reputation over at Group Five — the divisional response group, chasing other agents' or agencies' requests for assistance — he was also the division's firearms officer, administering instruction and examinations at the shooting range, and its physical fitness officer, coordinating the physical conditioning program and personally jogging anywhere from five to seventeen miles a day.

Dick Gregorie liked the choice. In April, Kennedy had sent Grilli to Dick to take over the ongoing Medellín Cartel investigation and the two had hit it off. Within six months, Grilli would put together what was then the largest real property seizure in south Florida history against the cartel as part of the work for Gregorie. The big Italian kid from Brooklyn — six feet four, two hundred thirty pounds, former holder of the Albany (N.Y.) State University record in the discus throw — was indeed hot. By June, Gregorie had already made it clear to Kenny that he wanted Steve to go after the General as well.

Grilli, however, still hadn't a clue what was up when he reported as ordered. "I had no real idea of who fuckin' Manuel Noriega was," he remembered. "And no idea that anybody was thinking of makin' a fuckin' case on him. It was all a blank. I just knew Kennedy had somethin' he wanted to see me about down in his office and that was it."

Kennedy's office, by governmental regulation, measured out at exactly twice the square feet of floor space as the offices assigned the next lower pay grade, such as the Group Five supervisor's into which Grilli had first been called for notification of Kennedy's summons. Otherwise, the ASAC's office was undistinguished. GS-11s like Grilli didn't as a rule have contact with GS-15s like Kennedy, but Grilli had been in his office before, when Kennedy first sent him off to Gregorie to cover the cartel case. Kennedy's corner space with its floor-to-ceiling glass, sealed and tinted, was occupied by a government-issue desk parceled out from some General Services Administration warehouse, with two similar chairs facing it and a bulk purchase couch against the wall behind the chairs. Once inside, the enormous Grilli stood there looming over the furnishings until Kennedy, pear-shaped and stumpy, motioned him to a chair.

The first significant contact Steve Grilli had ever had with Kenny Kennedy had been in the aftermath of 85 Zulu One Seven some four months earlier, when the giant heroin bust had finally come down and the case was bound over for prosecution. At the time, Kennedy had approached Grilli in the office and praised him for his obvious smarts. Grilli didn't waste any energy being bashful in response to the compliment from his boss's boss, an otherwise unapproachable four pay grades his senior. He was chafing in Group Five, where he was assigned to bits and pieces of other people's investigations, mostly legwork. So he took the opportunity to make his argument straight to the ASAC.

"Then let me use my brain," he'd pleaded in answer to Kennedy's appreciation.

Kennedy only laughed, but he got the message.

Kenny started their June conversation by saying he had an opportunity for Steve to put his fuckin' brain to use if that's still what he wanted to do. To work on it, though, Grilli would be utilizing informants already developed by Group Six, whose specialty was air smuggling and where Danny Moritz had once been assigned, so Grilli would have to be transferred there out of Group Five in order to keep everything inside operational guidelines. His promotion to GS-12 would come soon as well.

Grilli, of course, had no problem with any of that. He was tired of kicking in doors or playing the goon in somebody else's buy-bust operation for a kilo or two. Special Agent Steve Grilli hadn't come to Elephant Country to hunt rabbits. He meant to be the best agent south Florida had ever seen and wanted nothing more than the chance Kenny Kennedy was about to give him.

In what would prove to be the pivotal moment in both their careers, not to mention the General's, Kenny Kennedy eventually reached into a drawer, then pulled out a file and tossed it over to Steve Grilli's side of the desk. The file contained the DEA-6 forms accounting the February interrogation of Floyd Carlton, Moritz's telex announcing the case to the rest of the DEA, and DEA-6s on the tiny pilot and several other captured airplane jockeys the station had accumulated in the DIACSA takedown the year before.

"I want ya to check this out," Kennedy told him. "Then let me know if you can make a case out of it or not."

Grilli took the file with him as he got up to go.

"And I want a yes or a no," Kennedy added. "Don't bring me back no fuckin' maybes."

— 2 —

More than anything else that June, Steve Grilli wanted to demonstrate a mastery that he hadn't yet managed in his life, despite all his trying. He called it "hittin' a home run." He knew he had it in him. And he wanted that accomplishment with the quiet desperation of someone who had already fallen short of his vision and been forced to start over once before.

Grilli's abandoned dream had been his studies toward a Ph.D., a yearning he had inherited from his father, a Queens meat-cutter who had always aspired to the academic life after his own college education had been interrupted by World War II. Steve's father eventually earned his bachelor's degree at night but got no closer to academia than moving his family out of the city to Long Island for most of Steve's childhood and then helping his son with his homework during the week. Sundays were always given over to tables of meatballs and canneloni being devoured by relatives who seemed to arrive from everywhere. At home, young Grilli was taught that family was everything.

Steve chose Albany State for his own run at the Grillis' academic dream, but, after earning a 1971 undergraduate degree in history, as well as three varsity letters in track, Steve first worked for three years as an officer with the New York State Parkway Police patrolling Long Island before he returned to the Albany campus to earn a doctorate. His specialty was European military history. When he married his wife, Patti, a secondary school teacher, in 1975, he was working on his masters and soon took a job teaching, then another job working for the campus police at nearby Rensselaer Polytechnic Institute. He was devoted to his intellectual dream, but by the time his daughter was born in 1981, Steve could read the financial handwriting on the wall. There was no way teaching school and studying history was going to pay his family's bills, and now, sixty units into his doctorate, he hadn't even begun working on his dissertation yet. He figured he had no choice but to find something else to do.

If not a "failure," he accounted his lost shot at the Ph.D. as a "falling short" at the very least.

To start over, Steve Grilli returned to law enforcement. Working as a parkway police officer had been a good job as far as he was concerned, though the endless patrol was brutally dull. Steve also liked the detectives he watched on television, bringing their minds to police work, and, not long after his first child was born, he applied to the Drug Enforcement Administration, making a trip to New York City to be interviewed by a panel of agents. Before his application could be acted on, however, the Reagan administration declared a hiring freeze, and Grilli's hope to become a federal detective was put on hold. Instead, on a vacation in Florida visiting his parents after their retirement to Boynton Beach, his cousin Sonia — who worked for the police department in Coral Springs — told Steve that the Coral Springs P.D. was hiring and offering starting pay a third again higher than anything he'd ever made as a teacher. Grilli signed up in short order and decided to abandon the Northeast for good.

The change in his life was, needless to say, abrupt. So much so, in fact, that it was a year before Patti moved from upstate New York to join him and, for a while, it was not clear that she would come at all. In the meantime, Coral Springs put Grilli in a cruiser working late hours in the boondocks, dealing with little of note that wasn't just turned over to the Detective Squad. For family life, Steve relied on phone calls to Patti or hung around with his parents. Then, with little notice, Steve Grilli got a call from the Drug Enforcement Administration. They said his deferred application had been approved. The War on Drugs was going into high gear, and agents were needed. Grilli accepted the DEA offer with alacrity and was sworn in on May 24, 1984, in Fort Lauderdale. And, just as Patti and their daughter finally arrived in Florida and settled into the Grillis' new house in Deerfield Beach, Steve was ordered to the Federal Law Enforcement Training Center in Georgia for twelve weeks of basic agent training.

Older than most of the other recruits and already an experienced policeman, Steve was one of the class stars at Basic Agent Training. He also first seeded his reputation as a "conehead" there, when, in response to a query on a standard DEA psychological profile asking him to list the last book he had read, Steve actually wrote down the title of a volume on military history instead of the pulp fiction everyone else listed. Steve began his special agent career posted to Elephant Country by virtue of his outstanding record at Basic Agent Training. He was proud and excited. "This job was gonna be nothin' like I had ever experienced in my life," he remembers, "and that was exhilarating — sort of looking at the roller coaster, anticipating the ride."

On the other hand, it had to have been at best an ambivalent moment for his wife. Patti already had severe doubts whether Steve's narcotics policing was a sufficient reason for her to sacrifice a normal family life — an outcome of which the Drug Enforcement Administration notified her ahead of time, quite literally. In order to complete the paperwork for Steve's new employment, both she and he had to sign three waivers. The first attested to their recognition that as a condition of employment, a DEA special agent was subject to postings anywhere in the world at the DEA's discretion. The second attested that Grilli would also be expected to work long and unpredictable hours, again at the DEA's discretion. The third and final waiver attested that both partners in their marriage understood that the divorce rate among DEA agents was almost eighty percent, far higher than the national average.

Patti and Steve signed off on all three and then, as predicted, Steve proceeded to disappear. He sometimes joked that DEA stood for "Don't Expect Anything" and it must have seemed doubly true from where Patti stood. In his own words, Grilli was "a workaholic type guy." He missed his daughter's basketball games when he was off kicking in doors with Group Five on arrest forays, and, though he managed to make it for his son's birth in January 1987, he was off again working seven-day weeks on 85 Zulu One Seven almost immediately. Needless to say, it was far less than Patti had hoped for.

From Steve's point of view, however, his approach was working. It wasn't just that he was smart. It was also his dogged devotion to his assignments that had allowed him to emerge from the pack and catch the ASAC's eye. That meant more long hours on top of those he had already put in, whatever the consequences for his family life.

And now, thanks to that sacrifice, it looked as if Steve Grilli might be about to get a shot at the biggest Elephant in Elephant Country.

Steve Grilli did not look the part of the smartest agent Kenny Kennedy had at his disposal. Indeed, the combined impact of his hulking size and Big Apple accent was such that he almost always played the gorilla when working undercover, masquerading as some hired muscle named Guido, the goon sent by the other end of the pipeline to pick up the goods. Grilli was also partially deafened in one ear from having a gun go off next to it, so he often tilted his head slightly to lead with his good ear and sometimes worried that he talked a little louder than he meant to. Appearances aside, however, Special Agent Steve Grilli knew just what to do once he'd given the General's file a first read.

"It didn't take no rocket scientist to figure out that Carlton was the key," he remembers. "If Carlton's for real, then you can shoot the fuckin' moon. But if he ain't, there's no case and no hope of making one. I had to see the guy."

That, however, would take a while. Witness Protection had long since moved Floyd Carlton out of the Submarine and into concealment at some other federal facility somewhere else in the United States. Once Grilli filed his request with the U.S. Marshal's Office, it would be more than two weeks before the marshals could produce his witness. In the meantime, Steve checked a few things out, read the file several more times, and mused. There were two facets in particular to *United States v. Manuel Antonio Noriega* that drew him:

The first was its differentness. "I thought I was a different kind of agent," Grilli remembers, "so I wanted a different kind of case. And this was a whole different kind of case than DEA usually made. You gotta understand that DEA is a proactive single-mission federal agency, the only one of its kind in the United States. They don't, as a rule, start investigating after a crime had been committed. They start before it's committed and get themselves in it so they can bust it just as it goes down. The DEA is also statistics-driven. They put all institutional value in numbers of arrests, quantities of interdicted drugs, and the value of assets seized, period. The rule of thumb I was taught at the academy to separate good cases from the mediocre ones was 'powder on the table and bodies in jail,' the more the better. I mean they didn't even teach RICO at the academy. And this case had none of what they were lookin' for. It was *reactive* not *proactive* — we weren't goin' to insinuate ourselves into some fuckin' dope deal involving Manuel Noriega. We had to reconstruct a crime that dated back five years. And when we did, we weren't going to bust any powder on the table and we wouldn't get any more than one arrest out of it, if that. This was a historical conspiracy, a kind of case that was well off the DEA's beaten path. But I liked that. I liked that a lot."

The second lure for Grilli was how the case fit in with the larger picture. "Since I had started workin' the Medellín Cartel for Gregorie, I had been studyin' all the evidence from the first two indictments and I could see right away how the fuckin' General fit in the picture. The first work I ever did in Miami right outta the academy was for Group Four, the laboratories group, who were hiding tracking devices in shipments of ether headed for cocaine manufacture in Colombia. And all of it went through Panama. Now I find all this cartel shit is goin' back and forth through there too. It was like *All Roads Pass Through Panama,* you know what I mean? And once I got this case, I found out nothin' happens in Panama without the General's permission, so it all fit together. I could make a case on him as an extension of the cartel RICO, which is the way Gregorie wanted it made. And I was intellectually fascinated. I wanted to be the guy to put that puzzle together. Assuming, of course, that Floyd worked out — which was still a pretty big assumption for me. Like I said, I had to see the guy."

— 3 —

Steve Grilli's first encounter with Floyd Carlton finally took place during the afternoon of July 7, 1987, in the Submarine. To get there, Grilli drove east from the Miami office in the backwash of the Dolphin Expressway — his car windows rolled up tight and the AC on maximum to fend off the furnace outside — all the way to Interstate 95, then caught a downtown exit, made a quick run up a side street to a steel gate that had been raised at his approach, and then down a ramp into the high security underground parking garage beneath the Federal Courthouse Annex, just a short jog from Biscayne Bay and its cruise ship terminals.

According to the DEA's internal tracking system for agent activity — the backbone of which is a Form 352 filed by every agent to account for every working day — Grilli's July 7 afternoon and early evening were devoted to an ancillary investigation of the second cartel indictment, out of Group Six, involving cocaine smuggling. He was just back from four days off — the three-day holiday weekend plus one more day charged against his annual allotment of nineteen vacation days. It amounted to Steve Grilli's longest such off-duty stretch of the summer, preceded, typically, by working at least ten hours a day for ten of eleven days. Steve had spent those four off days with Patti and the kids hanging around the house in Deerfield Beach, trying to make up for lost family life. Now, on his first afternoon back, the heat was lifting off Miami Avenue in sheets, imparting a sense of relief to the explosion of shade inside the garage, but Grilli was too focused to notice. He had been looking forward to this afternoon since long before his days off.

Steve Grilli was joined in the garage by a Spanish-speaking agent and the assistant United States attorney from Gregorie's office who was running the DIACSA prosecution. All three of them then approached a plain solid steel door in the parking garage's back wall, unmarked except for an intercom plate and a closed-circuit security camera on watch above the entrance. After activating the intercom, each of the three was asked to approach the camera and hold up their identification. When all three had been checked against the list at the other end of the video and their badges examined, the door was buzzed open and they stepped into a long windowless concrete corridor, all of it — walls, floor, and ceiling alike — painted with a generic gray paint that the General Services Administration likely purchased by the acre foot. The door slammed shut and locked behind Grilli, the last man through, and he wouldn't see daylight again until he passed back out going the other way. From this point on, the world was lit with fluorescent tubes, the air refrigerated and pumped in and out through ceiling grates.

After turning a couple corners down the hallway, Grilli and the others reached the outer perimeter of the Submarine itself, where the passage was sealed by another solid steel door like the first, again monitored by an intercom and a camera. Here, for the second time, the three visitors displayed their badges, identified themselves, and were buzzed into an antechamber or sallyport, facing another plain steel door that was never opened until after the other door locked behind them. This third door, when unlocked, admitted them to the innards of the Submarine, the highest-security detention facility in the Southern District of Florida, containing three "public rooms" in addition to the cell block hidden behind yet a fourth solid security door beyond which visitors were never allowed. The first public room was the squad bay for the team of marshals on duty, all of them armed for instant response to any threat. The other two rooms were a larger "conference room" and smaller "interview room." Grilli could have either, they told him, so he took the smaller one, better to tower over the diminutive informant.

Floyd Carlton, for his part, did not miss Grilli's body language once he'd been brought in from the Submarine's cell block. Floyd had spent most of his adult life playing the tick bird to someone else's rhinoceros, so he picked up on such messages quickly. Like Grilli, he was also much more than he seemed — which was fortunate because, on first glance, Floyd did not look like a whole lot. He padded into the interview room wearing flip-flop sandals, jogging shorts, and a dirty T-shirt, unshaven, with a Tupperware sheen to his skin generated by the collision of overhead fluorescence with Floyd's own jailhouse pallor. Whenever the opportunity arose, Carlton smoked a menthol cigarette and the smell lingered on his breath. That first afternoon together in the Submarine, Gregorie's assistant made the introductions and Grilli stood up just long enough to cast a shadow over the short and skinny Floyd before folding back into his chair.

Grilli told Carlton that he knew Floyd had been working with Danny Moritz but Danny was gone now and he, Special Agent Steve Grilli, would be running this investigation from here on. What Floyd and Danny had done back in February was good enough for the initial debriefing, but what he and Floyd were going to do over the next few months would involve a whole lot more. Grilli had a case to make, and that meant he had to learn everything Floyd knew and then he had to corroborate it. And whatever he couldn't confirm would be worthless. So he didn't want any off-the-wall stories. And he didn't want Floyd tellin' him stuff just 'cause he thought Grilli might want to hear it. Grilli wanted real information, period. He'd deal squarely with Floyd if that was forthcoming. But, if Floyd fucked with him and told him lies, Grilli promised to bust his balls. Steve reminded his new snitch that his charges had only been reduced to a maximum of twenty years and that how much time out of that twenty Floyd would have to do would depend on what Steve Grilli said to the judge.

That yank on Floyd Carlton's chain was enough to provoke him to protest in a burst of gutter Spanish to the effect that he would never tell no lies — not to Grilli, not to nobody. Then Floyd pointed out that if Grilli was in charge now, he better look after Floyd because these marshals weren't doin' a good job of it. They hadn't fed him anything except gringo fast food since they brought him back down here and now, Floyd complained, he couldn't even take a shit, not even drop a little rabbit turd. The television didn't work right neither.

The snitch went on like that for another fifteen minutes, winding up with a tearful tour through his pain at the absence of his family.

When that flow of grievances had ebbed somewhat, Steve redirected Floyd's attention to the stories he had told Moritz back in February. Grilli wasn't looking for a thorough rendition — that would come later, in spades. That first day, he just wanted to get Floyd comfortable, see the way he handled questioning, assess his familiarity with the material, and size him up. So Special Agent Steve Grilli spent the afternoon doing just that, later scribbling some of the conclusions in his ever-present notebook:

Floyd was obviously bright. You could see it in his fucking eyes and how quickly he picked up on what was wanted of him.

Floyd was also going out of his gourd down in the Submarine. He had nothing to do but talk to Grilli, so he would eventually look forward to it, which would make him open to telling even more than he wanted to.

Floyd remembered detail. Floyd even remembered shit like airplane tail numbers and exact load sizes and dates, exact dates. That would provide a gold mine for corroboration purposes.

Floyd's memory was consistent. When Steve stopped him with a question and forced him to go back over statements made fifteen minutes previously, the story stayed the same.

In assessing Floyd's motivation, Steve guessed the chance for revenge against the General was high on the list. Floyd obviously hated the son-of-a-bitch for not having saved his ass down in Costa Rica when he had the chance. Vengeful as he was, Floyd would have to be double- and triple-checked for exaggerations and invention.

Lastly, Floyd was often hysterical with self-pity. And he was fragile. On both those issues, Grilli noted he would have to be indulged up to a point, but only so far. The guy had it coming, after all.

It was dark in the security garage when Steve finally emerged from that first encounter in the Submarine, the night outside afloat with deep-fry smells, carbon monoxide vapors, and the scent of brake fluid.

The last thing Grilli told the marshals on the way out was that he'd be back on Thursday.

Grilli returned to the Submarine as promised, then returned the next day too, and again the following Monday — all the time just conversing with

Floyd and hearing his stories of the good old days in Chiriqui while the air-conditioning vents rattled overhead and the light tubes hummed and Floyd got used to talking to him. Then on Tuesday, July 14, 1987, Steve Grilli brought a polygraph machine along, with a DEA specialist to administer a lie detector test. The exam itself was a series of questions referencing the events involving Carlton, the Medellín Cartel, and General Manuel Antonio Noriega between 1982 and the present, which Floyd had first described last February. Carlton was now asked to attest to the truth of what he'd said.

Carlton did so emphatically. And the polygraph — geared to rate the informant's responses on a scale from "definitely truthful" through "somewhat truthful" and "somewhat false" to "definitely false"— rated everything Floyd Carlton said as the very maximum on the "definitely truthful" end of the scale.

"That was instant hard-on," Steve Grilli remembers. "The guy was off the fuckin' chart."

By the next day, Grilli had made his mind up and stuck his head in Kenny Kennedy's office up on the Miami Divisional Office's second floor to give the ASAC a response to the question he'd left Grilli with when Grilli took the file during June. There was indeed a case to chase in this, Steve was now convinced.

Kennedy was behind his desk, the glare at his back smothered in window tint.

"The answer is yes," Grilli told him. No fuckin' maybes.

On Friday, July 17, 1987, *United States v. Manuel Antonio Noriega,* the four hundred and thirty-seventh investigation opened by the Miami office that year, officially commenced. Special Agent Steve Grilli was immediately posted to the case full time.

Exactly two years, five months, three days later, when a detail from the American invasion force — reeking of the torched rubber and spent cordite churned up in the very short battle that had consumed their morning — kicked in the General's door and stumbled upon his abandoned altar, festooned with candle wax and chicken entrails, the soldiers would find Steve Grilli's name written right near Dick Gregorie's on the General's list of targets for bewitching.

CHAPTER 2

THE WASHINGTON SIDE OF THE STORY

— 1 —

The other strand in the General's outcome began in Washington, D.C. during the first week in June, among the luncheon crowd at Maison Blanche, a trendy restaurant then at the top of the capital's food chain. Tables here were hard to come by and the crowd generated a murmur just loud enough to make the room feel safe, but never so loud as to prevent business from being conducted. Much of the side talk overheard around the restaurant that day was about the Iran-contra hearings, under way for the last two months, and before which the State Department's one-time boy wonder, Elliott Abrams, had just testified in what was thought by most to have been an epic episode of stonewalling, if not outright deception, featuring, as it did, yet another denial that he had done anything untoward in the course of Bill Casey's Nickawoggwha campaign. The hearings were already dominating the *Washington Post*'s front page and the most widely anticipated witness in Washington's recent memory — the late Casey's acolyte at the National Security Council, Oliver North — had yet to testify.

Virtually unnoticed in the hubbub, off to one side of the room, two men were seated, talking. One of them wore a uniform. That was Fred Woerner, fifty-four, United States Army, three stars on his shoulders, in town to pick up his fourth star before heading south to his new posting as general commanding SOUTHCOM, the United States Southern Command, a 15,000-man outpost headquartered in the Panama Canal Zone with military responsibility for all countries due south of the American border. For Woerner, now referred to as "CinC SOUTHCOM" —

Department of Defense shorthand for commander in chief of that military district — as well as perhaps the army's foremost "Latin Americanist," his new command was a dream come true, all the more precious for having almost eluded his grasp.

Woerner, a Philadelphia native, West Point '55, had expected his career would end with his previous three-star post at the Sixth Army in San Francisco — at which he'd stayed barely a year. To rise any higher than three stars, he had to follow his specialty and, a year ago, SOUTHCOM, the only four-star Latin American posting in the army, had looked as though it would be filled until after Woerner reached mandatory retirement age and left the service. His prospects had changed suddenly earlier that spring. A public gaff by the American general heading NATO had resulted in a resignation that set off an internal army reshuffling in which Woerner's SOUTHCOM predecessor was dispatched to Europe to fill the unanticipated NATO vacancy. CinC SOUTHCOM was then given to Woerner, in no small part because, having finished a four-year tour in Panama only the year before, he was already up to speed.

Fred Woerner sat at the restaurant table that day in June during his brief Washington stopover looking anything but extraordinary — medium height, medium build, with a noticeably straight back and an otherwise plain vanilla air that was a reasonably adequate reflection of the deeper recesses of his largely plain vanilla self. Though Fred was an intellectual of sorts, at least by military standards, he had always soldiered pretty much by the book.

Woerner's host for lunch was one Gabriel Lewis, fifty-seven, a Panamanian national planted at the table with the smooth ease of someone both very knowledgeable and very rich. Lewis hailed from Panama's upper economic stratum known colloquially among the Isthmus's dark-skinned underbelly as *rabiblancos,* literally the "white butts," the rich who had traditionally controlled Panamanian affairs, both economic and political. Lewis's family owned a bank and a number of other capital enterprises, a stake first begun a generation earlier, and to which Gabriel himself had added considerably under the regime of the General's PDF mentor, Omar Torrijos, of whom Gabriel had been a confidant. Lewis had also served as Torrijos's ambassador to the United States for a while and was Panama's principal negotiator in the talks that created the new Canal treaty. He spoke English as if it were his first language and, though he no longer had any official post representing Panama, he still visited

Washington regularly and was on a first-name basis with a number of the town's players, particularly on the Hill.

Fred Woerner thought of Gabriel as a kind of *caudillo* figure, his power generated by an unmatched knack for suspending a seemingly infinite number of important people in the web he spun with incredible grace and charm. The two had first met during the new SOUTHCOM commander's previous posting in Panama as a one- and then two-star general, commanding the 193rd Brigade, which was the backbone of SOUTHCOM's military force. Gabriel, having identified the brigade commander as someone of potential influence, began to pay court to him to better make the American's acquaintance. At one point, he ferried Woerner and his wife, Gennie, on one of the Lewis yachts out to one of the Lewis family compounds on one of the several islands the Lewis family owned off the Pacific coast of Panama, for a long and very pleasant weekend. As always, Gabriel insisted on picking up the tab and professed that he, of course, "expected nothing in return." In May, when Lewis learned of Woerner's promotion to SOUTHCOM command, he got in touch and suggested they have lunch when Fred was in D.C. at the start of June.

Gabriel Lewis was his usual charming self that day, playing the gracious host, incessantly chewing ice from his water glass with the driven quality other men might have brought to chain-smoking. Not very tall, thick but not fat, Gabriel was always high voltage and a very difficult man not to like. His voice sounded something like gravel shifting around in the back of a dump truck. Over lunch at Maison Blanche that afternoon in June, he caught up a little on old times with the new American commander and then launched into his own briefing on the state of affairs in his native country. Gabriel spoke mostly about General Noriega's Panama Defense Force, complaining about the close relationship Woerner's predecessor had maintained with them, and hoping that Woerner would not "fall into the same trap."

"Gabriel made it very clear he thought General Noriega was going to be a problem," Woerner remembers. "He was upset about him but he didn't complain about human rights or drug-trafficking or any of the rest of the stuff that was usually brought up. Instead, Gabriel was outraged at the way the General had been expanding the PDF's business enterprises into new territories, often in open competition with existing businesses. He mentioned the hotels they were building, their aircraft servicing contracts at the airport, and their control of the duty free zone at Colón as cases in point." Gabriel did not mention that in the last nine months the General had screwed the Lewis family out of two very lucrative real estate deals as well, but even without bringing up his personal losses, Gabriel had no difficulty communicating his high outrage on the subject of General Manuel Antonio Noriega. According to Woerner, "Lewis also made it very clear that he was speaking for his fellow *rabiblancos* when it came to the General." There was definitely going to be "trouble," Lewis warned, so Woerner should be prepared.

Before lunch ended, Gabriel Lewis got even more specific with his advice. Woerner had better start planning how he was going to use his forces "to remove the General from power," Gabriel suggested, because, sooner or later, that was what it would come to.

Fred Woerner let that last remark pass as if he hadn't heard it — though, of course, he had and was not at all pleased with its drift. Woerner thought Lewis was barking up the wrong tree if he expected Fred Woerner to back that kind of military gambit — let the damn *rabiblancos* handle their own business with Noriega instead of deputizing the United States Army to do it for them. But Woerner kept his thoughts to himself at the Maison Blanche.

Instead, the two men just parted after dessert and coffee with warm handshakes and promises to see each other again soon down on the Isthmus, both pleased with themselves over how they'd handled their encounter.

The talk about General Manuel Antonio Noriega circulating in places like Maison Blanche was minimal at best in the first week of June. Despite his front-page treatment by the *New York Times* the year before, the General was still largely off the capital's daily radar screen. But what scuttlebutt there was mostly assumed that the Department of Defense for which Fred Woerner would act as point man in Panama was — along with the CIA — at the top of the General's list of remaining "friends" around town.

The future General Manuel Antonio Noriega first appears in Defense's institutional memory in the early 1960s, when he briefly joined the department's payroll under the budget for military intelligence. Noriega was a cadet at a Peruvian military academy at the time, thanks to the good offices of his older half brother, a homosexual and former leader in the nationalistic Panamanian student movement, who had taken upon himself to look after his middle-class father's impoverished bastard by the family's maid, and, using his influence as an officer in the Panamanian foreign service, had secured the young Manuel Antonio the academy appointment. Since Panama had no institution of higher military learning of its own, all its future officers studied abroad and the Peruvian academy was one of the more prestigious options, drawing cadets from all over the hemisphere. Cadet Noriega first connected to the gringos when he got into trouble while carousing and, faced with charges for assaulting a whore, needed money to settle the case before it got to court. At that point, a Defense intelligence operative, on the lookout for young talent among the Latin American military, offered some cash and recruited the ugly young Panamanian to supply information about his classmates.

The Department of Defense had been tracking Manuel Antonio Noriega ever since, following his career once he was commissioned in what was then the national guard and would eventually become the PDF, noting his adoption for patronage by Omar Torrijos, tracking another violent incident with a whore, and then his marriage to a woman he courted in Chiriqui during those days he was also hanging around with Floyd Carlton and César Rodríguez. The rising young Manuel Antonio Noriega graduated from SOUTHCOM's School of the Americas' courses in Jungle Operations, Infantry Command, and Military Intelligence during the late 1960s and, after assuming the reins of G-2, was given a VIP tour by the army when he first visited the United States in 1974.

A secret Department of Defense Intelligence Information Report on the then Colonel Noriega, recorded on a form DD 1396, was prepared by SOUTHCOM in 1976. This DD 1396 described the Panama Defense Force's future *comandante* as

> intelligent, aggressive, ambitious, and ultra nationalistic, [a] shrewd and calculating person [who, while] loyal . . . and respectful to his superiors . . . berates peers and subordinates, often in the presence of others. . . . He is a persuasive speaker and possesses rare common sense [and] is considered to be a competent officer with excellent judgment. . . . [He is] an aggressive leader . . . respected by friends and feared by enemies, [who] possesses almost unlimited military and/or political potential.

Colonel Noriega was also known to enjoy intellectual banter with Americans, to love eating hot dogs and drinking expensive scotch, and to reflexively chew caramels. A later addendum to the DD 1396 added that, "Noriega is a non practicing Roman Catholic, and is possibly a follower of the Rosicrucians and has studied Buddhism." Five foot seven, 170 pounds, and a "mulatto [with] kinky, black hair," the General to be was, by SOUTHCOM standards, "a neat dresser who enjoys natty clothes." He was also judged "an astute political observer [who] enjoys demonstrating this knowledge. . . . [He] will exercise the power necessary to gain his objectives. . . . He is a man of action who is not afraid to make decisions." Cited as proof of the latter was an incident in 1970 in which the future General had summarily executed an airplane hijacker in the course of an arrest. According to the DD 1396, Noriega's favorite exclamation was *"chueletas"* — Spanish for "porkchops." He also held a black belt in judo, was "an accomplished parachutist," including free fall drops, and "an avid reader" who could "discuss Latin American revolutions at length."

This secret 1976 report advised in conclusion that, "in the event of a confrontation [with the United States], Noriega would be a capable adversary," but never anticipated that such a circumstance would ever occur.

During the 1980s, more bits and pieces about the General showed up among the scuttlebutt along the more informal edges of Defense's institutional intelligence: he kept mistresses, often several at a time, and was still a regular client of whores as well; the death of his older half brother in 1984 had been a profound loss, according to those who knew the General well; in addition to his three daughters by his Chiriqui wife, the General had a son by one of his mistresses, an offspring he recognized and supported; the General maintained a collection of at least three hundred custom-tailored military uniforms; the jeweler and front man who often traveled with the General was said by some to do double duty as the General's homosexual lover; the General owned two BMW 735s, a custom-built luxury van, a $50,000 Corvette, and several airplanes. By 1985, hints about the General's involvement in drug-trafficking were added to his file as well.

Still, as June 1987 began, what the Department of Defense knew best about the General was that he was as good a landlord as SOUTHCOM could have ever expected under the circumstances. In a country where resentment of gringos was rampant, SOUTHCOM had nonetheless been allowed to ignore the new Canal Treaties' provisions that would have prevented the United States from using its bases in Panama for anything but the defense of the Canal, and, instead, do whatever it needed to support its Central American wars and hemispheric operations, using SOUTHCOM as a military platform and staging area. The General's forbearance made all that possible. It was a sweetheart deal of the first order.

And, as far as the Department of Defense was concerned, Fred Woerner's most obvious responsibility upon assuming command down there was to do everything he could not to fuck up that sweetheart deal.

General Manuel Antonio Noriega was, of course, no stranger to Fred Woerner. Fred's previous tour at the helm of the 193rd Brigade had overlapped with the General's last year as G-2 and first three as *comandante*. While not particularly close, the new CinC SOUTHCOM and the General were certainly well acquainted.

"When I was at the 193rd," Woerner remembers, "I had as much contact with him as anybody in the American military, for several reasons: I was serving under commanders then who didn't particularly enjoy dealing with Noriega so they handed responsibility for contact with me; with my professional reputation as a Latin Americanist plus speaking Spanish as I did, I was the natural point man for him to contact as well; my home during that tour was on Fort Amador which we shared with the PDF and where he kept his office; and, of course, by virtue of my post at the 193rd, I was the 'owner' of most of the resources that he might want us to provide, so relating to me was in his best interest. I guess I saw him every month or so for almost four years. That contact took a lot of venues, but formal meetings were very rare. Usually it involved some protocol function like a ribbon cutting or the Christmas ball. The rarest exception in our relationship was a 'let's get together and talk' session. Still, I felt like I knew him."

Fred Woerner felt particularly well equipped to understand the General as well.

Woerner was no novice to the Latin circumstance. On his last tour there, he and his wife, Gennie, an American national who had grown up in Bolivia, forsook the insulation of Canal Zone society for involvement in the local culture — a relatively unusual posture for American officers — and socialized with Panamanians. Fred had been fluent in Spanish since his training at the Defense Language Institute in the early 1960s, had earned a masters in Latin American history, and had served four years as director of Latin American studies at the U.S. Army War College. He had also studied at the Uruguayan Military Institute, lived and traveled in Colombia, and advised the Guatemalan army on the use of military forces in socioeconomic development. Though an Airborne-qualified Ranger who had served two combat tours in the Vietnam War, Fred Woerner had risen to four stars on the strength of his reputation as a "diplomat" and scholar. Had he not been at SOUTHCOM and the army had wanted to know something about the southern hemisphere and how it worked, they still might very well have called Fred Woerner to find the answer.

While Woerner was in Washington before reporting to the Isthmus, Panama hardly registered as a dilemma on his professional radar screen. "It's an easy place to take for granted," he remembers, "plus there was a lot on SOUTHCOM's plate. There were almost two dozen countries in which we maintained missions. There were wars in Central America and, of course, within a year, we would be staging maneuvers in Honduras, just close enough to the Sandinistas' border to send a message. And in South America, a whole new day seemed to be opening up as the military in places like Argentina and Chile and Brazil were stepping away from power. That transformation, in fact, was my passion and I also meant it to have my highest priority."

The uproar over Panama and its commanding general would eventually make that wider focus impossible, but hadn't yet. In Washington, the first week of June 1987, when the subject of General Manuel Antonio Noriega came up during his various briefings over at the Pentagon, Fred Woerner's view of the General was obviously knowledgeable, if somewhat dismissive.

"Noriega is a thug, no doubt about it," he pointed out, "though he can be charming as well. He is naturally a very hidden man. He has a way of disappearing behind his physical ugliness, like it's a wall. I think 'inscrutable' is the word for his demeanor. It is hard not to feel watched in his presence. His character, of course, is over the edge, the living antithesis of everything I believe in. But he is more than that. He is the first ruler of Panama to ever make it up from the very bottom and that has made him powerful enemies. He is a crook, but hardly the only one. A former President of the Republic of Panama once described the place as not so much a nation as 'a tribe of pirates' and I have to agree. In any case, Noriega is Panama's problem. If Panama doesn't want him, let Panama throw him out. That's not our job."

One of Fred Woerner's final Washington meetings during his stopover that June was with Elliott Abrams. They met in Abrams's office at the State Department, a formation of concrete and glass slabs on the leafy downslope where 22nd and C streets intersect. Their encounter would seem to portend a great deal when examined in retrospect — the opening contact between what would eventually become the standard-bearers for the two opposing agendas inside the government over the issue of what "to do" about the General. But the meeting was actually meaningless in the present tense of that afternoon in early June — a courtesy call by Defense's new regional commander on the assistant secretary of state for the same region — standard operating procedure, no more, no less. Woerner considered it "opening lines of communication" and would meet with Abrams on future visits to Washington as well.

For his part, Abrams was his better self that day when he first made Woerner's acquaintance — friendly and engaging, easy to make conversation on generalities, obviously intelligent, yet intent on extracting as much information as he could while revealing as little of his own hand as possible. There was none of the abrasive and pointed arrogance that had made so many enemies for Abrams during his tenure as Assistant Secretary of State for Inter-American Affairs. His talk with the new head of the Southern Command ranged all over South and Central American topics, but it remains unclear whether Panama ever even came up. Woerner no longer remembers if it did or not and Abrams refuses to comment on the subject. In any case, their meeting was of far more interest for what was not mentioned rather than what was.

Abrams's own situation was the most obvious of the unmentioned subjects. The assistant secretary was at the nadir of his State Department career and, even though he refused to act like it in front of a visitor from the Department of Defense, everyone in town knew it. That summer, with all eyes on Iran-contra, Elliott Abrams was, after Oliver North, the second most visible figure left standing amid the still smoking wreckage of the late Bill Casey's Nicaragua strategy. During his testimony before the Select Iran Contra Committee, Abrams, the so-called King of Latin America, had made it very clear that he did not intend to apologize for anything, nor was he going to admit to having done anything the least bit improper, openly ignoring a streak of very dramatic prevarication over the previous year that was now a part of the public record.

"As an official responsible for U.S. policy in the region," he testified instead, "I have tried to keep not only the letter but the spirit of the law in mind. . . . There was no directing [of contra activity] . . . no coordinating going on by Colonel North or anybody else under his direction in the U.S. government."

Many of the senators and congressmen on the committee were incredulous at Abrams's assertion, but, when questioned in detail, Abrams regularly repeated, "I don't know," "It never occurred to me," and "I didn't ask"— to such a degree and with such vigor that one of the impaneled congressmen described him as the only man he'd ever met who "takes pride in not knowing anything."

It was altogether a far from persuasive appearance. One senator publicly volunteered afterward that Abrams's testimony had made him "want to puke" and speculated that Abrams might very well have some "slammer time" in his future. One hundred and twenty-nine members of the House also signed a petition calling on Abrams to resign, and one standing Senate subcommittee refused to allow him to testify before it on the subject of hemispheric affairs, even though that continued to be his State Department turf. "As far as Congress is concerned," the subcommittee chairman pointed out, "Elliott is a man without a mission. There's no reason to believe anything he says." By the afternoon when Fred Woerner, the new CinC SOUTHCOM, came by to say hello, word was beginning to circulate around town that both the White House chief of staff and the new national security adviser would like to show the assistant secretary the door. "Abrams is finished," one administration source would soon tell *Time* magazine.

Abrams wasn't finished, of course, not by a long shot, but if Abrams had been anything less than a protégé of the secretary of state himself, he might have been. That June, Elliott Abrams desperately needed a strategy for redeeming at least a fraction of his previous reputation and recouping, if not his status as a boy wonder, at least a margin of his former job security. Abrams will not discuss it, but, in retrospect, he seems to have spent the month of June intent on securing the means to rescue himself. And he had already concluded that the unseating of General Manuel Antonio Noriega — the same General whose flanks he had zealously defended for the last year at the behest of Casey and North — might very well provide that means.

For the second time in as many years, Elliott Abrams was about to change his tune where the General was concerned.

Abrams, of course, made no mention of any of this to Fred Woerner during the latter's courtesy call. And, when Woerner left, Abrams — who likely had already sized up his visitor as a potential adversary in the gambit he was now looking to launch — quite disingenuously wished the new commander good luck.

— 2 —

Panama, Fred Woerner's dream posting, describes an S-shaped wiggle of jungle where South and Central America meet, 400 miles long and 30 miles wide at its most narrow, native territory to a population roughly the size of Brooklyn's. At the time Woerner arrived, this Isthmus was perhaps the oddest foreign posting in the army. Its oddness lay largely in the irony that it didn't feel foreign at all. The Canal Zone, spanning some ten miles astraddle the Canal from one side of Panama to the other, contained twelve American bases that had been there almost as long as the Republic of Panama had existed and had been maintained throughout that period as an outpost of American Dixie by the Army Corps of Engineers — including trimmed lawns, white picket fences, and, until the 1960s, de jure segregation. Even now — when, under the provisions of the new Canal Treaty, parts of the Zone had already been handed over to the Panama Defense Force, with the entirety scheduled to be surrendered to Panama at the end of the century — the Zone still felt like home. The Republic of Panama was then the only other nation in the world to use the American dollar as its own currency, so incoming Americans didn't even have to trade in their money for someone else's.

Woerner arrived there in one of the perks of his new command, a large executive transport jet, part of whose cabin was walled off into a private office that included a raft of top-secret communication systems and a security safe. The flight from Washington, much of it over the deep blue shimmer of the western Caribbean, took some eight hours, and the new CinC SOUTHCOM sat at his desk, working on his speech for the upcoming change-of-command ceremony, until his jet bumped down on the Canal Zone runway and taxied to the honor guard standing at attention in his honor, the air around them pleated by the rush of heat off the blacktop.

Fred Woerner brought with him great expectations of extending American influence throughout SOUTHCOM's regional bailiwick, in what he predicted would be a seminal stretch of history for the entire hemisphere. Looking even farther south, to the abdication of political control now taking place among the largest militaries of the region, Fred thought the time was ripe for an American military man with a diplomat's flair to influence what was perhaps the most profound development Woerner had seen in his area of specialization over the course of his entire career. His own professional creed centered on civilian control of the military with an almost religious devotion, and he now saw a chance to convert half the continent to his faith. By all evidence, however, Panama didn't figure much in his initial vision of transformation, no more than as a kind of idiosyncratic backwater incidental to the larger point that was being made elsewhere. The new commander considered it far more important to first address the hemisphere in general.

Accordingly, Woerner meant the speech he had written on the trip south and was about to deliver when he officially assumed command in the Canal Zone on June 6, 1987, to be a clear presentation of his country's military credo as both an abstract and practical ideal. He knew his speech would be his most visible statement, perhaps of his entire career, so he didn't farm the address out to some aide to draft. Every word in the text had been carefully selected by the new CinC himself. He intended to make a broad statement to all of the United States' neighbors and allies to its south, about the role of the military in its highest philosophic incarnation — not, he would later point out, as a specific criticism of anyone in particular in any country in particular. Woerner still professes mystification that his host, General Manuel Antonio Noriega, could have taken the new SOUTHCOM commander's public remarks on June 6 as a personal rebuke. But that was exactly what happened. And in the end, only the General's upset would be remembered.

At the time, the General had a lot on his mind. The restiveness of the *rabiblancos* was already visible in Panama City. Civic groups had been formed among the well-to-do to promote a return to civilian rule, and demonstrations against General Manuel Antonio Noriega had already been staged and more were being planned. Needless to say, the General was in no mood for a public lecturing from the gringos to boot.

The occasion itself started out as nothing more than another protocol function, like the many at which Woerner and Noriega had previously brushed shoulders when Woerner was still with the 193rd Brigade. The ceremony and its attendant speech were held in a vacant United States Air Force hangar, outfitted with bleachers, past which units representing all of the Southern Command's elements paraded. While the hangar was hot, even with its doors opened wide to catch any possible breeze, it was far cooler than the surrounding tarmac, despite the relatively early hour. An air-conditioned reception was scheduled for a nearby officer's club to follow the CinC SOUTHCOM's speech. A number of foreign missions sent delegates to attend the function, and the largest group by far in the crowd of some two hundred, from the Panama Defense Force, was led, of course, by the General himself.

Fred Woerner's address began with an extremely ragged opening, thanks to Woerner's brand-new aide, who forgot to put a copy of the commander's speech on the podium. So Woerner, sporting his new fourth star, strode up to the microphone to find nothing to read. Once he recovered from the shock, the incoming CinC was forced to give his entire speech from memory, off the cuff, and, in his confusion, managed to violate protocol by failing to offer compliments or even polite salutations toward his hosts, the General and the PDF delegation. Then Woerner went on to pay tribute in both English and Spanish to the armed forces of the United States and their commitment to democratic civilian control of military force. "Never in our history have we ever had a man on horseback [seize power]," he pointed out. "[Instead, we] have always been subordinate to civilian authority as elected by the populace. This ingredient of legitimacy is a fundamental underpinning of a [truly] professional military."

By the time Fred Woerner reached the end of his impromptu remarks, the General and the rest of the PDF delegation were seething. The Panamanian officers, led by their *comandante,* immediately stomped out and neither approached to shake hands nor attended the reception afterward.

Within forty-eight hours of Fred Woerner's debut, the "trouble" Gabriel Lewis had predicted over lunch at Maison Blanche broke out in earnest all over Panama City.

As *Time* magazine later characterized events:

> [T]housands of Panamanians defiantly took to the streets of the capital. Their demand: dump General Noriega, who is not only the country's military commander but its de facto dictator. . . . Helicopters monitored events from above, hundreds of [PDF] riot police fanned out through the streets, controlling the crowds with nightsticks, tear gas, and volleys of bird shot. . . . As the [Noriega] government digested the latest threat to its authority, concern was growing in Washington that one of the closest allies in the hemisphere was headed for a long period of instability.

The incident that had finally precipitated this outbreak was set off by the General's most recent consolidation of power. On June 2, 1987 — the same day Elliott Abrams was on the stand fending off the select congressional Iran-contra investigation in Washington — the General summoned his chief of staff to the *comandante*'s office at Fort Amador, in the PDF sector of the Canal Zone. The chief and the General were two of the three colonels who had assumed power inside the PDF — and thus Panama — when Omar Torrijos was killed in a 1981 plane crash. At the time, the three had agreed to take three consecutive five-year terms as *comandante,* each handing off to the other. The first of these colonels, the General's predecessor, resigned from the PDF early to run for president and rule as a civilian, only to have his campaign then torpedoed by Noriega and end up out of power entirely. General Noriega's own agreed-upon term at the reins of the PDF was to be over in 1988, when the chief of staff was scheduled to ascend. That schedule was changed unilaterally on June 2. Noriega simply informed the chief that the chief was retiring immediately, whether the chief liked it or not, and that the General was about to be appointed for another five years as *comandante* by the PDF General Staff.

Noriega's suddenly former chief, essentially powerless to contest the move, stewed over the termination briefly, then called several reporters among the Panamanian opposition press and began describing the General's transgressions in what became a running two-week public discourse, full of revelations about the *comandante.* Many of these were delivered from the former chief of staff's home where he holed up, the doors barricaded and the street outside full of PDF, just watching and making no immediate moves to storm the building. At one point in his ramblings, the chief talked openly of the General's role in firing his first president and said that the PDF had executed the hero Hugo Spadafora, under orders from General Manuel Antonio Noriega himself. At another point, the chief declared that the General had also been responsible for the plane crash that killed Omar Torrijos.

The public response was almost immediate and continued sporadically for the next month and a half. One Florida daily reported on June 14:

> Panamanians defied riot police and combat troops . . . to turn out in large numbers for a sixth consecutive day, but an indefinite general strike appeared to be crumbling. . . . Business leaders, who have played a key role in the campaign of nonviolent protest against the

> government, held meetings throughout the day in an effort to shore up support for the strike. . . . [Otherwise] there was no sign of slackening. . . . Thousands of Panamanians went into the streets at noon and again at 6 P.M. dressed in white to symbolize their opposition to the regime. They banged pots and pans, and caravans of cars flying white flags raced through the city with horns honking. . . . Witnesses reported sporadic clashes between riot police and protesters. . . . They said police fired tear gas and buckshot at demonstrators and blocked roads with burning tires and garbage. . . .
>
> In the afternoon, hundreds of people streamed through downtown Panama City in cars and on foot to attend Mass at the Don Bosco church. To get to the church, protesters crossed through lines of soldiers armed with M-16s, tear gas guns, and rubber truncheons. Riot police, nicknamed the Dobermans, were positioned on the street. Two military helicopters mounted with machine guns circled overhead, making low passes over crowds that overflowed the church. . . . People in the crowd responded by waving white handkerchiefs. . . . Leaflets distributed outside the church urged Panamanians to boycott stores that opened for business and to refuse to pay taxes as well as electric and telephone bills. . . . The protests appeared strongest in the city's middle and upper class neighborhoods. . . . While disenchantment with Noriega seems widespread, the [*rabiblanco*] opposition appears to have been less than successful in mobilizing support across class and racial lines.

The uprising drew two different American responses inside Panama itself.

The ambassador at the United States embassy in Panama City welcomed the renegade PDF chief of staff and the spontaneous rebellion with open arms. The ambassador, recently widowed, even allowed his grown daughter — who was staying with him following her divorce — publicly to visit the chief at his home in a gesture of support and endorsement. The ambassador's daughter also reportedly joined in demonstrations, beating a pan and waving something white.

Fred Woerner, on the other hand, thought the ambassador was totally out of line letting his daughter behave like that, compromising the embassy's primary mission. Woerner already considered the ambassador incompetent at best, and nothing that happened later during his tour at SOUTHCOM would change the CinC's mind. Woerner also warned the chain of command to keep the former PDF chief of staff at arm's length. Woerner had known the chief during his tour at the 193rd Brigade, when the chief seemed to be "everything Noriega was not," but the chief had changed in the year since Woerner was last on the Isthmus. The PDF officer was now under the influence of an Indian guru, the guru's eighty-six-year-old disciple, and the disciple's beautiful thirty-six-year-old American "psychic consultant." Abjuring meat and alcohol for tofu and vegetables, the chief had suddenly lost thirty-six pounds, become a yoga enthusiast, and, until his recent "resignation," kept a framed photo of his personal swami on his PDF office wall. Frankly, Woerner thought the chief was "not himself" and had "lost a few marbles," so something less than an embrace from the United States was appropriate.

Woerner was also skeptical of the entire campaign undertaken by the *rabiblanco* opposition. He knew the street action in Panama City had been covered by American news video, but he warned against making too much of how that coverage made the situation appear. All the video was compromised by the melodrama of its presentation. He pointed out that the people who were demonstrating were accustomed to a degree of comfort that boded ill for their staying power as a political movement. Several *rabiblancos* whom he knew personally had sent their maids out to demonstrate in their stead. They would "want to make revolution on the weekends."

And, the SOUTHCOM commander predicted, when they fell short of bringing the General down themselves, as would inevitably be the case, then they would be asking the Americans to do it for them.

Neither the ambassador nor Fred Woerner was in direct contact with the General during this "crisis," but, during its opening days, Woerner felt that the General sent him an indirect message, whose form and content were "pure Noriega."

The episode opened with Woerner still arranging his new office in the Southern Command's main headquarters building, a two-story wooden structure not far from July 4th Avenue, the thoroughfare separating the Zone from Panama City. The location was known as Quarry Heights, for the abandoned rock quarry on whose edge the SOUTHCOM installation perched, occupying a slope overlooking parts of Panama City and the *comandancia* there, headquarters of the PDF. Woerner's office was on a second-floor corner, with windows on the two exposed walls that commanded some officers' quarters across the way. While unpacking several office storage boxes that hadn't been touched in the year since he had left Panama the last time, Fred came across a memento from the General that had been delivered the day in 1986 that Woerner had departed for his new three-star posting stateside. The package had arrived by messenger from the General's office, wrapped in some garish Panamanian paper.

The present inside was a photograph, done up in a boxy manufactured plastic frame. The photo had been taken several days earlier, at a reception after Woerner had been awarded a Panamanian medal for his service with the 193rd Brigade. It showed Woerner, with his new award around his neck, surrounded by Noriega on one side holding a champagne glass, and by the PDF chief of staff on the other, also with a glass raised. It was inscribed "Congratulations" in Spanish, "from your military friends," and signed by the General and his then chief. Since he was about to depart when it arrived, Woerner had thrown the picture in the nearest handy box and never saw it again until he unpacked that box a year later as SOUTHCOM commander.

At the time, Woerner did not want to hang the rediscovered picture of himself and the two PDF officers on the CinC's office wall, for fear someone would think he was trying to declare that he had some special relationship with Noriega. So the new commander finally hung the photo in his private latrine, a bathroom reachable only by walking in Woerner's office's sole entrance, crossing the office, and opening the bathroom's only door.

Within days after the picture was hung, another messenger arrived from the General, without warning or explanation, just like a year earlier. The package the messenger left was wrapped in the exact same paper as the present delivered in 1986. It also contained a photo exactly the same size inside the exact same kind of boxy plastic frame as the first. This photo was from the same 1986 awards reception, but featured Woerner with his medal, side by side with the ugly little PDF general and no one else. The General was holding a champagne glass just as in the first photo. Finally, this second photo was inscribed with the exact same message, except in the singular, and signed by Noriega alone.

"I had no doubt whatsoever that the second present was a statement," Woerner remembers. "Noriega was telling me two things: First, 'I have penetrated your headquarters,' and second, 'There is a new power structure and you are dealing with me and me alone.' It was very clever and very very Noriega. He never said anything else about it, but the message was clear."

— 3 —

Fred Woerner was soon contacted directly by the General's *rabiblanco* opposition as well.

On the evening of June 12, Gabriel Lewis telephoned the new CinC SOUTHCOM, the two men's first talk since their Washington lunch. Woerner took the call at his Canal Zone home, known as Quarters One, a two-story clapboard structure that dated from the original Canal construction, with a corrugated tin roof and enormous verandas wrapping both stories. The house was a three-minute walk from the office, and Lewis, of course, had the CinC's home number.

Woerner remembers Lewis that evening as "the most upset I'd ever heard him."

Lewis explained that this had been the worst day yet.

That morning, the General himself had called Lewis at his family's Panama City compound. The General told him that there was no need for Panamanians to be at each other's throats. At the very least they ought to talk it over. Would Gabriel Lewis be so kind as to arrange a meeting of the opposition with the General's representatives hopefully to start a "dialogue," just see if there wasn't some way "to resolve things" between himself and the demonstrators?

Lewis responded that there was no hope for such a resolution without "everyone making a sacrifice." Then he scheduled a meeting for that evening. Lewis would later describe his own proposed role in the conclave as that of "mediator."

In the meantime, Lewis went into downtown Panama City to take care of some family business at the Lewis family bank, El Banco del Istmo, and to meet with one of his brothers, the financial institution's chairman. Shortly after Lewis drove away from the bank, his business with his brother concluded, three truckloads of the PDF's feared "Doberman" riot police invaded the Banco del Istmo, broke its plate-glass front window, roughed up the employees in the lobby, and arrested the bank manager.

The Doberman raid on the Lewis family bank was, of course, another of the General's messages. Of the cruder variety, but to the point. He likely wanted to make sure Lewis understood just what "making a sacrifice" could look like.

All the intimidation did, though, was piss Lewis off. He was furious when the General's delegates, two PDF colonels and a civilian, showed up at the Lewis compound for the scheduled negotiation. By that point, the street in front of the Lewis house was lined with PDF regulars, just watching. To represent the opposition in the negotiations, Gabriel had summoned one of its recognized leaders and three other civilians who were critical of the General. The ensuing session lasted some ninety minutes. Despite his later claim at mediation, "Gabriel was not a neutral party," one of the opposition delegates remembered. "He was very strong in saying that Noriega was the symbol of everything wrong in Panama and needed to be taken out." Lewis also reportedly described the General as "the most hated man in Panama" and argued that the chief of staff's disclosures had revealed why.

The colonels from the PDF defended their General and described the chief of staff, still holed up in his house giving radio interviews, as "a lunatic." They also argued that removing the General would weaken the PDF, potentially creating a situation where the officer corps might have to stand trial as it had in Argentina when they stepped down from power. When the meeting ended, however, the officers promised to get back in touch with a direct response from the General himself.

Instead, the General's delegation had been gone for less than an hour when an intelligence officer from the PDF's G-2 phoned the Lewis house and berated Gabriel. "You can go to hell," the man from G-2 screamed. "Omar Torrijos made you rich. Now you are betraying the homeland." As a consequence, he swore, Gabriel Lewis was now "Enemy Number One." The consequences of that designation were left to Lewis's imagination as the officer rang off.

At that point, by now the middle of evening, Gabriel Lewis phoned Fred Woerner over in Quarters One on Quarry Heights. As he recounted the day, Lewis spoke breathlessly without being out of breath and the gravel in the *rabiblanco*'s voice came over the wire as both higher pitched and more ragged than usual. Woerner could tell right away that the ordinarily suave and gracious Lewis was in a state of distraction at the very least.

Lewis eventually told his "old friend" at SOUTHCOM that he needed a little help. "Gabriel was afraid Noriega was going to have him killed," according to Woerner, and Lewis had made arrangements to leave Panama by private plane in the morning. In the meantime, however, he needed to bolster his "security."

Fred Woerner immediately allowed that SOUTHCOM could be of service. "As CinC, I had a personal security detail," Woerner remembers, "which I found cumbersome and somewhat embarrassing. It seemed a lot more bother for me than it was worth, so I immediately told Lewis that I would loan it to him. I ordered the security detail to his house right away in uniform, but I also put them under orders not to wear side arms, though I expect they had them in their vehicle. In any case, the irony of me having to give that order was that it was necessary in order not to violate the Canal Treaty that Gabriel himself had negotiated. I instructed the detail to make itself very visible and I thought that would be enough to keep the PDF from doing anything silly."

Just in case Woerner didn't follow through on his promise, Lewis also called the senior Democratic senator from Massachusetts up in Washington, one of Lewis's closest gringo friends of long standing, who called Woerner's boss, the chairman of the Joint Chiefs of Staff, who later rang up Woerner just to double-check.

The next morning, a limo from the Costa Rican embassy under protection of diplomatic immunity drove into the Lewis family compound. The ambassador to Panama from Costa Rica was inside the car. He fetched Gabriel Lewis, his immediate family, and their luggage, and then drove to the airfield in caravan with a black panel truck full of the CinC SOUTHCOM's personal security team. The PDF only watched them go. The General would later tell reporters that "when [Lewis] left, he had no problem of any kind," and there was no reason to flee.

At the airport, Gabriel Lewis boarded a private prop plane owned by an American businessman, which flew him to Costa Rica. There, Lewis switched to an executive jet owned by another American businessman and flew on to Washington, where he would spend the duration of the General's story, in exile.

Two days later, the *Los Angeles Times* reported the Lewis migration:

> An industrialist who tried to mediate Panama's political crisis has fled the country after calling privately for the ouster of military strongman Gen. Manuel A. Noriega, well informed sources said Sunday. Gabriel Lewis, a former ambassador to the United States flew [to Washington via Costa Rica] on Saturday . . . telling friends he feared for his safety. . . . The collapse of talks between the military and civilians came as strikes and rioting against the government controlled by Noriega entered a second week. At least two protesters have been killed, scores injured and hundreds arrested. . . . Lewis, [a self-described] apolitical businessman, . . . told the Spanish news agency EFE that

> he . . . left Panama, "not as an exile, but as an ambassador for [the opposition]," seeking the [Noriega] regime's diplomatic isolation.

"Ambassador" was an understatement.

Gabriel Lewis's return to the District of Columbia was a signal event in the General's Washington story. The *rabiblanco* moved into a very comfortable home on exclusive Foxhall Road cluttered with telephones and fax machines and began working the Hill, much as he had in securing American ratification of the Canal Treaties some ten years earlier. Almost immediately, scuttlebutt about Panama was being passed around in places like Maison Blanche, and the word was almost all to the effect that the General had to go. And most of the talk was traceable right back to Lewis. He was close not only with the senior Democratic senator from Massachusetts, but also with the senior Republican from North Carolina, despite the Republican's outright hatred for the Canal Treaty Lewis had previously negotiated. Lewis became an almost instant force to be reckoned with on the Hill, and, fueled by daily television footage of rampaging riot police on the Isthmus, he managed to essentially corner the issue.

The first concrete sign of the magnitude of Gabriel Lewis's impact in the American capitol was Senate Resolution 239, up for a vote on June 26, 1987, less than two weeks after the *rabiblanco*'s arrival. That resolution called on "the government of Panama" to restore constitutional guarantees that had been suspended because of the recent demonstrations, provide genuine autonomy for civilian authorities, investigate charges made by the "resigned" former PDF chief of staff, and "direct the current commander of the Panama Defense Force and any other implicated officials to relinquish their duties pending the outcome of an independent investigation."

Gabriel Lewis described the measure as "a start."

Senate Resolution 239 passed, 84 to 2.

— 4 —

There is no record of how closely Elliott Abrams watched that vote, but he couldn't have failed to note that its margin alone qualified the General as the foreign leader the Senate would most like to see deposed. Since the assistant secretary of state was already the American government official the Senate would most like to see dealt with similarly, the benefits of allying himself with the Senate's antipathy to the General had no doubt become obvious to Abrams. By the time Resolution 239 passed, he had already initiated a shift in State's stance, backing his ambassador's approach to the former PDF chief of staff and adopting the demand that the chief's charges be investigated. And it's likely he found the switch personally satisfying as well as opportune. General Manuel Antonio Noriega was an easy figure for Abrams to despise and, of course, Bill Casey was no longer around to suppress that impulse.

The shift in attitude toward the General that Elliott Abrams had been crafting ever since his Iran-contra committee appearance was greeted by those working under Abrams as a remarkable transformation. Suddenly, he echoed the arguments inside the department that he had savagely suppressed only a year before. At the time, his support of the contras had seemed paramount. Now, however, the reformulated assistant secretary abandoned his previous rote anticommunism, in which overthrowing the Nicaraguan Marxists had been the highest possible foreign policy goal, and now put State forward as the champion of participatory democracy throughout the Americas. All authoritarian regimes had to go, be they left or right, Argentina or Cuba, Nicaragua or Panama.

Abrams's switch allowed him to keep Nicaragua on the front diplomatic burner — since the contra guerrillas were still making raids out of Honduras, now with congressional funding — but also allowed Abrams to reincarnate himself as the champion of Panamanian liberty and perhaps keep the congressional wolves who were chasing him at bay. The model for action he now proposed for the Isthmus was the mass political uprising, such as in the Philippines, in which the American government's leverage on its foreign client had been critical. At the time of the Senate vote on June 26, Abrams was already looking for an opportunity to seize the issue and run with it.

And then the General provided him with one on the very last day of the month.

It was, in some sense, predictable. Manuel Antonio Noriega's professional specialty was intimidation, and he exalted the use of it as a military weapon in *Operaciones Psicologicas,* a seventy-eight-page training manual on the fundamentals of psychological operations written by Noriega in 1975, when still G-2. The point, he argued, was to defeat your enemy before ever reaching an actual battlefield. According to Noriega, Genghis

Khan had been the best at it, ever. And in the General's own strategy of psychological war, the intimidation inherent in Senate Resolution 239 demanded an answer. So, on June 29, the Republic of Panama's Legislative Assembly, controlled by the PDF's political party, passed a resolution declaring the United States ambassador *persona non grata* and accusing the gringos' Senate of meddling in internal Panamanian affairs that were none of their business.

On June 30, the General then lifted the State of Emergency ban on public demonstrations, just as Resolution 239 had demanded. And the first such demonstration into the streets came up the main Panama City thoroughfare, Avenue Balboa, until it reached the American embassy.

Back in Washington, Abrams followed the ensuing action with the embassy's cable traffic.

"As of midday 30Jun87," one cable reported,

> the pro government demonstration stretching from in front of the U.S. Embassy along . . . Avenida Balboa, continued to grow with some estimates of the crowd in excess of five thousand. . . . Once in front of the Embassy, the crowd became more volatile by throwing rocks and debris taken from nearby garbage dumps. The pavement of the . . . surrounding streets is being broken up to use the cement as rocks. The Panama police, previously stationed around the Embassy, are not interfering with the rock throwing crowds. There appears to be a group of around some hundred persons who are moving around the Embassy building, throwing rocks and trying to stir up trouble. As of 1240 hrs, the main crowd started to dissipate from in front of the Embassy and moved . . . toward the center of town. Some small groups of rock throwers remained behind attempting to knock out Embassy cameras and windows.

Altogether, two embassy buildings, a consular library, and nineteen cars parked near them were damaged.

One of the embassy's advisory cables the following day speculated that, "barring additional accusations by U.S. legislative members and depending on whether Noriega perceives his position as being strong, the level of anti-US protests should gradually subside. Meanwhile, the political opposition [in Panama] will probably maintain a low profile, at least for the near term."

Elliott Abrams, however, was about to do the opposite. There couldn't have been a better opportunity to seize the high ground facing the General, and Abrams did so without hesitation.

First, he cleared a public State Department response issued to the world press. Though largely diplomatic boilerplate, it made the point:

> The United States is protesting in the strongest terms to the Government of Panama its unmistakable involvement in demonstrations . . . which resulted in significant damage . . . and put U.S. diplomatic personnel at risk. . . . It appears that the Government of Panama lifted the State of Emergency yesterday . . . primarily in order to orchestrate a demonstration against the United States Embassy. . . . It is [also] clear . . . that a decision was made at the highest levels of the [PDF] not to protect the Embassy. Actions of this kind will have a significant and negative impact on relations between the United States and Panama.

Then, inside Washington, Abrams also took up the issue personally. By fortuitous coincidence, Abrams had been previously scheduled to address the World Affairs Council here on the evening of June 30. It presented the perfect opportunity to make public his switch on the General. The appearance was one of his first since his testimony to the Iran-contra committee, he was one of the most recognizable men in town at that moment and, whether they liked him or not, much of Washington wanted to hear what he had to say. Among the messages the assistant secretary delivered that evening was the headlined comment that U.S. policy toward Panama had to change and he was going to make sure it did.

"The old [American] complacency . . . over the inevitable dominance of the Panama Defense Force in the nation's politics is gone," he announced. "[Panama's] military leaders must [now] remove their institution from politics [and] end any appearance of corruption."

The demand drew applause, which Abrams welcomed.

Henceforth, it would be the stated mission of the State Department and its assistant secretary for inter-American affairs to pry General Manuel Antonio Noriega loose from power, the sooner the better.

By July 17, 1987, when Steve Grilli officially launched *United States v. Manuel Antonio Noriega* in the Southern District of Florida, the demonstrations in Panama City were subsiding into uneasy calm — just as Fred Woerner had predicted — but the new initiative undertaken by State toward the General was well under way. Its most active forum was the administration's Policy Review Group on Panama, composed of representatives from the Department of Defense, the CIA, the National Security Council, and the Department of Justice, as well as State. A memo sent to Elliott Abrams in August by State's representative to this task force memorialized the new strategy:

> I would summarize the conclusions [of the Policy Review Group] as:
>
> We should continue the "gradualist approach" for the time being, ratcheting up pressure on Noriega as the circumstances warranted. We should look for ways to strengthen the cohesion of . . . the [Panamanian] opposition. . . . We should consult with the Congress . . . to try to keep Congress from taking charge.
>
> [This] gradualist approach . . . would be the logical extension of current policy — keeping the pressure on Noriega but not getting too far in front of the opposition. Doing everything . . . except asking Noriega for a departure date. This [approach] suited . . . the others around the table. . . . The CIA representative painted a picture of a standoff between Noriega and his various opponents, with the [opposition's] momentum down . . . CIA had a slightly more optimistic outlook [for Panama] than other observers . . .

This memo to Abrams also provides the first documentary evidence that Washington knew that the General had a Miami story going on as well:

"One of the most interesting comments during the meeting," the State Department rep reported to his assistant secretary, "was made by [the representative] of [the Department of] Justice. The best current Justice estimate is that an indictment of Noriega could come as early as November 1."

Elliott Abrams immediately grasped the leverage such a criminal charge might provide.

CHAPTER 3

THE INVESTIGATION BEGINS

— 1 —

From the get-go, Steve Grilli went after this case as if somebody was watching. He didn't know who or why or what in particular they were interested in. What he did know is that if word got out about the events he was looking at and that word then spread to the General, any trace of the evidence Grilli might need that was still in Panama would disappear. So Steve wanted the fewest possible people to know what he was up to, for the longest possible time, and wasn't bashful about saying so. Kennedy, of course, got an earful on the subject right away.

At immediate issue was the telex Danny Moritz had sent in April about Carlton's February debriefing. Grilli could not figure out what had possessed Moritz to do such a thing. "I mean this fuckin' telex went all over hell and gone," he remembered. "He gave it the widest possible circulation. Can you imagine what could happen to that kinda document in a place like fuckin' Colombia? What that information would be worth? That's like a loaded weapon aimed at the case. The last thing you want if you're really gonna try to make a case like this is people sniffin' around the details. There was a lot of agendas out there and I didn't want 'em all messin' around with my crime scene. It was already old and fadin'. I didn't need nobody sweeping off the trail, faint as it already was. I told Kenny we had to contain Moritz's damage and do it fuckin' quick."

Kenny agreed and sent out an immediate order advising all of its recipients to remove the Moritz telex from their files and shred it.

Not surprisingly, this was just one of the organizational problems Kennedy had to grapple with as he put together a base for the case inside the Miami offices's bureaucratic pyramid. To start with, though Grilli was now assigned to Group Six, Kennedy pulled him out of the normal chain of command to work under Kenny's direct supervision, making Steve the only GS-11-soon-to-be-12 in unintermediated organizational contact with a GS-15 — certainly in the Miami Divisional Office, and perhaps the whole DEA. Kenny did it anyway. He wanted Grilli relieved of as much of the normal lower-echelon workaday static of dealing with his group supervisor as he could. That way, the big Italian kid could chase the General without distractions.

Aside from Grilli, the only manpower assigned to the "Noriega task force" was an agent on "desk duty," awaiting action on a disability claim from a back injury — who was fluent in Spanish and moonlighted as Grilli's interpreter whenever the pain in his spine allowed — and a kid right out of Basic Agent Training, who stayed perhaps seven weeks and had the skills to make coffee and little else. They set up shop in a partitioned portion of one of the Miami Divisional Office's unused training classrooms, where Grilli worked at a portable table and used a reinforced closet to house his Top Secret safe. His slapped-together office had several phone lines, but none of them was scrambled. As skimpy as this arrangement was, Kenny'd had trouble scaring up even that. Absent powder on the table and bodies in jail, there was little institutional interest in a RICO that was more than four years old, whomever it was about.

That July in 1987, the famously good-natured Kennedy just laughed off the trouble involved in making such a weird case, quoting an old DEA aphorism.

"Big cases," he pointed out, "big problems; little cases, little problems; no cases, no problems."

Perhaps the most difficult of these "problems" for Kenny and Steve to figure out remained the issue of "confidentiality and information control." Beyond containing Moritz's telex, somehow the stories Floyd Carlton was currently telling down in the Submarine also had to be secured from circulation. Otherwise, both Kenny and Steve were convinced they were bound to surface somewhere they might do the investigation harm. According to normal DEA procedure, all of the information Carlton provided to Grilli would have to be recorded on a DEA-6, a yellow-paged manifold form. Once signed off on by Kennedy, as procedure required, those yellow sheets would then circulate into the upper reaches of the Drug Enforcement Administration, making the investigation an open book to the entire organization. Both Grilli and Kennedy could foresee the outcome of *that* arrangement.

"I can't make this case with half the fuckin' world lookin' over my shoulder," Steve complained.

Kenny consulted with a GS-14 on the Cocaine Desk at Washington Headquarters about the dilemma, and the GS-14 suggested the answer. There was a provision in the DEA operations manual mandating the "secure containment" of sensitive material, a classification left in the hands of the local bureaucracy. Using that mandate, Kennedy could take the case off yellow paper and file it on white paper instead. Then, rather than circulating, the regular reports filed on white sheets could be stored away from common knowledge in the safe of the station's special agent in charge until such time as the case's circumstances allowed the information to be passed up the chain of command. And, the GS-14 pointed out, Kennedy, as ASAC, had the authority to initiate the shift from yellow pages to white.

Kenny Kennedy exercised that option immediately.

The arrangement did not, however, conceal the case altogether from the rest of the DEA. It was soon known that Grilli was working on something with a cartel angle, somehow involving Panama — that much was unavoidable — and since it was about Panama, there would be the natural speculation that it might involve the General, The Man in all things to do with the Isthmus. But that Grilli had already targeted the General and the full extent of the evidence he was accumulating against him remained a mystery to the chain of command above Kenny Kennedy until the Southern District of Florida began calling witnesses to the grand jury, some three months after the case officially began, at a point when quashing the investigation from on high would be so potentially scandalous as to be impossible.

This decision by Kennedy to control the flow of information about *United States v. Manuel Antonio Noriega* while it gestated would be resented by his superiors in Washington — almost all of whom felt Miami's secret would have been safe with them and let him know as much in no uncertain terms.

After the investigation had been back circulating freely on yellow paper among the agency's upper reaches for more than two years, however, the invading American infantry who finally kicked in the General's Panama City door, arrest warrant in hand, would find — in addition to his altar and bewitching list — at least one DEA document on this case, marked "DEA Sensitive," stashed in the General's personal file cabinet.

"Some fuckin' DEA Sensitive that was," Steve pointed out.

To further conceal its objective, this case was not yet even named *United States v. Manuel Antonio Noriega.* That title would not come into open use until the Southern District produced its indictment, in February 1988. The DEA itself wouldn't officially adopt the name until January 1990, after the General was in American custody, down in the Submarine where Floyd Carlton had once lived. The case's given name when it began on July 17, 1987, was *Escobar Ochoa, Luis Fernando, et al.,* tracking number 87-0487.

DEA procedure required any case in the making to be named for its highest-level perpetrator and, in this instance, that was Escobar Ochoa, a member of the cartel who was suspected of being the ultimate source of supply for the 350 kilos of cocaine seized off Panamanian waters by a Colombian coast guard vessel in early March 1986. The boat carrying the cocaine was the *Krill,* a forty-eight-foot motor yacht of Panamanian registry passing through Colombian waters on its way to the United States. Though the DEA's Barranquilla Resident Office had known about the seizure of the *Krill* and had been interested enough to copy portions of the Colombian national police's investigative file, no domestic American investigation had been attached to the incident until Grilli's. Steve figured *Escobar Ochoa, Luis Fernando* provided a number to put on his Form 352 that gave nothing away but was still close enough to the ballpark as far as what Steve was actually doing, to pass bureaucratic muster.

The connection that allowed Grilli to use such a cover came from Floyd Carlton. And Floyd provided it during one of the interviews before he'd even been polygraphed.

The snitch was not particularly snarly that day, padding around the interview room wearing his flip-flops under the long strips of heartless light that never blinked, whatever time, day or night. But Floyd was weepy as hell. This morose bent soon landed him on the subject of his wife, and then he wouldn't let go: sweet Maria, Maria of my dreams, Maria, mother of my children, light of my life. That he had been torn away from Maria was a pure agony, he wailed. That he could not hold Maria in his arms was more than he could bear. If he had all the millions of dollars that had passed through his hands, he would give it all for the comfort of her presence. Floyd also sniveled that he, Floyd Carlton, was a pile of pig offal for having fucked up and now maybe lost her forever, Maria, center of his universe . . . And on like that for some fifteen minutes.

Finally, Grilli managed to nudge Floyd off that tack and onto his remembrances of his old friend, the late César Rodríguez. That threw Floyd back to César's last days before heading off to the "Venezuelan border" to score cocaine, a venture from which César never returned. Floyd told Grilli that he'd met with César in Panama City during the time preceding his death, right after Floyd finished doing his ninety days for the DENI and before he fled to Costa Rica.

César was in a smuggling venture right then with the General, Floyd declared. He had told Floyd so.

Grilli pushed him for more, and Floyd responded that he didn't know all that much.

Then he recounted what he did know: César wanted to get Floyd involved, but Floyd didn't need it. He was already hip-deep in shit. But César told him stuff about what he was up to anyway. He knew César was partners with two brothers, because he had met with them that day in the Holiday Inn. He knew the two brothers, one of whom died with César, were the sons of the General's predecessor as *comandante*. He knew César and the brothers' smuggling that March also involved a vessel named the *Krill* that César had once owned. César had told him that the fix was in for the yacht to take on its load from a local vessel at an island off the Panamanian coast, right near Colombian waters. He said the General had a piece of the scam and the General's G-2 was handling the security. This fuckin' boat of coke had bought César a slab in the Medellín morgue, and Floyd claimed that he knew the General, "that son-of-a-bitch who never did nothing to help me," had set César up to die that way, off in the bush with some *chingadera*'s pistol stuck in his ear.

Grilli already knew how Floyd felt about the General, so he was worried Floyd would get deep enough into badmouthing that he'd end up over the edge for the next half hour. Grilli interrupted.

So what else did César tell ya?

What else? What else Floyd knew from César was that the business was some kind of drugs-for-guns swap after which the coke was to be ferried from an island between Colombia and Panama into Panama itself, where it would be ferried on to the States by air. If that was true, the guns would have had to come from the PDF, Floyd insisted. Only the General moves guns in Panama, no exceptions.

That was it?

The only other thing Floyd remembered was that César had told him that he had mounted a portrait of the General in the *Krill*'s cabin so that everyone would know under just whose protection they were operating.

Those memories were enough.

Grilli filed everything Floyd had to say about the *Krill* smuggling venture that didn't involve the General on yellow paper and sent it up the chain of command as proof of his work on the *Ochoa* case, and then filed the relatively enormous mass of information Floyd relayed about the General and the *Krill* and any other circumstances on white paper as part of *Ochoa* being stored in the SAC's security safe. From outside the Noriega task force, it all looked very much as if the cartel case agent was doing nothing more than making another Colombian case on yet another seizure of cocaine.

And, for the rest of the summer, no one in the DEA besides Steve and Kenny was the wiser.

— 2 —

There was, of course, a second chain of command looming over this case, but about which Steve and Kenny weren't nearly so worried. That parallel structure belonged to the Department of Justice and its regional incarnation in the Southern District of Florida, headquartered down at 155 S. Miami, a nondescript building whose sixth and eighth floors were given over to the United States Attorney's Office. There, *United States v. Manuel Antonio Noriega* carried a lot more weight.

And Grilli, for one, was impressed with the rank of his new Justice associates. "You gotta understand," he explains, "I was just a nothin' GS-12. A GS-12 usually has trouble gettin' even the most lowly dipshit assistant U.S. attorney to return his phone call, much less remember his name. So here I am suddenly meeting with fuckin' Gregorie, who is the star of South Florida, you know what I mean? And I'm meeting with his crew, this brain trust at the top of that office, and I'm doin' it all on a daily basis. Forget gettin' a call returned, I don't even gotta call, they're callin' me. They're leavin' me messages to the tune of Steve this or Steve that. Even Gregorie's boss, fuckin' Leon Kellner, is callin' me up and addressing me by my first name. It was heady stuff. From my perspective, I was keepin' some high-altitude company. And I suppose it pumped me up that I was, made me want to do this in a big-time kinda way."

Grilli was also caught up in the chemistry of the process in which business was done on the sixth floor where Gregorie kept his office, right next door to the United States attorney's. It was a very collegial shop in its uppermost echelon. "Gregorie operated with this brain trust," Grilli remembers, "these two other senior lawyers in the office, I forget their official titles. One was the legal genius, the guy who figured out how to do what we needed and ended up doin' the actual writin' of most of the cartel indictments. The other we called Dr. No, because whenever you thought you'd figured somethin' out and then ran it by him, he'd always see the flaw. I mean he'd pick it apart. And this case was put together that way, up on the sixth floor, ideas bouncin' off the walls, free-form discussion, no intellectual holds barred. For me, goin' over there was liberation from havin' to hide my conehead. This was like a coneheads' convention. I ended up feelin' more at home there than I did back in my own organization.

"And, believe me, Dick Gregorie was the guy who made it all work. It wasn't that he was the brightest of the lot, but he had the energy that made it happen. He was the Jedi Master, if you know what I mean. He brought this faith and sense of righteousness. He was fightin' a crusade to save America's children from all this white powder floodin' into the country and he didn't fuckin' apologize for having a sense of urgency. There wasn't an ounce of back-off in him, you know what I mean? But he was gung ho without being anything but a regular type guy who just happened to be on a mission from on high. Gregorie was the best, everybody said so, at least in those days, and I felt like I was better for workin' with him. I started carryin' candy in my pocket to revive him when his blood sugar got too low. I was never worried about Dick undercuttin' what we were doin' like I eventually became about DEA headquarters. We were countin' on Gregorie's juice at the Justice Department to provide cover for us all. The bottom line was that I always thought this was Dick's case, even when I did most of the makin' of it."

Of all Dick Gregorie's qualities, however, the one without which this case would certainly have stopped in its tracks that July was simply that *he had backing.* And that backing came in the well-dressed and somewhat rounded form of Leon Kellner, forty-one, the United States Attorney for the Southern District of Florida, and the fourth member of Gregorie's office collegium.

Dick and Leon were bonded, though their relationship only went back as far as when Leon's predecessor brought them both to Miami some five years before to spearhead the return of law and order to south Florida. Leon Kellner had arrived as first assistant to his predecessor, with whom Leon had once roomed when they were both law school students, and his predecessor's recommendation had assured Leon's appointment to the top job — that, plus Leon's own political connections, which were considerable. Unlike his predecessor, as well as unlike Gregorie, Kellner was anything but a Justice lifer. He was on leave from a very lucrative civil practice in Washington, D.C., in which he was also a mover and shaker in Republican Party politics, and being United States Attorney amounted to a kind of busman's holiday for him. Kellner had inherited the office's collegial approach and reveled in it, always managing to be present in the critical moments of the Southern District's big cases. He had also inherited Gregorie and his pre-existing grant of unfettered latitude to pursue "the bad guys" up the cocaine chain of command. Kellner not only maintained that backing, but expanded it by naming Gregorie his first assistant.

"I always kept Leon informed," Gregorie remembers, "and he was always involved, but he pretty much followed my lead when it came to prosecutions. We weren't that much alike, but I always thought we worked easily together. I liked Leon and he liked me."

Kellner's nickname among his other subordinates was "Neon Leon." The United States Attorney, though not an egotist in most things, liked being seen at the center of events and played that role with a certain amount of flash, hence "Neon" seemed appropriate to those working under his direction. The only time the nickname assumed a certain edge had been during an incident in the aftermath of the first cartel indictment, when the United States Attorney's Office had received a phone threat from an unidentified Colombian who claimed to be aggrieved at the office's attempts to extradite the cartel. The caller said he intended to kill the fucking gringos who were doing this. Given that the cartel had already assassinated the Colombian justice minister, Kellner took the threat seriously, not only announcing that it had been made, but then abandoning 155 S. Miami and holing up behind barbed wire at a nearby air force base. The paramount federal law enforcement officer's flight to a high-security refuge out of the reach of the cocaine gangsters was widely reported in the local press as well.

While Kellner was "in hiding" for his own protection, Gregorie, the one who had actually made the cartel case and pursued their extradition, showed up at 155 S. Miami Avenue every morning to run the office. At one point in Leon's absence, the First Assistant was approached by some of the other assistant United States attorneys there who demanded to know what was up. If it wasn't safe for Neon Leon to be in the office, what were all of them still doing there? Gregorie told them not to get their noses out of joint. He was here with them and if they got blown up, he'd go too. That ought to be proof enough they were safe.

Neon Leon was back on the sixth floor in another week.

Leon Kellner remained relatively invisible to the Southern District's public at large after that, until just the last few months before *United States v. Manuel Antonio Noriega* got under way, when Kellner returned to the political stage, this time cast as the lead Miami angle on the biggest national story of the year, the Iran-contra scandal. In June, Kellner had even been grilled by the Iran-contra committee and, though the committee cleared him of any culpability, he was still very much under a cloud of suspicion. He would remain under investigation by another congressional body, the Senate Subcommittee on Terrorism, Narcotics, and International Communications, for the next year and a half.

At issue was just what Leon had or hadn't done about a case developed by one of his office's young assistant United States attorneys during early 1986, when Bill Casey's Nicaragua strategy was at its zenith. The young assistant had stumbled onto a series of gunrunning and other apparent legal violations that, while committed in the Southern District on behalf of the so-called contras, seemed to have been masterminded by some marine lieutenant colonel named Oliver North in Washington, D.C., working at the White House for the National Security Council — and of whom no one in the United States Attorney's Office had, at that point, ever heard. While encouraging the assistant to pursue his leads, even agreeing to send the attorney down to Costa Rica for a week to investigate, Kellner eventually balked at allowing him to take the case to the grand jury. In May 1986, Kellner even went so far in that direction as to rewrite his assistant's case memo justifying the grand jury request, so the rewritten memo instead reached the opposite conclusion. Then Kellner sent the memo on up the Department of Justice's chain of command, over his assistant's alleged signature without the assistant's knowledge.

This secretly rewritten memo was immediately used against the administration's congressional critics to prove there was no substance to the allegations of contra legal abuses. Some three months later, Oliver North bragged that the rewritten memo's Miami gunrunning investigation was one of the cases he had "dealt with." The two FBI agents assigned to the investigation also submitted a memo to their superiors that summer accusing Leon Kellner of suppressing the inquiry and sandbagging their efforts. Three more months after that, in the fall, just days after the Iran-contra scandal had been ignited by the C-130 crash in Nicaragua, Kellner reversed his position on pursuing this prosecution and suddenly gave his assistant carte blanche to indict the gunrunning case. The assistant did so, but a judge quickly quashed the charges for lack of evidence of any criminal act, one of the reasons given by Kellner for his refusal to proceed earlier.

Nonetheless, in the investigative feeding frenzy that followed the exposure of the administration's subterfuge, the accusations of sandbagging against Kellner had left their taint. The accompanying innuendo and gossip were the only blemish ever in his otherwise scrupulously upright professional record. And it pained him deeply. By July 1987, defending himself against the whispers in circulation back in his hometown had stripped much of the Neon from Leon's style. The heretofore affable United States Attorney now kept to himself more and often brooded.

The day Dick Gregorie came in from his office next door and announced he wanted to turn Steve Grilli loose to round up an indictment against the General, Leon Kellner was sitting behind his desk with his suit coat off, but his expensive dress shirt still buttoned at its collar and cuffs and his tie cinched tight, his expensive suspenders on display, the way he often worked. The window behind him overlooked the burrito parlors and dime stores occupying most of Miami's faded downtown. In the days when Leon Kellner and Dick Gregorie had first arrived here, Immigration had maintained an office on 155 S. Miami Avenue's ground floor, and the line of refugees waiting to talk to somebody about a green card circled the block. Immigration had moved since, so the sidewalks below were now clear, if littered. The view from behind Leon's desk up on the sixth floor captured mostly boiled air of the palest blue shade and the total absence of clouds. Leon himself looked soft and sedentary sitting there, but also slick and exceedingly well groomed.

Leon Kellner was not surprised at Gregorie's announcement. Leon had personally tracked the extradition and initial interrogation of Floyd Carlton. He knew the case was brewing.

Nor was Leon upset. Indeed, later, Gregorie's detractors would claim that the first assistant had only made a case against the General in order to rescue Kellner's damaged reputation and demonstrate that his boss was not the kind to sandbag any prosecution, anywhere, anytime, now or ever, even if his political allies wanted him to.

In any case, there was no apparent agonizing on Leon's part over the implications of such a bold step into territory heretofore reserved for diplomats. Nor did Leon seem the least worried about what Justice in Washington might think of what the Southern District was about to do.

Instead, Leon Kellner, the one man still in a position to kill this effort before it ever got rolling, greeted Gregorie's intention to hunt the General with apparent relief.

"Go get him," Leon said.

— 3 —

The extended interrogation of Floyd Carlton — the heart of the evidence the Southern District would eventually take to the grand jury — began at 9:00 A.M. on July 23, 1987.

The day was thought a big enough occasion that Gregorie was there along with Grilli and the interpreter, locked into the Submarine's larger conference room with Floyd, who looked his usual disintegrated self in his usual jailhouse attire. Dick told Floyd the time had come to either put up or shut up as far as the General was concerned.

Otherwise, the actual interrogating of Floyd was left largely to Steve Grilli. Where Floyd's original sessions with Danny Moritz the previous February lasted for three days, between six and ten hours a day, Steve Grilli's lasted some nine weeks, anywhere from two to twelve hours a day, as many as thirty days running without a break. Throughout it all, Steve moved back and forth over Carlton's memory, like some giant vacuum working a seabed, churning up the grit of past happenings and digesting it into a series of yellow legal notepads in thick flurries of note-taking.

Grilli walked his snitch through event after event, guiding himself by another yellow pad full of notes he made at night back at the station, after their sessions were over for the day. He often halted Floyd's narrative in midstream to ask for a clarification, thereby forcing Floyd to backtrack over something already said so Steve could check for discrepancies in the story. Then he swung back through the same events a week or two later and made the check all over again. Before long Grilli had taken to describing Floyd Carlton's facility for recollection as "prodigious" and his potential testimony as "cast iron."

There were two significant limitations on this daily debriefing process down in the Submarine under the courthouse annex. The first was Steve's interpreter, without whom Grilli, who understood only a little Spanish, was helpless to interrogate Floyd in detail. The interpreter's back had been torqued by a falling bale of marijuana during a raid several years earlier, and now simply sitting in a chair for an hour was a physical challenge. He ate pain medication during their sessions but still sweated profusely, often wiping his brow with a hand that trembled. Many days, Grilli cut the interrogation short to let the Spanish-speaking agent recover.

The other limitation was Floyd himself. Some days, he was plagued by headaches, on occasions so bad they made him vomit. Other days, he was prone to long bursts of self-recrimination, berating himself out loud and refusing all attempts at consolation until he finally reached an emotional meltdown during which he sobbed uncontrollably. Even when less than distraught, Floyd was constitutionally uncomfortable with the role he was playing and consequently balky and closemouthed on occasion. To manage the snitch's performance, Grilli used a short leash. He had little sympathy for Floyd's pissing and moaning and reminded him regularly that the judge still hadn't passed sentence yet. Any bullshit, and Steve would see to it that he had a lot of time to wish he'd been more forthcoming. Grilli had few problems playing the hard guy. He figured Floyd had asked for what he got and if he were let free today, by tomorrow night he'd be right back talking shit and making loads.

"Carlton had done it all and lost everything," Steve remembers. "He was dejected and lost and there was no way back for him. Here was a guy who was sheepish and soft-spoken with the most fantastic story to tell I had ever heard. It seemed out of place with the guy telling it, this thin little guy, with a manner more like Mr. Rogers on children's television than Al Pacino in *Scarface*. Floyd's looks didn't fit the role he had played.

To be honest, I didn't know what to make of him most of the time. He was a chameleon. And he was fuckin' unstable. I couldn't plan much ahead of time because I didn't know where his head would end up the night before. He could be a giant pain in the ass and usually was."

On those pain-in-the-ass days, Grilli felt nothing but relief when he finally got out of there and exited through the parking garage next to the Submarine, squealing back into the stink of traffic on Miami Avenue, the glare so hard it pushed his eyeballs into the deepest part of their sockets.

There were also times when Floyd Carlton was a gold mine.

July 29, 1987, was one of those. That was the day Steve and Floyd solved the case's venue problem, an essential for any formal criminal charge to ever be made against the General. Even if Noriega had acted as an enabler for the international cocaine conspiracy run by the Medellín Cartel, American law only had jurisdiction if Grilli could prove that the General knew that the cocaine he allowed to pass through the Isthmus was destined for the United States. With such proof, the United States had venue, sufficient legal standing to prosecute, and without it, the whole investigation might end up inadmissible in American courts. Establishing venue was, hence, a very big deal.

Steve and his interpreter logged in with the marshals' desk on the other side of the third solid locked door at 8:50 A.M., and, as usual, Floyd looked like roadkill and had a bitch going. This time he was whining that whatever the marshals had fed him for breakfast was sitting on his stomach like it had crawled in there to die.

Grilli told Floyd to suck it up. They had work to do.

Steve had arrived that morning with venue on the brain, and to that end directed Floyd back through the last of the cartel smuggling business for which he had arranged the General's protection in late 1983, the scam for which Noriega had demanded $250,000 and then claimed to have been shorted on the first payment.

Floyd immediately pointed out that when he had delivered that original sealed box full of what was supposed to be a quarter million dollars to the General's bagman, a PDF captain, Floyd had joked with him that, all wrapped up in electrical tape as it was, the package looked like a bomb.

And the bagman had quipped in response, "Let's hope it doesn't turn into one."

Since, for all intents and purposes, the box of money had done just that, setting off another dispute with the cartel, Floyd found the irony amusing enough to laugh out loud.

Grilli didn't follow suit. Instead, he told the snitch to stop dicking around, go back to the beginning of the smuggling job, and start the story from there. Steve had heard only truncated versions of the contact Floyd had made with the General while arranging for this last transshipment. This time, Steve wanted Floyd to elaborate all the details.

As Floyd recounted the episode again, he said he had spent most of the summer of 1983 away from Panama, in Europe. While he was gone, the cartel had attempted an unsuccessful smuggling venture through the Isthmus without the General's permission, and the PDF had busted the operation. It had fallen to Floyd to try to put the cartel's relationship with the General back together, so Floyd sent a message to his old buddy from Chiriqui that he needed to talk.

In early December 1983, Carlton's message had been answered by the jeweler who acted as the General's front man. He instructed Floyd to go immediately to the beach house at La Playita. Floyd did as he was told and was quick enough at it that he arrived before the General did, so Floyd waited until Noriega eventually drove up in his usual short parade of sedans and well-armed outriders. After their customary hug, the two old homeboys went inside to talk. The General made it very clear very early in the conversation just how pissed he was at the Colombians. He told Floyd that he would help his old *compadre* out by allowing one more flight, but it would be the last and he wanted $250,000 for it, cash in front as usual.

In his soft-spoken, kiss-ass way, Carlton then tried to mediate a little. He said that while he understood what the General was saying, the Colombians, on the other hand, were complaining that they had expected protection by virtue of all the money they had already paid and were worried their cash was buying them nothing.

According to Floyd, the General bounced off the wall when he heard that.

"Do they think Panama is just some jungle full of fucking Indians?" the General snapped. "That they can just come and go without telling anybody?" The money he was asking from them was nothing. Did Floyd know how much money these Colombians were going to sell this shit for in the United States? Maybe $40,000 a kilo, that's how much.

Then the General asked how much Floyd was making for one of his four-hundred-kilo trips.

Carlton told the General he was being paid $150,000.

The General immediately pointed out how stupid that was. A hundred and fifty thousand was chicken feed. As he pressed the point, the General assumed the verbal posture of a far more important older man sharing wisdom with the younger, less substantial one. This, he lectured, was why César Rodríguez, their mutual homeboy, was always ahead of Floyd in business. César at least was making a pile of money. Floyd should recognize that this opportunity came once in a lifetime and he should use it to set himself up. It wasn't going to last forever. . . .

Grilli interrupted.

The General had said that the cocaine was being sold in the United States, was that right? he asked.

Floyd answered that it was. Then, he resumed the narrative.

While sitting down together at La Playita, Floyd continued, the General had also instructed Floyd not to fly this load to the Calzada Larga airstrip he had been using. Someone else had reserved it. Then the General warned Floyd that he better not catch the same disease as these Colombians and try to operate in Panama without checking with the General first. "If anything goes wrong," the General told him, "I'll stick it to you."

At this point, Grilli broke into Floyd's narrative again.

Was Floyd sure that the General had said that the cocaine was going to be sold in the United States?

Floyd was irritated at being interrupted yet again and answered directly in English, without waiting on the interpreter. "Yes, Steve," he growled, "I am sure. The son-of-a-bitch said, 'Do you know what they are going to sell this shit for in the United States?' "

Bingo. *United States v. Manuel Antonio Noriega* now had venue.

Steve could hardly wait to get up to 155 S. Miami Avenue to let Dick Gregorie know what he'd found.

There were also days when Floyd told Steve more than Steve wanted to know.

The most notable of those happened one afternoon when Grilli took a break in the narrative in order to quiz Floyd about a claim made by the tiny pilot who'd landed Floyd's Cessna out on I-75 almost two years earlier. The pilot, currently in the Federal Correction Center downtown, claimed that he had flown a load of money in 1984 from the cartel in Colombia to Panama where he was told it was destined for the General.

Grilli took it from there, his interpreter slumped next to him and Carlton slumped across the table. What did Floyd know about that payoff? he asked.

"Only what I've heard," Floyd answered. He'd never had anything directly to do with it.

So what had he heard?

Floyd said he'd met with several of the cartel men in Panama City during the spring of 1984 and one of them had told him that they'd paid Noriega four million for the privilege of hiding out in Panama. At the time, Colombia was in an uproar over the cartel's assassination of the justice minister and they needed a refuge. The arrangements had been made through the General's front man, the jeweler. Floyd said he had also heard from one of the cartel's top employees that they had paid the General's PDF bagman another four million for protection of a new cocaine lab they were building out in the jungles of Darien Province, near Panama's border with Colombia. But that deal had come apart when the PDF busted the lab anyway, before it even got into production. By the time Floyd heard about it, he also heard that the cartel men were actively discussing having the General killed for ripping them off. Floyd was unsure why nothing had come of that idea but, by the fall of 1984, the cartel's members had left Panama to hide out elsewhere, traveling on Panamanian passports, just like the cartel man Gregorie had tried to extradite from Spain.

Floyd Carlton told Steve Grilli that the cartel men had the run of Panama while they were there. Sometimes when Floyd saw them, they had PDF guards to supplement their own gunmen, all of them openly hoisting automatic weapons. Floyd also claimed that two of the cartel's most significant members even used to walk down Panama City's Avenue Balboa every day for exercise, all the way from their hotel, past the American embassy — where the DEA's Panama Country Office was housed in a room that overlooked the promenade — and back again. And what was most amazing, Floyd chuckled, was that the DEA never had any idea they were there. Here were the most wanted guys in gringoland, and the DEA never even recognized them outside their own window.

At that last remark, Grilli accused Carlton of talking out of the side of his head. No such thing ever happened.

No shit, Floyd insisted. This was the real deal he was telling.

Floyd then laughed hard enough to jostle his McDonald's cup and splash soda onto his pale legs.

Grilli changed the subject when the laughter stopped, hoping the snitch hadn't picked up on just how disconcerting to him that last revelation really was.

Perhaps the biggest investigative disappointment of the entire case first emerged when Steve and Floyd had been working steadily for little more than two days. And it came out of the blue, after a big lecture from Steve on corroboration, delivered once Floyd had finished his fast-food lunch.

Corroboration, he instructed Floyd, was everything. Not just something, fuckin' everything. If Steve couldn't confirm the critical mass of whatever Floyd had to say, it would amount to no more than another jailhouse story — a giant jack-off. Floyd had to give Grilli the details that would let him find proof somewhere outside the Submarine. Did Floyd have any hard evidence to back all this up?

Floyd was anxious to please that day and responded with uncharacteristic alacrity. He did have evidence, he said. Most of his records had been taken from him when he was arrested by the DENI in late 1985, but he still had some stuff, including his old passports and personal address books. And he knew about a whole lot more than that. To further make his point, Floyd said he even knew about tapes.

Tapes?

Audiotapes César Rodríguez made of the General himself, talking dope deals, past and present, with César.

Grilli had to hold on to the side of his chair to keep from jumping to his feet. "What?" he snapped.

Tapes of the General, Floyd repeated. César made them without the General's knowing, around the time the whole *Krill* thing was being put together. César had played one of them for Floyd the last time Floyd had seen his best friend alive. When they talked that day, César was obsessed about not ending up like Hugo Spadafora, and said he had "insurance." That's when he produced the tapes. They were in a shoe box in his closet. César said, "I've been recording the son-of-a-bitch all along. I won't end up like Hugo." And if anything did happen to him, César said, motioning at the shoe box in the closet, "all this will be public."

That, Grilli explained, "was an instant hard-on. Can you imagine? Tapes of the fuckin' General talking about their smuggle on the *Krill*? I'd have him dead to rights, a fuckin' smokin' gun. I instantly wanted those tapes as bad as I've ever wanted anything."

Getting them, though, was not simple. Since sending him back personally to search was out of the question, Floyd would somehow have to locate the tapes over the phone to Panama. So, once Steve arranged with the Marshals Service to have calls patched through a cutout number in case anyone was trying to run a trace, Floyd called his wife, Maria. He was going to get her to do his legwork, but Grilli told him that was stupid. If she was being watched by someone interested in what Floyd was up to, she might end up leading the General to the tapes. Instead, she had to get someone she trusted who was outside suspicion to make the inquiries. Carlton and Grilli finally agreed to let Maria make a few investigative forays personally. Among those was delivering a message to the late César's former secretary, with whom Floyd led Steve to believe that he had once conducted an affair. Floyd's message instructed the secretary to use someone else's phone — since hers might be tapped — to call him back at another cutout number the marshals had set up on which Floyd could receive calls.

Down in Panama, Maria did as she'd been instructed, even going so far as to have the closet searched in César's house where Floyd had last seen the tapes. All to no avail.

After a week or so, the secretary finally called back as well. It was late at night and Grilli had already left the Submarine. The marshals had to fetch Floyd from his cell to take the call in the control room.

When Floyd told the secretary what he was interested in, she became very skittish.

Yes, she said, she knew about the tapes. She had engaged the secret tape recorder for many of them, recorded through the phone system in the Bank of Boston tower office that she supervised. She'd seen the tapes in the same shoe box that Floyd had seen as well. She said that she'd had them for a while after César's death before passing them on to one of his relatives.

Then, sounding somewhat shaken, she rang off.

The secretary called back again minutes later. This time, even more shaken, she told Floyd she didn't know anything about any tapes and that he should never get in touch with her about them again.

Floyd gave Steve the bad news the next morning.

Grilli took Floyd's account with a shrug at the time, but he would secretly yearn for those tapes for years thereafter.

And the tapes would never be found.

— 4 —

Of all the days he spent under the courthouse annex, one after another after another, August 3, 1987, was the only one of them Floyd had dreamed of ever since he'd arrived in manacles from Costa Rica. This was the day when he got to see his Maria again at last.

Floyd had been pestering Dick Gregorie about such a visit for months, insisting that his wife was in danger in Panama and had to be included in his Witness Protection arrangements as soon as possible. Gregorie was willing, but the bureaucratic process was anything but instant. Gregorie had to call the Marshals Service, which connected him to the Witness Security program and a particular woman there who always handled the Southern District's requests. Even then, the process had only begun. Anyone to be included in Witness Protection had to submit a lengthy application document establishing who they were and what risk they were under. That was followed by an investigation.

The biggest hang-up to Maria's application as August began was Maria herself. She was anything but excited at the prospect.

Maria Carlton was of Swiss extraction, thin and blond, and had lived in both Panama and Europe as a child. In Panama, when Floyd had been on his roll, she was a woman of standing. "She was used to living like an aristocrat," Dick Gregorie remembers. "And you can't live that way in Witness Protection. They just take you out in some town, usually out in the middle of nowhere, set you up, and there you are. The lifestyle was decidedly middle class and she was used to being rich. I don't think she wanted to give it all up for a life of driving back and forth to some suburban grocery store and shopping mall. She wasn't even sure she needed protection. And I don't think she considered Floyd worth it, to be frank."

That last impulse on Maria's part was reinforced by the fact that she hadn't cohabited with Carlton for a number of months preceding his Costa Rican arrest and theirs was, in fact, a separation more than a marriage. Given all Floyd's moaning about his darling Maria, Steve Grilli found their marital state a surprise when he learned as much from the marshals. On this front, Floyd seemed rife with self-delusion. Still, his monologues about her and about their love together continued on a regular basis. In the end, part of the reason for Maria's trip to the United States was so Floyd could discuss coming into Witness Protection with her face-to-face, part so she could carry up some of the documents from Panama that Floyd had promised, and part just as a reward for Floyd, what Gregorie hoped would be a little morale booster. The marshals arranged to sneak Maria out of Panama through SOUTHCOM and kept her in a secret Miami safe house before bringing her to the Submarine.

Grilli was there when she first arrived inside the high-security confines of her husband's new life, stepping through the third door along the Submarine corridor in a delicate $600 summer frock, with gold on her wrists. Steve figured right away that Floyd was in trouble. Even to a perfect stranger, Maria was obviously pissed. She made no secret of the fact she did not want to be where she was, doing what she was doing. She didn't like being whisked around by marshals almost as if she was a prisoner, and she made a point of staying as far from her escort as she could, eyeing her surroundings as if she'd been dropped into a sewer. Waiting impatiently for Floyd to appear, she seemed even blonder under the tube lights. Grilli thought she looked as if she had married Carlton for his money and now he was like last week's shit on her shoes.

For his part, Floyd was dressed in his best slacks and shirt for their reunion, looking like a preppy out for an afternoon at the yacht basin, clean shaven for perhaps the only time Grilli had ever seen him.

At first approach, Floyd Carlton wrapped his wife, Maria, in a hug and she responded like a board, looking past Floyd's face at the far wall. Steve left the couple by themselves for a few minutes in the Submarine's conference room. When he last saw them, she was sitting bolt upright with her arms folded across her chest and Floyd was stooped toward her, half on his chair and half off, tears already running down his face.

When Steve returned, their postures were exactly the same only Floyd was now sobbing uncontrollably.

Maria, on the other hand, was still "cold as fuckin' ice," Grilli remembered. "She blamed Floyd for this mess and wanted him to put things back the way they had been. And poor Floyd looked like he woulda done anything else she asked, but was helpless to do anything about it. He was bawlin' his brains out and she was sittin' there like a piece of furniture. It was fuckin' sad. I mean, for once even I felt sorry for the guy."

The next day, Floyd presented Grilli with a new demand. Carlton now wanted his kids' nanny included in Witness Protection as well as Maria and the kids themselves. His eyes were bloodshot and the marshals said he'd been crying off and on all night.

Nanny? Grilli exploded. Did Floyd think this was the fuckin' *Lives of the Rich and Famous* or what? Nanny? Did he want the marshals to put him up on a fuckin' yacht too?

No, Floyd told him, if the nanny didn't come, then Maria for sure wouldn't come, and if Maria didn't come, Floyd might have second thoughts about "helping himself" by talking the way he'd been.

Steve was out of his chair and in Floyd's face in an instant.

If Floyd stopped talking, he warned, Floyd was going to spend the rest of his life in some maximum-security cell somewhere so far from Maria that it would take a month to reach her by postcard.

Having made that clear, Steve also began filling out the required paperwork to include the nanny in Carlton's Witness Protection package. "Floyd," he pointed out, "was too important a witness to risk over that kinda bullshit."

CHAPTER 4

MAKING THE CASE

— 1 —

It's hard to say when exactly this case hooked Steve Grilli. It might have been that first day back in Kennedy's office, just because he knew something big was up. It also might have been later, after he and Floyd hit their stride and Steve began to accumulate the various pieces of evidence that would eventually be stitched together into an indictment. In any event, by the second week in August, Grilli's obsession with *United States v. Manuel Antonio Noriega* had considerable purchase on his life.

"There's a kind of hunger you get," he explained. "Where you can't get enough of it, you gotta know. You wanta examine every little bit of evidence over and over and you're always wantin' the next bit you still haven't found. The case becomes an all-encompassing-type deal. You get immersed in it and then, pretty soon, there's nothin' else. At least I was that way. I was goin' full bore in my most idealistic mode, straight outta the academy in my mind-set. I was gonna get the Mutha of all Elephants. It's the kinda job I know now is just bound to consume anybody who touches it.

"Also, you gotta remember that the DEA was a dog-eat-dog kinda place. There is literally only one hero allowed per case — when they dole out credits, only the case agent scores — so that makes a kinda solitary work, work where you gotta be obsessed or else. There's no fallback position, you know? And ego is always a big part of the job. Ego keeps you alive out on the street. To do the work, you gotta believe that you're the toughest muthafucka in the jungle. It takes a certain element, not just anybody can do it. You gotta be half crazy. Some of us control it a little better than others, but after a while it's hard not to feel invulnerable, just from swallowin' so much of your own adrenaline if nothin' else. And once a case gets its claws in you, it won't let go.

"But I went into it with both eyes wide open. I liked this work. Nothin' before this job had ever given me the challenge I was lookin' for. And this job was nothin' but challenging, inside and out. My police friends told me before I got in that the DEA was the best law-enforcement agency in the world and I was going to be part of the elite — only seventy people a year in the whole country are selected to train as special agents. I came to the DEA already confident in what I had between my ears and what I had between my legs. And I got more that way. Once I'd bagged my Elephant, I was sure I was gonna be part of the elite of the elite. I didn't know any better at the time.

"At that tender age, I guess I believed all the shit they taught us in agent school about being able to do anything. So I went for it. It's the kinda work that has to be a spontaneous, take-it-as-it-comes life experience. I was ready for that, even though I'd always been a planner. I wanted to make a difference, and if I couldn't make a difference, I wanted to make a statement. Almost as soon as I started this work I realized I wasn't going to come out of it the way I went in. It just asks too fuckin' much of you to be any different. Later in my career I learned the trade secrets — if you weren't fightin' with the bad guys, you were tryin' to manipulate your bosses, many of whom were only interested in gainin' an advantage for themselves. And when you weren't arguin' with the bosses tryin' to get a piece of the precious few resources that are available, you are arguin' family values and priorities with your wife. But I only got a clear picture of all that later.

"At the time, I still didn't know shit. I was my most gung ho. The challenge egged me on. I mean, look at the fuckin' odds against it: We were gonna make a case on the ruler of Panama — the very same place where his part of the conspiracy had been committed, so he had complete control of most of the potential evidence against him — and we were gonna have to make this case without any help to speak of from any of the rest of the DEA. And the whole scene just crawlin' with politics the whole while. Go figure. I can't believe we ever pulled it off.

"That summer, though, I had no doubts we would, despite it all. I was ready to dedicate everything to the cause. Before long, I was sleepin' at the office some nights. I had the smell of that big Elephant in my nose everywhere I went. I guess it paid off, but, in the end, it just cost me too much any way I figured it. Check it out: I ended up knowin' this fuckin' general in Panama, who I'd never laid eyes on, better than I knew my own son, who I was livin' with out in Deerfield Beach. There's gotta be somethin' sick about that."

The legal yardstick with which Steve Grilli's obsession would be measured was well known to him by that August. He'd had to master it on the fly, since RICO was not part of the agency's training curriculum, but Grilli learned quickly and had Gregorie and his brain trust to brush him up on any fine points.

In essence, before a grand jury could vote a true bill, thus formally indicting the General, it had to be satisfied that the investigation had established the four major elements of the Racketeer Influenced and Corrupt Organizations statutes:

First, that the General had been part of an "association in fact" that functioned as a criminal enterprise.

Second, that the General had committed at least two "predicate offenses" from a statutory list that included importation of cocaine, distribution of cocaine, money-laundering, and more.

Third, that those predicate offenses committed by the General were part of some "common scheme, plan, or motive so as to be a pattern of criminal activity."

And, finally, that those predicate offenses were also committed as part of the General's participation in the affairs of the "association in fact" which he had joined in pursuit of their mutual criminal enterprise.

From the very beginning of the case, Steve Grilli visualized that "mutual criminal enterprise" as a kind of current circulating in a figure-eight pattern that connected Colombia and the Southern District of Florida. The figure eight crossed in Panama. Flowing northeast, the current carried cocaine through the Isthmus and on to Miami. Flowing southwest, it carried both money to be laundered in Panama and chemicals for cocaine manufacture to be transshipped into the Colombian wilderness. The General charged toll on everything that passed and, in the eyes of RICO, that toll-taking "association in fact" meant he was guilty of the entire process circumscribed by the rest of the conspiracy, whether he personally engaged in the other violations or not. By inference, he was among the biggest cocaine-traffickers on the planet.

All Grilli had to do was prove it.

— 2 —

The General was potentially liable for this RICO from his first act on the cartel's behalf back in 1982 until he disavowed further participation — the meter ran until it was explicitly turned off. In this instance, Grilli thought he might have proof that the General had at the very least continued his association in fact well into 1986, when he participated in the *Krill* venture, attempting to smuggle cartel cocaine.

That end of the evidentiary trail was freshest, so the *Krill* was the first lead Steve explored during the time he wasn't down in the Submarine with Floyd. Also, since the true nature of his investigation was still hidden to the organization around him and the *Krill* inquiry was out in the open, it allowed him to utilize other DEA resources without compromising what he was really up to — making this lead the most easily accessible as well.

That access initially translated into a chance to peruse the intelligence file on the seizure of the *Krill* that had been prepared by the DEA's Bogotá office. This report identified one of the suspected principals in the smuggling venture as a swarthy-looking Colombian known as *El Turco,* the Turk. So, in a standard investigative step taken shortly after Maria Carlton had come and gone, Grilli put out a request on the police wires for any and all information regarding this Turk and got very lucky almost right away. At that moment, the Colombian he was looking for was being held by the Immigration and Naturalization Service in the Miami Metropolitan Correctional Center.

According to the INS, the Turk had fled his homeland after the *Krill*'s seizure and then entered the United States illegally. Earlier this year, he had been busted attempting to purchase two handguns and was now about to be deported to Colombia, where he was wanted on smuggling charges. According to the INS people dealing with him, the Turk was not at all pleased to be headed back. Grilli got in touch with the Turk's lawyer straightaway and inquired if his client might like to trade what he knew about the *Krill* for a chance to stay stateside.

To conceal the Turk's intent from his fellow prisoners, it was arranged for him to be hauled in the daily defendants' bus over to the courthouse annex, where he could be taken from the annex's holding cell for a clandestine meeting with Grilli without attracting any suspicion from his fellow inmates. That meeting took place on August 17, 1987, in a room in the old courthouse Grilli referred to as "the Igloo" because its air conditioning always created indoor blizzards — even on days like this, when the sun outside barbecued anything that stepped out of the shade.

Right away, Steve sized up the tall, thin, and twitchy Turk for a certified scumbag with a nose jones for the cocaine he'd been moving. The Turk also had a lot of bad-guy smartass in his manner, but behind his bravado, he was eager to deal. He eventually said he was prepared to tell everything he knew about the *Krill,* as well as wear a wire and collect evidence on the other parties to the scam who were loose in the Southern District, in exchange for granting him immunity, dropping his gun charge, and issuing him a green card.

At that price, Grilli growled, the Turk better have something pretty interesting to say.

As it turned out, he did.

For starters, the Turk told Steve that he never would have gotten into this scam if it hadn't been for his specialization in "transport vehicles"— just one of the "things" at which Turk claimed to be very good. The Turk was known for finding boats for people "in the business" and was approached by a smuggler he knew who wanted to move maybe 350 kilos of coke to the United States in a private yacht. That's when the Turk first learned of the *Krill.* He was told it was owned by the two sons of the General's predecessor, César Rodríguez's partners.

According to the Bogotá station's report that Grilli had seen, by that point in the Turk's story, the brothers and César were planning to use the *Krill* to haul several loads of M-16 military assault rifles, some one thousand in all, to trade in Colombia for cocaine, which the *Krill* would then ferry into Panama for further transport to the United States. The Turk said that the brothers had transported the boat back from the Pacific side on a canal pass from the General himself.

When the Turk inquired about purchasing the *Krill,* the two brothers introduced him to César Rodríguez in Cesar's suite atop the Bank of Boston tower, and César immediately referred to the boat as his own. The sales agreement César then negotiated essentially merged the purchasers' smuggling venture into his own. César bragged that his portion of the *Krill*'s load would just be the opening round in an operation in which César and the two brothers expected to be moving eventually six hundred kilos through Panama every two weeks.

This, according to the Turk, was where his story really got good. Word was already out in the jailhouse that the feds were interested in information about the General, so the Turk focused on that subject.

Everybody in this smuggling deal, he claimed, understood from the get go that the Panama end of things had the General's protection. The Turk mentioned the same portrait of the General on the boat that Floyd had cited, without any prompting from Grilli. The Turk said he knew that the picture had been given to César by the General himself, a fact later confirmed by Floyd as well. The Turk also said that everyone involved was too scared of the General to have lied about whether they had his permission. Even César.

The Turk had personally laid eyes on Noriega himself only once, at another meeting in César's Bank of Boston office. The ugly little *comandante* was sitting at a table with César and the two brothers when the Turk entered with two of his principals.

Once everyone was seated, the General spoke, but only to César.

"Who'd you sell the *Krill* to?" he asked.

César pointed to the Turk and his principals and said the arrangements had been made. Then César turned to one of the brothers and asked, "How many pieces?," meaning how many kilos of cocaine were scheduled for transport.

The brother said they were still working on the final number.

The General shrugged. "Move the boat quickly from Panama," he said to the room at large.

At that point, the Turk claimed, he and his two principals were asked to leave for a moment, and when they returned as scheduled, the General was gone.

A week later, when the *Krill* was on its way to Colombia's Rosario Islands to be loaded, the Turk, back in Medellín, received a phone call from Panama telling him that César had disappeared and no one could find him. The Turk claimed to have immediately dispatched one of his friends to search around town, and that friend eventually found César and the missing brother in the morgue. The *Krill* set sail with only half its expected load two days later, and the Turk was still in Medellín when the Colombian National Police pounced on the boat. At the same time, *El Turco* learned that the Panama Defense Force's G-2 had been out to Colombia to "investigate" the Panamanians' deaths. Several papers controlled by the PDF in Panama City had already printed the

Turk's passport photo with a story that he was a prime suspect in the killings.

But the Turk swore to Grilli on his mother's grave that he had nothing to do with no murders.

To test his authenticity, Steve had the Turk brought back to the Igloo several days later for a second meeting. Steve then produced a display of ninety-six photos on twelve pages and required the Turk to go through and pick out the people with whom he claimed to have dealt. The Turk passed with flying colors. In addition, when taken back to his Miami apartment under escort, he produced his Colombian passport, stamped in and out of Panama on exactly the days he said it would be, and several canceled checks endorsed by the late César Rodríguez and others, pursuant to the boat deal, as well as a bill of sale for the *Krill* itself.

Grilli was, at that moment, impressed and promised the Colombian that once he told his story to the grand jury, he would never have to leave the United States again. And that, of course, was what the smuggler wanted most of all.

Even so, things never quite worked out for the Turk. He died four years later, in a fiery crash after a high-speed car chase through Miami the day before his planned testimony against several of his other partners in the *Krill* venture. The Turk's unidentified pursuers escaped. The mangled corpse of the Colombian informant was finally laid to rest in a Miami grave paid for by the Drug Enforcement Administration. And Special Agent Steve Grilli would be one of the few mourners present at the interment.

The Turk tied the General into the 1986 chain of events surrounding the *Krill,* but a far larger concern to Grilli in the summer of 1987 was nailing down the heart of his case, dating from 1982 through 1984. And before he could hope to convince a grand jury to endorse a RICO indictment for all that Floyd claimed had gone on during those years, Steve would have to have an answer to the question, "Where's the dope?"

Grilli needed to demonstrate that somewhere along the flow through the figure eight of criminal enterprise he had visualized, sometime around the events Floyd described, actual cocaine had been seized. Otherwise, the case lacked substantiation. Steve's starting point was two stories told by Floyd down in the Submarine independently of each other on two separate occasions.

The first emerged on one of Carlton's headache days, and it was just about all Steve got from him that session before having to cut the interrogation short so Floyd could return to his cell to lie down. The story came out while discussing the $250,000 payoff and the smuggling that was consummated in early 1984. Steve assumed out loud that this had been Floyd's last smuggling trip through Panama for the cartel, but Floyd corrected him and proceeded to tell the story of one more smuggling venture several months later, in which Floyd had handled the arrangements on the ground inside Panamanian territory. But, Floyd complained, even though he had completed the unloading and delivered the cocaine to the cartel's Panama operation, he had never been paid. The cartel had explained only that they couldn't pay because the dope involved had later been seized when it reached the United States.

The second story came out on one of Floyd's better days, after he'd been talking for hours.

This time, Grilli raised the subject of the former Panamanian diplomat who had been Floyd and César's boss at the air service. Floyd responded that the former diplomat had been one of the General's front men as long as Floyd had known him. He claimed one of the companies the diplomat owned back in 1984 was a freight airline called INAIR that specialized in shipping home appliances from the Colón Free Zone, through the United States, to third countries.

As Floyd recounted it, INAIR came up for discussion once when Floyd was out for a stroll in Medellín with one of the cartel men, guarded front and back by bodyguards packing automatic weapons. At some point, their little caravan ran into the diplomat on the street in a remarkable coincidence. After several *mucho gusto*s and hugs, they went their separate ways. Floyd and the cartel man then started discussing the former diplomat whom they'd just encountered. Floyd insisted the diplomat was someone with whom the cartel ought to do business.

In fact, Floyd advised his companion that the cartel ought to buy the diplomat's INAIR company. It would be a perfect smuggling vehicle for them, and Floyd had little doubt the diplomat would be amenable to some kind of financial arrangement.

The cartel man chuckled and, when Floyd responded with a quizzical expression, the cartel man explained.

"We already own it," he said.

With those two stories in hand, Grilli started looking for dope. His first step was to run INAIR through the Miami Divisional Office's computer, locating an August 1984 bust of a cargo the Panamanian air freighter INAIR had landed in Texas in order to clear customs before flying on to Miami. Almost a ton of cocaine had been seized, secreted inside seven Philco refrigerators which had embarked from the Colón Free Zone, listed on their U.S. Customs manifest as transshipping on their way to South America. The inspection that led to the bust had been prompted by an anonymous tip to the Miami office over the phone from Panama.

Steve's first conclusion was that INAIR must have been how the coke — which Floyd Carlton had flown into the Isthmus from Colombia with the General's permission between 1982 and 1984 — had moved on to the United States. Given what Floyd had been told when he asked the cartel connection for his money and the proximity in time between that incident and the INAIR bust, Grilli was convinced that part of what was seized in Texas was very likely the same load Floyd had handled in late June. Since the cartel had also bragged of owning the air freight company prior to that, chances were that the three previous loads Floyd cleared through the General had been moved the same way.

After calling up the file on the INAIR case and reviewing it, including a stack of photos of the pile of seized cocaine bundles, Grilli met with the special agent from the Miami office who had handled the 1984 investigation in the seizure's aftermath. This case agent noted that one of the unsolved mysteries of the investigation was the packaging of the dope. Each of the kilo-size bundles that had been discovered hidden in the Philcos was marked with one of a half-dozen or so distinctive symbols. But the case agent still didn't have a clue what they meant.

Steve ran the mystery of the markings past Floyd the next day in the Submarine, but Floyd wasn't much use on the subject, since he claimed that he never opened the duffels full of coke he hauled and had never seen the actual packages or their markings.

Steve remained stumped by the INAIR package markings for the rest of the summer until he was trolling for new leads one day and got a look at a photocopy of the Colombian National Police files concerning a March 1984 raid on a massive cocaine factory inside Colombia at a spot in the jungle known as Tranquilandia — including copies of the cartel's seized ledgers and photographs of the seized dope. Steve already knew of this raid as a legendary landmark in the history of the War on Drugs. It had been conducted by the Colombian Justice Ministry and revealed the most concrete proof yet that cocaine had gone industrial. The Tranquilandia laboratory was by far the largest ever uncovered, marking an exponential increase in productive capacity. In response to the loss of their enormous factory, the cartel struck back and assassinated the Colombian justice minister who had ordered the raid. Then the cartel was forced to flee next door into the arms of the General while things cooled off.

The first thing Grilli noticed in the photos of the dope seized at Tranquilandia was that the packaging, identical to that in the INAIR seizure, was also marked with the very same set of symbols.

To determine just what those markings meant, Steve routed a request through the Marshals Office and had Witness Protection deliver up Brooklyn, Gregorie's snitch for the second cartel indictment, to the Miami office for some questioning. Brooklyn was apparently being kept close by because it took only a couple of days to summon him. He showed up tan, with a gut hanging over his belt, and wearing cowboy boots, his trademark. Brooklyn was the Southern District's resident expert on the operations of the cartel, for whom he'd been a high-level operative from its inception until Brooklyn's own arrest. In addition to freedom and Witness Protection, he would eventually earn rewards of more than a quarter million dollars from the federal government for his assistance seizing the cartel's Florida properties.

Grilli showed the snitch the pictures from both the INAIR and Tranquilandia busts and pointed out the marks on the packages.

Brooklyn lit up. Those? Sure, he knew what those were. The marks were how each cartel member tracked his own dope among their common loads, he explained. Individual members owned separate pieces of cocaine even though they engaged in mutual manufacture, transport, and, often, distribution. That was how a cartel worked, at least for them. Brooklyn then ran down each of the cartel members for whom the symbols stood. He said they only started using the system of markings seen in the pictures after the Tranquilandia lab was opened.

This final scrap of information, strung together with all the others from Floyd and elsewhere, would allow Steve to point to actual cocaine before the grand jury. In fact, samples of the cocaine were still stored in a DEA high-security evidence warehouse. And this cocaine could be connected to the criminal enterprise served by General Manuel Antonio Noriega — as the coke was manufactured in Colombia, passed through Panama, and then on to the United States, source to destination, completing the northeast flow along the figure eight — all within the time frame during which Floyd could testify in first-hand detail about the General's involvement.

Bingo again.

— 3 —

By the middle of September, it was obvious the investigation of *United States v. Manuel Antonio Noriega* was about to shift away from the Submarine. The days of synthetic light and recycled air were coming to an end. Seven weeks into his interrogation, Floyd Carlton had little left to say, and the focus now was almost exclusively on chasing the leads Floyd had provided rather than trying to coax more out of him. This transition might have been a sentimental moment for Grilli and his snitch, after such an intense confinement together, but it wasn't. Theirs was a use relationship, pure and simple. And, in his sentimental moments, Steve thought a lot more about the witness who wasn't there than the one who was.

"Don't get me wrong," he explains. "Floyd was a great fuckin' witness. I mean bar none, a great witness. But can you imagine what it woulda been like if I'd had César? Or even just César's tapes? César was the main man in all this. He was the mover. He was the one who had all the goods on the General. Floyd just had a small piece. César would have busted Noriega's balls. César sold his access to the General as a regular part of his operation. Floyd mostly just used the General for a favor here and there. César had a corporation in which the General was a full blind partner, for Christ's sake. He had the best seats in the house. Floyd's evidence was only third best. But, since first best was dead and second best was the suspect himself, third best was not bad, to say the least. Floyd almost had enough all by himself to indict, but I woulda traded Carlton straight up for the chance to flip César. You know he knew the whole fuckin' bazooka.

"Even dead, César's ghost was all over this case. He was like a shadow in every episode. Everything Floyd had to say was part of this trio kinda thing. And bein' down there in the Submarine with him was like watchin' endless reruns of *The Floyd, César, and Manuel Antonio Show,* you know what I mean?"

Perhaps Grilli's favorite episode in that underground series was the time in 1983 when César had convinced Floyd to buy a Learjet 25, tail number N281R, a.k.a. November two eighty-one Romeo.

The actual convincing happened at a condo César owned in Miami. The cartel had sent Floyd there to shop for a Learjet, and Floyd was using César's place when suddenly César himself showed up without advance warning. He, too, was on the lookout for a Learjet. He told Floyd that the General was so hot to have such a plane that he couldn't bear it and wanted César to find him one. César's suggestion was that they combine their missions and use the same airplane to satisfy both their customers. Floyd used the cartel's money to make the $700,000 down payment required.

Back in Panama, César and Floyd presented the Learjet to the General as his to use, so long as César and Floyd could put the plane to work when the General didn't have plans for it. The cartel went for the idea because they figured the General would provide camouflage. The General went for it because he wanted a Learjet badly and thought he was getting a cut of all the plane's side action as well. And there was no small amount of the latter. When November two eighty-one Romeo wasn't being used to haul Panamanian delegations on the General's business — including, on at least one occasion, official visits to the United States — César used it as part of his booming money-laundering service, available to all comers, flying money from the United States to Panama and meeting each load on the runway with an armored car to be dispatched to whichever among Panama's 140 banking houses César's clients chose, though César himself always used the General's favorite, the Bank of Credit and Commerce International. Soon, César, through his C.A.R. Corporation in which the General was a silent partner, was employing six different pilots — including the tiny pilot eventually busted out on I-75 — making regular cash flights from Fort Lauderdale to the PDF's principal military airfield in Panama City.

But, unbeknownst to the General, there was more to it. Without the General's permission, the cartel had built secret compartments into November two eighty-one Romeo and used those compartments to transport several hundred kilos of cocaine into Miami on the trips where Floyd flew suitcases full of twenty-dollar bills back to Panama. Floyd objected, but the cartel shrugged the objections off, arguing that Floyd couldn't expect them to fly their plane empty on half of a round trip. Though queasy about it, Floyd wasn't bothered enough by what the traffickers had done to inform on them to the General, but Floyd's worst worries were soon realized.

When one of the General's flunkies discovered the secret compartments, the jig was up. The DENI immediately detained Floyd Carlton for an interrogation that lasted some twenty-four hours, during which the General's old Chiriqui homeboy made no mention whatsoever of his high-ranking patron and claimed no knowledge of the compartments. Then, once Floyd had been released, he received a phone call from the jeweler, the General's front man. He said Floyd should tell the cartel that they could get their airplane back for $250,000, cash in advance. Floyd notified the cartel and sent word to César.

César called back, half frantic.

"It's a rip-off," César warned him. The General was never going to let November two eighty-one Romeo go. He liked having a Learjet too much. Noriega's plan, according to César, was to take the money and just keep the plane anyway.

When Floyd passed that warning on to Medellín, the cartel told Floyd to tell the jeweler that they would pay the ransom for their airplane, but that no money would be given to the General until the Learjet was actually in the air headed for Colombia.

That condition was the deal breaker. The jeweler called Floyd back and told him the offer was off the table and there wouldn't be any others.

Afterward, the cartel summoned Carlton to Medellín to explain what had gone on, which Floyd said he did as well as he could. At that meeting, Floyd noticed that one of the cartel members present was writing a list with the General's and César's names on it. He told Floyd he would ask the former diplomat who ran INAIR to find out what was going on. Then, two other cartel members entered the room. The man making the list greeted them. "Now let's forget about the plane," he told them. "Let's forget about Panama and let's go on to business in Mexico."

According to Floyd, he never heard about that Learjet from either the cartel or the General again. And the plane itself just disappeared.

The first time Steve Grilli heard the story of November two eighty-one Romeo from Floyd, Steve just shook his head.

"I'm amazed the General didn't blow César's brains out a long time before he did," Steve told Floyd.

On another occasion, Floyd and Grilli got around to the subject of just why the General cut César so much slack.

The were "close," but even when it had been easy between those two, Floyd admonished, it never really was. To make his point, he told another story about the General and César:

The three homeboys from Chiriqui still saw a lot of each other socially until Noriega rose from G-2 to *comandante* and became the PDF's one and only general. Among the old friends' regular rituals was meeting regularly to discuss their sexual conquests. The General in particular seemed to enjoy these sessions and insisted on hearing all of the details of every screw César or Floyd mentioned. During the year before buying November two eighty-one Romeo, César fell in love with a gorgeous model from Indiana whom he'd met through an American marijuana smuggler whose $35 million surplus César was then washing, several millions at a time. César was so smitten with the model that he had her flown down to Panama almost every weekend. After a while, the General started hitting on César to set him up with her too. César didn't want to, but Noriega put the squeeze on him enough that he finally gave in. The General then spent a weekend with César's Indiana sweetheart in a suite at the Panama City Marriott. Afterward, the General took great delight in telling the crestfallen César all the details, several times over.

And, Floyd observed, it got even weirder than that.

To make this last point, Floyd told yet another story. He said he got the account straight from César, right after it happened.

César and the General were on a flight inside Panama, returning to Panama City, alone, with César at the controls, when, without warning or foreplay, Noriega reached over and unzipped César's pants, pulled the pilot's cock out, and, despite César's protests, commenced giving him a blow job. When César neared climax, the General ordered him to put the plane in a dive while he finished César off.

Floyd was on the tarmac when the two landed. He told Grilli that César looked almost as white in that instant as Floyd now was after months underground.

The first law enforcement officer to hear that account of fellatio besides Grilli and his interpreter was Dick Gregorie, to whom Steve passed it on.

The story generated chuckles but not a lot more. Only evidence held Gregorie's attention for long. Gregorie agreed with Grilli about what a bombshell César Rodríguez would have been as a witness, even if that particular airplane flight was likely inadmissible, but he warned him that they had no time to waste trying to raise the dead. By the third week of September, Gregorie was already pushing the pace.

Floyd had now been thoroughly milked. The moment was ripe "to get the grand jury involved in this thing," Gregorie announced. And he was taking steps to do so immediately.

CHAPTER 5

THE GRAND JURY

— 1 —

At this point in his story, it is unclear whether General Manuel Antonio Noriega even knew what a United States grand jury was, much less just how vulnerable he was to it.

Indeed, the grand jury remains a somewhat obscure institution even to most Americans. It first entered the United States' legal antecedents in thirteenth-century medieval England as a response to abusive prosecutions by the crown. With the introduction of the grand jury, a body of ordinary citizens was inserted into the legal process, charged with determining if charges were warranted and, originally, with hearing and deciding the subsequent trial as well. Those latter functions had long since been separated from the grand jury by the time the United States declared independence, but the institution survived in American law as a citizens' panel assigned to inquire into crimes and make accusations binding people over for formal trial.

Those accusations take the form of an indictment, referred to officially as a "true bill" and defined in the United States Code as "a plain, concise, and definite written statement of the essential facts constituting the offense charged." In its investigations prior to voting a true bill, the grand jury has the power to subpoena witnesses and compel their testimony, operating almost always under the direction of a prosecutor. All of the grand jury's proceedings are secret, again under penalty of law, and the defendant has no right of representation before it, or even notification of the grand jury's inquiry if he isn't called as a witness.

The particular grand jury in the Southern District of Florida to whom Dick Gregorie would bring *United States v. Manuel Antonio Noriega* was one of a half dozen then impaneled at the behest of the United States attorney's office. Most were hearing information dredged up in the War on Drugs. The General's grand jury had twenty-three members, all unpaid volunteers, with a schoolteacher as its forewoman. They would meet every Thursday, always in the same grand jury room off the first-floor lobby of the courthouse annex, just up the block from 155 S. Miami.

Grand juries are often belittled as nothing but instruments of the prosecution, which, of course, in basic function, they are. Some defense attorneys even joke that the United States attorney could get a true bill on a ham sandwich if he asked the grand jury for it, but Dick Gregorie argues that the case against the General bore no resemblance to anybody's ham sandwich.

"There was no way this grand jury or any other grand jury was going to indict the de facto ruler of Panama without serious substance," he points out. "And I wasn't looking for a soft touch. I knew I would have to run this indictment through Washington before I got it. And the rule there was simple — if you go after the king, you've got to hit him with the first shot. I had to have the goods on Noriega because if I didn't I knew I would get the whole thing shoved right back in my face. There was a lot of dicey territory to cover before we got to a grand jury vote. Believe me, this indictment would be no gimme."

— 2 —

Dick Gregorie was in a rush to jump-start the grand jury process because he sensed the "politics" surrounding the case beginning to close in. Two incidents in September 1987, as Floyd's interrogation was winding down, confirmed as much.

The first of those was a phone call Gregorie received from an investigator with the Senate Subcommittee on Terrorism, Narcotics, and International Communications. By then, of course, the subcommittee and the United States Attorney's Office for the Southern District of Florida were no strangers to each other. Among other things, the subcommittee was the source of most of the accusations of questionable behavior raised against Gregorie's boss, Leon Kellner.

A derivation of the Senate Foreign Relations Committee, the Subcommittee on Terrorism, Narcotics, and International Operations had been commissioned the previous January, following a yearlong campaign by the junior Democrat from Massachusetts to force an investigation of illegal activity by the contras, including cocaine smuggling. The junior Democrat's effort was another of those which Oliver North had prematurely bragged of thwarting a year earlier. Finally, after making common cause with the senior Republican from North Carolina and agreeing to enlarge the scope of the inquiry to cover all drug influence on foreign political processes, including, of course, the General — whom the senior Republican could not stand — the subcommittee was born. And by that September, it had already knocked sparks off the Southern District over three witnesses the subcommittee had recruited.

The first of those was the wife of a Colombian involved with the cartel. She told the Senate investigators that she had seen planes from Southern Air Transport, the CIA's airline, loading cocaine at an airfield in Barranquilla, Colombia. The subcommittee eventually sent an eleven-page proffer on her claims to the Department of Justice, and Gregorie was ordered to interview her in Miami. Gregorie thought the subcommittee's witness was "as wacky as they come" and quickly concluded that, even if by some astrological coincidence she was telling some portion of some truth, there was no jury he could possibly impanel in the Southern District of Florida whose members would believe this woman beyond a reasonable doubt — which was what he reported back to Justice.

Gregorie's second disagreement with the subcommittee came over the subcommittee's star witness at an open hearing it convened that July, a former cocaine-trafficker who was a prisoner held in the Southern District and with whom it had just completed long drawn-out negotiations for a plea bargain. The trafficker testified that the contra leadership and two representatives of the CIA had recruited him to their cause when he was facing two separate drug-running indictments, offering to keep the law off his back in exchange. Under their direction, he claimed to have piloted a series of six flights round trip to Costa Rica. Departing Fort Lauderdale and Opa-Locka airports in Florida loaded with weapons, and returning to the same strips loaded with a total of some $35 million worth of cocaine, the trafficker moved through those airports without any legal interference on all the contra smuggles. The arrangement stopped only because the trafficker was busted on a separate smuggling venture of his own and ended up in extended negotiations with the Southern District of Florida before he could tell his story. He also claimed that Kellner's office had done its best to suppress his testimony before he finally made contact with the subcommittee.

Dick Gregorie described these latter accusations as "bullshit," about the strongest word in his vocabulary. The plea negotiations had taken so long because the witness had kept refusing to tell his story before making the deal, and that was the only reason.

The subcommittee also held another, closed-door hearing in July. Its featured witness for that secret session marked the third collision between the Senate panel and the Southern District. This witness was a Cuban American accountant from Miami who was apprehended attempting to leave the country in 1983 carrying some $5.5 million in cash and was now serving a thirty-five-year prison sentence. The subcommittee had discovered him with the assistance of a film crew from CBS News to whom the accountant granted a jailhouse interview. He told the subcommittee that he and Noriega had been money-laundering partners, handling $2 billion a year on a 1.5 percent commission. He claimed his arrest had occurred because "General Noriega very adroitly used the American law enforcement agencies to surgically extract me from the [money-laundering] operation while leaving the operation intact for him and his cronies to continue working."

By July, the subcommittee had already attempted to push the accountant onto Gregorie and the Southern District as a prime candidate to trade time off his sentence in exchange for testimony, and Gregorie had rejected the offer out of hand. He knew all about the accountant down at 155 S. Miami. This guy had been trying to turn informant since his arrest in 1983, only then he'd had an entirely different story, all about drug-running by the anti-Communist Cubans. He came up with reformulated stories regularly thereafter, usually coinciding with the appearance of news accounts of the same subject on which he offered information. The Southern District not only refused his services but also prepared a nine-page affidavit announcing it had "declined to base any court proceedings on his testimony" because doing so would "violate our ethical obligation to present truthful and reliable information."

Needless to say, when the investigator from the subcommittee phoned in September, his employer and the Southern District were, in Gregorie's words, "at odds." The investigator had not, however, called to pick a fight. He framed his request as a way the two could "work together."

At specific issue was Floyd Carlton, though the subcommittee did not yet know his name. The investigator had heard that the Southern District had a witness they were using to make a case on the General. The subcommittee wanted to talk to this witness and, eventually, put him on the stand.

Dick didn't pause a beat before saying no.

"Why should I risk my witness?" he later explained. "I suppose things like the subcommittee have a legitimate purpose, but not at the expense of the Justice process. They were just making a public show and, for all intents and purposes, had no standards of evidence. I, on the other hand, have the rigorous task of meeting demanding standards of proof in a adversary process. And anything a witness tells them goes on the public record and can be used to discredit him when he testifies in court for me. That's a no-brainer. Law School 101. Any attorney wants the least possible public record on his witness. All of it is leverage against you. So why should I weaken my case for the subcommittee's purposes? But I didn't say all that when they called. I just said that my witness was still being debriefed."

Dick then tabled their request into the indefinite future.

The subcommittee investigator promised he'd be back in touch.

The second incident that resonated of approaching "politics," at least to Dick's ear, occurred one September afternoon in Leon Kellner's office on 155 S. Miami's sixth floor. Steve Grilli was notified of the meeting with a phone call asking if he could come up to Leon's right away. In addition to Kellner and Gregorie, a third man was there as well, whom Grilli recognized as a reporter for the *Miami Herald.*

Steve took a chair and Leon turned the floor over to the reporter, who got quickly to the point. He said he had written a story, which the *Herald* would soon run, revealing that the Southern District was pursuing the General and would take its investigation to the grand jury. He claimed to be informing the three of them ahead of time in order to solicit their comments, if they wished to make any, and, of course, as a matter of courtesy. For effect, as the reporter said so, he produced a computer printout of the story's text that he allowed to unfold in a flourish of paper reaching all the way from his chest to the floor.

Dick Gregorie made no secret about his desire to keep that story off the newsstands, but Grilli felt somewhat differently. While Gregorie negotiated with the guy from the *Herald,* Grilli quickly read the computer print out. He thought ninety percent of it was off the mark and that the only real information the *Herald* article had came from Washington, likely someone over their heads in Justice — a conclusion the reporter would later confirm to him. If it had been up to Grilli, he would have told the reporter to go ahead and run it and forget about any deals. He didn't think the story would hurt them that much.

Gregorie, however, thought otherwise. And the reporter left that day having agreed to hold his story in exchange for the promise of an exclusive scoop whenever an indictment was in the offing.

Gregorie was in no mood to take chances, at least where this subject was concerned.

— 3 —

At 9:30 A.M., on October 1, 1987, the grand jury hearing *United States v. Manuel Antonio Noriega* commenced its deliberations behind closed doors. For experienced Miami courthouse observers, just the sight of Dick Gregorie entering the private grand jury rooms off the courthouse annex's lobby was a sure sign something was up, but no one knew what.

The first witness whom the First Assistant United States Attorney called to testify before his new grand jurors was Floyd Carlton. Floyd, dressed in his yacht-club-looking civilian clothes and freshly shaven, was loaded on a secret high-security elevator that connected the Submarine to the grand jury chambers and, traveling with an escort of marshals, unloaded in a secure waiting area adjacent to the three separate chambers in which grand juries convened. The General's grand jury gathered in the windowless one farthest from the locked door leading to the annex's lobby, because the marshals thought it the easiest grand jury room to defend. All twenty-three members were waiting for Floyd, seated on loge chairs bolted to the floor in a small lecture hall that looked as if it belonged on some junior college campus.

Under Gregorie's direction, Floyd started with his meeting with the cartel back in Medellín in 1982 and began to recount the smuggling for the cartel he had arranged with the General's permission. It would take more than one Thursday for Floyd to tell the whole story. He would eventually be followed on the stand by the tiny pilot and then more than a dozen others Grilli had already rounded up to be paraded into the grand jury during the Thursdays that followed through the fall.

From that first day in October, Steve remembers, "everything was for keeps. We'd crossed the fuckin' Rubicon."

On most of those Thursdays, late in the afternoon, after the grand jury had finished meeting, Dick and Steve usually repaired to Tobacco Road, a bar and grease dive on the other side of the drawbridge south of the courthouse and 155 S. Miami. The roadhouse had a beer garden out back that caught the mild breezes, which now ended most days as the tourist season approached. Sometimes Kenny Kennedy joined the two of them there as well. Kenny, always up for a "brewski," would use the gatherings as an opportunity to catch up on the case. Dick and Steve would use them to strategize, plan, or just blow off steam.

At one of those sundown sessions in the beer garden, Grilli, in a knit shirt and jeans, leaned back in his chair and indulged his own sense of amazement at how far their case had come in what seemed such a short time. He also expressed wonderment at the unprecedented stature of their target.

"I can't believe it," he said. "Are we actually gonna indict this guy?"

Gregorie, in his shirtsleeves, with his tie half undone and his suit coat thrown over a nearby chair, laughed.

"Steve," he answered, "what else do you think grand juries are for?"

CHAPTER 6

THE BLANDON PLAN

— 1 —

Thus far, the only ripple on the surface of this otherwise invisible case had been the August 4, 1987, article in the *Los Angeles Times,* datelined Washington, D.C. Under the head "U.S. Reported Probing Noriega Link to Drugs," the *Times* described the General as

> the focus of a major federal drug conspiracy investigation . . . by a federal grand jury in Miami . . . into whether he has been providing protection to cocaine trafficking and money laundering operations. . . . [This] disclosure . . . comes only two months after [the U.S. attorney general] and other Justice Department officials praised Panamanian law enforcement . . . for seizing . . . drug profits. . . . One law enforcement source . . . rated as "very strong" the evidence gathered so far. . . . The Colombian cartel allegedly linked to Noriega is . . . suspected of supplying as much as 75% of the cocaine sold in the United States. . . . Senate sources said that Noriega has no State Department backing [anymore] and little Justice Department support, but is still backed by the Pentagon and CIA.

The story ran on the front page and jumped inside for some thirty column inches — devoted almost entirely to the testimony heard in "secret" by the Senate Subcommittee on Terrorism, Narcotics and International Operations — but the news drew little notice among either other media or the public at large.

Even so, the August 4 *Times* story's impact on the General's eventual fate was enormous — all because of its effect on one man, Jose Blandon, the Republic of Panama's consul general to New York City.

Blandon had been the General's chief political adviser, cruising the Gulf of Panama with Noriega and Oliver North two years earlier, dickering over assistance to the contras. Now, in a move some interpreted as a reward for loyal service and others thought was a well-cushioned demotion, the General had appointed Blandon to the New York consul generalship, considered a financially lucrative posting, full of opportunities to skim profits off official business. Short and prematurely white-headed, Blandon had risen from humble beginnings and had no doubt he would accomplish great things, wherever he was. He also made little secret of his faith in himself — often speaking with the air of someone who expected his words to be inscribed on marble walls some day. Jose Blandon was described in State Department cables as "Panama's leading Marxist theoretician" and was still close enough to his boss to later claim, "I had access to General Noriega any time I wanted, as often as I wanted."

Ensconced in his consulate office in Rockefeller Center in midtown Manhattan, Jose recognized right away that the implications of that snippet of news carried in the *Los Angeles Times* were potentially earthshaking. Such inquiries by the legal authorities might very well lead to a formal criminal indictment, and Blandon knew enough about the American political system to understand that such a formal charge could potentially make the situation dangerous. Grand jury indictments could not simply be retracted with no one the wiser. And if Noriega waited until he had actually been indicted to address the possibility, the pressure inside the American government to "do something" about the General would inevitably increase, while the ability to resolve the situation smoothly, behind the scenes, would almost evaporate.

Having recognized the implications, Jose's first conclusion was that the General's window of opportunity was still open, though there were no assurances it would stay that way for long. Blandon had tracked American coverage of the disturbances in Panama over the summer and knew of Elliott Abrams's intention to unseat the General. He expected Abrams would use such a criminal charge like a weapon whenever it became available to him.

Blandon's second conclusion was that this moment was also a window of opportunity for Jose Blandon, and within two weeks, he committed to leaping into the breach and making the best of the General's dilemma. Telling himself that history belongs to the bold, Jose booked a seat in first class on the next commercial flight leaving New York for Panama City. The time had come to see the General and make his point face-to-face. Jose Blandon believed he was on no less than a mission to secure the orderly transition of power among the political heirs of Omar Torrijos.

Landing in the evening, on August 21, Blandon's sense of urgency was such that he ordered the driver to take him straight to the *comandancia,* the headquarters garrison of the PDF, downtown in the shadow of the Zone and SOUTHCOM's Quarry Heights command center. The opposition demonstrations that had paralyzed portions of the city for parts of June and July had ebbed into uneasy calm, though there was still litter from the action in some gutters. The sense of crisis here had dimmed considerably, in sharp contrast to Blandon's own mood. He believed that if the General let this legal situation with the gringos wait too long, he would set off a chain of events in which the continuation of the PDF and its political party — of which Blandon himself occupied the left wing — might both be threatened as well. It was not a matter he felt comfortable putting off even long enough to stop by his house and drop his bags.

At the *comandancia,* Blandon's pass admitted him past the sentries, and when he reached the building where the General kept his offices, Blandon found Noriega holed up on the second floor, drinking scotch with several of his PDF cronies. Blandon told him they had to talk, but the General wasn't interested. He was winding down. He said Blandon should have some scotch and wind down himself. They could talk business the next morning.

Jose Blandon would eventually cite this lack of urgency on the General's part as a sure sign that, where once he had been driven and irresistibly cunning, General Manuel Antonio Noriega's mastery of the situation had now begun to slip.

Nonetheless, the General and Jose met the following day, August 22, 1987, as the General had promised.

According to Blandon, "Noriega was serene. I was talking to the real Noriega [this time], the guy who thinks things through, the guy who knows that he is in trouble." Blandon later claimed that right away, he told his boss, "I think the moment has come to negotiate.

"I said, 'General, this is the best moment to resolve the problem with the United States. There are no indictments, [though] we had information that they were coming. The United States is at a loss as to how to resolve this crisis. The administration has its own problems with Iran-contra [which are distracting it] . . . so we have to make a proposal of our own. . . . And it starts with your willingness to realize that the time has come to make your exit. I'm not saying that it's your fault. [But] politically, the top man pays the price for the errors of his subordinates.'

"He said, 'I agree with you. But I'm not going to leave because the gringos are pushing me or because of the opposition.'

"I said, 'Now is the time, when the opposition is at its lowest level, when the gringos are without a plan. A proposal from us will yield the maximum that we're able to get. It is when we will have to make the fewest concessions.'"

The General gave Jose no immediate answer, but the next day, at the Panama Defense Force ceremony honoring his fourth anniversary as *comandante,* the consul thought he detected signs that the General was thinking about what he'd said. In the General's speech on the occasion, he referred to the current "troubles" and repeated several times that the situation required a "Panamanian solution," not an American one.

Two days later, Blandon and the General met again, this time for almost three hours. Though no record was made of just what was said, obviously the General was now prepared to consider his options. Before Jose returned to New York, Noriega gave him a secret assignment to search out whatever deal the gringos might be willing to take in exchange for stopping any indictments and cleaning the General's legal slate.

Not surprisingly, Jose Blandon took that brief and ran with it.

— 2 —

Jose Blandon had always been proud that he was not some *rabiblanco* born to the hallways of power. It was far better, he said, to have earned his way there instead, as he had. His father had been a worker in the furniture factory owned by the family of the late hero Hugo Spadafora. And Jose himself was a kind of boy wonder, Panama style. After graduating first in his class from high school in Panama City, the young Blandon had won a scholarship to the University of Mayaguez in Puerto Rico, where he graduated *magna cum laude* as an agricultural engineer. Then he did some graduate study in economics, eventually wrote a treatise on the economic history of Panama, and gained a reputation as a leftist intellectual of the more strident nationalist persuasion. Like a number of others who had risen off the Panamanian bottom, Jose Blandon came to government service in the republic after Omar Torrijos of the National Guard seized power in 1969. Jose started as Torrijos's head of agricultural reform and soon emerged as his somewhat legendary political adviser.

Blandon had first become familiar with the General when Noriega was still the G-2, and one of Blandon's responsibilities as chief of political intelligence was to share information with the G-2 at regular meetings. Occasionally the two traveled together on official business as well. Under Torrijos, Blandon was thought of as his boss's "brains," while Noriega was referred to by Torrijos as "my gangster." The General gained enough respect for Blandon's abilities in those days that, when he came to power in 1983, he enlisted Blandon's help almost immediately. Noriega's new regime was faced with the first election of a civilian government for Panama in more than a decade, set for May 1984 as part of a schedule for democratization to which Torrijos had committed the country before his untimely death. Blandon was assigned the task of charting a course for the PDF's political party through a campaign in which the PDF's candidate for president was eventually "elected" with only a little ballot stuffing.

When, eighteen months later, the General wondered if the time had come to discard his president, he again summoned Blandon. Jose's role in that 1985 ouster was typical of the confidence the General had come to place in his operative. Shortly before the president's resignation and shortly after Hugo Spadafora's headless corpse had been found floating over the border in Costa Rica, Blandon, in Panama, received a phone call from the General, who was on a European trip, about to leave Paris for New York. He instructed Blandon to fly up to New York to meet him the next day at the Helmsley Palace Hotel on Madison Avenue in Manhattan. They had business to discuss. At the time, the General had already received reports of some visible protests demanding the investigation of Spadafora's killing and word that the civilian president whom the General had "elected" was considering giving in and staging such an inquiry. The General wanted an up-to-the-minute report on the lay of Panama's political landscape from his adviser before he flew on to Panama City himself.

During their talk at the Helmsley Palace, according to Blandon, the General told him that he hadn't killed Spadafora, but named the PDF major who had. Then, as they drove in their limo to La Guardia Airport where the General's Learjet was waiting, the General raised the subject again. However the killing happened, he pointed out to Blandon, Spadafora "deserved to die."

The General and his adviser spent a lot of time in particular during the flight south assessing the popular reaction to a "witness" who had recently surfaced in Panama City claiming to have evidence that Spadafora had, in fact, been killed by Salvadoran guerrillas. The General said he had arranged for this "witness" with a phone call to the CIA station chief in San José, Costa Rica, but Blandon told him it had been a wasted effort. He said no one was going for it, and the CIA's fiction had already been exposed as a sham. The rest of the flight was spent mostly thinking out loud about what options remained.

Their conclusions soon became obvious. Within forty-eight hours after landing back in Panama, the General faced down Elliott Abrams and secured the resignation of Panama's civilian president.

Jose Blandon was given the assignment of making an official response to the change in government on behalf of the president's political party and dutifully announced that the resigned president had conspired with "rightist elements within the military and civilian opposition," outside "financial interests," as well as the CIA and the United States embassy, to hand Panama over to "foreign control and neocolonialism" by staging a coup against his own party and the PDF. Blandon then went on to Washington as the chief spokesman in a lobbying campaign on the General's behalf, designed by an American political consulting firm.

If Blandon's subsequent appointment as consul general to New York was indeed a reward for loyal service, he had it coming.

In this instance, of course, the General expected more of the same. Jose Blandon was a veteran member of the *comandante*'s inner circle by the time he flew into Panama City in a lather over the gringos' investigation. And his proposal didn't sound like a bad idea as far as it went. Noriega's modus operandi under any circumstances was to determine whatever someone was prepared to offer, and Blandon seemed a natural to play the cutout role with the gringos to which he had nominated himself: Blandon was able, trusted, and well positioned to make inquiries outside normal channels, through the back doors where the General no doubt expected that the best deal would be proffered. To the General, it seemed a no-lose proposition. At the very least, he expected Blandon would get the Americans to tip their hand a bit and keep them off balance, unsure of the General's thinking.

What the General had not expected, however, was that Blandon would play a double game, pretending to act as the General's loyal agent while secretly attempting to force the General out.

Blandon likely hadn't expected such a transformation himself. Indeed, there is no evidence Blandon had such betrayal in mind when he confronted the General that August with the need for action and secured the General's secret brief to represent his interests and inquire on his behalf. If anything, Blandon seems to have been unsure exactly how next to proceed. But there is no disputing that Blandon slipped into disloyalty relatively quickly once he'd returned to New York and embarked on his quest.

Part of Blandon's switch in motive was rooted simply in character: his self-absorption made it easy to assume that he was now in charge of the Panamanian succession. And once Blandon landed in that intellectual territory, a double game was almost inevitable.

The other influence on Blandon's switch in loyalties was the company he began to keep. This double game was not Jose's doing alone. He had two significant partners.

The first was an American political consultant with whom Blandon had first worked on the 1984 Panamanian election and again in the aftermath of the 1985 presidential firing, when the consultant had been in the General's hire. Jose called the consultant, then living in Washington, as September began. A significant player in both the Democratic Party and the Carter administration, he had ended his work in Panama more than a year earlier, when he and the General had a final falling out.

The impetus for the consultant's break with the General had been a seventy-five-page memo he had submitted to his boss circa early 1986, concerning the General's political standing in the United States. The memo advised that both the presidential firing and the Spadafora murder had provoked "a disproportionately strong reaction from the U.S." and that Noriega, hip-deep in Casey's still secret Nicaraguan scheme, should not simply count on his backers at the CIA and Department of Defense to protect him. "Casey is a real friend [and] Defense and CIA [certainly] have clout," the memo observed, "but they are not as strong as Panama believes." The real problem was that the General's own government "stumbles from crisis to crisis [and] appears stalled and defensive." And the General's enemies were multiplying in the meantime. Previously, the General's critics had all been right-wing Republican ideologues still upset over the Canal Treaties, but they were now being joined by the left wing of the Democratic Party, "creating real problems." Simply put, the

General's standing in Washington was, according to the consultant, anything but that of "a caring sympathetic leader," and he was in far more trouble than he wanted to believe.

The General had not responded well to the consultant's perspective, a fact that came across quite clearly when the two met several weeks after the memo was submitted, and within days of the overthrow of Ferdinand Marcos, the dictator of the Philippines. The consultant immediately pointed out to his boss what had happened to Marcos and warned the General point-blank that he ought to burn any documents that might prove compromising right now, before the situation worsened.

The General had answered with frost in his voice. General Manuel Antonio Noriega, *comandante* of the Panama Defense Force, he declared, did not have those kind of problems.

The consultant, in turn, had felt compelled to point out that Marcos, of course, had thought the same thing.

At that, a PDF colonel who had been sitting in on their meeting interrupted and read the consultant the riot act for talking to the *comandante* as though he were some schoolboy.

From that point on, the consultant had found his access to Noriega reduced to almost nil and, within a few weeks, learned that the General had turned a sympathetic ear to Oliver North when North suggested that the consultant was conspiring behind the General's back to overthrow him. Upon being told that the General had repeated North's allegation to a meeting of his PDF General Staff, the consultant denied the charges and then, choosing discretion over valor, packed his bags and left the Isthmus, never to return. And, rid of his competition, North, still at the height of his power, had taken over the General's Washington protection for himself.

When Jose Blandon reached the consultant that September in 1987, explained the brief the General had given him, and asked for help on the Washington end of things, the consultant was quick to sign on to Blandon's pursuit of a solution to the General's dilemma. The consultant's one condition was that Blandon include a third partner in this enterprise as well, without whom the consultant claimed this all would be pointless since he pretty much had a choke hold on the issue up on the Hill. That third partner was, of course, the ubiquitous Gabriel Lewis.

Had the General any idea that Blandon was about to consult with Gabriel Lewis, the PDF's Enemy Number One, he might very well have withdrawn Blandon's negotiating commission immediately. The idea was to deal with the Americans, not the *rabiblancos.* But the General had no idea what his consul general was up to, and Blandon met with Lewis anyway, knowing full well he was stepping outside the General's envelope when he did so.

Their meeting took place on October 3, 1987, in Washington, at Gabriel's place on Foxhall Road. The consultant was there as well. At one point, Gabriel and Jose had both been leading lights of the PDF's political party — Jose on the left wing and Gabriel on the right — and, that day in Washington, each began the encounter still somewhat limited by the stereotype through which he viewed the other. Blandon knew Lewis as the stalwart of the privileged class who had abandoned the General's cause. And Lewis knew Blandon as the ideologue who, though perhaps the brightest of the General's henchmen, was a henchman nonetheless. Now, both men had landed on complementary strategies at the same moment. Like Blandon, Lewis was ripe for a "Panamanian solution" and had concluded that the possibility of the General's indictment by the Americans might very well provide the leverage necessary to pull it off.

Having discovered their new commonality, the three men met again some three weeks later in a hotel in New York City. Here, they brainstormed about the particulars of such a "Panamanian solution" and, afterward, assigned the consultant to write up the consensus strategy upon which they'd settled. This nine-page document, written over a forty-eight-hour stretch, was originally titled "Thoughts on a Panamanian Political Solution," but would be remembered as "The Blandon Plan," after its instigator.

Having been sent on a fishing expedition for a deal, perhaps trading some form of voluntary resignation for legal immunity — Jose Blandon's effort was about to become a concerted effort to force the General to make such an exchange, whether he wanted to do so or not.

"The Blandon Plan" was a double game on its face: written in two parts, Part One was designed to be shown to the General, and Part Two was intended to be kept secret from him under all circumstances. Indeed, it was understood that if the General ever laid eyes on Part Two, the jig would be up.

Part One, "Consensus on Objectives," the larger of the two parts, laid out the terms to be presented to the General: a series of structural political changes inside Panama, along with a series of personnel "reassignments" that would accompany them. The goal was identified as laying the groundwork for a genuinely democratic election in 1989 that would give Panama a new civilian government with the power to truly govern. And the provisions included retiring not only the General, but the six most senior members of the PDF under him, a group of officers Blandon described in private as "the Empire"— a takeoff on the science-fiction movie *The Empire Strikes Back*. The plan also placed the selection of future *comandantes* in the elected civilian president's hands rather than those of the PDF General Staff. The only high-ranking member of the current PDF-controlled civilian government who would be retained on an interim basis was the current president — the second, of course, to hold that post under the General. This second president, "elected" as First Vice President in 1984, was in daily secret contact with Blandon and was someone Blandon thought he could deliver.

As envisioned in Part One, the General, having ordered all the previous provisions of the plan into effect, was to announce his retirement, which would take place "absolutely no later than the first week of April 1988." In return, the General "would be granted immunity from criminal prosecution in Panama and the United States," safe from indictment in Miami or anywhere else.

Part Two, "Selling the Plan to Noriega," was all about how to force the General to accept Part One, like it or not. "Sustained pressure must be put on Noriega," the plan argued, and it had to be applied by a united front, advancing

> from every direction. . . . The problem today is that no one has a clear idea of what a meaningful, sensible resolution [to this situation] might be. Noriega has the least idea [of all]. He is now resigned to fight because he sees no way out. He has in fact become somewhat schizophrenic in his own analysis. On the one hand, he concludes the U.S. cannot be trusted, that they want to put him in jail and then, on the other hand, he feels the CIA and Pentagon in reality — secretly — support him. . . . [This Plan will] make clear to Noriega that there is a solution which takes into account his personal future. . . . If this explanation is timed with a series of events which remind him of his tentative hold on Panama, we will be successful.

The "series of events" Part Two postulated included a laundry list of possible activities, ranging from "street demonstrations" in Panama to further "U.S. press stories on drugs, etc.," to an inspection tour of Panama by a "Senate delegation," all woven into a strategic sequence and coordinated with several face-to-face messages delivered to the General in rapid succession, each to the effect that Part One was the best deal he could hope for and that he ought to take it while it was still available. Altogether, Part Two of "The Blandon Plan" was a recipe for the manipulation of the General.

And the need to hide it from him was considered obvious to all three of the men who drew it up.

Gabriel Lewis was so taken with the draft of the plan the consultant delivered to him three days after their New York meeting that he refused to allow its author to hold it long enough to clean up the prose and correct the spelling errors. Instead, Lewis immediately took the still sloppy draft, Parts One and Two both, over to the State Department, where the *rabiblanco* "ambassador" had been cultivating contacts. At State, the document precipitated a meeting in the first week of November between Jose Blandon, Gabriel Lewis, and one of Assistant Secretary Elliott Abrams's undersecretaries.

The attractions of "The Blandon Plan" to the State Department were obvious. The proposed pressure campaign in Part Two amounted to a slight escalation of the Policy Review Group's so-called gradualist approach, which had previously framed State's Panamanian policy, and the extent of the housecleaning outlined in Part One was considered appropriate. This was definitely an approach with which the undersecretary was convinced his boss, Elliott Abrams, would want to run.

Indeed, the greatest hesitancy of any expressed at this first meeting with the State Department came from Jose Blandon. His doubts were about just what would happen to *United States v. Manuel Antonio Noriega*. Jose told the undersecretary that the only possible flaw in his plan was whether or not the United States could actually find "a legal mechanism to stop the indictments" and thus deliver on their part of the General's bargain.

The undersecretary dismissed Blandon's worries with a shrug.

If that was the only problem, he promised, the State Department would "take care of it."

CHAPTER 7

TELLING WASHINGTON

— 1 —

At the time Jose Blandon first crossed the Beltway intent on translating the General's possible Miami indictment into leverage on the Panamanian succession, the Drug Enforcement Administration headquarters over at 14th and I streets remained almost entirely ignorant of the Florida case's particulars. The pile of white typewritten pages that might have explained what was going on was still sequestered at the Miami Divisional Office in a high-security safe.

That, however, began to change during the last week of September, a few days before the grand jury meeting on the ground floor of Miami's courthouse annex first heard from Floyd Carlton. The occasion was a visit to the city of Orlando in central Florida by the DEA's number two, the administrator's right-hand man. Upon arrival, the number two summoned Kenny Kennedy and Steve Grilli to fly up for a personal meeting, posthaste. Kenny, an old Washington hand who knew the number two from those days, took the invitation in stride, but Steve was a little starstruck. "This was another of those this-isn't-supposed-to-be-happening-to-me experiences," he remembered. "More of the kind of fairyland I seemed to be livin' in, you know what I mean? You gotta understand that Face Time with the ranks above you is the fuckin' lifeblood of the bureaucracy. And Face Time with the number two? That's a fuckin' GS-12's wet dream. Here I am gettin flown up there with Kenny in a DEA plane because what he's gotta talk to us about is so important no one wants to wait for us to drive there. This was a real big cheese kinda deal. I'd never experienced anything quite like it before."

The meeting took place in the DEA's Orlando office. He was respectful and pleasant, but got quickly to the point. The number two knew of Moritz's telex and had read the *Los Angeles Times* story, as well as followed all the leaks coming out of the Senate subcommittee. He told Kenny and Steve that it was time they took their investigation off white paper and let the rest of the DEA in on what they were up to. Following standard procedure, they should file it on yellow pages, like normal DEA-6s, so the information could be circulated. The number two reminded his two agents that he had personally written the provisions which allowed for a case to be classified and isolated as theirs was. He understood the necessity. But, at this point, enough was enough.

Kenny and Steve flew back to Miami that afternoon and the number two to Washington the next day.

On October 8, 1987, Special Agent Steve Grilli officially filed the first of three very lengthy DEA-6s on the interrogation of Floyd Carlton and Grilli's subsequent investigation. It was immediately circulated upward in the Drug Enforcement Administration.

Two weeks later, Steve got a call at the office from Dick Gregorie down at 155 S. Miami. Dick informed him with obvious agitation that the *Washington Post* was about to run a story exposing Floyd's existence and some of what he'd been telling the government. Leon had just got a call about it from somebody he knew up in D.C. Their trump card was now uncovered.

— 2 —

The final ritualized end to the isolation that had incubated *United States v. Manuel Antonio Noriega* began in Miami on November 3, 1987 — during tourist season, when the last warm dark of early morning was still beading dew on sawgrass leaves. Steve was up and gone from Deerfield Beach before Patti or the kids woke. He left his car in the lot at Miami International, where he met Dick and Kenny just as the first pink stripe was lifting out of the Atlantic. The three stalwarts of the Noriega task force were ticketed on the first shuttle to National Airport, Washington, D.C. By starting early, they beat the crush of incoming vacationers who would swarm the Miami terminal like army ants for the rest of the day. As it was, the airport was still thick with South American passengers changing planes. Kenny eventually managed to catch a little sleep as they waited for their flight to be called. Once in Washington, the delegation from the Southern District was scheduled to brief the administrator of the DEA and his "advisers" after lunch. Then, they would do the same with the number three man at the Justice Department. The idea for the trip had been hatched between Gregorie and Leon Kellner, then worked out over the phone with Justice. It was time, Leon had insisted.

The first part of their day inside the Beltway was spent touching base with their respective bureaucracies. Gregorie stopped off at the Justice Department on Pennsylvania Avenue and the two agents went down the block to the DEA. Kenny had some ASAC things to deal with there, separate from this case, and Steve had arranged for some technical assistance that morning from headquarters staff, preparing charts for that afternoon's briefing. Kenny's instinct was to approach the visit as a sort of homecoming, full of backslapping and lots of "how ya doin'?" but he was disabused of his fantasy in short order.

One of the first persons he saw back in the hallways he used to trod was the head of the Cocaine Desk, a former chum who oversaw the broad reach of all cocaine investigations inside the agency. The head of the Cocaine Desk was also one of the agency executives who were under orders from the administrator's office to attend the briefing about the case against the General. The invitations had gone out the day before and his had blindsided the head of the Cocaine Desk. This briefing was about a cocaine case and he knew nothing about it, not one fuckin' thing, having received no warning at all from his old buddy Kennedy.

"The guy was furious," Kennedy remembered, "I mean pissed off to the point of being red in the face. He was like sputtering he was so mad. I knew I'd fucked up. I tried to explain that the meeting was Gregorie's doing and that I was just along for the ride, but he was in no mood to listen to any excuses. He was too fuckin' pissed."

The head of the Cocaine Desk demanded to know how Kennedy dared send a cocaine case straight up to the administrator without even so much as giving him a shout? What kind of asshole strung his friends out like that? This was the Cocaine Desk's turf, for Chrissakes. What Kenny'd done was a major violation of the way things are supposed to be done, not to mention a major violation of their friendship. So Kennedy should get used to the fact that he was now on the official Cocaine Desk shit list. He shouldn't bother to call for any favors ever again.

With that last sputter, the chief of the Cocaine Desk wheeled and headed off down the hallway.

Kenny just stood there in a state of shock for several minutes afterward.

Then, for the some four hours that remained before the meeting with the administrator, Kenny tried every ten minutes to reach the Cocaine Desk chief, both on the phone and dropping by his office, but could never find him and ended up just leaving a stack of messages. Each one of them began with "I'm sorry about. . . ," all to no avail. The head of the Cocaine Desk would stay pissed at Kennedy for months to come.

The briefing of the administrator convened on the eleventh floor of DEA headquarters, shortly after 2:00 P.M. Gregorie rendezvoused there with his investigator and his old task force buddy, already carrying something of a defiant air. Kennedy, chastened by his morning encounter, was subdued. Grilli, however, about to log Face Time with the top guy himself, felt, in his own words, "so stoked I thought I was gonna hyperventilate."

When they filed into the nondescript conference room next door to the administrator's office, the administrator and more than a dozen other executives from headquarters were already grouped around the oval table. The greater ranks were at the table itself and the deputies grouped behind them in chairs. The three men from Miami found seats at one end. The headquarters contingent included the obviously disgusted head of the Cocaine Desk and the even more disgusted-looking head of Intelligence. Steve had been dealing with the Intelligence staff all morning, as its shop prepared the charts for his coming presentation, and they had made no secret that, from the top down, Intelligence didn't like the case Steve was making. Dick thought the entire headquarters group looked to be "a very unhappy crew." Kenny noticed the same thing, and it seemed to rattle him a little bit. He managed only a fidgety fifteen-second introduction before handing the meeting over to Steve and, thereafter, remaining completely silent.

All those years in front of a classroom teaching school had prepared the enormous Grilli well for tasks like today's. He stood next to his new charts with a pointer, both authoritative and confident. On the first chart, General Manuel Antonio Noriega, de facto ruler of Panama, was represented by a circle almost at the center. Over him was the apex of a triangle labeled "Medellín Cartel." Floyd Carlton was a smaller circle on one flank and INAIR was a larger square on the other, with a circle inside it named for the former diplomat turned Noriega front man. All of these major shapes were color coded and flanked by various subsets of other violators or witnesses, all connected to each other in a web of lines.

This was not your standard drug conspiracy case, Grilli began, by any measure. There was no powder on the table and no perpetrator standing next to it waiting for the cuffs. The General was not going to be caught red-handed in the same room with the cocaine, but it wouldn't have got there without him. And he could and should be charged with it. The way to do so was under RICO. As soon as Manuel Antonio Noriega signed on with Floyd Carlton in 1982, he joined the cartel as a facilitator and could be held responsible for the whole network of cartel activity. That included the INAIR seizure, the botched *Krill* smuggling venture, and a growing list of other events and enterprises. Grilli also ran down a list of airplanes and pilots he had been tracking along their document trails and described several other witnesses who had Face Time with the General as part of this "association in fact." The law required that the existence of the cartel be proven, that Noriega had signed on with it, and that he had never extricated himself from that arrangement. And they could already prove all those elements in a case that was "multifaceted, historical, and episodic." Eventually there would be an indictment with a large number of counts.

It was, Grilli admitted in closing, an unusual approach. But to make unusual cases, unusual approaches were essential.

For a moment, the complexity of it all seemed to stun the audience. Then the room full of "advisers" began to look at each other, projecting a lot of irritation. The administrator said nothing at all, with body language or otherwise. Finally a desultory "discussion" broke out.

By far the most negative response came from the head of Intelligence, his intensity mounting as he talked, sometimes pounding his hand on the table. He said flat out that their case was bullshit. They would never make it and it was not even worth trying. Even if they got an indictment, there was no possibility of ever bringing it to trial. And, on top of it all, the guy they were after was "the best goddamn friend the Drug Enforcement Administration has in South America," bar none. They should shut their investigation down, the sooner the better.

As intense as the head of Intelligence was, he wasn't the most combative among the men around the administrator's conference table. That title belonged to Dick Gregorie.

While Steve was obviously very aware of where he was and who all these guys were, engaging in the appropriate bureaucratic obeisance, Dick exhibited no such awe. "I didn't really give a damn whose toes I stepped on among those guys," he remembered. "As far as I was concerned, they had already been sandbagging this investigation and I wasn't going to cut them any slack."

On several occasions, Gregorie let the room know that the Southern District of Florida was going to make this case and they weren't about to let anyone run them off it. And he didn't care who tried, no matter how hard. On this one, the War On Drugs was coming home to roost.

After one such outburst, Steve kicked Dick under the table, then leaned over and whispered in his ear.

"Jesus, Dick, cool it," he pleaded under his breath. "You keep this up and you'll get me shipped out to fuckin' Nome, Alaska."

Dick backed off with reluctance.

The administrator's briefing on November 3, 1987, lasted an hour all together. The administrator managed to say absolutely nothing throughout, except to thank the men from Miami for coming as the meeting was about to break up. The rest of the headquarters group looked even more unhappy than when the meeting had begun.

For their parts, Steve still looked stoked, Dick unrepentant, and Kenny like he couldn't wait to get outta there.

The last stop on the Miami delegation's November 3 visit to Washington was at the Department of Justice. There, they had an appointment with the Department's number three. After waiting several minutes in a mahogany-paneled anteroom with French doors, embellished moldings, and an oil portrait of former Attorney General Robert F. Kennedy, the delegation was ushered into a large office with a desk, a couch, and stuffed chairs, and more portraits on the walls. The number three told his secretary to hold all his calls then closed the door. He and Gregorie had already spoken of *United States v. Manuel Antonio Noriega* on several occasions over the phone and the number three let it be known right away that he was among this case's backers here at Justice. Still, he seemed decidedly edgy about discussing the grand jury probe out loud and in person. After returning to the door to make sure it was well shut, the number three conducted the entire conversation in a hushed voice, as though to avoid being overheard.

The number three wanted to know about everything they had on the General, and Dick and Steve laid it out, talking in lowered voices as well, charts and all.

When they were done, the number three shook his head in a state of amazement. He agreed that they had the basis for a very big case, but they needed to get some more, and he took several minutes to lay out where he thought their evidence needed bolstering. He reminded them of the adage that if you went after a king, you couldn't just wound him. When they brought this indictment, they had to do so with all the goods.

Then, lowering his voice even further, hunching forward toward his visitors and beckoning them to do the same, as though his words might then be contained in the huddle, the number three offered in an almost whisper that they should go ahead and make the case.

Having received this faint blessing, the men from Miami felt as if they ought to tiptoe out when they left the building, so that as few people as possible might notice their presence.

Outside on Pennsylvania Avenue, looking for a cab back to National Airport, Steve exhaled and then framed the question that had been on his mind throughout the entire meeting. He didn't really expect an answer.

"Who the fuck is he so worried might be listening?" Grilli asked.

CHAPTER 8

PLAYING POLITICS

— 1 —

As the Miami delegation was leaving National Airport headed home, Jose Blandon was arriving in Washington from New York in preparation for his first meeting at State with the undersecretary. Jose now stayed in one of Gabriel Lewis's guest rooms out on Foxhall Road whenever he was in town, which was more and more frequently.

Another eleven days after that first visit to State, on November 18, 1987, Jose Blandon returned to Foggy Bottom for a 10:00 A.M. meeting with Elliott Abrams, the Assistant Secretary of State for Inter-American Affairs himself.

Again, the subject was "The Blandon Plan." "It was here in Washington," Jose later testified about the meeting.

> We met to discuss [my] political project and at finding a way out for General Noriega. . . . The only document I brought with me to Washington was [my] political Plan. [This] proposal [in Part One] contains . . . a general consensus [on how] to solve the problem [in Panama]. . . . It stated that the entire [PDF] group which appears there [in Part One of the plan] would [have to] disappear because, without eliminating that [PDF] machine, it would be impossible to have a democratic process in Panama. . . . The proposal set up mechanism for a free electoral process . . . also political reforms . . . which would guarantee . . . honest elections, fair elections. . . . But it is a very generous proposal, because what it proposes is that those individuals [who are to be forced from power] are not to be judged [by the

> law]. . . . We tried to find the least costly alternative for the people of Panama. . . .
>
> So the proposal was to give [the PDF hierarchy] a way out, and when [I] spoke with Abrams . . . I explained this proposal to him, putting it forward as a Panamanian proposal. . . . [Abrams] seemed pleased with it, but when I spoke of the immunity problem [for Noriega] here in the United States — I wish this to be very clear — [Abrams] never promised to do so. The only thing we were told was that they hoped that the proposal could be applied and that they would in due time give us their answer to that effect.

Nonetheless, within another week after that conversation with Abrams, Jose Blandon would be describing "The Blandon Plan" as the "de facto" policy of the State Department.

— 2 —

At no time in that process did Elliott Abrams recommend that Jose take his plan to the Department of Defense for their backing, even though one of the projected actions against the General in Part Two involved Defense's man at SOUTHCOM, Fred Woerner.

Specifically, the spine of Part Two's strategy was a series of man-to-man conversations with the General on the part of Americans who might have some influence on him, all speaking with "one voice," passing on the message that the time had come for the General to leave and this was the best deal he was going to get. The second of those conversations envisioned by the plan was between Noriega and Woerner. In the script brainstormed by Blandon, Lewis, and the consultant, Woerner was to insist that the General's three closest colonels be present at the meeting as well. According to the plan, "Werner [sic] should give same message. Important [for Woerner to] give [the message] to all 4 [at once] so Noriega has no freedom to freely interpret message to others. Message should be tough. [Woerner should] say [that Noriega] must deal with civilian U.S.G. [United States government]. Say there is no support in CIA or Pentagon for Noriega. U.S.G. has one policy. U.S.G., however, wants to help Noriega in transition. [We] feel that loyalty to him."

As things turned out, this confrontation between the SOUTHCOM CinC and the PDF *comandante* never actually happened. Nor was Fred Woerner ever consulted about the plan's projected approach or even made aware of the plan's existence until well after the fact. Indeed, had Woerner been asked about the plan's namesake, he would have described Blandon as "an opportunist of the first order," someone to stay away from.

Still, that fall, Woerner might very well have been tempted to sign on to "The Blandon Plan" anyway, just to have a role to play. There was a lot going on, but Fred could already sense that he was being left out of the shuffle and it pained him.

As Washington began to stir around the issue of the General that fall, the roots of Fred Woerner's disuse down on the Isthmus were several.

The first was simply an issue of turf with the State Department. Since Elliott Abrams had jumped into this issue with both feet, State had insisted on primacy in the overlapping Panama chain of command. Abrams did not want a repeat of the arrangement with Woerner's predecessor, who had essentially maintained his own diplomatic channel separate from the one maintained by State through its ambassador. For his part, Woerner was an easy mark on the issue. His overriding allegiance to the sublimation of military force to civilian control compelled him to cede the right to manage the communication of American policy and intentions toward the General to the ambassador without a protracted bureaucratic battle. This was no small concession for Woerner, since he considered the ambassador to be a man in way over his head, whose skills he doubted and of whose professional conduct he occasionally disapproved. Still, Woerner saw no choice but to concede that it was State's play to make.

The second obvious limitation on Woerner's potential usefulness in dealings with the General grew out of their roles as opposing military commanders, each obliged to engage and control the other and hence, by definition, hostile. Since the disturbances of the summer, General Manuel Antonio Noriega considered his Panama Defense Force to be engaged in a combat of posture, innuendo, propaganda, threat, and gesture with the giant American state, in which the brief siege of their embassy on Avenue Balboa had been only the opening round.

"The government controlled by military strong man Gen. Manuel Antonio Noriega has escalated its campaign of political attacks on

Washington," the *Washington Post* reported at the end of October, "with a series of actions to harass U.S. diplomats, servicemen and other citizens in Panama. . . . There has been no love lost between Washington and Noriega since the Senate passed a resolution on June 26 calling for the General to step aside . . . pending an investigation into allegations . . . that the General was involved in crimes. . . . Last week Noriega said U.S.-Panamanian relations have reached their 'lowest point.' "

During September and October, incidents between the two had indeed been rife. A retired American soldier was arrested for participating in an anti-Noriega demonstration and then deported. An economic officer from the embassy was arrested and detained for eight hours in clear violation of his diplomatic immunity. Nine off-duty American servicemen were arrested at a bar outside the Zone but right near Quarry Heights. The Canal Treaty required the Panamanians to notify SOUTHCOM within two hours of such arrests, but the PDF waited more than six. When SOUTHCOM sent twenty-seven visiting airmen from the U.S. War College in buses from the Zone to the embassy, the PDF-controlled television station described it as an "invasion" by two hundred troops in full combat gear and the republic's foreign minister denounced it before the United Nations as a "stupid provocation." All of this posturing was designed to irritate without a full-scale provocation, just enough to keep the gringos off balance and send the message that pressure worked both ways.

Fred Woerner would have liked to respond with a campaign in kind, thinking that at the very least his own skill at countering the General's psychological operations might lead to a mutual respect that would vitalize their relationship and open a potentially useful line of influence. Woerner, however, was under different orders. SOUTHCOM's assigned role from Washington was simply to absorb the General's abuse while avoiding incidents, and Woerner issued the commands to implement that passivity. After a while, his troops' irritation with being put in such a position found expression in nicknaming the Southern Command "WIMPCOM"— a derision that would dog Woerner's entire tenure at four stars, even though the behavior that inspired it was not of his own doing.

The final root of Woerner's disuse grew out of his own lack of chemistry with the General when they did communicate. While his predecessor and the General had got on famously, Woerner made no such bond.

"I never reached the point where I liked the man," he explained, "and I don't think he liked me. Noriega's reputation came with him, but in person he wasn't barbaric or especially gross. In conversation, he was polite, but it was always an effort and he was always hidden. And when he did talk, he was sometimes simply hard to understand. He mumbled and hardly moved his mouth when he talked. The word 'inscrutable' comes to mind when I think of him. He did have one character trait that was disarming, though. He enjoyed shocking people and, occasionally, telling the truth was one of the ways he did it, usually at the exact moment that you were expecting the big lie. I imagine I physically stepped back a little when he did so — just because I had mentally geared myself for some phony lecture. I'm sure he was candid like that for effect, to delight in the confusion it caused and momentarily gain the emotional upper hand. Even so, those moments were the closest I ever came to enjoying him."

Neither Woerner nor the General, however, was the kind to let personal distaste interfere with their duties, so the two talked with some regularity nonetheless. Usually those conversations were initiated by the General sending a message to Woerner through an intermediary, saying the situation required that they speak. At the insistence of the SOUTHCOM CinC, all such meetings were held in private, one-on-one. Woerner also warned that if Noriega ever violated the secrecy of their communications, he would not get the opportunity to do so twice. Typically, their rendezvous took place at Fort Amador, in the shared portion of the Zone, where the General kept an office and command bunker.

"He was using me as a vehicle [for] reminding the U.S. government of what a loyal ally he had been," Woerner later recounted, "and how he had helped us on a series of sticky problems: the shah of Iran, the intelligence-gathering activities, the counter–drug operations, et cetera. . . . I got the same lecture each time . . . the same speech about the [Torrijos] revolution that began in 1968 and would be completed with the elections of 1989, [including] full restoration of democracy. . . . Half of the talk would be straightforward. . . . And any day-to-day issues that we had were handled straightforwardly."

In hopes of probing deeper, Woerner often sought to touch the penchant for intellectual banter with gringo officers that had been identified in the General's DD1396, the Department of Defense's Intelligence Information Report. Woerner described the resulting conversations as "so much philosophic smoke." The most genuine the General ever got during one of those brief Fort Amador bull sessions arose in a discussion of the PDF's intention to "return to the barracks" and give up civil power after the election scheduled for 1989. Tired of Woerner's attempts to hedge him into detailing what exactly the PDF had planned for the years following 1989, the General broke out into a new lecture.

"Remember," he told Woerner, "this is not the United States. This is Panama. The democracy here will not be the democracy of the United States. It will be the democracy of Panama."

The General added that the PDF was going to have an important role for at least "the next year" after the 1989 elections.

Then Noriega paused to correct himself.

"No," he said, "for the next decade."

Pausing a second time, the General looked right in Woerner's eyes.

"No," he corrected himself again. "Forever."

On the basis of that conversation alone, had the SOUTHCOM CinC known what was afoot in Washington, he would likely have rated the chances of "The Blandon Plan" as somewhere between slim and none.

Gabriel Lewis had been working the Hill continuously since Resolution 239, including a couple more follow-up resolutions. He also mustered a coalition sufficient to dispatch a delegation of Senate staffers representing three Democrats and three Republicans, jointly authorized by both party leaders, on an immediate inspection tour of the Isthmus. The delegation's stated mandate was "to gather information on the situation . . . and report back to the Senate what progress, if any, has been made in restoring democracy and the rule of law to Panama." To make such an assessment, the staffers flew down to Panama City on a Thursday and left the next Monday, with nonstop meetings in between.

One of those meetings was with Fred Woerner at SOUTHCOM, at which Woerner again demonstrated a proclivity for the less than diplomatic.

The staffers' conclave at SOUTHCOM was preceded by a long and very tense session between the visiting delegation and representatives of the PDF officer corps who were, of course, behind their General to a man. The nine PDF officers present included four colonels and two majors, described collectively by one of the Senate staffers as "one smart guy and the rest thugs." Gabriel Lewis had pointed out ahead of time that this upper layer of the officer corps was one of the constituencies the General would have to satisfy in order to realize "The Blandon Plan" and guessed these officers might very well raise the most significant opposition the plan would have to surmount. Consequently, the staffers wanted to make sure these officers realized how set congressional opinion was against the current PDF rule, so the exchange was brisk, intense, and sometimes longwinded. Not surprisingly, the meeting ran well over its scheduled length, leaving Fred Woerner up on Quarry Heights cooling his heels.

Woerner was, by his own account, "furious" at this perceived snub — clearly beside himself, spouting to his aides about how he had a schedule too and wasn't at the disposal of every Tom, Dick, and Harry that Congress decided to send south. He was a four-star general, goddammit. At one point during his wait, Woerner had to be restrained from simply leaving so the congressional staffers would arrive at his empty office — a dose, the CinC thought, of their own medicine. When the staffers did finally show up, Woerner was primed for a fight.

It began when the staffers told him in no uncertain terms that the upcoming maneuvers scheduled between SOUTHCOM and the PDF should be canceled.

Fred Woerner felt that he did not need these Senate rugrats telling him his business and made that very clear, right away. In so many words, he asked who the hell they were to be instructing SOUTHCOM what it ought or ought not to do?

The exchange stayed testy like that for the rest of the conclave. The staffers eventually left under the distinct impression that the general running the Southern Command was a know-nothing red ass of the first order.

Later that evening, Woerner reached one of the delegation's leaders by phone from Quarters One and offered profuse apologies for his own short temper, but it did little to change anyone's impression. "This guy did not seem to realize we didn't even have to talk to him about these maneuvers," one of the staffers pointed out. "We could get them canceled with just a few phone calls around the Beltway."

Which was exactly what the delegation did when it returned from its tour. It also wrote a lengthy report for the Senate, recommending the passage of pending legislation cutting off Panama's aid and a list of other remedies, most of which sounded like cribbings from "The Blandon Plan."

At the heart of the staffers' recommendations was, of course, "reform of the Panamanian Defense Forces and the departure of General Manuel

Antonio Noriega on a mutually agreed upon date to be announced at the earliest possible time."

— 3 —

The only serious threat to Blandon's plan that November came while Jose was back in Panama, consulting with the General about the terms of Part One. And it arrived from a direction none of the plan's authors had anticipated. Just as Jose was making his presentation, a freelance gringo arrived in Panama City in his own personal Boeing 707 on a gambit to convince the General that he could deliver even more favorable terms than those Blandon had secured. The timing could not have been worse.

The gringo involved was a retired American naval admiral who had worked with Vice President George Bush when Bush ran the CIA, then moved on with his patron to the White House. The admiral's most recent assignment had been overseeing the vice president's South Florida Task Force in the War on Drugs. Now, he was out on his own in the public-relations consulting business and, as he later put it, arrived in Panama City looking "to make some money."

The retired admiral and his public relations-consulting first came to the General's attention earlier in the year when the admiral attended a Washington banquet hosted by a wealthy Korean businessman with whom the General attended cockfights when the Korean visited Panama. The dinner was in honor of the Republic of Panama's ambassador and, at it, the retired admiral offered a toast regretting the "unfriendly" policies the United States was pursuing toward Panama. That opening led to an invitation to visit Panama in August. When he came south, the retired admiral made sure the General understood that he had been briefed in advance by the Department of Defense, the CIA, the National Security Council, and, of course, the State Department, where he had spoken with Elliott Abrams himself.

The retired admiral later testified that on his first visit he told the General, "they were closing in on him [with a criminal indictment]. I told him why the United States had such a low opinion of him. I said, 'You're a drug guy, you're a murderer, you are considered a rapist, you are importing aliens into the United States, you're playing footside with Castro and possibly Ortega [in Nicaragua] and you're selling arms to the M19 [guerrillas in Colombia].' I said, 'You know that's the kind of reputation you have in the United States.' "

Jose learned about the admiral from the General the day the gringo returned in his 707 for a second visit. The General identified the admiral to Blandon as "Bush's guy" and was very impressed that just he and the General's old cockfighting buddy had flown down in their own jetliner — which, it later turned out, had been borrowed from an arms merchant then under indictment for violating the American arms embargo against Iran. To the General, such a big plane for so few people meant they must be on very serious business. Blandon left town to return to New York on the day the General and the retired admiral were scheduled to meet.

The admiral and the General's Korean cockfighting buddy — who had once been indicted in the United States for bribing congressmen and turned state's evidence to escape prosecution — had come up with their own plan for extricating the General. In it, Noriega would be required to make some "democratic reforms" and the Korean would use his considerable influence with the Japanese prime minister to get the Japanese to appeal to the Americans to ease their pressure on the General. The retired admiral advised the General not to worry so much about Elliott Abrams either, saying the assistant secretary, with whom the retired admiral had spoken just before the flight down, was not nearly the influential player he had once been.

The best news of all, as far as the General was concerned, was that the retired admiral did not think that the General would have to resign by April 1988, as "The Blandon Plan" specified. In fact, if the General played his cards right, he said, Noriega could certainly put off resignation until 1989 and, by then, George Bush might well be president. The admiral spoke knowingly about his former boss and suggested that under Bush, the situation might be altogether different.

Under a Bush administration, the admiral implied, the General might not need to leave at all.

Before the retired admiral and his Korean cockfighting buddy flew their 707 back to Washington, the PDF refueled it free of charge. Then the General left in his Learjet for a regional military meeting in Buenos Aires, Argentina, where he rubbed elbows with the rest of the hemisphere's military leaders, including SOUTHCOM's Fred Woerner. The General mentioned nothing of "The Blandon Plan" or the retired admiral to Woerner. But, while in Buenos Aires, the General did call Blandon from his hotel suite.

This gringo admiral who was Bush's guy, the General pointed out, had made it clear he was connected all the way up the ladder at all the right American places. The Americans had been sending him messages in this way for years — through Oliver North, for example. And Bush's guy had told the General that he might not have to leave until 1989, maybe later. What was all this shit that Blandon had been talking about only one deal being available? What the hell had Blandon been up to if this was the best he'd come up with?

Under the circumstances, all Blandon could do was keep up his imperious front and warn his *comandante* down in Buenos Aires not to be a fool. This admiral was just selling the General a lot of blue sky.

To himself, however, Jose had to have wondered just what the gringos were up to.

Jose raised the issue with Abrams as soon as he could get to Washington and secure an appointment.

What was going on? the Panamanian demanded. This retired admiral had claimed he was speaking for the State Department. What kind of double game was Abrams playing?

Elliott insisted that the retired admiral was just a lobbyist trolling for work. He'd only gotten a briefing as a matter of courtesy, nothing more. Blandon shouldn't worry. Nothing had changed.

The explanation was apparently sufficient.

Shortly thereafter, Blandon returned to Panama at the General's command to give a radio speech to which everyone in the PDF was under orders to listen. With the General's prior approval, the speech mentioned that Blandon was working on a "political solution" to the situation and that such a solution would have to include the opposition that had been demonstrating against the General in the streets. Blandon was convinced that by approving such a message, the General was preconditioning the PDF to acceptance of Part One of "The Blandon Plan" and he reported as much to Abrams.

By Thanksgiving of 1987, Jose Blandon was convinced that his scheme was coming together and he was going to pull it off.

CHAPTER 9

SPRINTING TOWARD THE FINISH LINE

— 1 —

Steve Grilli took Thanksgiving off — eating antipasti, zuppa, lasagne, broccoli rob, and turkey with Patti and the kids out at his parents' house in Boynton Beach, just up the Florida coast — but that was about all the off time he took that month. The sea breeze was up and every patch of sand seemed to be packed with bodies in various sizes and shades, ranging from pink to drugstore umber, but that meant little in the case agent's universe. Gregorie had put *United States v. Manuel Antonio Noriega* into overdrive as soon as they returned from Washington. And, as a consequence, Steve was everywhere but the beach, doing everything but getting toasted on both sides.

His most important task continued to be finding new witnesses to buttress the RICO construct they had laid out. Doing so took him all over the landscape. He found one witness as far away as Tulsa, Oklahoma, tipped off by a DEA intelligence analyst who had been questioning a Colombian popped for owning a hydroponic marijuana factory there. The Tulsa United States attorney had wasted no time sticking it to the Colombian, and he was already facing a sentence of ninety-nine years. Now, he was dropping the General's name, so the analyst gave Grilli a call.

Steve headed for Oklahoma on the next flight. "I'd go fuckin' anywhere to talk to anybody who'd had Face Time with the General," he explained. "And this guy had what I was interested in."

What Steve found in the lawyers' room at the Tulsa federal lockup turned out to be a Junior Scumbag — the son of a smuggler who had grown up to be a smuggler as well. His daddy was a big-time Colombian weed titan and Junior was a seven-figure player himself — well dressed and a little pudgy, looking spoiled enough to pass for the rich kid he really was. By the time Grilli showed up, Junior had already seen more of Tulsa than he ever wanted to see. This white-bread oil rig cow town was not somewhere a Latin who fancied himself hip could find a whole lot to grab hold of, and Junior was clearly foundering. He needed a deal, and giving Grilli the General was his best option for getting one; Junior talked as if the rest of his life depended on it.

He claimed to have started in this business six years ago, in 1981, helping with a few of his father's weed smuggling deals. Then he went out hustling on his own, found a niche supplying ether and acetone essential to the manufacture of cocaine, and became a cartel subcontractor, moving dozens of drums of chemicals from Merck & Co. in Germany to the Colombian jungles. Panama was an obvious transshipment point, and Junior claimed to have good connections there. His father had been friends with Omar Torrijos, as well as with the General's immediate predecessor. It was that predecessor's two sons who had connected Junior to the former diplomat whom Junior identified to Grilli as a Noriega front man. Then, in early 1984, one of the brothers called to tell the Colombian that the General had taken possession of a large shipment of ether and acetone that had been "left unclaimed" at Panamanian Customs. The brother told Junior that the General was prepared to sell all or part of the seized consignment. Was Junior interested?

Junior said it depended on the deal.

To work out the specifics, Junior and the brother met the General and the former diplomat at a very nice house in Panama City. Junior described the General to Grilli that day in Tulsa as "one ugly son-of-a-bitch" who knew how to get what he wanted. Junior said he and the General had talked around and around before settling on a price. Then Junior told the General that he had to take this arrangement to his cartel principals to finalize any deal.

In Colombia, the cartel said they knew all about this load of chemicals already. Those drums were a cartel shipment that the General had waylaid. Now he wanted to sell their own chemicals back to them. Sensing such a ransom was unavoidable, the cartel agreed.

The actual transfer took place at a PDF airfield in Panama City. The cartel flew in a DC-6 and it was met by a caravan of PDF trucks. Once the soldiers had loaded it, the plane took off for Las Llamas, Colombia, while Junior was paid $100,000 and the General, $250,000.

Junior claimed to have become even tighter with the General after that. He said it helped his standing no end when he started fucking one of the General's daughters for a while. Some two months after the ransom deal, his relationship with the Noriegas was good enough that the cartel asked Junior to act as middleman in another arrangement with the General. The cartel had blown away Colombia's justice minister and was having to relocate. As part of that relocation, they had cut a deal with the General to let them open a lab out in the Panamanian jungle of Darien Province. Now they were going to have to import chemicals to feed it and wanted Junior to negotiate terms with the General on their behalf.

Those negotiations took place in a three-sided conversation among the General, the former diplomat, and Junior. The price they settled on for the passage of a thousand barrels of chemicals was based on a calculation of how much cocaine these materials would be used to manufacture. The tab came to $4 million cash, in advance.

According to Junior, he picked up the money from the cartel in two black suitcases, each full of $100 bills, and passed them on to the General at the house where they'd met for the first time.

After that, his dealings with Noriega had fallen apart when the PDF busted the new Darien lab before it even began production. Junior said the story that he'd heard was that the General had ordered the raid because the lab was far larger than the one upon which they had agreed. In any case, the Junior Scumbag's Face Time with the General was over.

Before catching the next plane back to Florida, Steve told his new snitch that he thought they could work out a deal with the U.S. attorney. He also phoned Gregorie and let him know they could add a new count to the General's RICO.

The time pressure Steve was under made even such successes a double-edged sword. Besides continuing to advance the case, he had to maintain the evidence in a state of readiness, so each of the witnesses he accumulated had to be tracked, looked after, or put to work. Steve's weeks were now overrun with baby-sitting duty as well as the investigation itself.

In the case of Junior Scumbag, for example, Steve brokered a deal between the Tulsa United States attorney, Junior's lawyer, and Gregorie in order to bring Junior to the Southern District to testify to the grand jury. According to the terms of that arrangement, Steve took control of the Colombian for use against the General in exchange for using Junior in a big-time coke case with a venue in Oklahoma so that Tulsa could prosecute. Eventually, while working on Steve's leash, Junior brokered a three-hundred-and-fifty-kilo load that came north through Costa Rica, with a stopover to change planes in Tulsa, before ending in New York City. The Colombians who met the plane and the Colombian who sent the dope north would all eventually be captured and sentenced in Tulsa to life in prison.

Steve still had Floyd Carlton to deal with as well. Though Floyd was no longer the heart of Steve's workday, he needed to see him every now and then. Steve would call Witness Protection so he could be fetched from his secret location and delivered to the Submarine, and Floyd would be sniveling even more unmercifully than ever, mostly about whether Maria was going to leave him and what a shit soup he had made of his life. Steve was inevitably left with some wrinkle to iron out when they were done — just the ongoing price of doing business with Floyd.

Perhaps the baby-sitting that wore the worst was of the man from Brooklyn who was Gregorie's principal cartel informant. Brooklyn developed the habit of calling Steve at all hours of the night, usually waking him up out in Deerfield Beach. The snitch was in Witness Protection and didn't have Steve's home number but had a twenty-four-hour DEA hotline number, and the agency's switchboard would invariably patch him through to his case agent.

"Hi, it's Brooklyn," the snitch began, having dragged Grilli out of one of the few small patches of exhausted collapse he was now allowing himself.

On those occasions, sometimes Brooklyn was just lonely and wanted to shoot the shit, other times he was deep in Chicken Little mode and Steve had to talk him back to the ground.

Perhaps the worst of those paranoid incidents started with a single shattering ring at 3:00 A.M. Steve was stretched out next to Patti. He scooped up the receiver and slapped it upside his head before it could ring again.

"Hi, Brooklyn," he mumbled, assuming correctly that it couldn't be anyone else.

Brooklyn instantly communicated a state of absolute panic, breathlessly explaining that he had returned to his home and nobody was there. His wife had disappeared. He was sure that the cartel had snatched her. His wife was gone, he repeated in a scream. Did Grilli understand that?

He wanted the DEA to close the airports right away, seal the country so the cartel couldn't take her back to Colombia.

Steve moaned before answering.

"Let me get this straight," he finally growled. "You want me to seal the fuckin' United States of America?"

Before Brooklyn could affirm that was indeed what he had in mind, Steve exploded.

He told the snitch in no uncertain terms that he, Special Agent Steven Grilli, did not have the authority to seal an SPCA kennel, much less the whole fuckin' country. What did Brooklyn want him to do? Go down to fuckin' Miami International with a bullhorn and announce that the country was sealed?

"Nobody kidnapped your fuckin' wife, Brooklyn," Steve snapped as loud as he thought he could without waking Patti. "She left you. You don't need the country sealed, you need a fuckin' divorce lawyer."

With that, Steve hung up.

Laying there in the Deerfield Beach dark afterward, feeling his adrenaline slowly leak away as he groped to find sleep again, Steve had the premonition that if this pace kept up, he might very well be needing a divorce lawyer himself.

On top of all the rest, *United States v. Manuel Antonio Noriega* was not the only case Steve was working that fall. He was case agent for the cartel investigation as well and, driven as he was, didn't want just to baby-sit Brooklyn and leave it at that. He had set out to expand the cartel case even before he signed on to chase the General.

His first breakthrough at that task came at a brainstorming session with two of the DEA agents assigned to the Miami office's Intelligence Group who had been researching the cartel's local infrastructure, including front corporations and south Florida property interests. When Steve explained that he was looking for a way to pry loose even more information about the Colombians, they suggested he use the property seizure statutes to do so. Under these laws, the government could file a civil action against any piece of property it believed was involved in a crime or purchased with the fruit of criminal activity and seize it immediately. The burden of proof was then on the property's owner to go to court in Miami and prove that the property was not the fruit of some illegality before the property could be returned. In addition, the case surrounding the seizure would be conducted under civil rules, allowing the government to depose the property owners once they contested the action.

Steve thought the idea was brilliant and wondered why the intelligence agents hadn't made that case already. They responded by complaining they could never find an assistant United States attorney who was willing to do it. Steve said he could change that and went straight over to 155 S. Miami Avenue to see Gregorie.

Gregorie, in turn, went characteristically ballistic and began calling various assistants in his office and raising hell. He too thought this a great approach and couldn't believe no one in his office had picked up on it. At worst, they ended up with an uncontested seizure, so long as Steve did his legwork right.

After a half hour, Steve left Dick's office with a blank check to start pulling corporate records and identifying front men. He had the marshals bring in Brooklyn for a long interrogation and, throughout the fall, when he wasn't chasing the General, he was following paper trails on the cartel all over south Florida.

Finally, on November 30, 1987, a task force of DEA agents and federal marshals swept down on five different locations in south and central Florida and posted seizure notices on them all. The properties included a bay front luxury home in Miami, a condo in Miami Beach, a 210-unit apartment building in Plantation, Florida, a forty-unit apartment building in Miami Beach, and a thirty-five-acre ranch in Summerfield in Florida's horse country. Included with the ranch were a dozen purebred Paso Fino walking horses, reputed to be the prized hobby of the same cartel member who, according to Brooklyn, had personally ordered the assassination of Gregorie's fat pilot snitch. Altogether, the buildings and livestock were valued at some $22 million, a drop in the cartel's bucket, but nonetheless the largest such seizure ever conducted in south Florida. According to the papers filed by Gregorie's office, the seized properties had all been purchased using proceeds from the sale of at least fifty-eight tons of illegal cocaine.

At the press conference announcing the bust, Dick Gregorie, smiling like the cat who swallowed the canary, told the *Miami Herald* that if the owners were indeed innocent, "they only have to come to the United States and make us prove our case." It even sounded like a taunt when he said it.

To further make the point to the Colombians, Steve had a picture taken of one of the cartel member's prize show horses with a DEA baseball cap on its head. Then he wrote "The Newest Recruit" across the top of the photo — as though the cartel man's prize horse had now turned evidence as well — and autographed it, "Special Agent Steve Grilli," and mailed it to Medellín, addressed to the cartel.

Needless to say, Steve was back at work on *United States v. Manuel Antonio Noriega* the next morning.

"My mood was certainly more grim than it had been when I started out in the summer," he remembered. "Fatigue'll do that to you. I was starting to suck some wind. Also, about this time, I started takin' more shit down at the office."

Now that his prize case was off white paper, word of what Grilli was up to was all over the Miami office. So too was word that headquarters thought he was hunting down "the best goddamn friend the DEA has in South America." The result was a mixture of disapproval and outright vilification, usually delivered in a backdoor way.

Some were simply resentful of the rarefied bureaucratic altitude at which this GS-12 had been working. They asked him snide questions about whether he was spending just a little too much time with the ASAC and not enough with the other 12s. *Who does fuckin' Grilli think he is?* made the rounds. What did he think he was going to prove with all this bullshit, agents wondered out loud. A couple unsigned notes were left in Grilli's office suggesting in various ways that he try to make "a real case" for once.

Typical of the more formal institutional response Steve also faced was that of the group supervisor who, now that they were on yellow paper, was required to review the DEA-6s which Grilli was now filing on his case.

Where was this going? the supervisor demanded. Wherever that was, he continued, answering his own question before Grilli could, it wasn't putting any bodies in jail or any powder on the table, and it was a giant fuckin' waste of the Drug Enforcement Administration's time and money. Whom was Steve trying to kid? Even to make an arrest on this case would take a division of the United States Marines. All this shit Grilli was putting in his 6s was pure fiction, the great American novel or something. Nobody was ever going to put General Manuel Antonio Noriega in jail, plain and fuckin' simple, period. The supervisor's speeches on the subject tended to go on and on like that in the same vein.

While the volume of this backwash was insufficient to stop Steve, it couldn't help but add to the drag he had to overcome just to keep the case moving.

Meanwhile, of course, Gregorie was insisting Steve go even faster.

In the midst of this sprint to the finish line, Steve also managed to trade access to Floyd Carlton with the U.S. attorney's office for the Central District of Florida for access to one of their snitches, a thirty-five-year-old American who had been at the top of the marijuana importation pyramid in south Florida when he'd been busted in Tampa, Florida, in June 1984. Facing a 285-year sentence, the gringo weed king had finally cut a deal with the Central District the previous June. The FBI was running his case and had him secreted in a special federal facility in south Florida reserved for informants, which is where Grilli finally made contact.

Steve was certain the gringo weed king would be a knockout witness after they'd spent barely five minutes together. This scumbag was handsome, yuppie-looking, obviously bright, and very articulate. Starting from a kind of Haight-Ashbury approach to weed, he'd become a multimillionaire. His sentence had now been reduced to a maximum of twenty years and he was trying to work the remaining penalty off before he had to serve it. When the FBI tested him, the weed king had some problems on the polygraph, registering several slight deceptions, but Steve believed him anyway.

The weed king claimed his Face Time with the General began in late 1983 and grew out of a serious dilemma facing his operation. He was, quite simply, overrun with cash, most of it in small-denomination bills. His smuggling enterprise was grossing in the neighborhood of $80 million a year and he couldn't count the bills fast enough to keep up. His overwhelmed money counters even began suffering lead poisoning from the currency's toxic ink. For a while, the weed king had farmed the problem out to a bank in the Cayman Islands, but the bank couldn't handle the volume either and began refusing to take bills under $50. Eventually, he was keeping several houses in south Florida in which he stored his cash by the roomful. Altogether, the weed king had more than $35 million in immediate need of laundering, and foresaw another $300 million more over the next few years.

Finally, a friend in the business told him that Panama might provide the solution to all his money-laundering problems. His friend said that the man to see in Panama was one César Rodríguez, the General's old Chiriqui drinking buddy.

As soon as César met the weed king and heard him repeat the numbers involved, César jumped like a trout on a black fly. He and the weed king were sitting in César's office in the Bank of Boston tower and César immediately offered that for a mere 5 percent, he could provide full service banking and the best protection Panama had to offer. Then, the weed king later testified, "Rodríguez informed me that the leader of Panama was a man named General Noriega. . . . He was not the president but the head of the military, and they, in fact, retained all the power in Panama. If I wanted anything done or we wanted to attempt anything, we had to have clearance from General Noriega. He informed [me] that General Noriega, himself and [the jeweler, the General's front man] were partners."

César then introduced the weed king to the jeweler and the three of them visited the General that afternoon. The weed king brought along an aluminum briefcase with $300,000 inside. He explained to the General what he had in mind to do with César and the General "seemed very pleased over it." When it was time for the visitors to leave, the weed king walked off, leaving his briefcase next to the chair in which he'd been seated.

The General shouted after him that he had forgotten his bag.

The gringo weed king shook his head. "No," he told the General in Spanish, "that's for you."

From that point on, the weed king told Grilli, he and the General got on famously: He called the General "Tony" and the General called him by his alias, "Mr. Brown." The weed king quickly bought into a holding company shared between César, the General, and the jeweler; the gringo bought a helicopter for the PDF; the gringo put down $500,000 on a Boeing 727 airliner the General said he wanted to use for money-laundering; the weed king loaned the General his Learjet whenever he needed it; the weed king bought a house just around the corner from the General's; the weed king gave jewelry to the General's wife and gave the General several antique guns valued at $20,000. In return, the weed king's cash began flowing steadily through the Panama City airport and straight to the local branch of the Bank of Credit and Commerce International without ever passing through Customs; the weed king traveled on three different

Panamanian passports issued in two different names, one of them diplomatic so the weed king could not be searched at borders; the weed king was warned by the PDF when his plane showed up on the DEA watch list; and the weed king drooled over the future possibilities.

"It was obvious to me," he testified, "that there were no limits to what we could do in Panama. . . . I was quite impressed with what I had seen. . . . [With] the right connections, which it appeared that we had, Panama could provide us with a number of important contributions to our operations, which it did."

At the same time that he had become close to the General, the weed king had also maintained a close relationship with the cartel, from whom he often bought large quantities of marijuana. By the spring of 1984, the weed king and the General were discussing a scheme whereby the two of them would go partners in providing full-service money-washing for all the cartel's cash flow. The commission on such traffic alone would prove an astronomical figure. According to the weed king, the General was all for it, and so was the cartel. He said what convinced the Colombians was how well the gringo had dealt with the crisis that erupted when the PDF raided the cartel's new lab in the Darien. Almost immediately afterward, one of the cartel's operatives called the weed king and asked to come by and talk.

He told the weed king that the cartel had paid the General's bagman $5 million to protect that lab. The bagman was saying he gave the money to the General and that, instead of blaming him, the cartel ought to blow the General's brains out. What did the gringo think was going on?

Needless to say, the weed king's ear perked up at the mention of killing what looked to be his golden goose. He told the cartel man straight out that if the money had actually reached the General, the lab would never have been busted.

The cartel man then asked the weed king to see what he could do to work it out and, the weed king told Steve, he had. The subsequent deal was run through the jeweler and César and involved returning the bribe, the cartel workers who had been arrested, and much of the lab equipment. According to the weed king, the cartel was so pleased that they asked him to handle all of their Panama money-laundering.

The weed king claimed to have been gearing up for the task when he got arrested in Tampa on an outstanding smuggling charge. And the rest, he told Steve with a shrug at his surrounding circumstances, was obvious.

When they were done, Grilli called Dick Gregorie from the lockup and said, with this guy, they had the money-laundering counts nailed down.

Gregorie was more than pleased. He now thought they were about ready to turn this all into a true bill.

— 2 —

On December 5, 1987, Dick Gregorie stepped into Leon Kellner's office next door to his own on the sixth floor of 155 S. Miami and told him the case was ready. It was finally time to ask the grand jury to indict the General.

This, of course, came as no surprise to Leon. He had continued to track what Steve and Dick were finding along the General's trail and he had always known this moment would come. Still, he had Dick run through the evidence one more time in a final review. Then Leon got on the phone with the number three at Justice while Dick sat on the other side of the desk. The number three had been worried about having enough evidence when the delegation had visited Washington a month earlier, and Leon expected he would be only somewhat less worried now.

After a few pleasantries, Leon informed the number three that the United States Attorney's Office for the Southern District of Florida was prepared to ask the grand jury for a true bill in the matter of *United States v. Manuel Antonio Noriega*. Gregorie had the goods. It was time to indict.

The other end of the line responded with complete and utter silence for at least sixty seconds.

Finally the number three found his voice. "O.K.," he said.

But before any indictment was presented to the grand jury, Justice wanted a complete and detailed prosecution memo, laying out the entirety of the case, as though Gregorie were about to step into a courtroom with it — a work product that would take some six to eight weeks to produce. When that was ready, the number three insisted that the team from Miami would have to come up to Washington to defend it to the lawyers at the Justice Department. He also wanted to review the draft text of the indictment as part of the same Washington process. The number three pointed out that, just so the Southern District didn't feel picked upon, this kind of screening was standard practice on all RICO actions, no exceptions.

Leon told the number three they'd be up to see him in Washington in a couple months and relayed the conversation to Dick once he'd hung up.

And Dick got after this new task as soon as he was back in his own office, where the desk was a shifting landscape of documents, legal notebooks, annotated transcripts, pink message slips, and irregular paper scraps with scribbles on them, almost completely obscuring the desktop itself. His first step was to find the phone and call Steve Grilli to let him know they were in the home stretch.

CHAPTER 10

THE FINAL WITNESS

— 1 —

As Dick Gregorie's plan approached fruition, Jose Blandon's was coming undone.

The last sign of hope for "The Blandon Plan" arrived on December 9, when the General cabled his New York consul, describing the plan as "valuable" and "well ordered." He urged Blandon to be "careful, cautious, [and] conceptual in setting forth issues" and to ensure that any discussion of this plan be "kept under your strict control, so it does not appear as a formula of understanding on the part of the [Panamanian] government." When "we develop or create other points," the General promised, "I will send them to you."

Disaster, however, was just around the corner. The General's cable was followed some two weeks later by a political ambush in which "The Blandon Plan" was almost instantly reduced to smoking wreckage.

To Jose, the collapse felt at first like it had come out of nowhere, but he eventually concluded that it had been instigated in the third week of December from inside the Department of Defense in Washington. Someone at the Pentagon sent a purloined copy of the complete nine-page text of the plan — including not only the official terms of a deal but also the description of the campaign to pressure the General into accepting it — to a member of the PDF's "Empire," the core of a half-dozen officers to whom the General was, in some sense, answerable. None of them had seen the plan before and even the General, who had seen Part One, had no idea Part Two even existed. The complete text was quickly translated into Spanish, at which point the Empire learned that their futures were on the block in some secret negotiation the General was apparently conducting through the Communist Blandon. The Empire then confronted the General with their translated copy.

No record was made of the General's response upon reading the heretofore unknown Part Two for the first time, but when he reached the sentence, "If this explanation to Noriega is timed with a series of events which remind him of his tentative hold on Panama, we will be successful," the odds are the General screamed about that *chingadera* son-of-a-bitch Blandon, may dogs chew his dick off.

On December 21, 1987, Noriega called Jose in New York.

Jose immediately sensed by the tone in the General's voice that he was talking in room with others listening to his end of the conversation. Blandon suspected that at the very least the listeners included those Noriega cronies specifically identified for mandatory retirement in Part One of the plan.

Addressing Blandon as he would a disobedient subordinate, the General demanded to know what this "Blandon Plan" was. What kind of traitorous work had Blandon been up to behind his back? Blandon certainly hadn't been acting on the General's behalf. Eventually, raising his voice even louder, the General ordered Blandon to cease any activity on this plan. The New York consul general was not empowered to make any deals and never had been.

Blandon shouted back that the General could not talk to Jose Blandon like he was some damn sergeant in the PDF.

Jose also demanded to know if the General was alone. When the General ignored the question, Blandon told him to call back when he was by himself and could talk freely.

Then Blandon hung up.

The double game exposed, this was the last direct communication ever between General Manuel Antonio Noriega and the imperious white-haired intellectual who had once been his closest political adviser.

Like a snake with his head cut off, however, "The Blandon Plan" continued to twitch for the rest of the month, principally in the State Department's response to its sudden termination.

Jose called Elliott Abrams shortly after he called Gabriel Lewis to announce that Noriega had pulled the plug. Abrams thought the United States had to respond in some way and took the situation to the Restricted

Interagency Group, which had earlier been a clearinghouse for much of Ollie North's doings. What the group settled on for an immediate rejoinder was essentially a step that had been laid out in Part Two. The plan's version had called for recruiting a former CIA executive now at Defense who was reputed to be the General's best friend inside the American government, "to visit Noriega and tell him that the time has come for a political solution. [The messenger] must be tough, as only a good personal friend can be. [He should say], 'You must make a deal. It is the best route for you and your family! The U.S. wants to help you.'" The Restricted Interagency Group endorsed this same direct approach, only wanted to change the messenger.

In the group's deliberations to select a "more appropriate" person to deliver their message, each representative at the table had the right to blackball any suggested nominee, so, in the end, of all the names considered, only one assistant secretary of defense passed everybody's muster. The man was a weight lifter and former commando and widely held to be the right match to get along with an ugly thug like the General. The agreed purpose of the mission was to deliver an unequivocal notice that it was time for the General to retire, that everything could be resolved with a dignified exit that would be seen by the outside world to have come at Noriega's own initiative. The specifics of the style and substance involved in the language of the message itself, however, led to long hours of back-and-forth. The issues in dispute were whether to make the message soft or hard and then, whether to deliver it in a soft or hard way. The option that eventually prevailed was a hard message delivered softly. It was thought that such an approach would allow the General to react to the message itself rather than the messenger.

On December 31, 1987, the weight-lifting assistant secretary, accompanied by the American ambassador and a couple of aides, called on the General in Panama City, at the *comandancia*. To begin with, the weight lifter accepted the General's proffered hug rather than insisting on the more formal handshake which the ambassador thought would have been more appropriate. Then, when the General brought out a bottle of his favorite Old Parr scotch, the weight lifter drank with him quite affably. For sure, the messenger delivered his "hard" message faithfully, almost verbatim from the text he had memorized, but that took no more than a few minutes. The rest of their almost three-hour conclave was spent drinking and telling stories. The ambassador, who simply sipped a small toast, was appalled. "After a few drinks . . . they all wanted to be buddies," he recounted. "There were some friendly things said at that meeting that infuriated me."

Once the General finally escorted the gringos out, he reportedly held up the now empty bottle of Old Parr to his office staff like a token of victory.

Shortly thereafter, Noriega met with a number of PDF officers to brief them on the meeting with the Americans. In the intelligence reports that reached Fred Woerner at SOUTHCOM, the General was characterized as telling his cohorts, in short, "not to worry. All we have to do is lower our profile, cool it for a while. This will blow over." According to Woerner, the entire episode had to be accounted "a classic miscommunication. The General read the hug and the Old Parr. For him, that was the real message. He figured the rest was just an act to take the heat off somebody back in Washington."

— 2 —

Even with his plan dead as 1988 began, Jose Blandon was still a loose cannon on the General's deck. And he knew the information he had about the General was his best resource for wreaking havoc. No longer the kingmaker, Jose now adopted the role of the General's righteous exposer and Panama's Voice of Truth.

Indeed, he'd taken his first step toward such an incarnation before "The Blandon Plan" was even dead. During early December, when Jose was still playing the double game, an investigator from the Senate Subcommittee on Terrorism, Narcotics, and International Communications visited him at his office in the consulate at New York's Rockefeller Center. At the time, the investigator was still badgering Dick Gregorie, trying to get access to Floyd Carlton, and was on the make for more witnesses who could testify to the subcommittee about its new poster boy for international drug corruption, General Manuel Antonio Noriega.

"Blandon was receptive right out of the chute," the investigator remembered. "We already knew about a lot of the stuff about Panama that he told us, but he put the meat on it. I found him reasonably credible. Nobody ever tells you exactly what happened. Memory just isn't good enough. In my experience, the difference between liars and truth tellers is only about 15 percent and even the liar has to include some truth to make his spin work. I think Blandon was telling the truth. He missed sequences and misinterpreted some things, but the vast body of what he had to say had substance. Whatever the role that might have led Blandon to talk, it was definitely deep and not immediately obvious. He told a complicated story with inconsistencies, but how much truth do you need to be a credible witness? Like I said, I believed him."

Among the first work products Jose Blandon secretly produced for the subcommittee was a memorandum titled "Summary of the Most Important Facts Related to the Illicit Activities of General Noriega."

Such activities, according to Blandon, were managed by two groups. The "Civilian Group" included the jeweler, Floyd Carlton, the late César Rodríguez, and several others. The "Military Group" included a list of seven PDF majors and one captain, all of whom had worked in Noriega's G-2 before he ascended to *comandante*. The two groups operated in conjunction with each other and made use of the occasional involvement of a small list of Panamanian Air Force officers. Blandon also named several individuals or enterprises that operated as the General's business fronts or partners, including a Japanese investment firm and Mike Harari, a mysterious Israeli businessman who had "retired" to Panama after a career in the Mossad, Israel's foreign intelligence service.

"Noriega controls the government's most important institutions," Blandon wrote in his memo, and to substantiate his allegation, he also included a list of "officials who report directly" to the General, including the manager of the National Bank of Panama, the Panamanian comptroller general, the heads of Immigration and Civil Aeronautics, the attorney general, and the president of the Supreme Court. Not to mention the officer corps of the PDF.

This, of course, was just the teaser. Jose would have a lot more to say when the right time came.

Another obvious market for the stories Jose Blandon could tell was *United States v. Manuel Antonio Noriega* down in Miami. Gregorie was halfway through his prosecution memo by then, but always was on the lookout for more evidence.

That connection began being made on January 8, 1988, when Dick received a phone call from a producer at the television news magazine *60 Minutes*. Gregorie was in his office at the time, working longhand on a yellow legal tablet, drafting his memo, using files that were stacked on most available surfaces within reach.

"I knew the TV guy already," Dick remembered. "He explained to me that he was putting together a show on Noriega and he knew about Floyd and desperately wanted to interview him. I told him that was completely out of the question. By this point, I'd been turning down requests like that right and left. I was intent on keeping Floyd under wraps until after we got the indictment at least. I told him I wasn't making any exceptions."

The producer, however, was unfazed. He had expected this response. But what, he asked Gregorie, if he had a witness to trade?

Dick slowed down, suddenly no longer trying to get the newsman off the line as soon as possible.

A witness to what? he asked.

At that, the producer delivered his punch line:

A witness to the secret mediation between Manuel Noriega and the Medellín Cartel, conducted in Havana, Cuba, by Fidel Castro himself, the producer answered.

The offer stopped Dick dead in his tracks. His appreciation for this possibility was instantaneous. Linking the cartel, Noriega, and Castro together was a south Florida prosecutor's wet dream. No jury in the district would be untouched by it. On top of that, Gregorie knew that the Cold Warriors waiting for his case to run the gauntlet in Washington would be bowled over by such evidence, whether it ended up being used in a trial or not.

Dick told the producer he'd get back to him and then sat down next door with Leon Kellner and discussed a response. They decided to ask the producer to deliver some bona fides demonstrating that whoever this witness was could really back up this talk.

The producer then sent a photograph by overnight delivery as an offer of proof. Obviously taken with a point-and-shoot camera, the photo was set in what appeared to be the patio of a substantial villa with Moorish-style arches shading a stone porch looking out on an expanse of flat tropical grass backed by thick forest. In the foreground, left center, on a tiled courtyard beside a small table with four chairs, stood Fidel Castro and, perhaps two steps away, on the photo's extreme left, General Manuel Antonio Noriega. The General's PDF bagman occupied the photo's extreme right, with two unidentified men in shirts and slacks, one with dark glasses and the other a beard, floating further in the background. Castro, wearing a Soviet-style military dress uniform, was speaking toward someone off-camera, with a cigar in one hand and an authoritative expression on his face. The General was looking up at Castro, almost full profile, wearing a short-sleeved shirt and slacks. The top of the General's head barely reached the level of Fidel's shoulder boards.

Dick had the photo sent to the FBI laboratory for authentication and once they labeled it genuine, cut a deal with the *60 Minutes* producer, allowing the program to use Floyd Carlton for his very first on-camera interview.

In return, the producer supplied the name of Jose Blandon.

Jose Blandon was actually in Miami on January 9, the day after the producer first called, but Gregorie had no idea. Nor did he yet even know Blandon's name.

Jose had come to town from New York for what would be his final indirect communication with the General. Two of Blandon's closest associates from the PDF's political party had flown north for a secret sit-down, acting, as they told Jose, as emissaries of the General.

Seizing the initiative, Blandon told them that he needed his official position resolved, referring to the continuation of his tenure as consul general to New York. And he told them that the General had three days to do so, one way or another.

His old friends urged him to return to Panama instead and work it out, but Jose didn't even seriously consider such an option. He knew he had been publicly denounced in his homeland as a "traitor" and wasn't about to return under that cloud.

Blandon's final pronouncement to the General's emissaries was that they should do everything in their power to convince the General to resign. The fate of their political party, the Panama Defense Force, and the entire Torrijos revolution were in the balance. History was calling. If the General didn't step down now, they would all end up in ruin.

Jose also pointedly reminded his two friends that, should the General fire him as consul general, Jose would lose his diplomatic immunity and could then be legally compelled by the gringos to testify to the grand jury down here in Miami.

That statement hung in the air for a while among the three former political comrades, sounding very much like a threat. Which, of course, it was.

Blandon's two old friends flew back to Panama that same day to let the General know what Jose had said.

To no one's surprise, Jose Blandon was officially relieved of his post as consul general to New York almost immediately thereafter.

— 3 —

On January 20, the Southern District of Florida officially served a subpoena in New York on the Panamanian national Jose Blandon, requiring him to appear before the grand jury eight days hence in Miami. By then, Gregorie's prosecution memo was almost finished and an appointment to defend it up at Justice in Washington had already been scheduled for February 2, some twelve days away. Dick had been through a flurry of phone conversations, some with the staffers at the Senate subcommittee, even one with Elliott Abrams, as he tried to locate Blandon, but most with Blandon's newly acquired Washington attorney. The lawyer at first resisted having Blandon come down, but admitted he was already letting his client talk to the Senate subcommittee. He wanted asylum for Blandon and Witness Protection, to which Gregorie quickly agreed.

Finally, on January 26, 1988, Jose flew from New York to Miami, where he stayed in a private house occupied by a wealthy Panamanian publisher and ally of Gabriel Lewis. Blandon had now crossed the threshold from double game into open attack. That morning's issue of the *New York Times* ran a thousand-word story from the Foreign Desk on page 3 headlined "Former Aide Says He Can Detail Noriega's Corruption."

> A former top adviser to the Panamanian military ruler, Gen. Manuel Antonio Noriega, said yesterday that he would provide details on the general's involvement in drug and arms smuggling, corruption and money laundering, unless the general removed himself from politics. The former adviser, Jose I. Blandon, who was the Panamanian Consul General in New York until being dismissed by General Noriega several days ago . . . declined to give precise details of the extent of General Noriega's involvement in illegal activities, because he has been subpoenaed by a Federal grand jury in Miami. . . . According to Gabriel Lewis, a former Panamanian ambassador to Washington and opposition leader, Mr. Blandon knows more about General Noriega's activities than most [PDF] military leaders. . . . Mr. Blandon [himself] acknowledged that he might be putting himself in some personal

> danger if he challenged General Noriega directly or made public [all] his allegations. . . . Mr. Blandon [also] said he did not know whether General Noriega would step aside or fight. . . . "He can kill me, that's the risk," Mr. Blandon said. "But he can't kill what I know. . . . I have a lot of information about Noriega, probably more information on his arms trafficking, drug trafficking and the internal problems of the Defense Forces than anyone else. I don't want to be forced to use it. But if there is not any political solution, I will use it."

Blandon's first such "use" was already scheduled for the next afternoon, down at 155 S. Miami Avenue.

As part of the understanding Gregorie had reached with Jose's attorney, the Miami Divisional Office of the Drug Enforcement Administration would provide security for the new witness while he was in town. At first, Blandon had been a little hinky about having the DEA involved, since he considered them an agency in Noriega's hip pocket, but he accepted the arrangement anyway.

Kenny Kennedy organized the security detail and even worked one of its shifts. Kenny liked to get in on this end of the cases being made under him, as he had when bringing Floyd Carlton back from Costa Rica.

That first evening, while the ASAC drew guard duty out at the house where Blandon was spending the night, one of the occupants fell against a venetian blind in the living room, causing a racket. In response, Kennedy and the other agent on duty came crashing through the closed vestibule door, weapons drawn, safeties off.

Otherwise, Jose Blandon's first night as a government witness was uneventful.

At 3:00 P.M. the next day, Kenny drove Blandon from the publisher's house, where he'd spent the night under guard, to 155 S. Miami. The afternoon was warm and soft, with a trace of breeze that tickled the tourists' juices, but Kenny more or less took such days for granted and Blandon was preoccupied. Dick Gregorie and Steve Grilli were waiting in the First Assistant's office up on the sixth floor.

"Blandon wasn't particularly impressive lookin'," Grilli remembered. "He was short. And he reminded me of the character Costanza on *Seinfeld,* except instead of being bald, he had a thick head of gray hair. Otherwise, they looked a lot alike, him and Costanza, including the glasses.

You could tell Blandon was bright and that he was impressed with himself. Of course we didn't let on, but me and Gregorie were secretly droolin' over the guy. I mean, he was immediately believable by both posture and position. We had a lot of witnesses, but they were all nutted and gettin' out from under some jail time by telling whatever they knew about the General. This guy, though, was no scumbag. He was a fuckin' member of the government who had been on the very inside, with what seemed to be nothin' much to gain compared to the others we'd been takin' to the grand jury. The only downside to that was that he wasn't charged with anything, so we didn't have him in a twist, so there was no way to make him tell anything he didn't want to. Because of that, we were mostly stuck listening to whatever he felt like revealing. Fortunately, that didn't prove to be much of a problem because Blandon liked to talk — I mean, up one side and down the other, talkin' all the way."

The way Blandon framed the relationship, he, like Floyd Carlton and the late César Rodríguez, first met the General in the old days out in Chiriqui. Blandon was the hotshot young chief of planning for agricultural reform in the new Torrijos government recently installed by military coup and the General was then ranked major, a key ally in Torrijos's seizure of power, commanding the garrison at Chiriqui in the center of Panama's richest agricultural region. This initial contact between them was brief.

What Jose described to Gregorie and Grilli as his "political rapport" with the General began six years later, in 1977, after Blandon had become Omar Torrijos's "closest political adviser." Torrijos established a political intelligence office that year with Blandon at its head, working "directly and exclusively for the commander in chief of the armed forces of Panama and . . . given access to all intelligence sources in the country." Noriega was G-2 by then, so he and Jose had contact at least several times a week. In the late 1970s, Blandon did much of Panama's liaison work with the Salvadoran guerrillas — among other things, bringing orders for weapons back to Noriega who would fill them for a price and send Floyd and César off to El Salvador with planeloads of military hardware destined for dirt airstrips hacked out of the bush and lit by flashlights or torches. Blandon had been dispatched by Torrijos to sort out the situation when César crashed one of those loads and, though rescued by Floyd, abandoned a plane registered to Panama, provoking an international incident.

According to Blandon, during the last year of his life Torrijos became particularly suspicious of Noriega and had Blandon accompany his G-2 on several international missions, filing secret daily reports about Noriega's activities on audiotape for Torrijos personally. None of that, however, prevented Blandon from becoming Noriega's "closest political adviser" within three years.

Blandon ran on as he recounted his Noriega years, including his service during the election of 1984 and the president's resignation in 1985, but the Americans were getting antsy. "At first," Grilli recalled, "it was just kinda *This Is Your Life, Jose Blandon,* you know what I mean? The only time he got real emotional about it was when he started talking about the pressure they were putting on his son down in Panama. That clearly had him very pissed off. Which was nice, but it wasn't the reason he was there." With a little nudging, Blandon then got down to the subject at hand.

As far as he knew, he told the Americans, the cartel entered the picture shortly after Noriega's promotion to general in August 1983, though he had heard that the General had contact with them in 1981, when he was still G-2. That year, Colombian leftist guerrillas had kidnapped one of the cartel founders' children and the Panamanian G-2 had supposedly acted as an intermediary in arranging the child's return.

Blandon said his first personal eyewitness exposure to this aspect of the General came late in 1983, when Jose claimed to have stumbled over the General's money-laundering interests on a flight with César Rodríguez in the General's Learjet. Blandon was returning from a mission to Nicaragua, and César had swung by on a trip back from the United States to take Blandon home. Over the short flight, César had bragged about the money he was hauling in several suitcases and popped one open, just to watch Blandon's tongue fall out of his mouth. Cesar said the money was coming from the United States and belonged to "some gentlemen from Medellín." He also said that the General was in on the scam.

Blandon's next encounter with the General's cartel connection came the following spring. On election day, May 6, while Blandon was supervising the PDF political victory, he "became aware" of a secret gathering taking place simultaneously in Panama City, featuring the cartel and a former president of Colombia. The session was an unsuccessful attempt to negotiate a deal that would take some of the heat off the cartel back in their home country. Most of its members had by now taken refuge in Panama and those who hadn't would shortly. When Blandon learned of the meeting, he also learned that it had the protection of the PDF, and from that, he learned the cartel was under protection as well.

Blandon insisted to Gregorie and Grilli that he had confronted the General about granting asylum to these cocaine-traffickers and elaborated the potentially disastrous political consequences that might ensue from making common cause with them.

But, the General had objected. "They have to pay to stay here," he said. He had not made common cause with any of these Colombians and he was indignant his political officer hadn't credited the difference.

"They have to pay to stay here," Blandon repeated in Grilli's direction. The gringos want to know about Noriega? This was Noriega: "They have to pay to stay here."

Grilli was already convinced that they had struck pay dirt just as their Washington deadline loomed. "This guy already fit right in with the rest," he explained, "like the missing piece in a fuckin' jigsaw puzzle, and he wasn't even done talkin' yet."

Dick Gregorie pushed Blandon for specifics of the cartel's payoff to the General, but Jose claimed that the General had never mentioned an exact figure, only calling it "a high price." Blandon estimated that the bribe was somewhere between $4 million and $7 million, though he didn't reveal just how he landed on those numbers.

He also claimed that this was not the only payoff the cartel had made to the General that spring. He had sold them the rights to operate a cocaine lab out in the jungle in Darien Province as well, but Blandon himself had known nothing about the arrangements until the lab was busted by the PDF and Jose was called in to help clean up the aftermath.

At the time, the General himself was out of the country, on an itinerary with stops in Israel, Paris, and New York. In Israel, the General received a medal for having helped the Mossad smuggle arms to Iran for use against Iraq. He also met personally with the Israeli prime minister. Otherwise, the trip was largely recreational, and the General brought his wife, Felicidad, and several friends along, including the jeweler. According to Blandon, the General first learned of the lab seizure while still in Tel Aviv and César Rodríguez phoned him from Panama City with the news. Or at least that's what César told Blandon later, when they spoke about it.

In any case, the cartel response to the loss of their manufacturing facility got very heavy in a hurry. The Colombians went straight to the General's right-hand colonel, with whom they'd made the arrangements and to whom they had paid the money, and demanded to know what had happened. The right-hand colonel swore that he had given the General the money and, obviously, the General had decided to rip them off. The right-hand colonel then suggested to the cartel's representatives that they blow the General away. According to Blandon, the General had been tipped to this assassination discussion shortly after it took place by Israeli intelligence, acting through the "retired" Mossad agent Mike Harari. Among other things, Harari and the Israelis had reportedly designed the General's personal security detail.

Shortly after learning how heavy things had become, the General called Jose Blandon, and Jose's knowledge of events now became first hand. The General had reached Paris by then. He told his political operative that he needed him to go to "the island," their code word for Cuba. There, Jose was to meet with Fidel Castro, who had volunteered to act as middleman in a possible settlement with the cartel. The General said he would join Blandon on "the island" in a couple days.

Before leaving Panama for Cuba, Jose called César to see if the hustler up in the Bank of Boston tower had any take on the situation. César told him that the right-hand colonel would have to be sacrificed, the General would have no other choice. When they talked further, Blandon told Gregorie and Grilli, César made it clear the General was in the drug business. So was he, César told Blandon, and so was a whole lot of the rest of Panama.

Blandon claimed that when he got to Cuba, he was taken to see Fidel right away. It was not the first time they had spoken, Jose was careful to point out. As Panama's leading Marxist theoretician, Blandon had visited Cuba with some frequency. This time, the two exchanged pleasantries and talked a little Communist Party chitchat before Fidel got right to the issue posed by the cartel. He said that, as he understood it, $5 million had been involved, $3 million of which had gone to the General, $1 million to the colonel, and $1 million spread around the rest of the PDF. Castro pointed out that the cartel were "businessmen" who "don't want problems," but that, if not satisfied, "the cartel would transform Panama into a battle zone." He then said that the Colombians wanted their money and equipment back and that he recommended the General do so. There was a cartel representative here in Havana, and he suggested that Jose visit him to work out the details.

Jose met with the cartel rep some twenty-four hours later, in a comfortable private house right behind Havana's Palace of Non-Alignment.

The rep said the cartel didn't want any trouble, only a solution, and Blandon said the General felt the same way. He offered that he thought the General would want to give full restitution but, first, he needed to consult with the General personally, after he arrived the next day.

General Manuel Antonio Noriega, his wife, Felicidad, the jeweler, and half-a-dozen others flew into Havana from New York on a PDF passenger plane, having traveled from Paris to New York, flying commercial first class on the Concorde. Blandon met with the General after his arrival at the protocol house in which the General and his party were situated. Blandon told Gregorie and Grilli that he had never seen the General so antsy. Noriega hated situations that were out of his control, and this one certainly was. To fortify himself, the General drank at least "seven or eight frozen daquiris," until Felicidad told him to stop or he'd be stumbling all over himself when Fidel got there. In the meantime, Blandon briefed him on the deal and his conversation with Castro. Among other things, Blandon told the General that he had asked Castro if Castro could help get Noriega out of the narcotics business and that Castro had said that General Noriega would most likely be killed if he did. Blandon wanted to know if that was true.

The General answered that Jose should have asked that question to the Colombian he'd met with the day before. Only the cartel had that answer.

Fidel finally arrived to collect the General about 6:00 P.M. After socializing for a bit — during which Blandon circulated, snapping pictures, including the one the TV producer had furnished to Gregorie — the Noriegas left for an evening at the Tropicana, one of the few remaining nightclub floor shows left in Cuba. Blandon claimed that Noriega had an intense inferiority complex when it came to Castro, and when he left for the evening, the General, already half drunk, had the expression of a whipped dog.

Blandon next saw the General and Castro when they returned around midnight. The General was shaky on his legs and was escorted inside by Fidel. Blandon walked Fidel back to the door. Castro, still fresh, said, "The deal will be as we discussed," and left. Then Blandon returned to the house where the wobbly General was waiting.

"It was a mistake to take their money," the General allegedly told Jose. "We'll have to make good on everything."

According to Blandon, when the General and his party, Jose in tow, left Havana for Panama City, Castro sent along a dozen security troops to help defend the General should he encounter trouble upon landing in his homeland. The return, however, was uneventful. And the first thing the General did was cashier the right-hand colonel, just as Cesar had predicted.

Jose told Gregorie and Grilli that the last he heard about this affair was when the General mentioned that everything had been returned to the Colombians.

And that, Blandon admitted, was just about all he knew about the General and "the gentlemen from Medellín."

Dick exhaled in a moment of prosecutorial awe. Then he told Jose that he had to come next door with him and run through the part about Fidel again, this time so Leon Kellner could hear it.

Five hours after he first arrived, Jose Blandon left 155 S. Miami Avenue, again under Kenny Kennedy's escort. Biscayne Bay was now a wall of reflected glare on the verge of outright sunset. Kenny drove Jose to the house where he was staying and then walked him inside. Kennedy was surprised to find several Senate staffers from Washington waiting there for Blandon, most of them associated with the Subcommittee on Terrorism, Narcotics, and International Communications. They all greeted Jose like long-lost friends.

When Kenny got back to Gregorie's office, he told Dick about all the Senate people giving Blandon hugs when he arrived.

"What the fuck's goin' on with this guy?" Kenny asked.

Dick just shrugged in response.

— 4 —

On Thursday, January 28, 1988 — now just four days before the Southern District of Florida would have to defend its proposed indictment in Washington — Jose Blandon was taken to a security entrance underneath the courthouse annex and whisked up to the grand jury chambers. There, without having corroborated most of what his witness had to say, Dick Gregorie led Jose through the paces as he recounted his story again, this time testifying for the sealed criminal record.

His doing so would eventually generate some controversy.

"The Miami prosecutors were led into a significant error by writing charges . . . at the last minute based on the uncorroborated testimony of Blandon," one journalist from National Public Radio argued in his widely acclaimed book on the subject.

> Although Blandon indisputably had a major political role in Panamanian events and had inside knowledge . . . a significant number of his allegations defy confirmation and in some cases are implausible or demonstrably false. . . . I am [particularly] skeptical of Blandon's account [of the Blandon/Castro/Noriega/cartel meetings]. . . . A very high standard of evidence should be required to make a case that [Castro] would personally immerse himself in [such] a dispute. . . . Even assuming criminal intent on Castro's part, it is difficult to imagine him discussing [the cocaine business] with a low-ranking civilian [like] Blandon. . . . More important, the dates of other facts do not gibe with what can be established independently. . . . Other circumstantial contradictions also cast doubt on the story. . . . In short, everyone else [with knowledge of these events] would have to be lying or seriously deceived . . . for Blandon's story to hold up.

Dick Gregorie was nonetheless unrepentant. "What he told us," Dick responded, "the majority of it, was truthful. He didn't misrepresent who he was in the overall scheme of things, though he had some contradictions when it got down to the specifics of events. He was obviously someone with a clear revenge motive, but, otherwise, as far as where he came from and why he came to us, I didn't know the complete answer and didn't think I needed to. My biggest concern about Blandon when he came here to testify was that he was so chummy with the Senate staff. That concerned me greatly, but he brought corroboration with him and looked to be a great break. I knew right away he was going to help us in Washington."

To say the least.

"Prior to Blandon," Elliott Abrams explained, "had you asked people with access [to power in Washington], 'Do you think Noriega was involved in drug-trafficking?' none of those people would have said, 'Yes.' . . . [That changed and] I think the difference was Blandon."

CHAPTER II

RUNNING THE GAUNTLET

— 1 —

At first light on Groundhog Day, Tuesday, February 2, 1988, another delegation from the Southern District gathered inside the swarm of Miami International, next to the departure gate for the Washington shuttle. This time, they were five. In addition to Gregorie, Kennedy, and Grilli, one of the brain trust lawyers was along, and the group was led by the United States attorney himself, Leon Kellner.

Although Dick, Steve, and the brain trust lawyer were the ones who had spent the weekend at Gregorie's office putting the final touches on the new Blandon material in the revised prosecution memo — watching the Super Bowl on a dilapidated portable TV with aluminum foil for an antenna and eating pizza as they did so — everyone understood that this mission to Washington was Leon Kellner's moment more than anybody else's: Leon was the one among them who knew "politics" and how to play it; Washington was Leon's old stomping grounds, to which he would eventually return when he went back to private practice, so, for him this wasn't uncharted territory; and the political party in power was Leon's own as well, in whose service he had a long track record and in which he had enough clout to secure the job he now held, so he knew how to force the issue.

And Leon was motivated. On the phone to Justice over the previous week, he had already made it very clear that if anyone wanted this indictment blocked, they would do so over his own vehement public objections — perhaps even his resignation. Leon had no intention of being denied. And what he was about to do would redeem his reputation.

After the five of them landed at National Airport in Washington, they broke into two groups. The DEA agents took a cab straight to DEA headquarters, where the delegation's first formal meeting was scheduled. The attorneys took a separate cab to the Justice Department on Pennsylvania Avenue.

The lawyers were greeted on Justice's front steps by a flock of media, most of whom Leon had tipped off to his mission the night before, staying "off the record" but hoping to ensure the object of his visit would be public enough to restrict the options available to his potential opposition.

Not surprisingly, Kellner was asked by one among the throng of cameras if he was in Washington this morning to confer with Justice about the indictment of General Noriega.

Leon stopped and faced the camera. He said he couldn't comment on pending cases.

Then he wheeled and, with Gregorie and the brain trust lawyer in tow, proceeded up the steps. Once inside and off camera, their mission here accomplished, the three attorneys circled through the hallways of the Justice Building, exited by a side door, and flagged a cab to link up with Grilli and Kennedy over at the DEA.

The Miami delegation's stop at the DEA was "a courtesy call" on the administrator, to let the top man know what was about to happen. At this stage of the game, the DEA had no power to pass on *United States v. Manuel Antonio Noriega,* one way or another, so permission was neither being sought nor extended. Nonetheless, this Groundhog Day encounter resonated inside the agency.

The meeting was convened in the administrator's office, next door to the conference room in which Steve had briefed the administrator and his brain trust in November. This time, the administrator was all by himself, one-on-five with the visitors around a small table.

"I felt positively phat," Steve remembered. "I mean, this was the inner sanctum, where the Top Guy keeps all his personal stuff on the wall. A fuckin' GS-12 ain't even supposed to be able to imagine a place like that, much less sit in it. It was like I'd died and gone to narc heaven."

Caught up as he was, Steve sat through the meeting like a tourist, staring at his surroundings. Kenny, in the meantime, did his best just to disappear into the wallpaper. Even Dick didn't have much to say. This was all Leon's show.

Kellner told the administrator that the group from Miami was in town today for meetings over at the Justice Department and, when they returned to the Southern District, they expected to go to the grand jury and ask for a true bill on General Manuel Antonio Noriega of Panama. The DEA's head man had heard most of the case's detail already at the November briefing, so, besides filling him in on Jose Blandon, Leon didn't have to run through a lot of particulars. Among his generalities, he made a point of elaborating on how thoroughly the case had been made, while paying several loud compliments to the Drug Enforcement Administration for all its assistance, even though virtually no such assistance had been given. Leon then singled out the work of Special Agent Steve Grilli for particular commendation.

"By now," Grilli explained, "I didn't see how anybody could possibly have been phatter, you know what I mean? Here I was, not only in the inner sanctum but gettin a fuckin' personal commendation by the United States attorney to the administrator while I'm there. I figured I had accomplished something pretty spectacular and it was at this point I guess I expected that I would start gettin' the recognition I felt I had earned."

That it might not turn out that way at all, however, became almost immediately obvious.

Having received the news of the General's imminent indictment, the administrator thanked the visitors for their courtesy call and escorted the Miami delegation to his office door, shaking hands as he went — nothing if not gracious.

Steve was the last of the visitors to exit. Then, without waiting to ensure that the departing GS-12 was beyond earshot, the administrator dropped his graciousness and urgently called through the open door for his number two.

"Come in here right away," the administrator ordered. "We've got a problem."

We've got a problem?

Steve Grilli would chew on that last sentence for years to come.

"I mean, I made this case by the book," he remembered, "just like they instructed us at the academy. I went as far up the food chain as I could and bagged the biggest elephant I could find. That's what I was supposed to do. That's what I was taught to do. And they knew full well I was doin' it. Nobody ever said stop. So I went ahead and made a case on the highest-ranking cocaine conspirator ever, and what happens? 'We've got a problem,' that's what happens. I suppose it sounds a little dumb to say so now, but I never saw this comin'."

The meeting that afternoon at the Justice Department was not a courtesy call. Here, everyone was playing with live ammo, fully equipped to stop *United States v. Manuel Antonio Noriega* in its tracks.

The gathering took place in a conference room wall-to-wall with department lawyers, some seated, others standing. The entire Miami delegation attended, but Dick Gregorie did most of the talking, with a few assists here and there from Kellner. The meeting's purpose was to formally review Dick's prosecution memo and certify the case's legal soundness, as department policy required for all RICO prosecutions. Dick couldn't help but be a little antsy, given that the assembled group had the power to derail his case, and needless to say, Dick fully expected to have to fight for its survival.

He did not, however, encounter nearly the opposition he expected. And virtually all of what took place concerned technical points of jurisprudence.

The most heat erupted around the way the draft true bill was framed, labeling the entire Panama Defense Force an "association in fact" that comprised a corrupt organization under the terms of the statute. Dick and one of the department lawyers got into it, going back and forth in loud voices over whether such an arrangement constituted legal overreaching, not to mention an unacceptable intrusion into American foreign policy.

Eventually Leon interposed to smooth the ruffled feathers. The United States attorney agreed to have his first assistant redraft the true bill so that only the cartel was established as a corrupt organization. Leon conceded that naming the entire PDF was an issue on which the Southern District would have to give way to "politics," an unavoidable circumstance, and pointed out to Dick that they were probably getting off light. Otherwise, the session had been a cakewalk.

And, with it, the formal review process was now complete.

There was, however, an informal review process that also had to be completed. But, this time, in circles where only Leon would be allowed to tread.

2

While the rest of the Miami delegation dispersed, Leon Kellner was escorted by a deputy attorney general to a smaller conference room elsewhere in the building.

There, he met with what was known informally as "the deputies' committee," a regular gathering of assistant secretaries and the like from all over the government, just one level of clout below the National Security Council, on which most of their bosses sat. At issue was the case's final hurdle: whether or not forces outside Justice would ask the president to invoke Presidential Directive 27, allowing the chief executive to block a criminal indictment when the interests of different federal jurisdictions overlapped and wound up at cross-purposes.

One of the deputies' committee's more prominent members was Elliott Abrams from State. And, not surprisingly, this wasn't the first time the issue had been discussed among them. Several days earlier, when Jose Blandon was about to go before the grand jury and it was known the Miami delegation would soon arrive in Washington, the deputies had discussed the possibility of invoking Directive 27. Among the members, Elliott Abrams took the strongest position against doing so. One of those present at this first discussion described Abrams's arguments in support of the General's indictment as "impassioned."

General Manuel Antonio Noriega was a thug, Abrams insisted, a gangster, and a drugrunner. And, of course, according to the testimony of the General's closest political adviser — of which Abrams was more than well aware and already able to cite — the General was also a partner in crime not only with the Medellín Cartel but with Fidel Castro himself, America's archenemy. Noriega was in the way of everything the United States wanted in Latin America. He ought to be made an example. And this indictment would "drive him crazy" and "give us a terrific bargaining tool."

Abrams's position was not an easy sell, particularly among the representatives from the Department of Defense. They thought the General would prove "a tough nut to crack," who could make a lot of bad things happen as far as SOUTHCOM was concerned. Nor had their confidence in Elliott's approach been bolstered by the Restricted Interagency Group's botched attempt to deliver an ultimatum to the General on the last day of 1987. Nonetheless, one participant remembered, "Abrams turned the meeting around. He got everyone to agree to ratchet down on Noriega. Some were skeptical, but in the end, they were willing to give it a try."

By the time Leon Kellner was ushered in to the group, according to Leon, "it all smacked of having already decided whatever it had to decide," and the review itself came across as a kind of shadow play where everyone mostly acted the parts they wished to be seen playing, rather than speaking their minds. For his part, Leon had come expecting contentiousness. Unlike Gregorie, who usually credited no position but his own on the issue, Leon recognized there was a legitimate argument to be made for suppressing this kind of prosecution, and he expected to have to argue against it. Instead, virtually no opposition surfaced and the legitimacy of filing criminal charges against the de facto ruler of Panama went virtually unchallenged, even though Leon knew full well that more than a few of those present thought it was absurd to give a grand jury in the Southern District of Florida the right to shape relations between the United States and Panama as it was about to.

Almost all of the informal review meeting was spent dealing with more technical questions about the indictment itself. The deputies wanted to see a copy of the actual draft true bill, but Kellner pointed out that rule 6 of federal criminal procedure required all grand jury proceedings, including draft indictments, to remain secret.

Abrams himself said little while Leon was there, obviously feeling no need to make his impassioned argument against the General again.

About the only variance from the deputies' accepting demeanor was provided by the legal counsel from the National Security Council.

"Since when," he finally asked Leon with an edge on his voice, "does the United States attorney for the Southern District of Florida make American foreign policy?"

This barely veiled antagonism to the case was greeted by Leon with a certain relief, confirming reality enough to convince him this whole meeting was not a hallucination.

Leon answered that he wasn't making foreign policy. All he was doing was busting dopers, which is what the people of the United States paid their attorneys to do.

The NSC legal counsel thought Kellner was full of it, but, absent any other visible support for his position, dropped his protest. He, like Leon, finished the meeting amazed at how little of substance had been said.

The final stop on Kellner's informal review tour was the White House, where the deputy attorney general escorted him to a meeting of the National Security Council. Leon had never been to the NSC before and thought of it, appropriately, as the innermost of all Washington's recesses. His first take was that the room in which the council met was far smaller than what he'd expected. It was full to the gills when Leon arrived, the crowd a mixture of uniforms and civilian suits, everyone very collegial. If Directive 27 was going to be invoked, it would most likely be now or never.

This was not the first time the issue of the General's indictment had been raised to this group. After the November visit from the Miami delegation, Justice's number three had warned the NSC about what was in the pipeline. "I [told them] that we now had reason to believe that Noriega was a drug-trafficker," the number three recalled. "I told them the pieces of a case against Noriega are now lying around and we were working in a grand jury context to put them together. I told them we had probable cause. . . . [The case against the General] was not just speculation. It was not inference. It was not triple hearsay. We had witnesses, direct and circumstantial evidence. . . . [I told them] everything is coming out. . . . You can't keep secrets [about Noriega]. If you can't justify what you did, you better let us know. . . . Noriega might be a big guy now, but we might catch him running for his life . . . later."

When Leon Kellner showed up before the NSC on Groundhog Day to raise this issue again, the council was arranged in a ring of chairs around a long central table and a second ring of chairs against the wall. Leon started to take an empty chair against the wall, but the NSC man running the meeting motioned Leon to a spot directly across from the DEA and several chairs up from Central Intelligence.

"You're the reason we're here," he told Kellner, "so you have to sit up here at the table by me."

Leon took his seat with confidence. He figured he was holding all the cards; the deputies' committee had made that much apparent. This was no time to be standing up in public for shadowy characters in Central America, not, at least, if you valued your political future. So Leon made a point to relax and enjoy himself.

The council's immediate curiosity, just like their deputies', was about the exact terms of the indictment and the crimes with which the General was being charged, and Leon again invoked rule 6 and the secrecy of grand juries. All he could tell them was that a criminal indictment was indeed on the way. The Southern District expected to go to the grand jury for a true bill in two days, on February 4. The indictment would then be sealed for twenty-four hours. On February 5, the United States Attorney's Office would hold a press conference at which the indictment would be officially announced.

If anything, this review by the national security "big boys" was even more of a shadow play than the earlier meeting over at Justice. All the questions asked were either circumspect, banal, or seemingly disinterested. It appeared that they too had "already decided whatever they had to decide," though some were hardly pleased at the outcome. Indeed, once the United States attorney had left the room, there would be a series of exchanges among the group, many to the effect that it was an outrage to have Panama policy being set by a bunch of prosecutors and narcotics agents, but that day, with Leon Kellner in the room, no one revealed any of what they really had on their minds.

As the review finally wound down, the NSC man chairing the discussion surveyed the room for their explicit responses to the pending criminal true bill, *United States v. Manuel Antonio Noriega.*

"Does anyone have a problem with this indictment?" he asked.

No one said a word.

The last question Leon answered came from a man in a shapeless dark suit with a distinct edge on his voice.

In the course of his work, he explained, on occasion he had contact with General Noriega, whom, of course, Mr. Kellner was about to indict. The next time they crossed paths, he asked, "just what am I supposed to do?"

Leon went for a joke in response and referenced the first step in standard police arrest procedure. "You might try reading him his Miranda rights," he quipped.

No one in the room laughed. Not even a snicker.

— 3 —

The final word on the Miami delegation's Groundhog Day in Washington was said to Kenny Kennedy the next morning, February 3, when he stopped by the DEA to conduct a little ASAC business before meeting the others at National Airport for the ride home.

Talk was already all over the headquarters building that, yesterday, "the big boys" had met with the administrator in a crisis mode once the group from Miami left. And, first thing on this morning after, Kenny ran into an assistant administrator who had been one of Kenny's headquarters chums when he worked here and was also one of those summoned to the chief's conference room in the aftermath of yesterday's courtesy call.

The assistant was in no mood to backslap. He looked right through Kenny as he talked. And he got straight to the point. General Noriega was the best friend the DEA had in all of Latin America, he snapped, and this case the kid Grilli had made should never have happened.

"And whoever let him make it," the assistant administrator berated Kenny — knowing full well that the "whoever" to whom he referred was Kenny himself —"ought to be run out of the DEA."

CHAPTER 12

THE GENERAL'S TRUE BILL

— 1 —

Steve Grilli started the biggest day in his career with a swing by 155 S. Miami to fetch Gregorie. It was Thursday morning, February 4, 1988. Biscayne Bay was flat as a dinner plate, the nearby docks were readying for the weekend influx of cruise ships, and the two men were due down the block at the courthouse annex to present their true bill to the grand jury.

The Department of Justice had insisted that every possible measure be taken to conceal the indictment until the next day's press conference, so Steve secreted Gregorie on the floorboards in the backseat of his car, covered him with a blanket, then drove into the annex's gated underground garage without generating any attention from the press corps waiting out front. Had Gregorie entered the grand jury room by his accustomed path, through the public lobby and into the chambers' front door — or even if it were simply known Gregorie was in the building — the first assistant's presence would tip off the courthouse regulars that something big was up. And, given all the talk, that could only mean the Noriega charges.

Behind the chambers' closed doors, Gregorie greeted the twenty-three grand jurors, who, he explained, having met on the subject of the General almost every Thursday since October, were now at the end of their task. To make one final presentation, Dick called Special Agent Steve Grilli. Steve then held sway for the better part of two hours, reviewing the case with the aid of several large charts prepared for him at headquarters in Washington the day before yesterday. He reminded the grand jurors what they'd been told by Floyd Carlton, the Turk, the Junior Scumbag, the man from Brooklyn, the tiny pilot, Jose Blandon, and the rest, pointing to a large triangle marked "Medellín Cartel" connected by a web of lines to a central circle marked "Noriega." Steve made the entire two-hour presentation with reference to only the most minimal of notes, scratched on his usual yellow legal pad.

Then Dick presented the true bill itself:

It declared that,

> within the meaning of Title 18, United States Code Section 1961(4) [there existed] a group of individuals associated in fact which utilized the official positions of the defendant MANUEL ANTONIO NORIEGA in the Republic of Panama to facilitate the manufacture and transportation of large quantities of cocaine destined for the United States and to launder narcotics proceeds. [The General] exploited his positions to obtain substantial personal profit by offering narcotics traffickers the safe use of the Republic of Panama as a location for transshipment of multihundred kilogram loads of cocaine . . . by permitting the shipment of ether and acetone . . . by allowing and protecting laboratory facilities . . . by providing safe haven for international narcotics traffickers, and by allowing the deposit of millions of dollars of narcotics proceeds in Panamanian banks.

The true bill included some sixty predicate acts as required under RICO, all involving Floyd Carlton and the other cast of characters Grilli had assembled. General Manuel Antonio Noriega's personal profit in the enterprise those predicate acts served was estimated at "in excess of $4.6 million."

The indictment, officially titled *United States v. Manuel Antonio Noriega,* was some thirty pages long and included a total of twelve counts. Among the General's named codefendants were two members of the Medellín Cartel, one of the General's predecessor's sons, the former diplomat who had run the INAIR air freight service, the General's PDF bagman, and almost a dozen different pilots. If found guilty on all counts, the General stood liable for a maximum of 165 years imprisonment and $1,145,000 in fines.

During the grand jury's final secret deliberations on the true bill, Dick and Steve were required to leave the room and wait in an antechamber. Neither was nervous about the outcome. Eventually a message was passed to Dick that the General was now officially indicted, at which point he and Grilli exchanged high fives and then headed back for the garage to exit as stealthily as they'd arrived.

Meanwhile, performing the required ritual of its office, the entire grand jury carried the true bill, sealed in an envelope, out the front door of the chambers, across the lobby, and then across the courtyard that connected the annex to the old courthouse, where they were required to deliver their indictment to the clerk of the Federal Court for the Southern District of Florida. The sealed envelope was, of course, in public view during their short trek. Brief as the exposure was, however, it was enough for one of the old journalistic hands on the courthouse beat who was in the lobby when they came through. Sealed indictments were relatively rare, and the reporter knew that Thursday was the Noriega grand jury's regular day. His story went on the national wires that afternoon, announcing that the de facto ruler of Panama had been secretly indicted in Miami for crimes against the War on Drugs.

2

In the immediate moment, Steve found it all anticlimactic.

"Not that I didn't appreciate what we'd accomplished," he explained. "Don't get me wrong. I knew it was something pretty amazing to get this case to being an actual true bill. I knew how hard I'd busted my ass to get this done. And I knew there wasn't a fuckin' case like it. So I was relieved and satisfied. But I didn't do anything in particular to celebrate. I've never been much of a whoop-de-doo kinda guy anyway. This felt like just one more piece of business as usual, done the way we'd been doin' it for the last six months. I wasn't ready to make a big thing out of it. Besides, the case didn't feel like it was over. At least not in a way that registered for me."

That night, back home in Deerfield Beach, Steve did, however, announce the day's events to his wife, Patti. To her, he made it sound as though things would now be different in the indictment's aftermath, but Patti didn't buy it.

If this case is done, she pointed out, you won't be happy until you make another case. Nothing was about to change.

Of course, Patti was right.

The next day felt a lot more special, at least when it began.

The press conference announcing *United States v. Manuel Antonio Noriega* was scheduled for 11:00 A.M., and Steve drove in wearing his best suit. "I was dressed to lead the fuckin' Easter Parade," he remembered. When Grilli stopped for gas at Pompano Beach, he got a look at the newsstand's *Miami Herald,* with the headline "Noriega Indicted," and chuckled. This was indeed a big deal, Special Agent Steve Grilli was the man who'd made it happen, and the rest of the world was now about to learn as much. And, standing by the Regular pump in Pompano on the morning of his triumph, this pleased Steve no end, despite himself.

Grilli next stopped at the Miami office to hook up with Kenny Kennedy, and the two of them drove on downtown to 155 S. Miami, where they were to be featured players in the press conference that would be held in the downstairs auditorium. Four chairs were arranged there behind the microphones, and the room was already filling with national journalists and camera crews. As Kellner had requested, Steve and Kenny reported to his office up on the sixth floor, where Dick and Leon, the other two figures scheduled to be seated behind the mikes, were waiting. The office was suffused with a sense of accomplishment, and everyone greeted each other heartily.

Then the phone rang.

Leon took the call and it was brief, with Leon doing all the listening. When it was over, he turned to Kenny and Steve. "It was from Washington," he said. "They don't want you downstairs."

What?

The call was from the Department of Justice, Leon explained. The DEA administrator had just sent word over to the effect that no DEA personnel were to participate in the press conference down in Miami. Justice was passing the orders on. The administrator wanted no formal attribution of this indictment to the Drug Enforcement Administration. The closest thing to a reason given for this command was "concern over the safety of agents in the field." In any case, that meant Steve and Kenny were grounded and would have to wait here while Leon and Dick went down to face the press.

Steve thought Leon was up to some kind of practical joke, so he laughed and told Leon that he could pull his leg all he wanted, but Steve wasn't about to fall for that old line.

Leon smiled sadly. No, he insisted, this wasn't a joke. The order from the administrator was for real.

Steve sank down in one of Leon's stuffed chairs, stunned. "I'd been sold out," he remembered. "And I couldn't understand why. I felt like someone had run over me with a fuckin' truck."

Then, suddenly, it was time and Dick and Leon had to catch the elevator downstairs while Steve, who had made the case they were about to announce, had to stay behind, all spiffed up in his best suit, and watch CNN's live telecast of the press conference on Leon's television.

Meanwhile, Dick and Leon took their seats downstairs in the auditorium behind the microphones as the TV lights flashed on. There were still four chairs on the stage, as originally planned, and Dick, furious over the phone call, insisted that the two empties be left where they were, so it would at least be obvious that someone who should have been there wasn't.

PART THREE

THE ARREST

CHAPTER I

THE LAW AND MUCH MORE

— 1 —

While General Manuel Antonio Noriega's criminal indictment was certainly unprecedented, it was his subsequent arrest that made history. And, true bill or not, few, if any, in February 1988 expected that the General would ever feel the grip of American custody. Such an outcome seemed beyond the realm of possibility.

Indeed, years later, constrained by the wall of chain-link fence and razor wire dominating the only horizon visible from his cell block inside the Miami Federal Correctional Institution, the General must have still wondered — perhaps out loud while taking the sun on his tiny patio, or to himself, while laying on his prison issue mattress in the dark, tracking the sounds of another day's incarceration giving way to the night shift — just what kind of law was it that allowed his American captors to invade his country, seize him, and bring him to trial for his actions as the de facto ruler of Panama, all committed on sovereign Panamanian territory? Not only had the gringos never done such a thing before, it had been hundreds of years since an arrest like the General's had ever even been attempted, one nation to another.

The General's perpetual question, asked over and over for rhetorical effect, remains well taken — even today, a decade since his old headquarters a stone's throw from the Canal Zone was decimated in a firefight and then bulldozed, the equatorial stench of spent ammunition and torched shanties now scattered by the worn jungle air exhaled from the Isthmus itself.

But his question has also long since been answered in detail. Historic or not, the arrest of General Manuel Antonio Noriega, still almost two years away at the time of his indictment, would be legal under the laws of the United States.

Or so the Federal Court for the Southern District of Florida and then the Appeals and Supreme Courts after it would rule, in a definitive judgment first formally delivered in 1991, and titled, of course, *United States v. Manuel Antonio Noriega.* The decision would be elaborated in response to a petition from the General's lawyers to dismiss the charges against him and reverse his arrest. At the time this request was before the Federal District Court, the General himself was being held captive down in the Submarine, locked into the same windowless top-secret security cell in the basement of the courthouse annex that had once housed his old Chiriqui drinking buddy, Floyd Carlton. The lawyers' petition would muster a half-dozen major arguments challenging the legality of General Manuel Antonio Noriega's capture.

The first was an attack on the court's jurisdiction, claiming that "the extraterritorial applications of the criminal law [in *United States v. Manuel Antonio Noriega*] is unreasonable," but this argument went nowhere. Since 1804, in *Church v. Hubbart,* which affirmed that "[a nation's] power to secure itself from injury may certainly be exercised beyond the limits of its territory," American law had recognized such extraterritorial jurisdiction. The classic ruling on the subject, *Strassheim v. Daily* in 1911, stated simply that "acts done outside a jurisdiction, but intended to produce . . . effects within it, justify a State in punishing the cause of the harm as if he had been present at the effect, if the State should succeed in getting him within its power." And the Federal District Court in the General's case did little more than repeat those conclusions before moving on to the other arguments.

The second line of reasoning the General's lawyers would advance invoked a "customary international law, the doctrine of Head of State Immunity" providing that "a head of state is not subject to the jurisdiction of foreign courts." This was perhaps the General's strongest argument, particularly since the government's case was based almost entirely on the assumption that General Manuel Antonio Noriega was so omnipotent in the Republic of Panama that he and only he could sell the right to move cocaine through the country — the powers of a sovereign, "de facto" or not.

But this contention didn't pass legal muster either. "In order to assert Head of State Immunity," the Federal District Court decision insisted, "a government official must be *recognized* as a head of state [and] Noriega has never been [officially] recognized as Panama's Head of State either under the Panamanian Constitution or by the United States." On top of that, "to hold that immunity from prosecution must be granted 'regardless of his source of power or nature of rule' would allow illegitimate dictators the benefit of their unscrupulous and possibly brutal seizures of power. No authority exists for such a novel extension of Head of State Immunity [and Noriega's] claim to a 'right' of immunity against the express wishes of the [American] Government is wholly without merit."

The third argument was an extension of the second, this time seeking refuge in the Act of State Doctrine, enunciated in the 1897 decision *Underhill v. Hernandez,* establishing that "every sovereign is bound to respect the independence of every other sovereign State, and the courts will not sit in judgment on the acts of the government of another done within its own territory." This line of reasoning enjoyed no success either. Citing *Jiminez v. Aristeguieta,* a 1962 decision to the effect that "it is only when officials having sovereign authority act in an official capacity that the Act of State Doctrine applies," the Federal District Court found it impossible to imagine "how Noriega's alleged drug trafficking and protection of money launderers could conceivably constitute public action taken on behalf of the Panamanian state," and dismissed the argument out of hand.

The fourth and fifth defense arguments were rejected as well. The fourth pointed out that the General was carrying a valid diplomatic passport issued by the Republic of Panama at the time of his arrest and claimed he consequently had diplomatic immunity from prosecution. The court rejected this reasoning, noting that diplomatic status carrying immunity in American courts could only be conferred by the State Department, once the applicant had met certain statutory requirements, and Noriega had never sought nor received any such diplomatic recognition. The fifth argument postulated that the General's prosecution on criminal charges while in custody as a prisoner of war was a violation of the Geneva Convention Relative to the Treatment of Prisoners, but the court pointed out that, far from prohibiting such prosecution, the Geneva Convention in question actually made provision for how such prosecutions were to take place.

His attorneys' last legal stand and final argument alleged that the manner of his arrest — the dispatch of a 20,000-man army, sweeping into Panama City long before first light in a blaze of high explosives, burning down one entire neighborhood and killing at least several hundred

Panamanians, perhaps even several thousand — was itself "shocking to the conscience and in violation of the laws and norms of humanity" and also amounted to a violation of the due process clause of the Fifth Amendment of the United States Constitution. The rights that had been trampled in this enterprise were legion and the court ought to "exercise its supervisory authority and dismiss the indictment so as to prevent the Court from becoming a party to the government's . . . misconduct in bringing Noriega to trial."

The court spent a dozen or so pages in its decision gutting this last line of argument, much of it centered around the precedent of what was known as the Ker-Frisbie Doctrine, amalgamated out of two cases, *Ker v. Illinois* in 1886 and *Frisbie v. Collins* in 1952. These cases established that "a court is not deprived of jurisdiction to try a defendant on the ground that the defendant's presence before the court was procured by unlawful means." And, in order to make an exception to that precedent, the court pointed out, the violation of rights had to be of those personal to the defendant, not to hundreds or even thousands of violated third parties. In this case, the particulars of the General's personal arrest had been free of due process violations. Hence, the seizure of General Manuel Antonio Noriega was nothing but legal.

In any case, all of this dispute seemed little more than an abstract debate when it was initially joined. The first time the General's attorneys raised the possibility of dismissal — a year before the General's arrest, when he was still riding high inside the Republic of Panama, free to roam the countryside in his discreet armed caravan of sedans and sport utility vehicles, wearing one of his three hundred custom-made uniforms and a pair of shades — the Federal Court for the Southern District would grant an initial hearing on the subject. At it, the presiding judge predicted that while "this case [is] fraught with political overtones . . . it [is] nonetheless unlikely that General Noriega would ever be brought to the United States to answer the charges against him."

Looking back on it, the court's failure to anticipate anything else is easy to understand.

There would be a lot more than the law at work in the arrest of General Manuel Antonio Noriega, whatever the law might later say.

And, in the spring of 1988, when the ink on his indictment was still wet, most of that extralegal machination centered on Elliott Abrams, the State Department's one-time boy wonder and reigning King of Latin America.

— 2 —

On Thursday, February 4, 1988, as the grand jury in the Southern District of Florida was voting its true bill, Elliott Abrams was in his Foggy Bottom office, meeting with Fred Woerner, CinC SOUTHCOM, back in Washington for one of his regular visits.

Woerner, typically, was out of the loop on the subject of the General's criminal liabilities. He had heard all the rumors about the Miami investigation, many of them passed on in the newspapers over the last few days, but, otherwise, had no idea what was about to transpire. He had returned to town from the Isthmus for consultations at the Pentagon — something he did every two or three weeks — and was in Abrams's office making one of his usual stateside courtesy calls, just "keeping the lines of communication open." Woerner was hoping to discuss the entirety of Latin America with the assistant secretary, but, as was often the case between the two of them, the subject of Panama managed to intrude and dominate their exchange.

In this instance, the intrusion took the form of a telephone call.

When the phone rang, Woerner was sitting on the couch opposite Abrams's desk and Abrams was on the other side, seated in a swivel chair. The phone was behind him, so he turned his back to the SOUTHCOM commander to answer it. Woerner couldn't see Abrams's face as he talked, but he could follow Abrams's end of the conversation.

"No kidding?" Abrams exclaimed. "I don't believe it!"

After several more comments along those same lines, Abrams signed off and swiveled back to face Woerner.

"You won't believe this," Abrams began. "You won't believe this." Then he breathlessly explained that a federal grand jury in Miami had just indicted General Manuel Antonio Noriega on drug-trafficking charges.

To Woerner, it seemed that Abrams's entire posture and demeanor indicated that he had been completely blindsided by the Miami action. That Abrams had not only been aware of the indictment, but had actually argued strenuously on its behalf around Washington during the preceding week was not even hinted. And Woerner, by his own account, fell for the deception hook, line, and sinker. "He told me had no idea this was coming," Woerner remembered, "and I was convinced he didn't know."

The two of them then launched into a half-hour discussion about this development's potential implications for Panamanian policy. Both considered it as a piece of leverage for the opposition and as an embarrassment for Noriega and his supporters, but neither even suggested that it might eventually lead to the General's actual arrest. Abrams was able to maintain the fiction of his own ignorance throughout it all, and Woerner left State that day convinced that Abrams hadn't a clue what Miami had been up to until he received that phone call.

"Either he really didn't know," Woerner later suggested, "or he was one hell of a fine liar — perhaps the best I ever met."

CHAPTER 2

GETTING READY

— 1 —

Perhaps the only visible insistence that the General was a prime candidate for arrest during those first days after his indictment was generated by the Noriega task force in Miami. When Steve Grilli's wife, Patti, asked him what case he was going to chase next, he had sloughed the question off as premature.

"First," he told her, "we've got to bust this guy."

In immediate pursuit of that end, Steve filed a Wanted International Criminal warrant with Interpol, asking for General Manuel Antonio Noriega's "arrest with a view to extradition" to the Southern District of Florida, U.S.A. This notification would eventually be given a "Code Red" circulation to the police forces of 177 different nations, including the Republic of Panama.

That Interpol warrant began as a standardized form on which Grilli filled in all the empty spaces. He listed the General's birthdate as February 11, 1938, making him two years younger than the age attributed to the General by the Department of Defense, and described him as five feet six inches tall, 165 pounds, with black hair and brown eyes. Under DISTINGUISHING MARKS, Grilli wrote, "Pock-marked Face." In the space labeled ALSO KNOWN AS (ALIASES, NICKNAMES, ETC.), Grilli wrote, "Tony, the General, The Old Man" and identified the wanted criminal's passport as Panamanian #1247 D, a diplomatic credential. Under THIS PERSON CONSIDERED TO BE, Grilli checked the boxes labeled ARMED and VIOLENT. The General's OCCUPATION was listed as "De Facto Ruler of Panama." Noriega, the SUMMARY OF FACTS OF THE CASE went on, "is charged with violations of racketeering conspiracy, racketeering, conspiracy to import, manufacture, and distribute cocaine. . . . [Noriega] provided government services in furtherance of the cocaine manufacture, shipment, and money laundering activities of the . . . Cartel of Medellín, Colombia. Usually, Noriega's *modus operandi* made use of intermediaries who negotiated directly with [the] Medellín Cartel and who returned payment to Noriega for protection and permission to conduct trafficking activities in Panama."

"IF FOUND," the completed Interpol arrest warrant requested, "PLEASE DETAIN."

America's one-of-a-kind extraterritorial manhunt for General Manuel Antonio Noriega was now officially under way.

The case behind that warrant wasn't yet finalized, even if the grand jury was done. Grilli began February with a number of loose leads he'd as yet had no chance to chase, so his pursuit continued. The idea was to bolster the evidence available for trial, whenever that trial might come. Steve's relentlessness in that process was undiminished, but the attitude behind it had altered.

"I was spinning after that press conference," he remembered. "I hadn't expected that. I knew headquarters had their doubts about the case, but I thought they'd get down off all that once we'd brought the case home. I didn't think they'd just hang us out to dry. But that's what it felt like they'd done. For the first time I had to ask myself what the hell I was workin' for, you know what I mean? I didn't have an answer, but I was bein' carried along on the express train by then. I couldn't let go, even if I'd wanted to, and I didn't. I had nailed this scumbag and, even if they hated the case, I was in no mood to back off."

— 2 —

Although General Manuel Antonio Noriega considered his arrest out of the question, he nonetheless made two critical legal decisions during those first days after his indictment was announced, both of which would directly impact the case against him.

The first was to launch his own "independent" investigation of the allegations down in Panama, using the grand jury's true bill as a guide.

This provided Noriega with a convenient excuse to collect all the potentially incriminating evidence his troops could round up. None of that "independent" inquiry's "research" would ever surface after the General's arrest.

The other critical decision the General made was to retain American legal counsel. As far as Dick Gregorie was concerned, just whom the General chose for his lawyer told anyone all they needed to know about him. The criminal defense bar practicing in the Southern District could be divided into two distinct types, the legal talent and the mouthpieces, and the General retained a mouthpiece of the first order.

The General's new attorney was Ray Takiff, a polyester shyster if there ever was one, good enough at lawyering to service a midlevel scumbag but hardly of the skill or reputation that a man of the General's means might have hired from among the local bar. Gregorie figured either the General didn't know what he was doing or was even greasier than Dick had thought he was — or, of course, both. Ray Takiff was a fixer with one foot in the all-cash economy in which no one kept books except in their heads, and, for most of the last decade, various law-enforcement agencies had been trying to make a case on him. Gregorie himself was convinced Takiff was dirty as hell, though he had no evidence.

Perhaps Dick's most bizarre previous encounter with Ray Takiff had taken place several years earlier, under the regime of Leon Kellner's predecessor. At the time, Gregorie had come across Takiff's tracks when making one of his early offshore RICOs on officials in the Bahamas. Takiff was then representing two dope dealers who had bought an island there for transshipment purposes. The incident began when Gregorie's boss called him out of the blue at his office, then still on the eighth floor at 155 S. Miami Avenue. Gregorie's boss said that Ray Takiff, the sleazy mouthpiece, was out in the waiting room and ordered Gregorie down to the sixth floor immediately to deal with him. Gregorie's boss said Takiff had been raving to the receptionist about how the feds had people trailing him and demanding to know what the U.S. attorney was up to.

Takiff began to repeat his raving almost as soon as Dick got off the elevator. The six-foot-tall defense attorney was wearing baggy Bermuda shorts, a sport shirt, black silk knee-length dress socks, and well-polished black brogans on his feet. Gregorie thought Takiff was obviously in "a paranoid state." After listening to Ray's jabbering about the surveillance he was sure was stalking him, Dick told Takiff he was sorry if this was a disappointment, but he didn't have anybody on Ray's tail. If Takiff would like to confess to something, he should feel free, but otherwise, whoever was after him wasn't working for the Southern District of Florida. Takiff responded with disbelief, so Gregorie repeated himself. And with that, Takiff stormed out of the office as fast as his knee socks and brogans would carry him.

Not surprisingly, Gregorie's first response to Ray Takiff's appointment as the General's defense counsel was laughter. His second response was even more of the same.

Like Gregorie, Kennedy, and Grilli, Ray Takiff, fifty, was an immigrant to Florida from the Northeast — a native of south Philadelphia, where his uncle was a judge, Ray graduated from the local St. Joseph's College and then earned a masters in history from Villanova University. Ray left academia for "economic reasons" after his father died and later enrolled in the University of Alabama Law School, where he graduated with honors. At first he thought he might practice back in south Philly, but chose Miami instead and arrived in town with his nose open, looking to make as much money as he could and to join life in the fast lane without waiting for an invitation.

According to Ray Takiff's own account, Ray was a hit almost as soon as he hung out his shingle, pursuing criminal defense with what he liked to think was "a flair for the flamboyant." In his heyday, he was often seen around Miami Beach and Coconut Grove, driving a Caddy, tanned as brown as a dining room chair, wearing gold chains and leisure suits, and playing serious high-stakes poker whenever he had the money, which half the time he didn't. He also had a reputation as an operator who knew his way around the courthouse's darker aspects. His specialty as a trial attorney was calling attention to himself and what he termed "making a lot of noise." Typically, Takiff drew local headlines early in his career with his spirited defense of a ninety-one-year-old woman charged with cocaine possession who had fled the police and scaled a fence during the pursuit leading to her arrest. He got her off with probation.

Whatever Dick Gregorie thought of Takiff's legal skills, Ray liked to point out that he had no shortage of work at the time he took the reins of the General's defense.

Ray Takiff had secured the inside track on the General's legal business by virtue of being perhaps the only gringo lawyer whom the General had actually met face-to-face under friendly circumstances before his arrest warrant was issued. In the course of arranging "banking" in Panama for some of his Miami clients, Ray Takiff had encountered and eventually become close with the Panamanian attorney who handled the General's legal work in Panama City, mostly setting up shell corporations, moving sums of money, and the like. Takiff visited Panama as the guest of his friend, the General's attorney, in 1985 and, while there, he and the General met for the first time.

Some thirteen years later, as Ray Takiff lay dying of heart disease in a Boca Raton hospital, he was still General Manuel Antonio Noriega's faithful cheerleader and pronounced himself "absolutely awestruck" at their initial encounter. "We were in his office there in Panama City, at the PDF headquarters," Takiff recalled in a voice hardly loud enough to carry past the edges of his bed. "It had these big windows that looked out on the Canal. The General, I remember, pointed out the window at it. He told me, 'The Canal means everything here. Everything else is second in line.' The General had an incredible presence that just, sort of, emanated from him. The guy was short but you didn't notice it. He was definitely a heavy-duty individual. And right away, I was convinced he was a great man."

In early February 1988, as soon as news of *United States v. Manuel Antonio Noriega* began circulating, Ray Takiff called his buddy in Panama who had introduced him to the General and told him point-blank that he would really like to get the case.

Takiff was hired within hours of the call.

One of the General's new mouthpiece's strengths was knowledge of his own limitations, and Ray Takiff quickly assembled a team of other lawyers, more skilled than himself at the actual defending of his client. The most important among them was Frank Rubino, forty-two, a pugnacious former Secret Service agent turned trial lawyer, with a degree from Miami University Law School and a reputation only about half as questionable as Takiff's own. Of Rubino, the *New York Times* would later observe that "few had previously placed [him] in the upper reaches of Miami's criminal defense bar." Rubino's principal notoriety had come a couple years earlier in an example of what the *Times* would note as Rubino's "proximity to his sometimes unsavory clients." In this particular incident during 1986, one of Frank's clients, a smuggler of Colombian cocaine, rushed into Rubino's office and held the lawyer at gunpoint, threatening to blow Rubino's brains all over his fancy desk if he didn't sign over title to the yacht which the lawyer and his client had owned together. In addition to the boat title, Frank Rubino's client also took his lawyer's Ferrari sports car and his eighteen-carat gold Rolex watch.

Despite all that "gangster stuff," Frank Rubino was, according to Dick Gregorie, "a lot better lawyer than Ray Takiff." But that, of course, wasn't saying much.

In any case, Ray Takiff was in charge of the new defense team and, during the second week of February, he took Frank Rubino and a third lawyer with him to Panama City to consult with the General. In Panama, they waited two days at the Caesar Park Marriott Hotel before being actually summoned to their appointment with their client. A car fetched them from the Marriott to a PDF base where the General received them.

The treatment was typical of how the General would deal with his American lawyers for the entire two years leading up to his arrest. "We always got to see the General," Frank Rubino would later remember, "but it wasn't much of a priority for him. We usually had to wait two or three days and then we got a meeting of an hour or two." It likely wasn't until the very end, while being dog-walked in manacles down the long corridor to the Submarine, that the General came to truly credit the indictment as a force with which he would have to reckon. In the meantime, it was more an annoyance than anything else.

The American lawyers spent most of their first meeting trying to educate their client about American jurisprudence and explain the true bill from the Southern District of Florida, which they'd translated into Spanish. After that, Rubino remembered, "We formulated a plan."

Despite the General's ignorance of the ways of RICO and grand juries, this "plan" had a distinct Noriega touch. Far more about leverage than it was about law, the initial legal "strategy" concocted in Panama City that February amounted to a form of blackmail.

Ray Takiff gave public notice of what they were up to when the defense team returned from this first meeting and their plane was met by reporters at Miami International. Takiff fielded the media's questions, not so secretly savoring his first chance to make the national news, resplendent in a shiny sports jacket.

"We were given access by General Noriega to files which contain political dynamite," Ray Takiff asserted, "files which could effect the upcoming presidential election in the United States."

The General's new mouthpiece refused to elaborate, other than to imply that it was all embarrassing, "top secret," CIA kind of stuff, that there was a lot more of the same where it came from, and that the General was quite prepared to spread it all out to public view if the United States didn't back off and stop trying to put him in jail.

3

This barely veiled threat resonated with Dick Gregorie, even when delivered by a flyweight like Ray Takiff. As far as Dick was concerned, the case had only just begun. "I didn't indict Noriega to make some kind of abstract point," he explained. "I intended to put the son-of-a-bitch in jail and I prepared accordingly."

Gregorie had anticipated the defense's "plan" in his prosecution memo, written before the indictment. The memo's final paragraph, headlined "Problems," argued that it was quite likely the General's lawyers would introduce "unknown evidence of Manuel Antonio Noriega's activities with United States intelligence agencies. It is not clear at this time whether Noriega may choose to make some claim of being an agent of the United States in some or all of his activities. Sensitive materials may be sought on discovery from U.S. intelligence agencies, and potentially embarrassing testimony may be brought out at trial, [all of] which [is currently] unknown to prosecutors."

To explore this eventuality, Dick returned to Washington in the early spring to consult with a mentor of his, then the deputy chief of the Justice Department's Organized Crime Division. His old mentor knew more about those secretive "intelligence" interests — inside both the CIA and its sister organization, the DEA — than just about anybody else at Justice. In the 1970s he had been commissioned to prepare a top-secret internal Department of Justice report on "allegations of fraud, irregularity, and misconduct in the Drug Enforcement Administration," which had thrust him deep into Washington's shadow world. Willing to do whatever he could to help, the deputy chief pulled out parts of that top-secret report for Gregorie to examine there in the office.

Perhaps the most interesting information Dick found in his mentor's report was a long explanation of how a number of CIA agents had switched over to the DEA at the latter's inception during the Nixon administration. According to the report, there was evidence that those switched agents may have used their DEA postings to pursue the CIA's agenda. The report also included a summary of Manuel Antonio Noriega's drug activity in the early 1970s, during his first years as G-2, and revealed the existence of an internal DEA memo from those days before the General became the agency's "best friend," suggesting that the United States secretly assassinate Noriega before he made even more trouble than he already had.

Once Gregorie had perused the report, the deputy chief advised him to approach the CIA directly about Noriega. They might be spooks, he pointed out, but they were part of the same government as Dick and would have to respond to such a request, even if they didn't like it. He even volunteered to arrange the meeting for Dick himself.

When the deputy chief phoned, the CIA liaison with whom he spoke pledged the agency's full cooperation and scheduled a time for Gregorie to come by the following day and examine everything they had on the General.

"Good luck," his mentor advised Dick before he left. He didn't have to say that Gregorie might very well need all of it he could get.

The next morning, Dick Gregorie stood out in front of an address in Washington, waiting for a bus, even though he was in the middle of the block and there was no bus stop at the curb. After a short wait, an empty bus pulled up and took him as its only passenger. Once it pulled away from the curb, the bus didn't stop until it reached Langley, Virginia, and was waved through the high-security perimeter at CIA headquarters. Dick was deposited on the front steps. Then he walked inside and across the same imposing lobby that the General himself had crossed some seven years earlier on his first visit to Bill Casey's office. After producing his identification at the reception desk, Dick was directed to a conference room, where he was met by a geeky-looking agency legal counsel.

Closing the door behind them, the CIA counsel started by giving the First Assistant United States Attorney several nondisclosure agreements to sign.

Gregorie expected that the next step would involve the delivery of a number of boxes of paper to begin inspecting but, instead, the CIA counsel produced a very thin letter file out of his briefcase, marked "Noriega, General Manuel Antonio."

This was it, the counsel said, pushing the file across the table. Gregorie would be allowed to take notes on the material inside, if he wished, but the notes could not leave this room.

Incredulous, Gregorie opened the file. It held several clippings from the *Washington Post* and a single document, a photocopy of one of Special Agent Steve Grilli's form DEA-6s reporting on the case. The report had been severely excised with heavy black ink. Dick Gregorie already possessed a complete, unexcised copy of the same DEA-6 back in his desk in Miami. Gregorie closed the file.

This was it?

"You're kidding me," Dick exclaimed.

The man from the CIA didn't flinch.

No, he answered with a straight face, this was all of it. There simply was nothing more.

CHAPTER 3

ELLIOTT ABRAMS'S FINAL OFFENSIVE

— 1 —

By the time Dick Gregorie visited the CIA, General Manuel Antonio Noriega had become a fugitive icon in the American video pantheon, all over the evening news on a regular basis. And the parties inside the government with a preexisting stake in the General were already either hunkered down — counting on inertia and foot-dragging as a strategy — or on the attack. The Central Intelligence Agency was obviously in the former mode. Those in the latter were led by the assistant secretary of state, Elliott Abrams.

While Abrams had succeeded in saving his job, despite his role in the Iran-contra scandal, he had no hopes of serving in any more administrations after this one. And, since the upcoming presidential elections ruled out the last half of the year for any new initiatives, that left him six months in which to redeem his reputation before, like it or not, he was done with government service for good. It was the kind of challenge to which Elliott rose naturally. Never hesitant to take his best shot in what he considered the interests of the Republic, Elliott Abrams had recognized by January that it was now or never and had already begun to talk of raising a posse to go south and arrest the General.

This would be Elliott Abrams's final offensive.

His strategy was essentially a continuation of the pressure-on-all-fronts approach laid out in the failed "Blandon Plan." The assistant secretary intended to squeeze harder and harder until he had stripped the General away from all his supporting structure, then pluck him out of the Isthmus, under arrest, in a display of the reach and dedication of American force that he envisioned as an object lesson for the rest of the hemisphere.

To no one's great surprise, Abrams's principal Washington ally from outside the government that winter was the exiled Gabriel Lewis, fomenting the General's downfall from his home and headquarters out on Foxhall Road. Lewis too thought unremitting pressure was the only approach with a hope of working.

The plan to which both Abrams and Lewis committed their resources in the first months of 1988 had two initial tactical objectives. The first of those focused on the General's second president, the civilian who was formerly the vice president and now the official Panamanian "head of state," thus representing the high ground of constitutional legitimacy, even though he had assumed the presidency by the General's fiat, replacing a president whose own "election" had been fraudulent as well. To jump-start Abrams's final offensive, this second president would have to be split away from the General and convinced to exercise the president's theoretical "powers" to dismiss the *comandante* of the Panama Defense Force. Following such a "dismissal," exposing the illegitimacy of the General's authority for all to see, it was expected that the opposition would throw its forces back into the streets demanding the General's exit.

The second tactical objective was then to induce a suitable officer from the PDF to challenge the General's authority inside his own power base. At that point, Elliott Abrams expected the General would be ripe for arrest.

Gabriel Lewis later admitted that it all sounded "farfetched" in retrospect, but insisted, "we had to try something and this made as much sense as any other plan."

As it was, Elliott Abrams's final offensive would soon become the most serious challenge the General had ever faced from inside the Beltway.

— 2 —

Elliott Abrams kicked off his assault at a meeting with the second president, the official Panamanian "head of state," in a suite at the Waldorf-Astoria Hotel on Park Avenue in New York City during January. The second president was a *rabiblanco* with an enormous inherited share of his family's sugar dynasty, whose principal interest in life was his stable of racehorses. He was in New York that January on a trip to examine breeding stallions and brood stock. Having maintained back-channel contact with Jose Blandon throughout the life of "The Blandon Plan," the second president knew that the Americans had uses to which they wanted him put. He also knew he was already suffering personally at the gringos' hands. By virtue of congressional action taken at the end of the 1987 session under the urging of Gabriel Lewis, Panama's quota for sugar importation had been suspended, thereby eliminating the previous preference Panamanian sugar enjoyed in the American market, and the second president's inherited holdings stood to lose hundreds of thousands of dollars, perhaps millions, as a result.

At this rate, the second president noted in his meeting with Elliott Abrams, he would soon be the only Panamanian in history to lose money while serving as the republic's chief executive.

The second president also made it clear that he knew his former friend, Gabriel Lewis, was the one who had convinced Congress to target the sugar quota and, hence, himself. The second president's son had been married to one of Lewis's daughters, but at that moment, the couple was in the midst of an acrimonious divorce, so there was no shortage of bad blood at the second president's disposal toward his son's former father-in-law. He pointed out to Abrams that, while Lewis talked to the gringos all the time about democracy and the like, that whenever Lewis talked to him, it was always about money and how much of it General Manuel Antonio Noriega was costing the Lewises. The second president argued that, rather than letting Gabriel stick it to him, the Americans ought to be bolstering the second president and making him stronger, not poorer.

Elliott Abrams seized the opening. He would be glad to help the second president, Elliott allowed. All the second president had to do was "fire Noriega."

Fire Noriega?

The second president readily admitted — quite accurately — that he was no rocket scientist, but even he could see what a dead end trying to fire the General was.

No, he told Abrams, the Americans were barking up the wrong tree. Just let Noriega go. The General would sink of his own weight soon enough, then the PDF would chop him out and move on.

Elliott Abrams left this January meeting without any agreement, but he was by no means through with the Panamanian "head of state." The second president was thought to be as weak as he was dumb and Abrams was convinced he would eventually prove eminently useful.

The second president was also under severe social pressure among the only set that mattered to him.

The previous summer, when his fellow *rabiblancos* had taken to the streets in Panama City, the disfavor into which he had been thrown by his service to the General was brought home one day when the second president arrived at the city's exclusive Union Club, where generations of his *rabiblanco* family had been members, partaking of lunches, receptions, and social cotillions with the others of their uppermost class. On this occasion, his fellow wealthy diners, many of whom the second president had known since childhood, began shouting deprecations at him as he made his way across the dining room toward his table. Some threw chunks of ice from their glasses in his direction and even bits of food from their plates.

By the time Jose Blandon began testifying to the grand jury in the Southern District of Florida, the second president, worn down by ongoing derision among his peers and the relentless badgering of the Americans, had taken to telling his friends and family, and even the American ambassador, that if the *comandante* of the Panama Defense Force were actually indicted for drug-trafficking, then he, the lawful president, would fire him, just like the gringos wanted.

On the day the grand jury in Miami voted its true bill against the General, the American ambassador phoned the second president at his home in Panama City to remind him of his promise. The ambassador said that the General's indictment would be announced the next day, so if the second president really meant to fire Noriega, he ought to start preparing to do so.

The second president, as was now his usual response, just squirmed.

The next big squeeze on the Panamanian "head of state" was arranged by Gabriel Lewis, using the consultant who had not only co-authored "The Blandon Plan" but had, in 1984, managed the political campaign that had "elected" the second president and his predecessor. As the consultant remembered that electoral effort, the second president had been selected for the ticket because he was thought "a harmless cipher" but, in the immediate moment, had no doubt about the man's potential "usefulness." The consultant arranged to meet the second president secretly, during the third week of February 1988, when the latter flew from Panama City to Miami to see an American dentist. The dentist acted as the intermediary, and the consultant waited three days in a hotel for a phone call from the dental office to the effect that the second president had arrived.

When they finally met, the consultant remembered the second president as "scared shitless" and resentful at getting more pressure from Gabriel Lewis. He complained that Gabriel always wanted to control everything and everybody, including himself.

The consultant listened sympathetically and then took up the point he had come to Florida to make. Now was the time to act, he told his former client. Gabriel Lewis had arranged for a private jet that was waiting at Miami International. All the second president had to do was take it straight to a meeting of the Organization of the American States that was in session in Washington at that very moment. It had already been arranged that the General's second president would be allowed time on the floor, during which he could announce in a dramatic gesture, seen by the entire world, that General Manuel Antonio Noriega was officially relieved of his command of the Panama Defense Force. Only he, as president, could take that step. It would isolate the General, the consultant argued, and, in one fell swoop, symbolically seize the government back for the people and the Constitution, not to mention giving the second president himself a heroic role in the history of the Isthmus.

Despite the consultant's best effort, the second president wasn't going for it. The whole scheme required a level of daring of which he was still simply incapable.

Rather than accept such a stalemate, Elliott Abrams then flew to Miami himself and had his own meeting with the second president. At it, Abrams switched gears somewhat and encouraged the *rabiblanco*'s reluctance to go in front of the OAS.

Indeed, Abrams told him that, despite what the consultant had said, he would be far more useful back in Panama itself. The Panamanian Constitution required the country's "head of state" to secure the legislature's permission for any extended absence from the country and set a time limit for such trips taken without permission, after which, absence was cause for removal. The United States wanted the second president inside Panama and in complete concurrence with all such constitutional provisions, thus ensuring his uncontested legal authority when he fired the General. But, Abrams insisted, fire the General he must.

The second president squirmed again, then complained that the Americans had boxed him in with this damn indictment of theirs. Couldn't he offer the General the option of having the charges dropped if he left Panama?

Elliott Abrams said neither yes nor no that afternoon in Miami, but hinted strongly that, should this eventuality arise, the answer would be yes. He also suggested that perhaps a country like Spain might be willing to take the General should he decide to leave. Discussions with the Spaniards on the subject had already begun.

Before they could be completed, of course, the eventuality would have to arise and, by the end of this second meeting with Elliott Abrams, the second president still wasn't even up to raising such a question with the General face-to-face.

Abrams returned to Washington in the third week of February highly doubtful that the second president would ever act and he informed his patron, the secretary of state, of his doubts.

Nonetheless, as bureaucratic procedure required, Elliott Abrams also formally notified the Department of Justice that he would seek to have the president of the United States exercise the powers laid out in Presidential Directive 27 and quash *United States v. Manuel Antonio Noriega* if, by some chance, the Panamanian "head of state" actually convinced the General to go into exile.

Apparently, Elliott Abrams had underestimated the impact of his Miami persuasion on the second president. On February 25, 1988, the Panamanian "head of state" had a videotaped announcement delivered to Channel 5 in Panama City for broadcast on the 4:00 news and then disappeared into "hiding."

On the tape, the second president summoned all the *gravitas* he could muster and informed the audience that he was exercising his constitutional prerogative and relieving General Manuel Antonio Noriega, the PDF *comandante,* of all official duties, effective immediately.

Within eight hours of the broadcast, the Panamanian legislature, dominated by the PDF, had met, voted the second president out of office and, in accordance with the Constitution, installed a third president. Then, following the State Department's lead, the United States refused to recognize this new third president in Panama and became the only nation in the world to continue to recognize the second president as Panama's "head of state."

It was a remarkable development. For the three years leading up to the second president's dismissal, the United States had refused to recognize his legitimacy because of what it considered to be the illegitimate dismissal of his predecessor, whose election itself had, of course, been rigged. But now, for the first time since World War II, the United States recognized a government in exile devoid of any territory, a foreign-policy option previously eschewed even in the depths of the Cold War.

This exile government immediately named Gabriel Lewis its ambassador at large and Jose Blandon its representative at the United Nations. And Gabriel Lewis then compounded Abrams's victory by enlisting a Washington attorney to sue on the basis of the American recognition of the second president and win the right to freeze all of the Republic of Panama's funds in American banks, then some fifty million dollars — no small sum in a nation the size of Brooklyn. Coupled with a freeze on Panamanian transactions with the Federal Reserve initiated by State, this sudden impound acted like a load of gravel dumped in the gears of the Panamanian economy and, soon, back in Panama City, the republic's workers were being paid in uncashable checks and much of the nation's banking industry was forced to close its doors for want of currency.

By the second week of March, Elliott Abrams was telling everyone who would listen that the General was "done." The assistant secretary's final offensive had thus far swept the field before it.

As it did so, the second president who had provided Abrams's leverage was still in "hiding" inside Panama — sometimes staying at the American ambassador's residence in Panama City, often at a house on one of the Canal Zone bases controlled by Fred Woerner's Southern Command. The second president would be shuttled to the United States occasionally over the fourteen months remaining until the next scheduled Panamanian presidential election, on American military transports operating out of a Canal Zone airfield, but would never be absent from Panama longer than the Republic of Panama's Constitution allowed a president without legislative permission.

Otherwise, according to the SOUTHCOM intelligence reports reaching Fred Woerner's desk, the second president didn't do much while in Panama but sit around his quarters playing Hollywood Westerns on his VCR, often for as long as twelve hours at a stretch.

3

Much of the inertia resisting Elliott Abrams's final rush after the General was generated by the Department of Defense.

Fred Woerner, CinC SOUTHCOM and Defense's soldier on the spot in Panama, would act as point man for the department in this struggle with State. Abrams had identified the CinC as a threat early on, in part, at least, because Woerner still had his own independent communications with the General, even though they were only "informal" contacts in which Woerner was quite careful to make it clear that any statement of the American position was the prerogative of the ambassador, not himself. As always, those "soldier-to-soldier" conversations took place only after Woerner was contacted by one of the General's intermediaries and, when they actually met, the SOUTHCOM commander mostly just listened.

Fred Woerner was also the Department of Defense's lead adviser when it came to Panama, and he and the assistant secretary of state had very different opinions. For starters, Fred was considerably less than impressed with Abrams's opening gambit:

"We recognize a president once he has been removed, after refusing to recognize him when he was actually president because he was involved in illegally removing the previous president, who himself was illegally elected but recognized nonetheless?" Woerner asked rhetorically. "This is a policy? You need a damned encyclopedia to keep track of it."

Fred Woerner had also heard reports of Abrams's loose talk about sending American troops to enforce the indictment and arrest the General, and as March began, Woerner was already passing word up the Pentagon chain of command that this was the worst idea possible.

"I thought both the United States and Panama would be well served by Noriega's departure," he remembered, "but I felt that, while this was a legitimate objective of our policy, I disagreed with State's technique and strategy to implement it. I vigorously objected that this Noriega crisis was skewing our entire Latin American policy at a time when we had other issues of considerably greater importance. I felt Noriega's departure could be worked out with the U.S. playing an indirect role. This was Panama's problem, after all, and Panama should solve it. At the very least, the issue should have been held in proportion to our hemispheric interests. We were looking like buffoons and bullies for personalizing it, putting ourselves in a position where other Latin Americans could not support us even if they disliked Noriega. We were playing to our own stereotype, reinforcing the heritage of interventionism when we should have been taking advantage of the openings in the hemisphere to new approaches. It was the worst timing and the worst policy to achieve a good objective."

Elliott Abrams's displeasure with Woerner's criticism was obvious as March began and Abrams moved to sever all of SOUTHCOM's direct links with the General. As the assistant secretary continued to ratchet up the pressure, he wanted to make sure the General had no outlets to turn to besides the State Department, so he convinced his patron, the secretary of state, to insist to the president that Woerner stop all communication whatsoever with Noriega. Both the secretary of defense and the chairman of the Joint Chiefs argued against the move, insisting it was pointless to cut off Woerner's contact — the connection was harmless and might prove more than a little useful in some eventuality, when things needed to be said that the General would hear only from another military man, not an ambassador with whom he had only the most formal truck even under the best of circumstances. The secretary of defense and the chairman of the Joint Chiefs lost that argument, the assistant secretary of state was granted his request, and the Department of Defense ordered Fred Woerner to cease all conversation with General Noriega, without giving the Panamanian *comandante* any explanation for the break.

Shortly after receiving his new orders, Fred Woerner was contacted several times by Panamanian intermediaries, asking him to call the General and discuss the situation, as they once had done, but the CinC SOUTHCOM sloughed the requests off, without explanation.

Not surprisingly, Fred Woerner's invitations to talk with the General soon dried up.

— 4 —

By the second week of March, the pressure inside Panama that Gabriel Lewis had promised Abrams was under way as well. *Time* reported:

> As anti-government protesters gathered on the Via Espana in downtown Panama City last week, some of the women sported designer sunglasses and diamond-stud earrings to go with their smart dresses and slacks. Clapping in rhythm, the middle class crowd jeered,

> "Down with Noriega! Get out, and let us eat!" When passing motorists blared their horns in approval, riot police poured from their trucks bearing the painted image of Doberman attack dogs. Then from the side of the road rolled a truck hauling two water cannons.... Jets of water washed over [the demonstrators] while police fired volleys of bird shot and U.S. made tear gas into the crowd.... Fearing a run on their deposits, Panama's 120 banks remained closed. Thousands of retirees, unable to cash their social security checks, blocked traffic and angrily waved their pay slips in the air.... [Nonetheless] Noriega ... continues to vow publicly that "the only way this General is leaving is dead."

Time, however, like Fred Woerner, was doubtful that the demonstrators had what it would take to force the General out. "The country has not been gripped with the same volatile passions that ignited mass protests in Haiti, South Korea, and the Philippines in recent years," the magazine's correspondent observed. "Last summer's protests ... of fist-shaking Panamanians have [largely] given way to muted anger.... The demonstration last week ... never numbered more than 500.... Observed a veteran politician: 'Panamanians won't take the suffering [required to oust Noriega]. We are a bourgeois society.'"

Even if the Panamanian opposition wasn't quite up to the task at the moment, Abrams still considered it a more than adequate base for the next strategic objective in his final offensive. So Abrams now threw himself into finding a figure inside the Panama Defense Force who could cut the General away from his own base.

During the second week of March, the State Department cabled several of its Latin American embassies with orders to "inform Panamanian military attachés of U.S. desire to work with PDF, but inability to do so while Noriega remains. [Also express] desire to resume close cooperation once the PDF puts its house in order."

In effect, Elliott Abrams was now trolling for a coup.

Despite Abrams's hope for a PDF uprising against its *comandante,* when he actually got one within days of that cable, neither he nor anyone else in the United States government had any idea it was coming until after it was already over, fallen flat on its face right out of the starting blocks.

The target date for this unanticipated attempt to seize power was

March 16, the same day as the opposition had called for a general strike, to be supported by the government workers union, protesting the government's inability to meet its payroll because its bank accounts in the United States were frozen by the government in exile. While almost all the less than a dozen conspiring PDF officers involved in the coup had only recently returned from training assignments at American bases inside the United States, none of them made contact with SOUTHCOM or the embassy in advance.

Unfortunately, all of them except one were also without soldiers under their command. They were led by a colonel who ran the PDF's police wing and brought the insurrection its only sure troops. They also had little in the way of a plan and what little they did have centered on the assumption that the General would be spending the night before the coup at the *comandancia,* as he had informed one of the conspirators he would, and, thus, could be captured by seizing the base. Unbeknownst to them, however, the General stayed at his office in Fort Amador and sent his driver back to the *comandancia* early in the morning so it would seem as though the General himself had returned.

At 6:00 A.M. on March 16, the police colonel leading the conspirators kicked things off by placing the officer in charge of the *comandancia*'s armory under arrest and seizing most of the garrison's weapons. He then used the armory phone to call local radio stations and announce the coup. While he was on the line, however, the PDF officer he had arrested snuck out and locked the colonel inside the armory, the most secure building in Panama City, effectively eliminating the coup's leading figure in the first ten minutes.

Now, without any troops, the desperate officers who remained in the conspiracy met to discuss what to do in a room next door to where another of their PDF prisoners was being kept. This prisoner listened to all the details, then walked out of the *comandancia,* hailed a cab, and drove over to Fort Amador to alert Noriega, whom the conspirators still thought was sleeping in his *comandancia* quarters.

Finally, the coup plotters woke up the captain in charge of headquarters security and, at gunpoint, ordered him to instruct his men to place themselves under the conspirators' orders. The captain convinced the coup's remaining members that his troops would do so only if he assembled them and told them so to their faces. But, once they were called out, he ordered his troops to arrest the coup members instead. While that was being done, the captain fired a machine gun into the air to alert the rest of the garrison, the only actually shooting in the entire affair.

By 9:00 A.M., the coup was over, and the captured conspirators were on their way to the worst prison conditions Panama had to offer.

Elliott Abrams learned what had happened only later in the day, from an embassy cable quoting an official Panamanian government announcement of "a failed attempt by some officers to take and control the central [PDF] headquarters."

Undismayed by the failure of a plot in which he'd had no role, Elliott Abrams's plan for making a coup of his own emerged on the run, as his final offensive moved forward.

In its most developed form, Abrams's strategy called for establishing the second president and his government in exile in one of the portions of the Canal Zone designated for joint occupation by Panama and the United States. Included in that government, along with the second president, would be a new *comandante* for the PDF who would, if all went according to plan, convince his fellow PDF officers to abandon their General, thus enabling the second president to seize power. The government in exile's Canal Zone enclave — a beachhead from which Abrams expected the second president's authority would expand to encompass the entire Isthmus — would be protected from possible PDF retribution in the meantime by the existing SOUTHCOM garrison, reinforced by another six thousand combat-ready troops. If the General didn't give in right away, Abrams pointed out, with any luck, he would set off an incident in which his forces would be crushed and he would be arrested. Absent such a response, the United States would use a "surgical strike" by its commando troops to capture the General and, with extradition papers signed by the second president, spirit the General up to the Southern District of Florida to answer for *United States v. Manuel Antonio Noriega.*

When news of this plan eventually reached the Department of Defense, the reviews were unanimous. "Off the wall," "cockamamie," "comic strip," "sloppy," and simply, "bullshit" were perhaps the nicest things said about it there. Fred Woerner described Abrams's approach as "a harebrained scheme ordered into execution before anyone had any time or inclination to work out the details."

Nonetheless, the assistant secretary of state took his first steps to fill the critical role of the government in exile's new *comandante* of the PDF during the third week of March.

Elliott was assisted in this task, of course, by Gabriel Lewis. Together, they identified a PDF lieutenant colonel who seemed a perfect fit for the task they had in mind. Forty-six years old, a cousin of the late Omar Torrijos, and, like most of the PDF officer corps, trained largely by the United States Army, the lieutenant colonel was famous inside the PDF for not being on the take and was said to have a large following among the PDF's junior officers. He was also on the outs with the General.

As much was obvious, Gabriel Lewis no doubt indicated to Abrams, by their candidate's posting. The lieutenant colonel was currently serving as Panama's ambassador to Israel. In PDF terms, that duty station was equivalent to being stood up in the corner so that the General could keep a close eye on him. Noriega, Lewis pointed out, had a "special" relationship with Israel.

This "special" relationship was embodied in Mike Harari, the shadowy Israeli "businessman" and "former" Mossad agent who was thought to be the General's partner in a number of gunrunning enterprises, including sales to both the contras and the cartel, and who had also reportedly set up the General's personal security arrangements. When in Panama, Mike Harari was known as "Mr. Sixty Percent" for the size of his financial commissions. When in Israel, Mike Harari served as Panama's consul general, with an office right down the hall from the ambassador's office occupied by the lieutenant colonel whom Abrams now wanted to recruit. It was the Israeli Harari's job, of course, to keep an eye on this Panamanian for the General.

Despite that surveillance, on March 23, 1988, a messenger from Abrams visited the lieutenant colonel at his beach house near Tel Aviv and informed him of Abrams's plan. "Many people want you to help us," the messenger told him. "We have a problem with Noriega and we want you to fly to the United States to see what can be done."

Later that day, the PDF lieutenant colonel and the messenger from the State Department caught a plane to the United States, both flying first class but pretending not to know each other in order to keep their connection a secret.

Back in Washington, of course, Elliott Abrams's plan was in anything but the state of readiness his messenger to Tel Aviv had implied. Elliott as yet had no authority to set up his government in exile in the Canal Zone, no authority to protect them with American combat forces, and, of course, no authority whatsoever to snatch the General. Indeed, when the lieutenant colonel landed at Dulles Airport, the only elements in his plan that Abrams had in hand were the second president, his ambassador at large, his U.N. ambassador, and the lieutenant colonel, his potential armed forces *comandante*. All the rest of Abrams's plot still had to be approved at reaches in the government far more elevated than the assistant secretary of state of inter-American affairs.

What followed next one old CIA hand would describe as "Elliott Abrams trying to play covert action." The State Department "paraded" the lieutenant colonel "all over town," the CIA hand remembered. "Just about anybody around the District of Columbia could have figured out what they were up to."

And it didn't take the lieutenant colonel long to conclude that the State Department did not have its ducks in anything close to a row.

The day after he arrived from Tel Aviv, the lieutenant colonel was driven to the State Department for a meeting with a number of "civilian and military officers, all with very high security clearances" in a conference room just down the hall from Abrams's office. Abrams himself was not in attendance. The meeting lasted an hour and, by the time it ended, the lieutenant colonel's frustration was apparent.

"If you goddamn gringos are going to get serious and show some real resolve," he finally snapped, "we can work together. But we need you to let us know that you're not playing games."

The undersecretary chairing the meeting advised the lieutenant colonel to be patient and hang tight. There were a few details yet to be worked out.

To say the least.

— 5 —

In order to take his plan any further, Elliott Abrams would have to convince the layers of government above his own, a task for which he was at a significant disadvantage, despite his offensive's early success.

Perhaps the greatest portion of that disadvantage was a function of Abrams himself. One of the Central Americans with whom the assistant secretary did business that spring described him as behaving like "a fighting cock." "Elliott stepped on people's toes," a friend of his in the administration observed, "and, not only did that not bother him, he liked it." Abrams still thought himself the smartest person he knew and made no effort to conceal it, thereby alienating anyone smart enough to notice. On top of this knack for generating enmity, when it came to the subject of the General Abrams also delighted in rattling as many bureaucratic cages as he could. So much so that at one point, his patron, the secretary of state, called him in and asked, "Is there any cabinet member this week who doesn't want me to fire you?"

Abrams also overestimated his own strength and underestimated the weight and tenacity of his opposition.

That opposition was lead by the chairman of the Joint Chiefs of Staff, a sixty-three-year-old naval admiral who occupied the highest-ranking position to which a uniformed officer could be assigned. Only the secretary of defense and the president were further up the military chain of command. The chairman was an Okie born and raised, with a temper he kept carefully leashed, and no dummy. He had a masters from Stanford and a Ph.D. from Princeton, as well as having graduated from the Naval Academy in the same class as future President Jimmy Carter. A submariner who spent far more of his career in Washington than at sea, the chairman had risen through the service as a problem solver at the Department of Defense with a knack for mediation.

Abrams's act would not go over well with the chairman. The admiral described Abrams to one friend as "an arrogant young man, still wet behind the ears," to whom the secretary of state had given responsibilities "beyond his capability." He told another acquaintance that Abrams was little more than a "fanatic." Even years later, the chairman still professed to be mystified at how the secretary of state, a man the chairman respected, could delegate Latin America to the likes of this zealot of an assistant secretary.

The arena in which the chairman and Abrams waged their fight was the National Security Planning Group, a cabinet-level body in which the only full "members" besides the president were the vice president, the secretary of state, the secretary of defense, and the national security adviser, with "advisory" seats reserved for the director of Central Intelligence and the chairman of the Joint Chiefs. It was perhaps the ultimate power center in the Reagan administration. Often, when the secretary of state was absent on foreign missions, his seat was occupied by an underling from his department, a role filled at least once during that last week of March by Elliott Abrams.

It was this group that the assistant secretary of state approached for permission to implement his "plan" for dealing with the General. The critical meetings on the subject were held March 29 and March 31, 1988.

The chairman of the Joint Chiefs presented the Department of Defense's response to the proposal.

First, the chairman invoked the position first developed by Fred Woerner down at SOUTHCOM. Getting rid of Noriega might be all well and good, he admitted, but the question was who was supposed to do the getting. This was the Panamanians' fight, so let them fight it. Nor was it the right time for the United States to be throwing its military muscle around in the hemisphere unnecessarily. The chairman then noted that this "revolution" going on in the Isthmus was mostly peopled by the upper classes who themselves did not seem too eager to sacrifice for this cause.

"Why should good ol' boys from Peoria, Illinois go down and die for people in Panama driving in Mercedes?" he asked. "It just doesn't make sense."

The chairman's second argument was geopolitical. The United States currently leased military bases in Portugal, Spain, Turkey, and Greece. "In all those places there are sensitive political issues [surrounding that American presence]," he noted. "How do you expect those governments would react to the specter of the United States using its bases to overthrow a country's leadership?"

Thirdly, the chairman pointed out, doing anything like what Abrams had in mind would also leave the United States interests in Panama extremely vulnerable. The chairman pointed out to the group that not only would SOUTHCOM's facilities be in jeopardy, but that American command also had some twelve thousand dependents living off base in Panama and some sixty thousand American citizens living on the Isthmus. If the United States set off hostilities like the State Department requested, all of those people would become potential hostages. It would be impossible to defend them, and short-term evacuation was a logistical impossibility as well.

Abrams interrupted to challenge that estimate and demanded to know just what such an evacuation of dependents would require.

The chairman had anticipated the challenge and had already collected all the necessary data from Fred Woerner. When SOUTHCOM checked out this eventuality, the chairman pointed out to Abrams, all the moving companies used for transporting dependents and their possessions were booked up. It would be six months before a move of such magnitude could even be undertaken. And once it was, the evacuation would probably require as much as $100 million when all expenses were accounted.

The assistant secretary of state pronounced the estimate "unbelievable" and got very testy in a hurry. "When you disagreed with Abrams," the chairman remembered, "he turned things personal."

Sure enough, Abrams quickly began throwing the word "wimp" around in Defense's direction, implying, of course, that the military men simply lacked the gumption to mix it up with this two-bit Panamanian tinhorn.

The chairman restrained his anger at the insinuations and took particular delight in questioning Abrams's request for a "surgical strike" by commandos to seize the General and bring him back to face his charges down in Florida. There was no such thing as a "surgical strike," the chairman pointed out. All military operations are by definition messy. Only someone who had never been involved in one could imagine otherwise. As a military man, he was, quite frankly, frightened by such civilian fantasies about military action.

On top of that, snatching the General was not as easy as it sounded. This guy's security had been trained by the Israelis. He wasn't some goddamn rubber duck floating across a carnival pistol range. He moved around in an armed caravan, traveled without notice, slept any of a dozen different places, chosen at the last minute. To have any hope of making this kind of "extraction," at the very least the troops involved would have to know where Noriega was at any particular time, where he had just been, and where he was about to go. And as it was, SOUTHCOM usually only knew one of those three at best, usually after the fact. This "arrest" Abrams kept calling for was some kind of *Rambo* script he must have seen on TV late at night. It would be an embarrassing failure at best if anyone set out to attempt it.

When the smoke cleared, the argument went to the Chairman hands down.

On March 31, the State Department was denied permission to base its government in exile in the Canal Zone, denied permission to propagate Abrams's scheme with the intervention of American troops, and denied permission to dispatch commandos to arrest the General. Abrams was even denied permission to set up a radio station in the Canal Zone for his government in exile, the absolute minimum support he had requested.

Elliott Abrams's defeat could hardly have been more complete.

Needless to say, the rejection was a bitter pill to swallow.

"They were doing it the way the Pentagon always does it," Abrams complained. "They were just throwing in the kitchen sink in an effort to tell you that you couldn't confront Noriega. They were stonewalling, they were not saying no. . . . One understands that they are the guys that have to send out the telegrams that say, 'Your son was killed,' so one has to give them that. On the other hand, the way they [resist acting against Noriega] is with these ludicrous arguments. They stonewall. They don't say, 'We will not do this.' . . . They just set impossible preconditions.

"They would say, 'What if the PDF attacks the bases? What if [Noriega] makes it impossible to function? What if they put traffic lights and traffic checks and ID checks in seventy different places? We have thousands of solders in Panama. A certain percentage of them get drunk every night. What if [the Panamanians] start making trouble [over them]? The PDF can make life impossible. . . . They can attack. They can shoot at you, they can attack the bases.' . . .

"The Joint Chiefs of Staff wanted to know how we could defend [our] bases from the PDF. Give me a break. The PDF is like a Mississippi police force in the 1960s. It's vicious, corrupt, and incompetent. . . . It's not an army. . . . It is a group that never carried out a military operation. . . . The problem was a failure of nerve of the Joint Chiefs."

Bitter as it was, the defeat was nonetheless final. Elliott Abrams's last offensive was now done.

After a few more days holed up at the Key Bridge Marriott, in Roslyn, Virginia, the lieutenant colonel Abrams had recruited returned to Tel Aviv, where he was met by the Israeli Mike Harari and informed that the General had relieved him of his duties as ambassador. Shortly thereafter, the lieutenant colonel was back in the United States, in exile.

The second president spent the remainder of his term shuttling between Panamanian hiding places, preserving his status as the republic's "chief of state" and playing Hollywood Westerns on the VCR wherever he ended up.

Jose Blandon, the government in exile's United Nations ambassador, disappeared into Witness Protection.

Gabriel Lewis, the government in exile's ambassador at large, continued to invent new ways to attack the General from his home out on Foxhall Road.

And Elliott Abrams continued as assistant secretary for inter-American affairs. Though still the epicenter of the General's opposition inside the administration, the one-time boy wonder had obviously taken his best shot and come up short.

CHAPTER 4

LET'S MAKE A DEAL

— 1 —

Not surprisingly, the State Department had a fallback position that spring short of the outright assault to which Elliott Abrams aspired. Even in the throes of what the chairman of the Joint Chiefs considered his "fanaticism," when his final offensive was still riding high, Abrams recognized that, while he might be unable to escalate his pressure campaign into intervention — given the gauntlet of Defense opposition he had to run — that pressure still might be sufficient to convince the General to resign on his own. Signs of as much first materialized on March 16, 1988, the day of the abortive coup at the *comandancia* in Panama City.

Within minutes of learning of that failed PDF uprising, Elliott Abrams received a message from Panama, where the General was convinced that the plot he had just dodged was an American enterprise. Abrams immediately reported the contact in a "Secret/Sensitive... Action Memorandum" to the secretary of state, announcing that the General had just "expressed a desire to speak with me or my [undersecretary and right-hand man]." Abrams's memo also advised his boss that, "in light of today's events and General Noriega's request... it is imperative that we immediately initiate a face-to-face meeting between Noriega and a U.S. emissary."

The request to which Abrams was responding had not been made by the General personally, of course, but rather through his legal defense team in Miami. Ray Takiff, the General's lead attorney, had assigned the overture to the third lawyer on his team — a former assistant U.S. attorney and "top drawer" legal talent, who, unlike Ray Takiff or his cocounsel, Frank Rubino, had some contacts in Washington who could facilitate the connection. This third attorney quickly reached the State Department, and Abrams, of course, bit on the offer. A negotiating team was dispatched to the Isthmus that same day.

Though unanticipated, the General's offer to negotiate came as no big surprise to those at State on the Noriega watch. That spring, negotiations seemingly offered the General several obvious strategic enticements: His ugliness, both in body and in reputation, worked for him in that kind of physically immediate jousting, always keeping his adversaries a little unsettled and giving him a small but significant edge. Tactically, negotiating also suited the General's circumstance, allowing him to bluff and string his oversized opponent along if he wished, raising doubts and depressing the gringos' impulse to resort to the kind of "extreme" measures that Abrams was attempting to organize as negotiating began.

These talks would also let the General vent his own not-inconsiderable anger. Fred Woerner remembered that, immediately after the indictments, when the two of them were still allowed to converse, the General seemed "hurt" that the United States had done this to him. Noriega thought of himself as someone who had always given the gringos whatever they had wanted whenever they asked for it and had helped them with a number of seemingly intractable problems, not the least of which had been everything he had done for their Nicaraguan insurgency. To reward this loyalty by treating him as a common criminal was not only a danger, but an insult as well, and the General no doubt looked forward to at least responding with insults of his own when the time was appropriate.

Recognizing that the General would be a substantial adversary across the table, the American negotiating team included the undersecretary who was Abrams's right-hand man, another undersecretary who would act as the lead negotiator, and a psychiatrist whose assignment was, as Noriega later remembered it, "to psychoanalyze me by watching how many times I blinked and . . . cleared my throat . . . [so] they could figure out my weak points and set up psychological operations against me."

Counting supporting staff, the State Department delegation numbered some dozen people when they set out for the Isthmus from Washington at 7:00 P.M. on the evening of March 16 in an air force passenger jet.

The flight's first and only stop on its way south was in Miami to pick up the General's three-man legal defense team, whose presence at the sessions was a condition of the General's offer to negotiate.

No doubt the arrival of Ray Takiff and the other two lawyers during the brief Florida stop raised a few eyebrows among the relatively stuffy State Department crowd already on board. Ray had tufts of chest hair poking out of his open shirt front, as well as his customary jewelry, and looked every inch the Miami shyster he was. One of the undersecretaries later remembered Takiff as someone who "sweat a lot." The plane on which they all flew south was described by defense attorney Frank Rubino as "a gorgeous miniature of *Air Force One,*" the president's plane, and the sweaty Ray Takiff was like a tourist inside, goggle-eyed at everything he saw. "Who woulda thought?" he mused a decade later. "Old Ray Takiff from South Philly traveling around in a rig like that. I was like a kid in a candy store. I mean how many people ever get to ride in a plane like that? It made me feel genuinely big time, you know what I mean?"

Once everyone reached Panama, the negotiations were held in a house at the Canal Zone's Fort Clayton, one of the facilities that had already been turned over to the PDF under the Canal Treaty. The house was used for diplomatic purposes and, occasionally, when a very high ranking officer had a woman he wanted to fuck on the sly — otherwise, it sat vacant. Takiff and the rest of the defense team slept there during their stay, while the State Department crew was housed in quarters provided in SOUTHCOM's part of the Zone.

The first day, the State Department negotiators met with the defense team and the rest of the General's delegation, including some PDF colonels and a Panamanian negotiator with whom the American's lead negotiator had developed a relationship during the Canal Treaty talks a decade earlier.

The Americans used this opening meeting to lay out their offer: They were prepared to allow the General to flee Panama to a third country and would even promise not to seek his extradition when he did so, but he had to get out of Panama and do so immediately. In the words of their boss, Elliott Abrams, which they did not hesitate to pass on, "The only way this crisis is going to end is when Noriega leaves." And, as much as the United States sought such an outcome, they were not willing to trade *United States v. Manuel Antonio Noriega* for the General's departure. The indictment itself was not on the table and could not be dropped.

In response, the Panamanians made it clear that none of those terms was acceptable, particularly the last one. Panama was General Manuel Antonio Noriega's homeland and he was not prepared to leave it, certainly not with American criminal charges hanging over his head.

On the second and last day of these initial negotiations, the American delegation got the opportunity to present their proposal directly to the General himself. All of that day's talks took place around a large table in the Fort Clayton house's kitchen and were divided into two sessions.

At the first, according to one later account, the General "seemed frail, reticent, and shy. He was swimming in a [Panamanian shirt] that seemed a couple of sizes too big and his handshake was limp." He also did not like what he heard. After the Americans' lead negotiator laid out the basics of the position, Elliott Abrams's right-hand man took the floor and put it all in simple terms.

"Okay," the General remembered the undersecretary saying, "we have a plane waiting for you right here, gassed up and ready to go to Spain. You can leave, take all the people with you that you want; if you need money, we'll give you money; if you have friends you want to take with you, that's okay too. Anything you want. We'll even give you a medal for your service to the United States if you like. Just leave the country. The Spanish government agrees and is awaiting your arrival. It's all been arranged." According to Ray Takiff, the undersecretary also said specifically that he had two million dollars in cash to give the General to sweeten his exit, and that the General had forty-eight hours in which to leave Panama for good.

Defense attorney Frank Rubino recalled the undersecretary's presentation as "a grade B Western movie where the sheriff tells the bad guy to get out of town before sundown, or else. I could see the General was seething at being talked to like that but he didn't say anything right away."

The General reserved his response for the afternoon session. By then, according to a later account, he was "more confident and alert, [so much so that] the U.S. negotiators thought he might have taken some drugs . . . to boost his spirits after the morning session." Even when silent, "the General would slowly open and shut his reptilian eyes, always seeming as though he was watching for a passing insect to lash with his sandpapery tongue."

And the General was not silent for much of the session.

As he recounted to his ghostwriter in the memoirs published during his imprisonment, the General told the American delegation that "you obviously have come here thinking that this is your colony and that you can push us around like chess pieces however you choose. . . . [But] Panama is a sovereign nation and I am its military commander. I've always treated the United States equitably. You have no right to talk to me like this."

The way Frank Rubino remembered it, "they thought the General would capitulate but, instead, the General stood up at the head of the table and didn't sit back down for forty-five minutes. He lectured them. 'Who the hell do you think you are, coming to my country with these demands?' He went through a whole list of things that he had allowed the Americans to do at his pleasure. He just went wild, talking in a loud strong hard voice, his hands waving. He told the State Department guys off in no uncertain terms."

Ray Takiff concurred with Rubino, calling the afternoon session "little more than an old-fashioned ass-chewing."

It ended with the General giving the American delegation twenty-four hours to get off the Isthmus.

In fact, the Americans left even sooner than that, loading up their plane once the afternoon session closed, and heading for Washington, leaving Ray Takiff and the other defense attorneys behind to meet with their client by themselves.

During the State Department delegation's return flight, the two undersecretaries discussed the situation. The first undersecretary's view of what had gone on in the negotiations would end up in the *New York Times* shortly after their return to Washington. The General "hasn't come to grips with reality," the *Times* quoted an unidentified source close to the talks. "He still thinks there is some way for him to stay."

As they flew north over the Caribbean Sea, the other undersecretary and lead negotiator told his colleague, quite simply, "I never want to talk to that bastard again."

Nonetheless, over the next eight weeks, he would do so, more than a few times.

— 2 —

The Department of Defense tracked State's negotiations with the General throughout their duration, both openly and on the sly, using the offices of Fred Woerner. One of Woerner's most trusted aides acted as a translator for the American negotiators and, back at SOUTHCOM, filled in all the blanks in the sometimes less-than-complete official version of the talks, which State passed around the government for other departments' consumption.

Otherwise, Fred Woerner's only role in what was being called "the Panama Crisis" was as the front line commander coping with the "psychological war" being waged that spring inside the Republic of Panama and, on occasion, even inside the boundaries of the Canal Zone itself. That ongoing hostility was, of course, the backdrop for all American discussions with General Manuel Antonio Noriega.

The "pressure" applied by Abrams and company had ground the Panamanian economy to a relative halt, turning the Panama City skyline into a graveyard of half-finished high-rises on which construction had ceased and seemed unlikely to resume soon — a circumstance the gringos were constantly saying would change once the General was gone. For his part, the General began giving occasional public speeches at which he pounded the podium, shouting deprecations of the Americans, and waved a machete over his head, posturing himself as the embattled defender of Panama's sovereignty. He also began recruiting an irregular force of volunteers, eventually dubbed "Dignity Battalions," so "the people" could help repulse the American invasion the General insisted might soon be on its way. To arm those battalions, three Boeing 747s arrived in Panama from Cuba during March, each loaded with small arms, some fifty tons' worth, the mass of which was soon stashed around the Isthmus for use in possible future guerrilla actions whenever the Americans attacked.

Meanwhile, the General just tried to bother SOUTHCOM and keep the tension level up. He wanted to make sure the gringo troops could not relax, and he also wanted to tweak the Americans' noses, thus emboldening his own troops and humiliating his enemy at the same time. Most of that harassment involved penetrating the Canal Zone and probing SOUTHCOM's security perimeter. For several weeks after negotiations began, Woerner received reports from the field of small groups of unidentified intruders, operating at night, entering and exiting through the thick jungle that surrounded many American installations, always disappearing when SOUTHCOM's reaction force arrived.

It was a dicey business for both parties, and the most dicey it got was on the nights of April 11 and 12, around the borders of the 800-acre Arraijan tank farm, where SOUTHCOM stored fuel for nearby Howard Air Force Base. The tank farm's security was then in the hands of some four hundred marines who'd just arrived in country from Camp Lejeune, North Carolina. They spotted unidentified "bandits" with their night vision glasses, a total force of some fifty intruders who were then engaged by more than a hundred of the marines in a running series of firefights all across the tank farm, lighting up the darkness with muzzle flashes for some two hours spread over two successive nights. Afterward, there were rumors that this invader force had included Cubans, but there was no proof, since the only evidence left behind was a couple empty bottles of mosquito repellent and one trace from a wounded man's blood spoor. The heaviest weapons involved were a couple of mortars the marines brought into play out on the tank farm's jungle fringes.

The worst of the action involved a marine patrol that had split into two separate elements to chase a group of eight intruders through the dark. When a trip flare was set off, both elements of American grunts opened fire — on each other, as it turned out. After the smoke cleared, one of the marines was found, gut-shot by his own troops. He died while being rushed to the Zone hospital.

This casualty of friendly fire, a lance corporal from Santuce, Puerto Rico, was the first American to die in the manhunt set off by *United States v. Manuel Antonio Noriega.*

Before the General was actually under arrest, twenty-seven more American dead and some three hundred and forty-five wounded would follow.

— 3 —

Fittingly, it was at this moment that George Bush, the president who eventually chased the General to ground, entered this story — stage right, still vice president, but well into his campaign to be elected commander in chief.

General Manuel Antonio Noriega himself affirmed the significance of Bush's entrance. More than four years later, after a jury in the Federal Court for the Southern District of Florida had found him guilty on nine counts' worth of *United States v. Manuel Antonio Noriega* and the judge was about to pass sentence, the General addressed the court for the first and only time — and spent more of his speech talking about "George Herbert Walker Bush" than anyone else.

Altogether, the General orated for an hour, dressed in the uniform of the *comandante* of the Panama Defense Force, his words translated in fits and starts while he quoted variously from the Chinese philosopher Lao Tsu, the biblical prophet Jeremiah, and Hillary Rodham Clinton, wife of the man who was, by the time of this sentencing, attempting to unseat George Bush from the nation's top rung.

At one point in this singular oration, the General raised a picture of himself and George Bush, sitting side by side, for all to see.

"What is President Bush doing in this photograph with General Manuel Antonio Noriega?" he asked the court. "Noriega was not somebody strange [then]. He was not a criminal when [Bush] came to visit." But that was then. Now, "for my part," the General continued, "I accuse George Herbert Walker Bush of exercising his power and authority to influence and subvert the American judicial system in order to convict me. I accuse George Herbert Walker Bush of genocide for having ordered the massive bombardment of the civilian population of Panama and causing the deaths of more than five thousand people. I also accuse George Herbert Walker Bush . . . of planning the destruction of Panama's sovereignty and the destruction of the Defense Forces of Panama in order to retain those [SOUTHCOM] military bases . . . and in order not to have to return the Panama Canal to its true owners, the people of Panama. Of this and more, he is guilty, and today I denounce him before the United States people and the world. . . . [Having done so], I confess to the you and the world that I am at peace with myself."

In the spring of 1988, of course, the General expected far better of George Bush — largely because he considered Bush a fellow spy. George Bush had run the CIA briefly during the General's tenure as the PDF's G-2, and now was the first former director of Central Intelligence ever to run for president. On top of that, the General, of course, considered himself an intimate of that same CIA fraternity, still meeting with the agency's Panama City station chief as often as once a week. Indeed, when, some six months earlier, the retired admiral and public-relations consultant who had been "George Bush's guy" had suggested to the General that his former boss would likely deal lightly with him, the General had expected that might be true. The General assumed that men like he and George Bush, would, quite naturally, "look out for each other."

Otherwise, however, the two had nothing much in common.

George Herbert Walker Bush had been born into all of the status, wealth, and privilege to which the impoverished bastard Manuel Antonio Noriega had not. Bush's father had built the family fortune in investment banking and served as a United States senator from Connecticut, and George had spent much of his life attempting to prove himself independent of the advantages of the station his father provided — leaving Yale to win the Distinguished Service Cross as one of the youngest naval flyers to fight in World War II, and eventually moving away from the WASP habitat of upper-crust New England to Texas, where he started over "on his own" in the oil business. After two terms in the Texas congressional delegation, sandwiched between two unsuccessful campaigns for a Senate seat, Bush, the Texas preppy, had become a sort of Republican jack-of-all-trades over the next decade — serving Richard Nixon as ambassador to the United Nations and chairman of the Republican National Committee, and serving Gerald Ford as ambassador to China and then director of the Central Intelligence Agency. Bush's eight years of vice presidency under Ronald Reagan had grown from a failed effort against Reagan in the 1980 presidential primaries, a campaign most notable for Bush's coining of the phrase "voodoo economics."

Now, in 1988, George Herbert Walker Bush was back running in those primaries again, this time at the head of the pack.

George Bush and General Manuel Antonio Noriega had met face-to-face twice along George Bush's path towards the presidency, though, at first, Bush would attempt to deny either happened.

The first occasion was in December 1976, when George Bush was the lame duck director of Central Intelligence, about to leave office with the end of Gerald Ford's brief presidency. After this 1976 meeting was finally revealed to the American public in early 1988, Bush refused to answer questions about it, claiming he was bound by his oath as director to say nothing of his activities at the CIA, and has maintained that policy ever since — so the only public version of that encounter between the two principals is the General's.

The meeting reportedly took place at the Panamanian embassy in Washington, D.C., and the then CIA director came alone, a fact the General explained simply as "no witnesses"— except, of course, a translator. The subject to be discussed was several apparently terrorist bombings against the Canal, which had received wide publicity but caused no significant damage. According to the General, the bombings had originated when his boss, Omar Torrijos, had approached the CIA's Panama City station chief for advice on how to get negotiations over a new Canal Treaty moving along. The CIA station chief had suggested anything that raised American fears about how difficult it would be to defend the Canal against terrorism would be very helpful. The ensuing scheme, which the General claimed then Director George Bush signed off on, allegedly involved a team of Panamanians, trained in the United States by the CIA, who then infiltrated the Canal Zone and set off the explosions under the direction of a CIA operative. At their first meeting, "Bush," the General remembered, "needed to be assured that I was not going to spill the real story of the U.S. involvement in the bombings." But Noriega needed to do so "gently," to ensure the translator would not understand.

Thus, according to the General:

> [George Bush] said, "Have you done a report on the bombings?" What he meant, I am sure, was *I hope you haven't written a real report about what we did.*
>
> "Yes, I wrote a report and sent it to [the SOUTHCOM commander]," I told him. I understood this to mean *Don't worry, we're not talking.* It indicated that I had kept the information limited to what was already known and directed the facts to the diplomatically proper channel — the corresponding U.S. military authorities.
>
> "And he received the report?" Bush asked.
>
> "Yes, I made sure of that," I said.
>
> [The translator] never knew what to make of this conversation . . . [but] Bush had gotten the message. Sometimes, among intelligence operatives, no more than a word or a glance is needed to have a full understanding.

The two men's second meeting was both more public and more formal. It occurred in December 1983, during a thirty-minute stopover at the Panama City air terminal, during the vice president's whistle-stop tour of Central America promoting the American-backed war efforts in El Salvador and Nicaragua. The vice president was also then head of the Special Drug Task Force for South Florida, but the subject of drugs did not come up. "As they say about George Bush the man," the General remembered, "the meeting was so unmemorable that it did not even cast a shadow." At the time, the General had been a General for less than six months, and the meeting was organized as a consultation with the civilian president the General had inherited with his office, at which Noriega himself, who everyone knew was the actual power in Panama, was officially attending as this president's military adviser. Nothing formal was said in the General's direction, but, informally, the vice president approached him during a break.

"He congratulated me for having been named commander in chief," the General remembered, "and made a subtle reference to his request that the United States be allowed to use the Panama Canal Zone as a base for its counterinsurgency operations in El Salvador," as well as, of course, the contras. "'I hope you'll be supporting my old friends,' Bush said. 'Our pilots are already chosen and ready to start flying.'"

These pilots, the General pointed out, included the government witness Floyd Carlton, and the late César Rodríguez, "future cocaine traffickers [then] transporting Contra weapons in exchange for cocaine."

Before this thirty-minute meeting in 1983 ended, someone took a photograph of the principals all together. George Bush and General Manuel Antonio Noriega were each seated against the arm of an airport couch, catty-corner from one another, elbow to elbow with a side table and lamp wedged in between. Bush looked jaunty in a coat and tie, one leg folded over the other knee, and the General, wearing an open-necked Panamanian shirt, had a watchful, masked expression, seemingly nothing more menacing than a disingenuous attempt to appear submissive to civilian authority.

Until this photo surfaced in the spring of 1988, presidential candidate George Bush had claimed that he and the General had never met and thus kept the issue at political arm's length from his front-runner's campaign for the Republican nomination.

But, once he was obliged to "correct" himself and admitted the meetings in 1976 and 1983, there was blood in the political water and no shortage of sharks trying to hang responsibility for the General on the vice president and former CIA director: "BUSH-NORIEGA '88 — You Know They Can Work Together," one opponent's bumper sticker declared.

That spring, the George Bush for President campaign's biggest headache was their candidate's now well-known "association" with the ugly indicted fugitive drug thug who ran Panama.

— 4 —

The dilemma the General posed for George Bush came into sharpest focus around the negotiations which, having broken down during March, resumed again in April, thanks largely to the efforts of Ray Takiff's team of defense attorneys.

The lawyers commuted between Miami and Washington, keeping the connection alive until, a week or so after the first American casualty was taken among the midnight shadows of SOUTHCOM's tank farm, the undersecretary acting as lead negotiator returned to the Isthmus, without either the other undersecretary or the psychiatrist who had been present for the first round of talks. The Americans' lead negotiator and the rest of his supporting delegation met almost continuously over the next month with the defense team assembled by Ray Takiff to represent the General's legal interests and a Panamanian delegation appointed by the General to represent his political interests. All of their sessions took place in the General's windowless offices deep inside an underground bunker at Fort Amador, in the Panamanian slice of the Canal Zone. While talks were under way, the negotiators usually split into two groups, separately addressing the legal and political issues.

Each side made a significant concession relatively early in the process:

The General's concession was broached by Noriega himself when he came by, as he later claimed, just to "say hello" to the Americans upon their return. According to one journalist's reconstruction of this appearance, the General, looking troubled, said, "It's getting so I wake up in the morning and I think I am just going to go into the office and tell [the PDF], 'This whole pile of shit is your pile of shit. I'm walking away, *tranquilo.*' But, no, my people say that would be irresponsible and destabilize the country, and, of course, they are right. But that is how I feel."

This mention was, in the General's language, an invitation to raise the issue of his departure.

Which, of course, was just what the Americans had in mind. For the next two days, the two delegations went at it, hammer and tongs, over whether or not the General would actually resign power. The undersecretary was frank in saying that "if we can't reach an understanding on that issue, then there was no point in discussing anything else."

Finally, the General returned to the table and, seeming to choke on the words, allowed that he was prepared to resign on the upcoming fifth anniversary of his ascension to *comandante* in August, if the deal was right. Without elaborating further or even fielding any questions on his declaration, the General left the room again immediately thereafter.

The foremost concession the General's emissaries demanded in return for such a voluntary exit was the complete dismissal of *United States v. Manuel Antonio Noriega.*

The Americans, however, were at first adamant that the indictment was untouchable. They would certainly agree not to attempt to extradite the General from wherever he might take refuge. But the Miami true bill was, the undersecretary claimed, a "holy" thing whose abandonment would very likely yield a political disaster for an administration still wobbly from exposure in the biggest scandal of the decade.

Nonetheless, the General again returned to the table personally to insist on the point. "As long as those indictments are around," he reportedly argued, "you'll have to come after me. . . . I know what indictments mean in your country. I've spent [a] career rolling up men you've indicted. . . . You just grab a guy and put him on the plane to Miami. That's how it works. . . . If the day comes for me to step down and those indictments are still in place, I'm not stepping down. No deal."

In the negotiations that followed, Ray Takiff remembered, the General's defense team's position was that "the indictment should be dismissed on three levels: first, the General was a head of state, making him immune; second, that this kind of indictment would only yield an enormous backlash from the rest of Latin America; and, third, everything that Oliver North had shredded, Noriega had not, so keeping after this would only drag America's dirty laundry out for everybody to see."

By the last week of April, movement on the issue had reached the point where Ray Takiff and his team were drafting a possible motion to dismiss the indictment, and the American negotiators had essentially signed off on the question of *United States v. Manuel Antonio Noriega.* If the deal was right, they agreed, the General's criminal charges would be quashed and the warrant for his arrest withdrawn.

This matched pair of concessions remained "secret" until May 11, 1988, when the White House, after deflecting inquiries for two weeks about what kind of deal the State Department was making with the General, finally responded that the president was prepared to kill the indictment in the Southern District of Florida if General Noriega in turn agreed to step down, but that no deal was yet in place.

This news release was greeted in the George Bush for President campaign like a live grenade. The issue of the General and the vice president had already been raised by both Bush's strongest Republican rival and his likely Democratic opponent in the fall and, only earlier that week, Bush had "corrected" himself yet again on the subject.

This time the question had been whether or not the vice president was aware of Noriega's drug involvement before the indictment. The vice president ran a south Florida task force in the War on Drugs, this was a south Florida indictment, and the vice president hadn't known about this ahead of time?

Bush responded with his usual earnestness that indeed, he hadn't "known" anything about the General and drugs until the General was officially charged.

That statement hardly stayed afloat a week before the *New York Times* blew it out of the water with a story that revealed Bush had been thoroughly briefed on all the reports of the General's involvement with cocaine-traffickers and the like as early as December 1985, when he had such a session with the then ambassador to Panama.

The Bush for President campaign had no choice but to backfill again two days later. This time the candidate earnestly "clarified" that he hadn't meant that he hadn't heard *stories* and *reports* about the General before the grand jury indicted him, but that it wasn't until that grand jury action that he knew there was actual *evidence* to that effect.

The vice president came out of this series of corrections looking as if he might have something to hide and, then, with hardly time for his campaign to catch its breath, Bush was hit broadside by the White House announcement of the president's willingness to let the General off the hook in exchange for giving up his stranglehold on power in the Isthmus. Needless to say, the administration's position immediately drew fire from a lot of directions. The Panamanian opposition screamed about being left out of the negotiations and, before the week was out, the United States Senate passed a resolution against any dropping of the indictment in any possible deal.

Now, in light of the president's willingness to trade away criminal charges, the question being posed to Vice President George Bush was whether or not he thought that the government running the War on Drugs ought to grant amnesty of this sort to an indicted drug-dealer and let him walk away with all his illicit millions, olly-olly-oxen-free.

It was not the kind of question a vice president running for president enjoyed being asked.

The best advice Bush campaign strategists could come up with was for their candidate to use this as an opportunity to address his larger image as a sort of yes-man who had risen to power by taking on the colors of whoever appointed him. They argued that the way out of his seeming corner was to break ranks publicly with Ronald Reagan for the first time since the administration took office, and oppose letting any drug dealer off the hook, even if he was the ruler of Panama. This would both protect himself from the issue and establish in the public mind that he was indeed "on his own" now, worthy of being president himself. Long thought an almost servile company man on the administration's behalf, George could now individuate his candidacy.

So, while the undersecretary continued furiously working through more and more details with the General's delegation down at Fort Amador, feeling increasingly like he was on the brink of getting the whole deal done, Vice President George Bush, back in the White House, decided it was time to emerge as the foremost public champion of preserving *United States v. Manuel Noriega* and, at the last moment, attempt to stop the entire State Department negotiating effort in its tracks.

The vice president would do so with the endorsements of those who had constructed the General's indictment.

Special Agent Steve Grilli took the possibility of dropping the charges as an almost personal betrayal.

Assistant Special Agent in Charge Kenny Kennedy thought it would only compound the bad news this case had already added to his career, making the sacrifice for nothing at all.

First Assistant United States Attorney Dick Gregorie felt the same way he had already felt several times before, when his cases had been pulled out from under him, and his anger rose as he recognized the sensation. This looked like, once again, more of the same.

Gregorie first learned of the president's position from a television news broadcast he and Leon Kellner watched in Leon's office next door to Dick's own on the sixth floor of 155 S. Miami Avenue. And Leon was even more outraged than Dick.

While Gregorie sat there muttering oaths to himself, Leon immediately got on the phone to the attorney general of the United States and, according to Gregorie, "went bananas."

Why hadn't he been consulted? Kellner demanded when the attorney general came on the line. He had learned about what they had in mind for his indictment from the goddamn television.

The attorney general apologized for the oversight.

"This makes it look like a political indictment," Kellner complained. "It makes it look as if I was indicting this guy so that Washington could use it as a lever."

Again, the attorney general apologized and insisted that this didn't mean that the indictment had lost the Department of Justice's backing.

Before hanging up, Leon Kellner warned that the Department of Justice would have to fire the United States attorney for the Southern District of Florida if they expected him to go into court and ask that these charges be dismissed. He would never do it, period.

Leon Kellner did not stop with chewing out the attorney general, but next called a major national Republican financial backer who lived in Miami and was often credited with having "delivered" the state to the Reagan-Bush ticket in the last election. Leon asked this political benefactor, with whom he was close, to arrange an appointment in Washington with Vice President George Bush as soon as possible.

The next day, slightly before noon, Leon was ushered into the vice president's personal office in the White House basement. The two men had met several times before during the vice president's visits to south Florida to oversee his task force in the War on Drugs. Bush closed the door behind them, and Leon got right to the point.

Kellner told Bush that he was going to really put his foot in it if he was party to dismissing this indictment. The State Department's whole negotiating process was turning a true bill — whose impartiality and fairness were essential to the credibility of the entire criminal justice system — into something "politicized." This was not right. Furthermore, he warned Bush, if it looked at all like the vice president was playing footsie with this drug-trafficking dictator, it would be political suicide and George Herbert Walker Bush could kiss his chances of becoming president goodbye. Plainly put, if this indictment was withdrawn, "the voters are going to think that you're a goddamned crook and that the administration and you are being blackmailed."

According to Leon, Bush bridled at the insinuation, turned "beet red," and started denying any such thing.

Then, having calmed somewhat, the vice president explained the president's position and how the president thought this might be a small price to pay to get rid of a thug like the General. The president's chief of staff was even calling it the most "productive" plea-bargain imaginable. Bush portrayed himself to the visiting United States attorney as still undecided on what to do.

Kellner then said he could understand Bush's dilemma, but that Kellner himself planned to quit his job as United States attorney, with a full public explanation of why, before he would ever be party to pulling this indictment's plug.

After thinking about it for a moment, George Bush advised Leon to "do what you have to do," and pledged, "I'll support you."

Then, Bush called in a photographer, who took a picture of the two, which the vice president eventually sent to Kellner inscribed "with respect for your great record."

An hour or so after Leon left their May meeting, Bush went upstairs in the White House for lunch with the president and told his boss that he was going to have to break ranks with him over "this Noriega thing."

Near the end of that week, at a presidential campaign speech at the Los Angeles Police Academy, George Bush vowed, "Drug dealers are domestic terrorists, killing kids and cops, and they should be treated as such. I won't bargain with drug dealers . . . whether they're on U.S. or foreign soil."

George Bush's break with Ronald Reagan over how to deal with the General came to a head two days later at two meetings held over the weekend of May 21 and 22, 1988. Bush had started the ball rolling by asking that the undersecretary suspend negotiations in Panama and return to Washington to await further instructions while they had a chance to thrash this out at the White House. The request was granted and, on a warm Saturday, Reagan, Bush, and a host of cabinet members and their staffs gathered in the living room in the president's family quarters, around an unlit fireplace.

Among them, the only vocal proponent of finalizing a deal with the General was the secretary of state, who, while forceful on the issue, was nonetheless distracted. He and the president were less than a week away from the historic summit meetings with the Soviet premier in Iceland, at which they hoped to dismantle the Communist bloc and declare victory at last in the Cold War, and the secretary wanted, above all else, to make sure that this "Panama crisis" was done with, one way or another, before then, so nothing diminished the larger moment of presidential triumph over international communism.

In response to State's position, the attorney general argued that it was "the sentiment of the law enforcement community that making such a deal with an indicted drug dealer is like dealing with terrorists. . . . This will demoralize those on the front lines fighting against drugs if it is allowed to go forward." The attorney general also announced that his troops at Justice were already restive over the issue and cited Leon Kellner's threats of outright rebellion as an example.

The treasury secretary, who would soon resign his post to serve as the campaign manager of Bush for President, was even more vehement. This would sabotage the political base the Republican Party had built with the War on Drugs, he pointed out. They would end up looking like they were coddling the same people they had spent the last two terms vilifying. The treasury secretary reportedly went so far as to say that "the Democrats will eat us up on this."

Then the vice president spoke up. A little nervous at having stepped out of character and made this much of a fuss, Bush avoided any direct confrontation and tried to invoke the emotional landscape of the children whose lives were being ruined by drugs and the obvious duty to punish those who were responsible. Neither he nor the treasury secretary mentioned the George Bush for President campaign directly, but no one present had any doubts about the stakes for which George was playing on this issue.

For his part, Ronald Reagan said nothing at all before adjourning the Saturday meeting.

The president finally broke his silence when the same group met again the following evening. It was the only time in the entire process when Reagan spoke at length.

Elliott Abrams, who had accompanied his patron, the secretary of state, to both meetings, remembered this episode as the one and only "command decision" the president ever made on Panama. He also thought it one of Reagan's finest moments. "I've just never seen him so deeply engaged in a foreign policy argument," Abrams commented afterward. "You've heard all the stories about Reagan's general passivity, his lack of grasp of the facts, but if you had come down from Mars and seen Ronald Reagan on that day, you would assume all those arguments were made by morons."

Reagan declared flatly that the deal was the only option that made any sense at all. This indictment was just a piece of paper without Noriega in custody and, since extradition of any Panamanian from Panama was illegal under Panamanian law, and, even if that weren't the case, the man who would have to arrest him was Noriega himself, which made the prospect of actually getting him in custody nil. That so, this indictment wasn't worth a thing except what they could convince Noriega to trade for it. The choice was therefore between Noriega out of power or having a piece of legal paper to hang on the wall, and that was no choice at all.

Ronald Reagan admitted that a lot of people in the room weren't going to like his choice — causing more than a few participants to cast quick glances at George Bush sitting on the president's right. Then Reagan ordered the undersecretary back to Panama as soon as possible to finish cutting the deal.

Perhaps the most remarkable aspect of Reagan's presidential reasoning that Sunday evening was that the possibility of United States armed forces actually serving this arrest warrant on the General was considered such an off-the-wall possibility that Ronald Reagan never even bothered to explain his dismissal of it.

Vice President George Bush, the man who eventually did exactly what his predecessor refused even to consider, could do little at the immediate moment but swallow his disappointment.

The secretary of state, the winner of this intramural White House dispute, dispatched the undersecretary back to the Isthmus that evening, but with an added instruction Reagan had not mentioned at the White House conclave. The secretary told the lead negotiator that he had until May 25, when the secretary and the president were leaving for the Iceland summit with the Soviets, to tie this deal up and make a public announcement. That was three days. If he didn't meet the deadline, all deals were off and the talks would be dead on the spot. And there would be no extensions.

The secretary warned that he was tired of being strung along.

— 5 —

At the time, no one actually involved in the negotiations that had been taking place inside the General's Fort Amador bunker considered the secretary of state's deadline much of a challenge. The deal had been virtually set when the delegations broke for the weekend so the undersecretary could fly to the United States. Only a few loose ends remained for his return.

As structured, the deal called for the General to announce his resignation as of August 23, 1988, his fifth anniversary as *comandante*. The General would then endorse a statutory limitation on the term of all future PDF *comandantes* of no more than five years and, his own term over, depart Panama with all the pomp and circumstance due a national hero. According to the terms of the agreement, Noriega could return to the Isthmus for that year's Christmas, but otherwise had to remain abroad until after the next national elections on May 7, 1989, at which a new civilian government would be chosen and installed. In return, the United States would "seal" the indictment in the Southern District of Florida, with the provision that the indictment would never be unsealed so long as the General lived up to his side of the bargain.

"We had worked out the best deal in the whole world," Ray Takiff, the general's mouthpiece, remembered. "I mean, check it out — the government of the United States effectively drops the indictment and the General gets to take a trip around the world for a year and keep all of his money and his ladies and the whole bit just so long as he stays gone and out of politics for a year. That's a wonderful plea bargain."

Takiff and the rest of the General's team of American attorneys discussed the proposal with their client for several hours Friday, after negotiations broke, and then the General flew out to his house on the beach at La Playita "to think it through" over the weekend. He called Takiff from there on Saturday and asked him to fly out with cocounsel Frank Rubino and the rest of the defense team. A plane was waiting. When the lawyers reached the General's beach retreat, a party was going on, with some eight hundred guests, many of the men dressed in PDF uniforms. The General greeted his lawyers and took them aside briefly before joining the festivities.

At that point, the General told Ray Takiff — all buffed up in his best gold chain and rayon shirt — that "the terms" were, indeed, "wonderful," just like Ray had said. What the General now wanted to know was if Takiff sensed "any double dealing or blackmail." Takiff swore he did not and assured his client that "we all give you our word on that," motioning at the entire defense team, then repeated the assurance for emphasis. The only dissatisfaction the General expressed to Ray was with a particular provision in the draft agreement that required the General to sign the deal along with the undersecretary and then deposit the signed agreements with the papal nuncio, the pope's diplomatic ambassador to Panama City. He told Takiff he hated that weasely little papal son-of-a-bitch.

Then they all entered the party. After circulating for a bit among the Panamanians, Ray Takiff joined the crowd when the General called all eight hundred of his guests together in the house's courtyard. When the crowd was assembled, the General made a little speech thanking his attorneys and all the other members of his negotiating team and expressing how proud he was of the job they had been doing.

Then the General asked for the liberty to share with everyone a story about one of his lawyers. The story he told began with a little Panamanian girl who moved to Florida and was enrolled by her mother in Miami Country Day School, an exclusive private school, where, at first, she had a lot of trouble making American friends. Then another Miami girl took the Panamanian under her wing and helped her become one of Miami Country Day's most popular students. And that American girl who was so kind to a Panamanian stranger was none other than Averill Takiff, daughter of his lawyer, Ray Takiff.

With that, the General turned toward Ray and pointed him out to the crowd, who all clapped.

More than a decade later, when Ray Takiff remembered the incident, lying in his hospital bed with tubes running up his nose and more tubes running out of his gown, Ray glowed at the memory. He was on top of the world then, he pointed out. He had just negotiated what he was sure would be the most celebrated plea bargain in the history of the United States, certainly of Florida at the very least. And now he was getting enough strokes to make him feel like a Panamanian national hero.

"What a piece of luck," Ray recalled. "Finally all those endless school bills for my daughter paid off. I was amazed that the General even knew the story. I hadn't said anything about it myself. I didn't even know it had happened. I later learned that this little Panamanian girl in the General's story was rumored to be the General's daughter by some mistress of his. Anyway, thanks to my daughter, I now had it made in the shade. I thought to myself, 'I've got to buy my kid a bike.'"

That Saturday out at La Playita, Ray bowed and waved in response to his client's accolades.

Ray Takiff's illusions of grandeur began collapsing some seventy-two hours after the undersecretary returned and the negotiations resumed.

Until then, it seemed all the loose ends had been tied up. The General had notified his family that he would step down, and the secretary of state was expecting to announce the deal in Washington as soon as that day's final signing took place. The undersecretary had already assured him the deal was done. The only hitch had been a panic attack on the part of the General in which he had insisted the full text of the agreement might have been altered while the undersecretary was back in the United States. That distress was finally eased when both sides' copies were reviewed side by side, line by line. Otherwise, everything appeared to be right on track.

Then, early in the morning, with the secretary of state's final deadline barely hours away, Takiff received a call at his Panama City hotel from the General at the *comandancia*. The *comandante* asked his lawyer to hurry over. Takiff took a cab to the base gate, where the sentry paid the cab off, and drove him on to the General's office in a PDF jeep.

General Manuel Antonio Noriega was waiting for Takiff and, according to his lawyer, "had obviously been up all night and had obviously been very distressed."

"I can't take the deal," he told Ray.

"I asked him why not?" Takiff remembered. "And he said, 'My junior officers will kill me.' Not figuratively either. He meant literally. They were going to blow him away. He said, 'I can't do it. I'm going to have to tough it out.' "

"I said, 'General, do you realize what you're giving up here? Do you realize what you're giving up?'

"Then he said, 'Yes, I do, but I'm not going to take the deal.'

"So he didn't take the deal."

After notifying his legal counsel of his decision, the General called the undersecretary, provoking some three more hours' worth of frantic efforts between the undersecretary and the General to find a way out. The General insisted he needed more time to bring his junior officers around, finally saying he thought seventy-two hours more would be enough. Then he'd sign. The undersecretary believed the General was serious about signing, so the undersecretary called the secretary of state, who had already let the president go ahead to Iceland, while he delayed his own departure from Washington, planning to announce the deal in Panama he expected to be final at any moment, then catch up with the president before talks with the Soviets began.

When told that there was no signed deal in Panama yet and more time was necessary, the secretary of state ordered his negotiator to close up shop and come home. Then the secretary left for Iceland.

And with that, the one and only serious attempt by the United States of America to cut a deal with General Manuel Antonio Noriega short of outright arrest was over for good.

It had come "this close" to succeeding, the translator provided to the American delegation from Fred Woerner's staff told his boss afterward, holding up his thumb and forefinger to form a gap so narrow that light barely passed through it at all.

As things turned out, of course, that shortfall might as well have been by a mile. "Close" only counts in the game of horseshoes.

There would be days along the General's eventual path into the depths of the American criminal justice system — first in the dead air of the windowless Submarine, shuttling back and forth in the high-security elevator to the courtroom where he was standing trial, then, out at the Federal Correctional Center next to the zoo for the thirty-year long haul — when he was no doubt prepared to give everything he ever owned just to step back in time and say yes to the deal he had spurned on May 25, 1988.

But he didn't feel that way yet.

The American media, in fact, played the collapse of negotiations as the General's victory, by default, if nothing else. "Fiasco," *Newsweek* headlined; "The Grand Botch," *U.S. News & World Report* chimed in. Once again, it seemed the wily General Manuel Antonio Noriega had hung the bell on the clumsy American cat. "He screwed us," one presidential adviser observed for the public record. Deserved or not, humiliation was the administration's order of the day.

Had the General known better at the time, he might have hoped for a less abrasive conclusion. The gringos would eventually redeem their humiliation in spades.

What followed next, however, did not yet look at all like revenge.

Instead, the irresolution of the issue at the end of that May generated hiatus rather than renewed action. The General was out of the headlines within two weeks of the negotiations' end and the American economic sanctions were largely dissipated before summer was half done. It was as though the eye of the General's political hurricane had now moved overhead and the winds which had heretofore been blowing with deafening force were now instantly, eerily still. In early June, orders were dispatched from the Department of Defense to Fred Woerner, ordering him to put Panama "on the back burner until the election is over," and he did just that.

As far as Washington was concerned, *United States v. Manuel Antonio Noriega* was tabled until George Bush had a presidency of his own with which to pursue it.

CHAPTER 5

THE CASE'S DIMINISHMENT

— 1 —

Meanwhile, back in Miami, the First Assistant United States Attorney was in a fighting mood. Virtually every attempt Dick Gregorie had made to secure information from the rest of the government to bolster his case against the General that spring was rebuffed in much the same manner as exhibited by the CIA. The DEA "lost" his case agent's requests for computer searches and then "lost" his rerequests as well. The Department of Defense even insisted with a straight face that they couldn't provide Grilli with a satellite photo of Panama because they didn't have any such satellites. Gregorie's conclusion about the pattern was simple. "They don't want us to make this case," he barked at Grilli that April, "and they're going to do whatever they can to stop us, even now."

Dick didn't pause in his outburst to specifically define who he meant by "they," but Steve already knew that one of those at the top of Dick's list was the Drug Enforcement Administration.

Gregorie knew the DEA had sandbagged Grilli's investigation and done their best to make sure it died of information starvation when it was too late to kill it outright. He remembered how the administrator's brain trust had looked at them when they first went to Washington and explained that they were making this case. He had heard Floyd Carlton describe how the DEA's Panama station treated him when he first tried to turn evidence. He had seen how the DEA had denied their own agents the credit they deserved at the press conference on February 5. And Dick had already heard reports of the abuse being dumped on Kennedy and Grilli for having done their jobs chasing the General. All of this made

Gregorie at the very least unwilling to keep his feelings about what was going on at the Drug Enforcement Administration secret.

As much became clear that April at a Southern District of Florida awards ceremony convened in the Miami courthouse's jury pool room. All of the various law-enforcement agencies from the DEA to the FBI to Alcohol, Firearms, Tobacco were represented by their upper ranks, all gathered on folding chairs set up in front of a microphone and podium. The occasion was scheduled to honor the front line troops of federal law enforcement with the presentation of United States Attorney's Awards to various agents for outstanding work above and beyond the call of duty. One of the recipients was scheduled to be Steve Grilli, case agent for *United States v. Manuel Antonio Noriega.* Grilli's award was presented by Gregorie, for whom, of course, he had made the case. One of those in the audience was Grilli's boss, the associate special agent in charge of the DEA's Miami Divisional Office.

The presentation to Grilli was made by Gregorie, featuring what was planned as a short set of remarks. At first, Dick confined his statement at the microphone to describing how well Steve Grilli had done his job — pretty much standard fare, received with smatterings of applause. But then, Dick got on the subject of how much he would hate to lose Grilli and that, in turn, led him to the subject of how he had lost Danny Mortiz, his last case agent before Steve. Then, unable to resist the opportunity, Dick Gregorie began to dress down the DEA for having moved Moritz to Cleveland just when the investigation of the General had been getting under way. This transfer was, of course, very old business between the First Assistant and the DEA, but that status was not reflected in the vigor Gregorie brought to the subject at Grilli's award presentation. Dick's remarks quickly became a tirade against the DEA to a captive audience. Soon, silence descended on the audience, broken only by the uncomfortable shifting of folding chairs.

Finally, after Gregorie's tirade went on long enough to embarrass even those with no stake in the issue, the DEA's associate special agent in charge rose from his seat and stormed out of the room in a huff.

Paying no attention, Gregorie just kept railing away.

Steve found himself sinking lower and lower in his chair, wishing Dick would shut up.

"Dick just kicked one of my agency's elite local guys right in the balls," Grilli remembered, "right there in front of everybody in town who mattered. He didn't back off in the least. My first thought was, Holy Shit, are we in for it now."

The incident that transformed Steve Grilli's premonition of trouble into a full-blown reality began with a phone call on April 15. The call came to Grilli from a Panamanian who had once been Floyd Carlton's lawyer on the Isthmus and was, at the moment, visiting south Florida. Floyd had sent word to the attorney, suggesting he call.

Speaking halting English, the Panamanian claimed he possessed "documentary evidence that could be of great assistance," but would "also expose dangerous people on both sides." These papers, which the caller said were still down in Panama, allegedly included documentation of Floyd Carlton's business association with César Rodríguez and the General, plus records from accounts at the Panama City branch of the Bank of Credit and Commerce International that would shed light on various money-laundering operations, including the General's and "a lot of others." Floyd's old lawyer said he had shown many of these same documents to the DEA's Panama office some six months earlier, but the agents there "didn't react."

The same could not be said of Grilli.

Steve jumped on the offer without hesitation. If real, the bank records alone promised to allow the Southern District of Florida to locate the fugitive General's money and freeze it all, not to mention expose the insides of what was likely the largest money-laundering operation in the hemisphere. Steve told Floyd's lawyer to return to Panama and, over the following week, with Kennedy's help, Grilli came up with $2,000 of agency money to cover the would-be informant's expenses. The Panamanian was instructed to gather all the documents he had stashed, box them up for shipment, and deliver the package to the DEA office at the American embassy on Avenue Balboa in Panama City. The package would then travel north in a DEA plane.

Floyd's lawyer agreed to do as Grilli instructed him but wanted to be enrolled in Witness Protection in return. He told Grilli that if it were found out he had delivered this information to the DEA, his life would not be worth a nickel back on the Isthmus.

Once that protection had been promised by Gregorie, Floyd's lawyer returned to Panama, did as he'd been told, and, on April 26, 1988, delivered the box full of papers to a waiting DEA agent in a car down the block from the embassy, as had been arranged ahead of time.

It was at this point, as far as Dick Gregorie was concerned, that the plot thickened considerably.

The DEA agent from the Panama office who took possession of the box was at the end of his shift, so the agent just continued home with the package rather than returning to the embassy, and kept the sealed stash of documents with him overnight. When the box finally reached the embassy the next morning, it sat for another day and night, in a cabinet in the DEA office, where anyone with access to the embassy could reach it. Then it was finally loaded on a DEA plane and dispatched to Miami. Somewhere along that evidentiary chain preceding shipment, the box was opened and then retaped.

Finally, at 5:00 P.M. on April 28, Steve Grilli was notified that the box was up at the DEA Air Wing's office in Opa-Locka. Since the office there was about to close, he told the secretary who called him to lock the box up for the night, and the next morning, April 29, at 9:00 A.M., Grilli drove up to retrieve it.

Steve Grilli remembered being slightly distracted at the time. First hints of the deal the State Department was hatching with the General had begun to circulate in the press, and the rumors made Grilli wonder just why he was busting his ass so hard. Driving south along I-75 from Opa-Locka in a disgruntled state, he stopped first at the Miami Divisional Office, where the box was locked up again for an hour, then he picked up Floyd's lawyer at his hotel and hauled the would-be informant down to 155 S. Miami Avenue to meet with Gregorie in Leon Kellner's conference room.

There, Floyd's lawyer got very twitchy as soon as he saw the box.

Someone had opened it, he pointed out. The tape was different, an obvious patch job. What was going on? he wanted to know.

So, of course, did Dick Gregorie.

Dick had the Panamanian remove everything from the package, spread it out on Leon's table, and take inventory. When he did, the result was enough to send Dick through the roof.

Floyd Carlton's lawyer claimed that much of the best stuff was missing: most of Floyd Carlton and César Rodríguez's flight logs; the incorporation papers for César's C.A.R. Corporation including one original legal document signed by the General himself; several ownership papers for the dope ship the *Krill;* hotel records that substantiated the testimony of

El Turco; and, most important of all, an account list printout from the Bank of Credit and Commerce International that reputedly revealed the identities of virtually all of their money-laundering traffic, and for which Floyd's lawyer had paid a member of the PDF a thousand dollars.

At this point, as Grilli later noted in his official report of this incident, the would-be informant became "agitated" and volunteered to take a polygraph to substantiate his version of what had been packed in the box when he left it with the DEA's Panama office three days earlier.

Gregoric said that would be a very good idea as well.

So Floyd Carlton's lawyer-turned-informant was hooked to the lie detector within forty-eight hours of his inventory of the papers at 155 S. Miami. He passed on every document they asked him about.

And that was enough for Gregorie. As far as he was concerned, someone at the Panama office had their hand in the cookie jar and he vowed to get to the bottom of it, even if he had to challenge the whole DEA to do so. He was not about to "stand back and take it anymore."

Gregorie's first step in that direction was formally to impanel a grand jury for the purpose of investigating the Panama DEA office's handling of the box of documents.

Needless to say, this move had the impact of a howitzer round lobbed right into the middle of the DEA. Agents in Panama would be forced to return to the United States, retain legal counsel, and respond to subpoenas requiring their testimony. On top of that, of course, the Panama office's integrity was instantly impugned along with the DEA's in general. Panama City was a fast-track posting inside the agency, particularly for Hispanics, and the office's roster of alumni included more than a few major players currently staffing Washington headquarters. Gregorie, already dismissed among much of the agency for having pursued the General in the first place, "just to save Leon Kellner's bacon," was now thought of as "a squirrely little son-of-bitch" and agents in Miami were already telling Kennedy and Grilli they were little better for working with him. And the First Assistant's name was henceforth mentioned in most DEA circles with an attached prefix, as in "that fucking Gregorie. . . ."

For his part, Gregorie could have cared less what they thought.

"The DEA was too sensitive," he claimed. "They were used to operating inside their own little chummy scratch-my-back-I'll-scratch-yours world and suddenly had to get real. Being forced to testify under oath about their own behavior was a shock to them, I knew that, but I was so mad that there was no question in my mind that I was going to go to the grand jury. This kind of tampering was unacceptable, somebody was trying to kill this case, and I wasn't going to put up with it. It's called obstruction of justice, and it's against the law.

"The bottom line was I felt we had been betrayed. Here we were, trying to make the biggest case the DEA ever had, and not only were we getting no assistance, they might even have been outright working against us. With that at stake, it didn't bother me to subpoena agents, even if it put a blemish on their careers and got the DEA upset. I wasn't even sure if they were really working for the DEA or the CIA or somebody else. But whoever it was, I was going to make them take the stand and swear under oath that they hadn't messed with our evidence. I didn't do it to ruin someone's career. I was doing it because I wanted someone to tell me what the heck happened with that box. And I never did get a straight answer."

Well meant as it was, one of the very first effects of Gregorie's move was to make Steve Grilli's position extremely untenable. Steve couldn't be the case agent in a case against his own agency, even though being Gregorie's case agent was his job. It was a conflict of interest, not to mention a career disaster. Faced with this dilemma, Steve quickly decided he would have to keep working on Gregorie's other cases but leave this one completely alone.

Even officially recused from doing legwork for Gregorie's new grand jury, however, Grilli would nonetheless be reviled around the Miami office in the course of the shit storm Gregorie's inquiry set off. At one point, a retired DEA agent even met secretly with Gregorie to warn him that a number of guys at the office were saying Steve just might get "hit" over all this, though nothing ever came of the implied threat. It was, however, evidence of just how high feelings were running over Gregorie's "attack."

Steve laid out what he felt he had to do about this new grand jury in a conference call with Dick Gregorie and Leon Kellner on May 13, the day after the White House announced its willingness to trade *United States v. Manuel Antonio Noriega* for the General's resignation.

"I told Gregorie, 'You don't need an investigator. You need a fuckin' subpoena server on a fishing expedition,'" Steve remembered. "I was pissed. Dick was closing all kinds of doors on me by what he was doin'. You gotta understand. I'm getting feedback from the guys at the office regarding who's being thrown into the grand jury and 'where is this nut going?' and the like. I told Dick I wasn't going to sit there while this happened. 'I won't serve a single DEA agent,' I said. 'I can't wear that jacket.' It was a hard break to make. I mean really hard. I had paid the price and I was almost there, but I knew I had to walk from this case and the rest of this shit. At the time it felt like the end of the world. But I had to do it. I had no choice."

When he informed them, both Gregorie and Kellner responded that they had no problem with Grilli skipping this investigation while he continued to tend to the General's case and all cartel matters. Neither displayed any anger and both "understood" that Steve found the situation untenable.

And, just to reassure him, Leon Kellner even offered that if Steve ever needed any legal help in the future because of this, Leon would represent him himself, *pro bono.* Wherever Leon might be at the time, he promised he would drop everything and come running to help Steve.

Though Grilli said nothing when they were all on the line, afterward, he couldn't stop wondering about Leon's offer and just why Leon Kellner thought Steve might need legal representation and just where the United States attorney was going that he could even handle private cases, which such a defense would have to be.

And, when Steve couldn't answer those questions, he found himself, for the first time since he started on this case almost eleven months earlier, wondering if he just might be in over his head.

2

As it turned out, Dick Gregorie could hardly have chosen a worse time to pick a fight.

Indeed, had Gregorie known what was about to happen, he might have found a way to finesse the situation a little more, or maybe even just walk away from it. Then again, the way he felt, he might not have. In any case, he was about to lose the juice that had allowed him to make such a move against the Panama DEA office in the first place. Gregorie's power in the Southern District had always been his carte blanche backing from the United States attorney. But, unfortunately for Gregorie, Leon Kellner, worn down by his brush with disgrace, was about to retire, leaving Dick Gregorie without any backing at all.

The news of Leon's impending departure blindsided Gregorie completely. Dick learned of Leon's plans less than two weeks before Leon announced them to the public at large, some two weeks after Gregorie had decided to use the grand jury to put the squeeze on the Panama office. "Leon didn't consult with me about resigning," Gregorie remembered. "He just came to me one day late that May and said, 'In three weeks I'm gone.' I guess I was a little ticked off at him for that. I felt like he should have given me more warning and then gone to bat for me more afterward."

Dick Gregorie had always fantasized that, as Leon had moved up to United States attorney from his First Assistant's job, so in turn would he — but that fantasy would prove to be, by his own later admission, more evidence of Gregorie's own delusions than anything else.

Despite Leon's discouragement, Gregorie insisted on applying for the soon to be vacant top job, and Kellner promised to give him what help he could. When the attorney general came to town in early June to interview candidates, Gregorie was included in the process at Leon's request. Gregorie also tried to exercise whatever political clout he could muster, but the attempt was laughable.

"I was naïve," Dick recalled. "I didn't have the first idea how to proceed, but everybody told me that if I wanted to be United States attorney I had to go make connections, talk to people who have influence.

"I said, 'I don't know anybody that has influence. I've been doing this job my whole life, trying to stay away from people that have influence.'

"They said, 'You'll never make it if you don't have political influence.'

"So I said, 'Who should I talk to?' and a couple of friends told me who the big shots in the Republican Party were. I asked Leon for help and he arranged for me to meet with the guy who had arranged his meeting with George Bush."

The encounter was classic Gregorie.

The two men met in a high-rise office downtown, with greater Miami, all air-conditioned towers and the glittering bay beyond, spread outside the glass wall behind the Republican big shot, smothered in the last glare of spring. Otherwise, the sumptuous room spoke of money every direction Dick looked. Once they introduced themselves and Dick announced his attention to become the next United States attorney for the

Southern District of Florida, the first thing the Republican wanted to know was what Dick had done for "the party."

Gregorie, who had never registered with one political affiliation or another, had no idea what the guy meant and guessed he was talking about some social festivity he didn't know about.

"What party?" the First Assistant asked.

The outcome of Dick's quest to replace Leon was a foregone conclusion, despite the fact that a number of the assistant United States attorneys in the office signed a petition lobbying for Gregorie's appointment and sent it to the attorney general.

"Washington wanted someone they could control," Dick explained. "And that wasn't me, by any measure. They had been boxed in on the Noriega case and put in a position where they couldn't say no to it, and I was the guy who had boxed them in. They weren't about to risk that again. Miami was such a hot place, where things could blow up at any moment. They wanted someone they could call down to and say, 'This is what we want you to do and this is how we want you to do it.' I wasn't that kind of lawyer."

That analysis was more or less endorsed by Leon Kellner. "The office had become so closely tied to the drug issue and the political campaigns that year," Leon explained. "Justice wanted someone they felt they could work with, who would take instructions, and Dick Gregorie wasn't that guy."

Leon passed the news to Dick on June 10, 1988, several days before the new U.S. attorney was announced to the public.

"He said it didn't look good for my chances," Dick remembered. "I had already kind of figured as much but I still felt like someone had punched me in the stomach."

Leon's resignation and replacement would not only mean the end of carte blanche, but also the loss of Gregorie's First Assistant's role, after the transition in which the new United States attorney, a former state legislator, installed his own team.

Dick Gregorie's first encounter longer than five minutes with his new boss was as the recipient of a twenty-minute exposition on the importance of keeping detailed office time sheets. At that point, the only real option for Gregorie, unwilling to sink back into the ranks, suddenly seemed to be to leave. "I guess I knew I was going to have to go as soon as I didn't get the appointment," Gregorie remembered, "and I guess everybody else knew it too." This was still "the only job" he'd "ever wanted to do," but Dick Gregorie would nonetheless leave it at the end of 1988 and give private practice a try.

By July, when hiatus was everywhere manifest around the issue of the General in Washington, Dick Gregorie had become a lame duck down in the Southern District, no longer able to pursue the fight he'd just picked with the DEA, and his case, *United States v. Manuel Antonio Noriega,* was on the wane with him.

Dick Gregorie's only public statement in the course of his departure from the job of his dreams was made on July 12, 1988, some six months before he actually left. The new United States attorney for the Southern District of Florida had been in place over his head for some three weeks when Gregorie returned to Washington for one last time, to testify at the final set of hearings held by the Senate Subcommittee on Terrorism, Narcotics, and International Operations.

The subcommittee had already conducted almost a half-dozen similar sessions. The most widely publicized of those had featured, first, Floyd Carlton — testifying with a bag over his head, with cutouts for his mouth and eyes — and, then, Jose Blandon — now Washington's familiar short, white-headed expert on the General, testifying with such gusto and seeming credibility that the subcommittee called him back for a second appearance almost two months after his first.

The last set of the subcommittee's hearings, convened in July, was designed to be more generalized, addressing the larger issues. Gregorie was invited as the now almost legendary drug prosecutor who had nailed both the cartel in Colombia and General Manuel Antonio Noriega down in Panama.

Despite his new lame duck status, Gregorie's performance before the subcommittee remained in character.

First, he attacked the subcommittee cochairman's pet proposal urging "capital punishment for the dope trade." Gregorie pointed out that if they indeed applied the death penalty, "no country in the world would extradite a drug kingpin to the United States to face capital punishment. They don't believe in it and you have to get them to agree to extradition before you get it. The only drug kingpin you're going to get is some guy in Iowa who's been selling ten pounds of marijuana. And then you're going to put him to death?"

Having been skewered, the cochairman, Gregorie remembered, "hated my guts" for the rest of the session.

Gregorie followed that abrasive encounter by being blunt for one more time on his favorite subject of all. "The intelligence community is out of control," he later summarized his message to the senators that day. "There are no checks and balances on it — just a bunch of compartmentalized units doing whatever they want to do and, if you're not in their compartment, you don't know about it. I think the Congress or the president don't know half the things they're doing. The intelligence agencies have no regard for the law whatsoever. They think they're above it and can do whatever they want to do. This can't be what our Constitution had in mind."

Finally, Gregorie addressed the War on Drugs. His comments amounted to his valedictory, after six straight years as the lead battlefield commander in south Florida, originally called to the front in order to pursue the web of importation back as close to its source as he could, and now on the verge of leaving his post after having done more to extend the reach of the American drug prohibition than anyone in the country. Certainly no one could claim more expertise on just how that war was being waged.

"We have brought all the prosecutions that we have evidence to bring," he testified. "However, we are unable to get the highest level of the traffickers because they're in foreign jurisdictions. And, although we know where they are, we get information daily on their locations, there is nothing we can do about it. We can't bring them to justice in the United States. We, therefore, do not have [an actual] war. . . . We are certainly not using all the resources at the hands of the U.S. government to fight this drug problem. So, it is my opinion that there is no such thing as a drug war. We merely have a domestic police action, and it is impossible with a domestic police action to solve this problem."

That was the last Washington heard from Dick Gregorie.

Judging from the complete lack of notice with which his admonitions were received that July, no one in town was listening anyway.

— 3 —

"It was hard watching what happened to Dick," Steve Grilli remembered. "It was like a fuckin' train wreck, all taking place in slow motion right there in front of me. It was sad. I guess Gregorie's wreck felt like an omen for me too. Maybe I shoulda walked away right then. I quite frankly thought this would be the end of the case anyway, since Dick was the one who had designed the whole thing, at least legally. But we had an indictment and an arrest warrant and the powers that be were sort of stuck with it, even if it was a big flash with a little bang. In any case, without Dick, I felt sort of hung out there on my own."

On more fronts than one. Steve and Patti's hold on marriage was now openly tenuous. She was sick of being a DEA wife and he was sick of hearing about it from her. And, though they hadn't yet openly split, Steve was now spending stretches as long as a week without ever going back to see her or the kids in Deerfield Beach, sometimes staying in a hotel, often taking extra assignments at the divisional office that kept him away for days on end.

"I couldn't just say to my wife, 'Let's take some time off and get this thing right,'" he explained. "I couldn't jump off the speeding train — the same one Gregorie had ridden into the wall. So I just had to play it out. I was caught up in the momentum, for better or worse."

In July, that momentum carried Grilli back to Washington.

The same day the Senate Subcommittee on Terrorism, Narcotics, and International Operations heard from Dick Gregorie, it also heard testimony from the administrator of the Drug Enforcement Administration. A briefing session to prepare the administrator had been convened at the DEA's Washington headquarters during the week prior to his scheduled appearance, and on July 7, 1988, Steve and Kenny Kennedy were summoned north from Miami on short notice to participate in the administrator's preparations.

This was Steve and Kenny's third meeting with the Drug Enforcement Administration's big boss in less than a year. But there was more to the visit than just that. Headquarters had an additional "exercise" they wanted them to go through before the administrator's briefing that afternoon, of which Grilli learned only after he reported to the director of operations at 8:00 A.M. The director explained that before the session with the big guy, he had "some people who want to ask you a few questions" about *United States v. Manuel Antonio Noriega.* Steve later described the gathering as "the Inquisition."

After being notified it was taking place, he was told to return to the conference room in half an hour, and, when he did, he found it filled with "heavies" from around headquarters, most of them Hispanic, all GS-14s or better, all having served previous rotations at the Panama office. Copies of the general's case file were piled on the conference room table, with a chair at the head —"the hot seat"— reserved for the Miami case agent. Grilli had expected perhaps two or three others for an informal discussion and had no idea he was about to face a two-hour examination, but he defended the case as best he could. Kenny Kennedy, also present, said nothing throughout it all.

The session was opened by the GS-15 who had served as head of the Panama office during much of the time described by Floyd Carlton in his interrogations in the Submarine.

"We think Noriega's guilty, but not the way you have it," was the first statement out of the former Panama chief's mouth. It was a convenient opening, allowing the assembled group to maintain a law-and-order identity, thus deflecting any criticism for being soft on the General, but still able to swarm all over Grilli's case. This initial reference was, however, the only mention of any information they might have had about the General's guilt.

The rest, Grilli remembered, was all about his case: "This is wrong, this is wrong, this is wrong — a room full of detractors, all of them slam-dunkers from the old school. I was outnumbered more than Custer at Little Big Horn. They all had something to prove — that they hadn't been asleep at the switch as far as the General was concerned. Kennedy was exceedingly sheepish during the meeting. I was way out front, alone, and I knew it."

The first bone the inquisitors picked was over the fact that Grilli was not fluent in Spanish. Language capacity was, at the time, a hot issue among Hispanic agents, who were looking for extra pay for their linguistic skills. How could Grilli hope to be able to discern whether or not to trust a scumbag like Floyd Carlton if he had to relate through a translator? Not only did Grilli not have the language, but because he didn't understand it, he had no grasp of the culture either. How could he even be sure the translation was accurate?

The rest of the session only got heavier from there. The former Panama chief went on to point out that all of the agents assembled in this room could be called as defense witnesses for the General, because all of them had served in Panama and none of them could corroborate anything Grilli's informants said. On top of that, where was the fuckin' dope on the table in all this? And if there wasn't any, why the hell were they wasting their time on it? Then he asked if Grilli knew someone whose name Grilli had never heard before. This name was connected to INAIR, so why didn't Grilli know about him if he was such an expert on the subject? Then the former chief switched to the raid on the lab at Darien that Grilli's snitches kept talking about. He had been in on that raid himself. Rather than payoffs to free the people who were arrested, as Grilli's sources insisted was the case, "the Colombians who the PDF arrested in the jungle were all released because there was no crime in Panama for constructing buildings."

The longer the meeting lasted, the more pent-up Grilli became. "I could not believe that [this former Panama office chief] had a brain in his head," Steve recalled, "but I knew there would be no help from these other guys. Instead, they joined in, and then they all talked at me in rotation. I just sat there answering one question after another. I got more defensive as things went along. I mean, Jesus Christ, none of these guys who were actually on the General's turf had contributed shit to my investigation. They wouldn't even acknowledge my requests for assistance when I made them. We got zero from anybody down in Panama when we made the case. And now they do this? I thought they were supposed to be on my side. Instead, they just did their best to tear me down. I guess they figured that if my case was right, then it would look like they had been fuckin' the dog down at the Panama office all those years. They cross-examined me on all the white paper material, a lot of picky questions, one after another. After a while I started getting a little beside myself."

At around the two-hour mark, the former Panama office chief took the floor to work on Grilli a last time. The chief pointed out that he had been in Panama City when Grilli's informants said the cartel was there walking past the embassy every morning.

"If that's true, Steve," he demanded, "how come I didn't know it?"

Heretofore, Grilli, while defensive and brassy, had been as respectful and circumspect as he could manage, as was to be expected toward a crowd that all outranked him by two grades at least, but this last question pushed him over the edge into saying something he wished he hadn't.

"Because you were duped," Steve snapped.

He wanted the words back as soon as he said them. The former Panama chief's head recoiled and, as Kenny, who had been sitting there in silence, remembered, "that word 'duped' just echoed there in the room."

"I was tired and drained," Grilli later explained. "I wouldn't have said it if I'd been fresh. This guy was a GS-15, I mean a 12 don't talk to a 15 like that, under any circumstances. I was young then and full of piss and vinegar, but I could see right away that I'd stepped on my own dick big time."

The meeting broke up shortly thereafter, with Grilli now far worse off than when he'd begun it.

That trend continued at the administrator's briefing, though the antagonism there was more hidden.

"It was held after lunch in the administrator's conference room," Grilli remembered, "filled to capacity. There was an inside circle around the table and a not-so-inside circle on chairs against the wall. Kennedy and I were at the table with the big boys. I was a GS-12 and everyone else there was a GS-99, you know what I mean? This was the fuckin' stratosphere, the land of big beef. The administrator walked in with what we called 'his horse holder,' his administrative assistant. He sat at the table with his horse holder taking notes behind him. Then we went around and introductions were made for the administrator's benefit — each of the big boys, in turn, was identified, name and position recited. When my turn came, before I could say anything, the administrator says to me, 'How's the case going, Steve?' Can you believe it? 'How's the case going, Steve?' As soon as he said it, I could like feel the glare on my back from everybody else at the table. I mean, here are the beef boys having to re-introduce themselves and the big guy calls this smartass GS-12 by his first name? I could imagine the calls that were going to be placed to Miami about me while I was sitting there."

Otherwise, Steve Grilli was as silent as Kennedy while the discussion went around the table on various issues. Then someone raised the subject of one possible line of subcommittee questions concerning allegations from several informants currently on DEA leashes to the effect that all this cocaine traffic out of Colombia was connected in a conspiracy that included Cuba, the Colombian M-19 guerrillas, the Libyans, and who knew who else. It was suspected that the information had been leaked to the subcommittee. The big boys tossed the issue of such a conspiracy around a little for the administrator's benefit, then the administrator suddenly turned to Grilli.

"Well, Steve, what do you think?" he asked out of the blue.

Grilli didn't defer the question to his seniors, as a more politic agent might have, or even hesitate much. He told the administrator he thought information could be developed linking the General into this "bigger picture" and offered the testimony from his informant Jose Blandon about the intercession of Fidel Castro in the General's dispute with the cartel, as an example.

Several around the table noticeably sucked wind at the audacity of the Miami agent's response.

"This," Grilli later pointed out, "immediately sent my insignificant little GS-12 ass to the shit list the big boys were mentally putting together, if I wasn't on it already."

After the briefing was over, the head of Intelligence immediately jacked up Kenny and Steve in the hallway and demanded to know why he hadn't been informed of any of what Grilli was going to say beforehand.

Similar treatment was waiting for Kennedy and Grilli when they flew back to Florida later that same day.

At the Miami office, they were greeted by an associate SAC who was immediately in their faces. The associate had been fielding calls from Washington for a while at that point.

And the first thing he demanded to know was where the hell Grilli came off talking directly to the administrator like that.

— 4 —

Assistant Special Agent in Charge Kenny Kennedy, of course, tried to shield his agent from this harassment as best he could.

"Grilli was asked a direct question by the administrator and he gave the administrator a direct answer in return," he told the associate SAC that July. "So what's the fuckin' problem?"

But, try as he might, by then Kenny was in no condition to provide much in the way of cover for anyone. And it would only get worse. The bureaucratic counterattack was under way, and Kennedy's career was now sinking like a rock — far more so than Steve Grilli's. At least Grilli was considered a foot soldier acting under orders in his pursuit of "the best friend the DEA has in Latin America," and, indeed, Grilli himself would point out, no one ever told him to stop. As a consequence, when the time came later in the year at which, under normal conditions, it would have been appropriate to advance Grilli one rank to GS-13, he was promoted, despite the resentment of him and his case.

Kenny, on the other hand, bore the full organizational brunt. The true bill against the General was considered bad for the agency, and Kenny could have made it disappear without a trace, but had nourished it instead — so the blame was on him. On top of that, he was also the old strike force buddy of Dick Gregorie, who, in addition to being the author of the General's indictment, was a DEA anathema of the first magnitude by virtue of the subpoenas he was serving on the Panama office.

And Kennedy would never escape the taint. When Kenny first arrived in Miami — fresh from Washington, promoted to GS-15, and on a roll, seemingly ticketed for a three-year rotation as Miami's ASAC then further promotion to the elite Senior Executive Service — he was posted immediately under the special agent in charge: in the chain of command, the second most powerful operational rank at the entire Miami station. In the next fifteen years, the station would add an entire layer of associate SACs between the ASAC and SAC and expand the number of ASACs by a factor of three, but Kenny Kennedy would nonetheless remain at the exact same location in the organizational chart as he began. Even after the General's arrest and the DEA's sudden adoption of *United States v. Manuel Antonio Noriega* as its signature victory in the War on Drugs, nothing in Kenny's standing would change one way or another. His career would remain stopped dead in its tracks until it was time for Kenny to leave.

Those around Kenny Kennedy in the fall of 1988 already noticed a new morose side of the previously hail-fellow-well-met ASAC who was now in the permanent organizational doghouse. There were the long stares at the wall, the extra beer or two after work. Kenny didn't snivel about his fate, but Grilli picked up on it nonetheless.

"This had to be hard on Kenny," he remembered. "Washington didn't get on the phone and complain to me. They got on the wire with Kennedy and yelled at him. It was a case of shit running downhill, if you know what I mean. Kenny was a guy who liked to be liked and he was gettin' nothin' but dumped on instead."

The only other outward evidence of Kennedy's hard times was a sign he posted on his office door, printed on his computer and done up in a government-issue picture frame. It said simply, "THE BEATINGS WILL CONTINUE UNTIL MORALE IMPROVES."

Dick Gregorie spent his fall effectively hamstrung. He tried initiating more investigations, but got nowhere.

"I interviewed this one witness," he remembered, "who had been flying dope for the cartel and had been busted in Colorado. He talked about the Free Trade Zone in Panama, alleging that we had people in our military down there who were on the take for a lot of illegal ventures including sharing money in the dope transiting through. I immediately wanted to investigate but I couldn't get anybody to do it. The DEA refused, saying that the allegations involved stolen goods and a lot of other things that were not under their jurisdiction. I went to the FBI, and they said it was part of the DEA's investigation, not theirs. I went to several more agencies as well, and nobody would touch it. That's the way they kill a case. Once I got Noriega, they couldn't stop it, but they weren't about to let me start something else."

Dick Gregorie's last significant act on behalf of *United States v. Manuel Antonio Noriega* was on October 17, 1988, when the lame duck First Assistant and his case agent traveled to the Federal Correctional Institution at Sandstone, Minnesota, to stand up on behalf of Floyd Carlton. Floyd had finally gone before a judge in the Miami courthouse annex the previous June for sentencing on his guilty plea to one count of cocaine smuggling, carrying a maximum penalty of twenty years, and been given a nine-year sentence, with credit for time already served, both in the United States and Costa Rica. The federal marshals had then shipped him off to Sandstone, where Witness Protection maintained its own high-security cell block. His time served made Floyd immediately eligible for parole, and Dick Gregorie and Steve Grilli came to Minnesota for Floyd's first hearing before the parole board.

Up there, of course, it was already freezing, and both Dick and Steve were shivering when they saw Floyd before the hearing began. They made the mistake of asking the snitch how he was and got a half-hour whine about how cold Floyd felt all the time and how he didn't have the right jacket for this temperature and how the food wasn't right for a place so cold and how the TV was fucked up and how they should never send a

Panamanian like himself to this kind of goddamn deep-freeze place. Floyd, it seemed, hadn't changed.

The hearing was held inside a very small penitentiary office, in front of three traveling parole judges. Gregorie and Grilli testified separately, with Dick bearing most of the load. He told the parole judges about the bargain he had made with Floyd Carlton and how Floyd had lived up to his end in exemplary fashion. He said that without Floyd's testimony to the grand jury, the Southern District of Florida would never have made its case and never have secured the indictment. Floyd had done everything he had been asked to and, Gregorie argued, earned his right to join Witness Protection out on the streets instead of inside the penal system.

Floyd was paroled shortly thereafter and returned to Florida, where he assumed a new identity under the authority of the federal government.

Dick Gregorie's own official connection to *United States v. Manuel Antonio Noriega* would end in January 1989, when he left prosecuting for private practice. After his departure, his files on the General were processed by a paralegal who, under orders from the new United States attorney, cleaned out Gregorie's old office. The collected papers on the Noriega case were then broken up and dispersed throughout the office's filing system, spread so far from each other that, within a month of Dick Gregorie's departure, no one in the office had the first idea of where they'd all gone.

On December 16, 1988, the DEA's Miami Divisional Office held its annual Christmas party in the large DEA training classroom across from their main office building in the Kroger Executive Center, recognizable by the forest of antennae on its roof. Outside, as the sun faded from glare to pink glow, the palm trees caught just a touch of warm breeze, barely enough to rattle their fronds, and everyone, as always, was in short sleeves, with some in Bermuda shorts as well. Special dispensation for the occasion allowed a bar to be set up for the Yuletide revelers, along with tables of food.

One of those present was the station's new special agent in charge, just transferred down from Washington, where he'd been among the beef boys around the table consulting with the administrator when Steve Grilli had last been there. The new SAC had been drinking for a while before he and Grilli got by themselves at the party for a brief chat, all initiated by the new SAC.

The SAC said he realized that Grilli had done a good job with the General's case, though it didn't mean a whole lot since the General was still "locked inside Panama" and unreachable. He said that he'd read something in the recent *Newsweek* to the effect that Ronald Reagan was considering pardoning Noriega just so that the new president, George Bush, wouldn't have to deal with the mess. In any case, they both knew the case was, for all intents and purposes, dead in the water. The Noriega task force had been disbanded and Steve was now back in the regular chain of command.

The SAC then complimented Grilli on his recent promotion to GS-13, senior special agent. In fact, the SAC told Grilli, he'd had to rule on the promotion himself before transferring to the Miami station and had decided to go with it. Grilli was a person with a job to do, he said, and Grilli had done it.

Still, the SAC warned, "You've got a lot of enemies in Washington." He suggested that Steve try to make "small cases for a change."

While the warning was hardly news, hearing it again from the SAC only added to Grilli's sense of depression at his prospects. Though he remained the official case agent for *United States v. Manuel Antonio Noriega,* by now Steve just wanted to get as far from it as he could for a while. Enough was enough.

And this attitude was apparent in his new perspective on the indictment's practical viability. Previously, Grilli had completely rejected the criticism that his investigation and the true bill it had generated were essentially pointless abstractions — little more than "pretend law enforcement"— because the General himself would never stand trial on the charges, a universal argument among the case's DEA detractors. That Christmas, however, even Steve despaired of the General's ever being brought to justice.

"So what are they gonna do?" Grilli joked. "Send the fuckin' army in to arrest him?"

CHAPTER 6

THE GENERAL'S HARBINGER

— 1 —

Sending in the army was, of course, precisely what "they" were going to do, though it was still anything but apparent.

Indeed, General Manuel Antonio Noriega likely figured he was sitting pretty in January 1989. Over the preceding year, he had survived the onslaught of Elliott Abrams and the State Department, endured the unprecedented strangling of the Panamanian economy, weathered an attempted coup, bested a succession of street demonstrations, nullified a government in exile, absorbed the betrayal of both his former chief political adviser and his former Chiriqui drinking buddy, and, of course, seemingly outlasted his own criminal indictment. It was hardly surprising the General thought he had the gringos' number.

So much so, in fact, that, as 1989 began, the General even took the opportunity to gloat a bit. On January 20, when George Bush was being inaugurated president of the United States in Washington, the PDF's political party staged a rally in downtown Panama City to "celebrate" the end of the Reagan years under banners boasting, "Reagan Is Leaving and Noriega Is Staying." The General himself even made a cameo appearance in front of several thousand supporters to thumb his nose good-bye to those in the North who had been after his scalp.

Three hundred and thirty-eight days later, when he sat manacled in the belly of an American C-130 transport plane droning through the moonlight over the Caribbean on a heading for the Southern District of Florida, DEA agents on either side, such provocative behavior seemed to have been extraordinarily foolhardy.

But, at the time he engaged in it, needless to say, the General hadn't a clue what was coming.

Viewed in hindsight, that ignorance illustrated just how poorly Manuel Antonio Noriega understood the gringos after all. In January 1989, the *comandante* of the doomed Panama Defense Force was in the grip of three significant miscalculations:

The first was the General's underestimation of just how badly Elliott Abrams had wounded him with his failed final offensive the previous spring. Even in defeat, Abrams had shaken what remained of Noriega's protection, serving notice around Washington that there might very well be a heavy political price to pay for insisting that the General stay put. And, once that precedent set in with those who had heretofore barred the door to military intervention, the political expenditure required to resist sending a posse after the General was enough to legitimize the prospect as soon as the president to whom it had been an anathema had passed from office, and the new one, to whom it was not, assumed the apex of the chain of command. Abrams had made the General into an ongoing American embarrassment, a kiss of death if there ever was one, though, again, no one quite recognized its import that January.

The General himself apparently expected that the end of Abrams's tenure at the State Department might well deflate such military adventurism, but, if anything, Abrams's departure only seems to have made the General easier to pursue. Before the new Bush administration even addressed making a policy toward Panama, the chairman of the Joint Chiefs — who had defeated Abrams's plans to arrest the General and now less than eight months from scheduled retirement himself still considered military intervention a piss-poor option in Panama — made it clear behind the scenes that he was making no such ferocious stand against Noriega's arrest this time around. In fact, the chairman told Fred Woerner in February that, while no one in the White House had yet said anything about it, and despite his own reservations, he had a feeling they were now on "a slippery slope." He urged Woerner to start very quietly preparing for a fight.

General Manuel Antonio Noriega's second serious miscalculation was his failure to appreciate the extent to which, as far as the gringos were concerned, he had become his own worst enemy.

A specialist at intimidation, the General had always encouraged his legend for evil among the citizenry of the Isthmus, figuring that legend alone would do the work of a PDF division in making his rule function. Unfortunately for the General, the reverse dynamic proved true as well. In that sense, the General amounted to a tragic figure, felled by the very force that had raised him in the first place. While he had made a legend for himself in the United States, becoming the very symbol of equatorial evil, that elevation also made him an obligatory target for anyone with a symbolic point to make — especially, it would turn out, George Bush. Cop dramas on American television were now featuring characters modeled on the fugitive Panamanian strongman, complete right down to the true bill. Expecting to intimidate, the General had instead made himself into a tempting figure after whom to dispatch armed men with handcuffs.

The third of the General's glaring miscalculations was, of course, his underestimation of George Herbert Walker Bush. Having finally won election on his own for the first time since carrying a Texas congressional district in 1968, George Bush still had a lot left to prove, president or not, and the arrest of the General offered just the proof Bush needed. As always, the new president's lightweight upper-crust style, full of boat shoes and polo shirts, made him an easy figure to dismiss, and he had hardly been in office a month before one national columnist characterized his as an "unserious Presidency," not unlike some modern-day Coolidge. Over his administration's first hundred days, that sense of weakness and ineptitude inflated into the renowned "Wimp Factor" that drew attention whenever the new president was discussed and his political standing analyzed.

And, when it eventually came time to redress that wimpy image and prove he had a real president's hair on his chest, George Bush could ill afford to cut the General any slack at all, and would not.

Beyond these three miscalculations, General Manuel Antonio Noriega's blindness to his onrushing fate was also evidence of just how little grasp he had of the operative Washington mojo that would decide the outcome of his story.

In this gringo political voodoo, in order to abandon a policy of military inaction, it was first necessary to personify the rejected policy and then dispose of that person in a ritualized cleansing — a sort of bureaucratic human sacrifice. So, had the General known whom to watch, it might have become apparent far earlier than it did just what was in store for him.

Again, hindsight would provide the answer the General couldn't find at the time. The revelatory pattern would turn out to be a common one.

"Usually," Marc Cisneros, Fred Woerner's two-star deputy at SOUTHCOM pointed out, "they find a uniform when it comes time to name somebody to blame."

In this case, the uniform in question belonged to Fred Woerner, CinC of the Southern Command. Having carried out his orders to avoid provocation and thus saddled with his "WIMPCOM" reputation, Woerner was easy to scapegoat. He was also the last remaining foot-dragger over possible military action, so getting rid of him would rid the chain of command of its remaining policy reservations as well. Thus four-star Fred Woerner, the United States Army's foremost Latin Americanist, would act as the harbinger of General Manuel Antonio Noriega's fate through the spring and summer, before finally exiting this story for good, stage left, in a state of semidisgrace.

And, at that point, the General's end would be imminent.

— 2 —

Like the General, Fred Woerner was also his own worst enemy. In Fred's case, however, this self-destructiveness took the far more pedestrian form of his penchant for inadvertently stepping on important toes.

And in late February 1989, Woerner stepped on those of his commander in chief, the most important toes of all.

The incident was set off by a speech Woerner delivered to the American Chambers of Commerce at their annual gathering of Latin American chapters in Panama, convened at one of SOUTHCOM's officers' clubs. When he first received the invitation, Woerner was drawn to the rare opportunity to speak to an audience of senior American businessmen from throughout the hemisphere. It seemed a perfect opportunity to articulate his vision of the American presence in the region. On the other hand, he was also worried that he would not be able to escape being questioned on the General's status and drawn into a discussion on American Panamanian policy.

He was eager to avoid such a discussion because, as yet, the Bush administration had no Panama policy. Indeed, the new president hadn't even appointed an assistant secretary of state for inter-American affairs to oversee the policy process. Such tardiness was a general state of affairs throughout the new administration, exactly the kind of behavior that drew the description "unserious." In the meantime, SOUTHCOM was sitting on hold while Panamanian events continued to compound themselves.

Woerner hated to refuse to answer any question when he gave a speech, but answering any inquiries about the General and the United States' approach to him would run the obvious risk of speaking out of turn with the chain of command over Fred's head. When Woerner shared his worry with his public affairs officer, the officer encouraged his boss to accept the invitation to speak, just specify that all his remarks were off the record. Woerner did so and made sure his public affairs officer also taped the entire proceeding so he could establish just what he had said, should his speech kick up any dust.

Having made all those preparations, Fred Woerner managed to stick his foot in his mouth nonetheless. And on exactly the subject he had worried about.

The first question, once the SOUTHCOM commander's formal remarks were over, concerned Panama. The questioner said that American businessmen in Panama were hurting because of sanctions that still remained in force from the previous spring. Now that there was a new administration in Washington, could they expect a new policy?

Fred Woerner tried to measure his words but, he would later admit, "in hindsight, it was dumb" to say what he did.

Woerner explained to the assembled businessmen that, at this point, "we have a vacuum in Washington" when it came to Panama policy.

As soon as the word "vacuum" was out of his mouth, Woerner realized he had better explain what he meant, so he went on to elaborate on how, in the complex process of making a policy, "you have to have a person or office carrying the policy through from concept to development, and as long as the position of the assistant secretary [for inter-American affairs] is vacant, there is no policy person there to take it to fulfillment."

Along the way, Woerner also, unfortunately, chose to elaborate on the consequences of the vacuum on the Isthmus by describing the United States as "ill prepared" for the Panamanian elections scheduled to be held on May 7, 1989, not even three months away. "We ought to know what we plan to do in the event of a reasonably honest election, a grossly dishonest election, a postponed election, or any other possible option," Woerner warned. That the United States had not done any of those things went unsaid, but not unheard.

None of that might have mattered had Fred Woerner's audience of American businessmen honored their pledge that his remarks would remain "off the record." Instead, however, someone secretly taped the speech and then gave the tape to the *New York Times.* And, when the *Times* ran a story featuring Woerner's criticism of the administration's "vacuum," all hell broke loose.

George Bush learned of his SOUTHCOM commander's quoted remarks while on the first state visit of his term, to the Far East, undertaken less than two months into his presidency and already being criticized as premature, since the new administration was not even yet completely staffed. On hearing of Woerner's statement, the traveling White House fired off a furious cable to the chairman of the Joint Chiefs. The chairman then called Woerner and began yelling into the phone.

"What the hell did you say?" the chairman demanded.

Woerner explained that he had it all on tape.

"Jesus, man," the chairman ordered, "send the tape up here as quick as you can. The president is ricocheting off the walls."

Woerner did as he was told, but it did not seem to ameliorate the situation much. Perhaps two weeks later, the SOUTHCOM commander was in Washington for a consultation with the chairman and the new national security adviser on the subjects of Argentina and Chile. When that was done, the two military officers rose to leave, the chairman first and then Woerner after him, but the national security adviser stopped Woerner while the chairman, unaware, went ahead.

Fred Woerner later remembered what transpired next as "the beginning of the end of the career I loved passionately."

"Fred," the national security adviser informed him, "you should understand that the president was infuriated with your speech."

Woerner had previously assumed he was off the hook since he'd heard nothing about the dustup since sending the chairman his tape. Woerner could do little in the moment but sputter in response that he had sent the recording and it proved that he'd said "nothing wrong."

The adviser allowed that what Fred had said was "the truth," but, nonetheless, "you should have never said it."

And with that, he saw Woerner out the door.

In the face of this ongoing policy vacuum, Fred Woerner maintained the passive position SOUTHCOM had assumed since all the troubles with the General had begun.

Such a stance remained difficult. Woerner's command had been barraged by more than a thousand separate incidents of "harassment" by its Panamanian hosts over the previous twelve months, the most serious of which — besides the marine at the tank farm gut-shot by friendly fire — involved the PDF's detention of nine school buses full of American military dependents for some three hours on charges of improper vehicle registration papers. It was all part of the General's campaign of "psychological war" to which Fred Woerner had never been allowed to do anything in response. His troops had come to jokingly describe the approach as "Kiss Ass and Take Names Later," the motto of "WIMPCOM."

At this point, the only formal contact remaining between SOUTHCOM and its PDF antagonists was a monthly meeting of a group of PDF colonels with Woerner's second in command, two-star General Marc Cisneros. The regular encounter was a format originally designed to communicate any complaints or comments about the operation of the Canal. Cisneros, a Texas Mexican by birth, raised on the legendary King Ranch in Premont, Texas, where his father was a foreman, was now the highest-ranking Hispanic in the United States Army and was not of a mind to put up with much of the bullshit the Panamanians were used to running on Anglos.

"By early 1989," Cisneros remembered, "these meetings had become very hostile. I spoke these colonels' language and that kind of gave me a ticket to call them on all their bluster and I did. Finally, relations had deteriorated so much the meetings just stopped."

What remained for SOUTHCOM to do as far as General Manuel Antonio Noriega was concerned that spring was mostly military planning. In all the Department of Defense's game plans for deploying SOUTHCOM in the Isthmus, they had never developed any plan for subduing the PDF and seizing its *comandante* until after the Miami grand jury handed down its indictment.

The strategy which Fred Woerner and Marc Cisneros then came up with was given the randomly selected code name Blue Spoon. Operation Blue Spoon called for a series of ritualized reinforcements of SOUTHCOM from the United States, all brandished for the PDF to see, each with accompanying demands for the General's surrender and deadlines that would trigger a further engorgement of SOUTHCOM until there was a full 20,000-man force in the Canal Zone, poised to strike. If the final surrender deadline was missed, the force would attack the PDF and seize the Isthmus, though Woerner, for one, thought they would never have to use this final strike. Just in case, Blue Spoon included various scenarios assuming that the General's forces seized hostages from among the resident American citizens in and around Panama City and others assuming the PDF retired into the jungle to fight a guerrilla war.

In addition to refining Blue Spoon that spring, Woerner continued to attempt to convince the chain of command to approve giving the General a dose of his own psychological warfare. The plans CinC SOUTHCOM eventually proposed were code-named Fissures 1 and Fissures 2.

"The object," Woerner explained, "was to create fissures. To strengthen the opposition to Noriega we had to separate Noriega from the solidified power base of the PDF, therefore we ought to do things to weaken his institutional base. So we developed a strategy with thirty-two different things we could do that included a lot of psychological stuff, like contact with the wives and families of PDF members and undercutting the businesses that the PDF officers were all involved in. I wrote a message in the plan's final paragraph: 'You must understand that this is a strategy in its collectiveness [sic], not a menu that you can select items from. This doesn't mean that you have to approve all thirty-two but it does suggest that if you remove one you ought to substitute for it because it is the mass of activities that will have the impact, not any individual one.' So, the only message I ever got back about my proposal was an order to execute number seven, one out of the whole damn package of thirty-two."

The number seven in question involved cutting off the electric power to a house inside one of the Canal Zone forts already in possession of the PDF that was used as a place of assignation by high-ranking officers and their mistresses.

Woerner protested to Washington that if they just did this one thing, with nothing else to restrain the PDF, the Panamanians might very well respond by cutting the power grid to SOUTHCOM's entire operation at the Caribbean end of the Canal, whose transmission lines flowed across Panamanian territory.

Washington repeated the order to do number seven and only number seven.

Fred Woerner did as commanded and, sure enough, shortly after the Americans disrupted the PDF officers' trysting spot that spring, the Panamanians cut off electricity to all of SOUTHCOM's easternmost operations. At that point, Washington ordered Woerner to turn the power back on and the PDF then responded in kind.

Unfortunately for Fred Woerner, embarrassment continued to be the Americans' order of the day.

The pace surrounding the issue of the General quickened inside the Bush administration the closer May 7 came. Those scheduled Panamanian elections — originally envisioned by the General's late patron, Omar Torrijos, as the moment when the PDF would finally step away from political control — provided the starting point for George Bush's policy toward the General and though as yet unwilling to pursue a more complete strategy or commit itself to the General's arrest, the new administration was anxious to make sure the right people won at the polls in May. In late February, $10 million was allocated to the CIA to be used in support of the opposition candidates in Panama, and in early April, a CIA operative was arrested by the PDF in Panama City preparing to establish a pirate radio station to broadcast against the PDF's candidate for president and, needless to say, the *comandante* himself.

Otherwise, Bush's administration still seemed in disarray as May began. "The United States and Panama are on a collision course," the *Christian Science Monitor* observed,

> and the time has come for top Bush Administration officials to forge a cohesive policy. . . . Forging [such] a consensus . . . will require firm leadership. . . . The battle lines are by now well defined: The Defense Department has favored diplomacy. The State Department has favored military pressure. The Drug Enforcement Administration has favored conciliation. . . . One way to punish Noriega, a joke [in Washington] goes, would be to make him sit in on an interagency meeting on how to deal with Panama. . . . [As a result,] long-term

> strategy . . . remains a question mark, [leaving] Gen. Manuel Antonio Noriega as entrenched as ever [and] President Bush continues on that course. [However,] as one US official put it, there are "time bombs" in the road ahead. . . . State Department officials say they are considering a range of options and that they need to see how events on [May 7] play out before they can get more specific.

The elections of May 7, 1989, were, of course, pivotal for the General as well. This was the plebiscite in which the General used to tell his late *compadre* César Rodríguez that he intended to be elected president himself, thus crowning his rise to power with legitimacy. Those plans, however, had certainly evaporated by the time 1989 began. Under the provisions of the Panamanian Constitution, the General would have had to resign his position as *comandante* by that January in order to be eligible to run for president, and the General did not. Part of the reason was captured by a poll, taken by an Italian polling firm in December 1988, among the Isthmus's voters. In it, 71 percent expressed "dislike" for the General, 5 percent said they "liked" him, and 81 percent wanted the General to resign and get out of Panama's government.

Instead of risking the kind of political humiliation indicated in such samplings, the General decided instead to repeat what he had done in 1984 and push through a candidate from the PDF's political party who would act as the General's front man. PDF officers were instructed to issue multiple voter identification cards to their supporters and install other rigging devices expected to be able to counteract an actual vote of even 67 percent in favor of the opposition.

Unfortunately for the PDF, however, this was not 1984 when a little bit of jiggering could secure an election. The actual legitimate vote on May 7 ran three to one against the PDF's candidate, and after the polls closed, the PDF had to dispatch its paramilitary forces to seize ballots before they could all be counted, an approach the General later described to his ghostwriter as "canceling the election" at the last minute. His stated reason for the "cancellation" was that American meddling had made an honest count impossible.

The most visible American role in Panama on May 7 was played by a delegation of observers featuring more than a dozen congressmen and senators, dispatched to the Isthmus by the Bush administration. Their assigned task was to assess the fairness of the vote and then report back to the president on their conclusions.

When the observers' Department of Defense transport first landed in the Canal Zone, having flown straight there from Washington, Fred Woerner and the American ambassador were on the tarmac waiting to greet them. The sun had turned the runway into a griddle, and both men felt like they were being cooked alive. And, once again, Fred Woerner's proclivity for stepping on toes was about to show itself in spades.

The atmosphere was already testy before the delegation even touched down. Woerner and the ambassador didn't get along under the best of circumstances, and this was surely not those. As far as Woerner was concerned, in fact, there was something of a crisis. All Americans entering Panama, even if they came in through the Canal Zone, required a Panamanian visa, and the Panamanians had refused to issue any in advance for this delegation. In addition, the government newspapers had been describing these incoming Americans not as observers, but as "invaders." That morning, Woerner had received an intelligence report with a "very high rating as to both reliability and source," straight from an informant in the PDF's G-2, to the effect that President Bush's observers were going to be denied entry and then arrested as illegal immigrants if they entered anyway. While he and the ambassador waited out on the griddle, Woerner insisted that the ambassador warn the delegation.

The ambassador, full of the State Department's desire to pick a fight and let the chips fall where they might, berated Woerner, characterizing his and Defense's attitude as "wrong all the way through." There "is no [legitimate] government of Panama," he informed the SOUTHCOM CinC, and nobody was going to turn this delegation away.

Woerner, still under strict orders to avoid any confrontation and maintain scrupulous conformity with the treaty provisions concerning the use and movement of American troops inside the Isthmus, pointed out that there might not be any legitimate government, but the PDF was obviously running things.

"Fine," the ambassador snapped, "but we don't recognize them. We don't have anything to do with them." And, in any case, there was "no way" the General was going to keep these American dignitaries from observing the election. Though, he allowed, he'd like to see Noriega try. If denied visas, the ambassador planned to send the delegation into Panama anyway, whether Noriega liked it or not. The belicose ambassador thought it was high time Woerner stopped letting this little tinhorn thug over at the PDF call the shots.

For his part, Woerner thought the ambassador was in the throes of a testosterone overdose and completely out of his head.

That the two were at odds with each other was obvious as they boarded the delegation's passenger jet, still dripping sweat from their wait out on the asphalt. The incoming observers were all seated when the SOUTHCOM commander and the ambassador addressed them, standing side by side in the airplane aisle, each obviously impatient with the other.

The ambassador greeted them officially, saying it was great to have the observers here, and stressing what an important moment this was for democracy in Panama.

Then he handed the floor over to Fred Woerner, who was incensed at what the ambassador had not said. "Not a word about the possibility of their arrest," Woerner would remember, "I bloody well couldn't believe it. I said to myself that this was fundamentally irresponsible and I wouldn't be part of it. So I told the delegation about the visa problem. I said, 'I would like to inform you that there is a possibility you could be arrested or harassed during this visit.'" Woerner also explained that, while he could not use his troops to intervene in that instance, such immigration problems weren't uncommon and there were procedures already in place for the quick release of Americans. "If it happens," he assured the president's observers, "we will immediately start the diplomatic process to get you freed."

Once again, Fred Woerner had stumbled over just the wrong thing to say to the wrong people at just the wrong time.

These presidential observers he was addressing were largely recruited from the ranks of the General's Washington opponents, many organized by the ubiquitous exile Gabriel Lewis during one of his continuing congressional lobbying campaigns. They were now on the ground in Noriega country, their blood up, and in no mood to be trifled with. Woerner, the chairman of the Joint Chiefs would later rue, "didn't realize what the hell was going on around him." The delegation fresh from Washington heard Woerner's welcoming speech as a statement that they were on their own and the Southern Command would offer them no help or safety.

That stance was particularly galling to the Republican senator from Arizona, a former naval officer himself, whom the chairman of the Joint Chiefs later described as "very vain and arrogant."

"General," the senator demanded, "are you telling me that you, as the American military commander, can't defend senators and congressmen of the government of the United States?"

"Senator," Woerner answered, "I have no authority to defend you by force of arms. What I am telling you is that whatever happens may be inconvenient, but it is not threatening. It happens all the time. We will get you out of jail if you end up there."

The senator from Arizona ended the exchange incredulous and infuriated at Woerner.

The issue of visa violations, however, turned out to be meaningless. One of Woerner's aides slipped a stiff bribe to a Panamanian immigration officer, while his boss and the ambassador were still speaking, and got the entire delegation's passports stamped with visa permits that conferred legality on their presence. But, in the meantime, Fred Woerner had, once again, made the worst possible first impression.

The SOUTHCOM commander last saw the senator from Arizona when the observers returned to his base two days later, on their way back to Washington to report to George Bush. The senator had been circulating among the SOUTHCOM officer corps and heard all the bitching about "WIMPCOM" and the like, and it had pissed him off. Pugnacious to start with, the senator was additionally inflamed at how he personally thought the Southern Command was tiptoeing around the PDF. During election day, he'd been furious when he was relegated to the second of two helicopters hauling the delegation, which was then grounded for mechanical troubles, and, when he demanded a replacement chopper, it had been delayed while official notification about the flight of the new chopper was given the PDF, as required by the Canal Treaties. The senator spent the rest of May 7 steamed, convinced that Woerner had seen to it that he was separated from the delegation's lead party. And, when that attitude was fed by his outrage at all the PDF thuggery involved in "canceling the election," the senator from Arizona arrived back at SOUTHCOM on his way out of country, mad as a wet rooster.

When Fred Woerner spotted the senator, he approached, intent on "telling him thanks for the job the delegation had done," but, Woerner remembered, "it was a cold reception."

To say the least. The Republican senator from Arizona was worked up and, early in their conversation, demanded in a loud voice how long it would take Woerner to evacuate all the Americans in Panama, so they could go after this son-of-a-bitch.

Woerner asked whether the senator wanted the numbers for an emergency evacuation or a more deliberate approach that allowed the dependents under his jurisdiction to keep their household goods, their cats and dogs and the like. The senator chose the more deliberate version and Woerner answered that the time had already been worked out and, citing the figure the chairman of the Joint Chiefs had used to defeat Elliott Abrams the year before, estimated six months more or less.

"Six months?" the senator shouted at Woerner. "What the hell are you gonna do? Send them on a goddamn slow boat to China?"

The senator's temper was still at a fever pitch when the delegation's plane returned to the United States.

The next day, the Republican senator from Arizona was at the White House reporting to George Bush. The senator, like the other observers, described the "canceled" election as a "fraud" at best. He also told Bush that they ought to get Noriega out of there. The senator from Arizona did not suggest they send a force in to arrest the General, but he did offer that dropping *United States v. Manuel Antonio Noriega* would be worth it, if doing so would convince the General to leave.

He also had some advice for George Bush on the subject of SOUTHCOM.

"You must replace the man in charge down there," the senator told the president. "That man [Woerner] is no damn good."

— 3 —

Fred Woerner later learned that George Bush almost fired him after that conversation, but had been dissuaded by a presidential adviser who argued that the president couldn't very well relieve a General for doing what he had been ordered to do. And Woerner, the adviser pointed out, had been ordered to avoid trouble if at all possible, which is just what he'd done.

At that point, the aborted elections had returned the air of crisis to the issue of Panama, and the Bush administration was feeling the heat. "The [Panamanian] opposition's leaders . . . are mostly afraid to call their supporters onto the streets," *The Economist* reported. "Such meetings as took place were small, in factories and supermarkets or outside churches. . . . In the military areas controlled by the Americans, troop movements and mock invasion exercises were in progress. They looked ferocious enough, but virtually nobody expects an American military move. . . . The General seems not to care. . . . Having gone so far and got away with it, he sees no reason to turn back. . . . When he reappeared [publicly after the elections] at a rally in Panama City, the sign above the stage said: 'With Noriega To The End.' "

Having decided not to fire Woerner that May, the White House discussions in the election's aftermath did, however, feature the first serious proposal ever presented to Bush that the United States simply invade and snatch the General. This option, opposed by both Woerner and the lame duck chairman of the Joint Chiefs, already had enough support that the chairman was able to back it down only by warning of the "body bags" that would start coming back home if such a move was made.

Both Woerner's reprieve and the invasion's were, of course, only temporary.

Fred Woerner certainly knew by that May there was no shortage of people looking to get him fired, even before the senator from Arizona added himself to the list. The CinC SOUTHCOM was now particularly disliked among Panama's dissident *rabiblancos,* for whom an American invasion was the preferred response. Speaking on the opposition's behalf, the papal nuncio in Panama City had even approached Woerner before the May elections and asked the United States to invade immediately. Woerner, however, remained dead set against such intervention.

"I was constantly signaling to Washington that I thought force was an inappropriate option," he later explained. "We were boxing ourselves in by absorbing full responsibility for the Noriega situation and absolving Panama of any responsibility, making it a U.S. crisis when it should be a Panamanian crisis, not ours. The use of military force would be a confirmation that the Bush administration was a clone of many historical administrations and not something new. I felt the *sine qua non* of our relations with Latin America had to be nonintervention — it was the one nonnegotiable issue south of our borders. So it made no sense for the U.S. government to build a policy around the arrest and removal of a de facto head of state. The precedent that set was not worth the cost involved. Instead of our solving the problem, it would only enhance Panama's dependence on us, exactly contrary to what we should be trying to accomplish. If we insisted the opposition solve the problem on their own, we would make the greatest contribution to Panamanian independence and sovereignty that we could. That would have been the right thing to do."

When the May discussions at the White House again made it clear that Woerner was not about to revise his position against military intervention, he remembered, "the *rabiblancos* not only turned away from me, they turned against me."

And none more so that Gabriel Lewis, the most important *rabiblanco* in Washington, D.C.

The fraternity with Fred Woerner that Gabriel had invoked when they lunched at Maison Blanche before Woerner flew south to assume the Southern Command was completely absent some two years later. On his regular monthly returns to Washington during the first six months of 1989, Fred Woerner had begun to pick up stories that were being spread about him around town. The worst of them alleged that the SOUTHCOM commander's wife was on the take and that his two grown sons were secretly in the hire of the PDF. And when Woerner traced the rumors, he claimed that most of them led to Gabriel Lewis, who now maintained his lobbying headquarters inside the Capitol at the offices of the senior senator from Massachusetts.

The CinC SOUTHCOM's last contact with Lewis was indirect and surprisingly tacky. Shortly after the canceled elections, while Gabriel was in Washington lobbying for Fred Woerner's dismissal, Gabriel's two sons visited Woerner down in the Canal Zone. They were seeking Woerner's assistance in helping one of the Lewis family businesses secure a contract with the Zone's commissary system and said their father had recommended they enlist the aid of his old friend Woerner.

Woerner, who knew full well what Gabriel had been up to back in Washington, was astonished at the Lewises' gall. "All that," Woerner remembered with some bitterness, "and he sends his sons to ask for business favors? I'd never known Gabriel to be quite that crass before. Maybe he just figured I was on the way out so he better get whatever he could before I left."

Fred Woerner refused the request and never heard from Gabriel Lewis again.

— 4 —

The only immediate change at SOUTHCOM in the aftermath of May 7 was a loosening of the rules of engagement under which Fred Woerner's Southern Command operated. This much was apparent in Washington's approval of an ongoing operation, code-named Sand Flea, devised and executed by Woerner's two-starred right-hand man, Marc Cisneros.

Cisneros, fifty, had designed Operation Sand Flea as a means of going on the offensive at last, conducting what the Joint Chiefs called "exercises that would enforce to the limit of the letter of the law American maneuver rights [inside Panama] under the Panama Canal treaties." Cisneros himself described Sand Flea as a way "to piss in Noriega's mess kit. It was provocative. We wanted to aggravate him, to be an irritant and cause the PDF to react so we could judge their reaction plan and also get moral ascendancy over them, showing them that we were willing to stand up. That was good for morale. It also provided a way for us to exercise our contingency plans. We started tightening up on our readiness and targeted reducing our response time for a general mobilization from six to eight hours down to two. It was training, but it was meant to aggravate him into a fight sooner or later and make it look like his fault."

This "training" spanned the summer of 1989, featuring maneuvers by combat-ready American troops near PDF bases, a convoy of American tanks suddenly rumbling along the street in downtown Panama City where the municipal courts were located, A-37 "tank killer" attack jets assuming holding patterns over PDF installations, and even the simulated defense of the American embassy, when a sudden armada of choppers crossed Panama City, hovered over the embassy, and disgorged commandos who slid down ropes, wearing face-black and carrying live ammo, and assumed a defensive perimeter.

The PDF often responded to American troop movement with its own units, usually armed civilians from the irregular Dignity Battalions with a few uniformed regulars, bent on maintaining tension and making propaganda points. In one case, such a group stopped an American convoy; in another, they tried to block access to one of SOUTHCOM's forts. The result, one officer commanding American troops in the operation recalled, was "young soldiers, locked and loaded, facing PDF, also locked and loaded, where any one person on either side could . . . do something wrong and start a fight. We did a lot of those intimidation games."

The most notorious of the Sand Flea incidents was directed by Marc Cisneros in person, hovering over the scene in a helicopter. The exercise began with a column of SOUTHCOM infantry and light armored vehicles maneuvering among the roads on the edge of the Zone, where the surrounding landscape was mostly jungle. Cisneros knew that the PDF had groups of irregulars and political workers shadowing significant American movements in hopes of catching the gringos in a violation of Panamanian territory and creating an incident. So, Cisneros later explained, he decided "to lure them in." He began by dispatching two light armored vehicles down the road to a small Panamanian town on the west side of the Canal. Their purpose, according to the statement later issued by Woerner's headquarters, was a reconnaissance to "check [the] condition of roads and confirm [the rest of the American column] could move along certain routes." Their real purpose was to attract the PDF pursuit crew that Cisneros knew was in town. His light armored vehicles were under orders to avoid capture but to stay close enough that the Panamanians would give chase.

Sure enough, a makeshift posse of police cars and PDF trucks took off after the Americans, who led them up a jungle side road until the pursuers had unknowingly crossed into a portion of the Zone restricted to American use only. At that point, Cisneros had a company of marines waiting in ambush. The marines then surrounded and captured a total of twenty-nine Panamanians — ten in uniform, all of them armed with everything from AK-47s to Saturday night specials — and held them for having violated American territory. No shots were fired. The Panamanians were led by a PDF major who was also General Manuel Antonio Noriega's brother-in-law. The other twenty-eight captives were lined up on their knees in the road under guard, but Cisneros, who had landed to inspect the scene, allowed the General's brother-in-law, the major, to sit in one of the marines' humvees.

The SOUTHCOM motorized column held the Panamanians for the better part of two hours until Cisneros received orders from the American embassy that he was to release the Panamanians and return their weapons. Cisneros told the embassy he would release the prisoners but he was not about to return their weapons without a direct order from the Department of Defense. So the Panamanians left unarmed, led by Major Brother-in-Law.

As he departed, the major got in Cisneros's face and told him just what a rotten son-of-a-bitch he was, calling him the gringos' hired Mexican, and several more kind of sons-of-bitches after that as well.

Cisneros just listened.

Some six months later, Marc Cisneros, "the gringos' hired Mexican," would see Major Brother-in-Law again. By then, Cisneros's reinforced 193rd Brigade had smashed its way into Panama City to the *comandancia,* effectively beheading the PDF, though missing the General himself by hours. Cisneros came across Major Brother-in-Law during a subsequent inspection of a "detention facility" for high-ranking Panamanians. The jail had once housed American enlisted men and was air-conditioned, clean, and relatively spacious. Cisneros's inspection consisted of having every one of the Panamanians brought out of his cell for him to see, to ensure that the terms of the Geneva Conventions for prisoners of war were being met. Major Brother-in-Law cringed when Cisneros approached him.

The Tex-Mexican general reminded the major in hardnosed border Spanish what kind of a son-of-a-bitch the major had called him the last time they met.

The major cringed again, expecting, at the very least, to be slapped around.

But Cisneros told him Americans didn't do things that way. Instead, Cisneros ordered Major Brother-in-Law transferred out of the air-conditioned jail and into a regular prisoner of war camp, outside in the reeking heat and bugs, where prisoners lived in tents surrounded by mud, military police, and barbed wire, and serviced by overworked field latrines.

Needless to say, Marc Cisneros got the last words between him and the General's brother-in-law. For the record, those six final words were "The gringos' hired Mexican, my ass."

One of the unanticipated side effects of Operation Sand Flea was that Marc Cisneros became something of a celebrity among the people of the Isthmus that spring and summer — thanks in no small part to the General's psychological warfare campaign. In response to the Americans' new bellicose "exercises," the collected media owned or controlled by the PDF singled Cisneros out for vilification, featuring him regularly in articles as a traitor to his heritage, the tool of North American imperialism, and as Panama's public enemy number one. A regular public demonstration by the PDF's backers involved burning a coffin labeled "Cisneros," photographs of which were on a number of Panamanian front pages the next day.

The nickname the PDF tabloids gave the Tex Mex was *El Pocho Maldito.* A *pocho* was the Panamanian slang for an American Mexican, and *El Pocho Maldito* means "the bad one" of those. *Pocho,* even by itself, "is not," Cisneros explained, "an endearing term," an expression similar to a number of those with which Major Brother-in-Law addressed Cisneros after his capture by Sand Flea. Cisneros was also featured as *El Pocho Maldito* for a while on a Republic of Panama billboard in downtown Panama City, along with some slogans for defending the Republic.

His immediate superior, Fred Woerner, viewed Cisneros's visibility as an asset and thrust his number two forward as SOUTHCOM's local spokesman, ordering him to give interviews to the Spanish-language press and to use those interviews to try to intimidate the General whenever possible — all, of course, with Defense Department approval. Woerner felt lucky to have Marc Cisneros. He was "a very good soldier" who was "tough," "thorough," and "scrupulous."

All the commanders Marc had served under felt pretty much the same way, which is how he had risen to be the highest-ranked Hispanic in the history of the United States Army. He had started as the captain of the Reserve Officer Training Corps at St. Mary's University in San Antonio, Texas, then accepted a regular army lieutenant's commission after graduation. Twenty-five years later, as a full colonel on the verge of being given his first star, he had been transferred from Alaska to SOUTHCOM at the request of Fred Woerner's predecessor, had stayed on under Woerner, and was soon given command of the 193rd Brigade, Woerner's old unit.

While Marc Cisneros would have seemed on paper to be a natural fit at SOUTHCOM, Cisneros himself ended up ambivalent at best about the posting that earned him two stars. Eventually, he even recommended to younger Hispanic officers that they avoid assignment to the Isthmus if at all possible.

"You end up in the middle," he explained. "To start with, relations with the Panamanians were never very good. They gave you a lot of anti-American shit all the time, like you're supposed to be on their side. That made for a lot of ugly arguments. There was no love lost between us. And when a situation like Panama starts developing, you get a lot of know-nothings on your own side who make the whole thing racial and treat you like you're one of the natives. You can't win. I felt like I was in the middle of the road taking arrows from both sides."

Still, Marc Cisneros played his assigned role to the hilt. And, as a consequence, he was also singled out that summer for an attempt at heavier intimidation than just being called *El Pocho Maldito* in the newspapers. The attempt, however, didn't last long.

It began one afternoon when Cisneros's wife drove to St. Mary's Church in Panama City to hear mass and the Panamanian police blockaded her car after she went inside, then waited for her to come out. When she saw what had happened, she tried to call her husband, but couldn't get through, so she just abandoned her car and went out of St. Mary's the back way with the parish priest, who drove her to SOUTHCOM in his own car.

Cisneros was enormously pissed off when he learned what had happened and told his wife to return to St. Mary's the next day. This time, however, she was accompanied by a squad of armed soldiers in civilian clothes, and SOUTHCOM also duly notified the PDF, as required under the Canal Treaties, that the Southern Command had mobilized an infantry company, its choppers already revved up to allow an immediate response in the vicinity of St. Mary's Church. He also notified the PDF that, should another incident like the one his wife endured happen, SOUTHCOM would treat the blockaders "as terrorists."

The message apparently got through. Marc Cisneros soon received intelligence that the pressure on his wife had been the plan of some minion, and that orders had come down from the General himself to lay off.

Henceforth, there was simply tension around Cisneros's presence whenever he crossed Panamanian turf, but nothing more. On his way to work every morning, he passed several PDF checkpoints, manned by Dignity Battalions, and every day, they pointed their weapons in his direction as he went by. They all knew who Cisneros was, so much so that he eventually secured the surrender of three-quarters of the Panama Defense Force by doing little more than calling up and identifying himself as *El Pocho Maldito* over the phone.

As June turned to July, Marc Cisneros also became the first authority along George Bush's chain of command to declare publicly that the United States was on the verge of getting a posse together to arrest the General. At the time, Fred Woerner was in Washington and Cisneros was running the shop at SOUTHCOM. Cisneros's statement was made in an interview with a Spanish-language press syndicate. He had already been widely quoted in the Latin American media calling General Manuel Antonio Noriega "a tinhorn dictator" and warning the PDF that their General "had been fooling them" and they "would be in trouble" if they didn't get smart. He had also described the General as "a coward who's afraid to fight."

This time, Marc Cisneros said that he had come to the "personal" conclusion that "the United States should impose a military solution that would give [Panama] an opportunity to have a government that isn't criminal."

Those words almost cost Cisneros his job.

When the quote was translated into English and reached the new secretary of defense, the secretary "went ballistic." No two-star general on the new secretary's watch was going to be making American foreign policy in the press, he declared, and wanted to relieve Cisneros of his command.

Fred Woerner was conferring at the department at the time and did his best to intervene on Cisneros's behalf, though Woerner by then hardly had any juice left at all. Cisneros's own defense was simply that he was under orders to use these interviews to intimidate Noriega and he was doing just that. Woerner called Cisneros twice from Washington while Cisneros's job hung in the balance, to keep him abreast of how the struggle was going, and, both times, the report didn't sound good. In their second phone conversation, Woerner essentially said he thought Cisneros was going to be relieved of his command.

That Marc Cisneros was not, in fact, relieved was due to the intervention of the Department of State, which objected in the strongest terms to Defense firing the man State called "the only general we've got down there who is willing to fight." So Cisneros stayed at SOUTHCOM, career intact, and continued Sand Flea.

The real job at jeopardy that July belonged to Fred Woerner.

— 5 —

The decision to relieve Fred Woerner of the Southern Command was made during July 1989, while the lame duck chairman of the Joint Chiefs was on a mission to Russia. When the chairman returned, he was told by the White House that Woerner was being fired and there was nothing the chairman could do about it. The only decision left to make was who his replacement would be. In the meantime, of course, the change at SOUTHCOM was to be treated as a secret.

For his part, Fred Woerner was not expecting it. In fact, only two months earlier, the army had approached Woerner with a request that he stay at SOUTHCOM beyond what would have been his mandatory retirement upon reaching thirty-five years service some eight months hence. That July, Woerner had not yet given the army an answer to their request, though, he remembered, "they knew I would say yes. I was just taking time to work it out with my wife. I was delighted. The last thing I wanted to do was retire."

Fred Woerner learned he was about to do so anyway from one of his close friends, then the United States Army chief of staff, once the "secret" was revealed to the chief "in confidence" by his boss, the secretary of the army. The chief of staff ignored that confidentiality, ordered up a military executive jet, and called Woerner at SOUTHCOM. The chief told his friend Fred that he was flying down right away and instructed him to meet him at the airfield. The chief would be turning around and returning to Washington as soon as they'd talked.

Fred Woerner's gut sank.

"I knew in my heart I was about to be relieved," he remembered, " but I didn't want to believe it. Relieved is such an ugly word in my profession."

Nonetheless, it was exactly the word Fred used when he called his wife, Gennie, after the chief of staff hung up. He told her he was sure that he was about to be relieved of his command. The chief of staff didn't just hop down to Panama to shoot the breeze.

What happened next was the nadir of Fred Woerner's professional life.

It was broiling out on the tarmac, in the middle of an afternoon well over a hundred degrees, with the heat lifting off the spongy asphalt in waves so thick that the jungle beyond fractured into disconnected layers, as though being seen from under water. The chief strode down the jet's ramp onto the black floor of this blast furnace and asked his old friend if there was some place out of the sun, where they might talk. They then walked, expressing pleasantries to each other, until they reached an air-conditioned guest room maintained by the air force in a building nearby.

When they were alone inside, the chief got serious. "I have some bad news," he said. "The president has decided to replace you."

At that moment, Fred Woerner's body went suddenly numb. Nothing like that sensation had ever happened to him before, not even in combat. Stunned, he nonetheless felt overwhelmingly grateful that his old friend had used the word "replace" instead of "relieve."

The only verbal response Woerner could muster was to ask the question, "Why?"

The chief answered that he didn't know. He said he had just been told himself by the secretary of the army and that he was "here telling you something now that I am not authorized to tell you." The condition of learning the news was that Woerner could not reveal to anyone except Gennie what was happening. Fred would have to feign ignorance for several more days until the chain of command notified him officially. His old friend said he thought Fred deserved to know ahead of time, which is why the chief had come personally.

As the chief's plane taxied back along the tarmac, through the heat ripples that warped its form into a smudge of military-issue gray, Fred Woerner felt as close to absolute despair as he'd ever been.

Woerner had recovered some by the time the official word was delivered. That delivery took place in Washington, of course, where he was summoned, and, throughout it all, Woerner acted as though he'd had no idea ahead of time.

His first stop was at the office of the chairman of the Joint Chiefs. Then the chairman took Fred over to the new secretary of defense.

"Fred," the secretary explained, "the president has decided to make a change."

Thanks to his secret forewarning, Woerner had already figured out what he was going to say.

"Mr. Secretary," he asked, "are you telling me I'm being relieved of my command?"

The secretary hedged, calling it a "retirement" instead.

Then Woerner disagreed. There was no way this could be called anything but relief, whatever they wrote it up as for the department's books.

"I have never been relieved of command in my life," Woerner pointed out. "I have served my country faithfully to the point that I have been entrusted with four stars and the responsibility for the Southern Command. You owe me more of an explanation than that."

"It has nothing to do with you," the secretary responded. "It's a political decision."

Fred said that wasn't enough of an explanation either.

The secretary said that was too bad, since that was all the explanation Woerner was going to get.

The rest of the meeting was spent working out the terms of Fred Woerner's "retirement." After a little dickering, the secretary, the lame duck chairman, and the lame duck SOUTHCOM commander settled on September 30, 1989, for the official change of command that would terminate Woerner's tenure at four stars.

With the exit of Fred Woerner, George Bush and his administration now considered the decks cleared for action down in the Isthmus.

And had General Manuel Antonio Noriega only been as smart about the gringos as he thought he was, he might have started worrying as soon as the change was announced.

CHAPTER 7

THE COUP

— 1 —

The new four-starred CinC SOUTHCOM, Maxwell Thurman, would eventually lead an American posse after the General. Before that, however, Thurman would manage the first major embarrassment of George Bush's presidency, a political landmark of oversized proportions that put Panama back in the American headlines and propelled Bush into his final decision to deal with Noriega "once and for all."

Tall and thin, Thurman, fifty-eight, was no Latin Americanist, nor was he a legendary fighter. Rather, Max Thurman had risen through the ranks from his start as a lieutenant from the North Carolina State University ROTC by being the epitome of what army lifers describe as "a staff weenie." The new SOUTHCOM commander — a confirmed bachelor, married to the service — had shone as a bureaucrat, rising to the army's assistant chief of staff on his knack for making administrative machinery function smoothly. Thurman's intensity along the way had earned him the nicknames "Mad Max" and "the Maxatollah" for his office tirades, and he was known as both a star and an autocrat of the first order. Max Thurman's greatest success had been his tour as head of army recruiting at the advent of the volunteer army, when he conceived the advertising slogan "Be All That You Can Be" and was widely credited with no less than saving the army once the country abandoned military conscription and recruiting had become the army's lifeblood.

Max was on his way out of the service, planning to live with his bachelor brother, also a retired general, when he was suddenly tapped for SOUTHCOM that summer and agreed to extend past his absolute retirement age. Washington wanted him at Southern Command because

Thurman knew how Washington worked, and Thurman amounted to the antithesis of a wild card. It was thought Max Thurman could be counted on to make whatever the president decided upon in Panama function well.

And the likelihood that presidential decision would include military force was a given before Thurman even went south. In fact, the new CinC SOUTHCOM spent a portion of his briefing period before assuming command initiating revisions in Blue Spoon, the SOUTHCOM battle plan for arresting the General. The new commander's biggest change was in overall approach. Where Woerner's battle plan featured a series of public reinforcements intended to pressure Noriega to leave on his own, Thurman understood full well that, as far as Washington was concerned, the time for diplomacy and negotiations had passed. No one was now interested in changing Noriega's mind. In Thurman's revised plan, almost all the same forces were employed in much the same manner as Woerner had envisioned, but they were all to arrive on the field of battle at the same time, in one massive stroke, delivered with no warning at all. The object was now to break the PDF's back in one fell swoop.

The chairman of the Joint Chiefs, just two days away from his own retirement, had given his old friend Max his marching orders right before the new commander flew to the Isthmus to take the reigns of the Southern Command.

"Max," the chairman told him, "you're going down there to fight a war. I don't know exactly how and when, but we're marching up on it and it may happen right away. Your prime responsibility is to get that place ready to hit Noriega."

Which Thurman did, of course, but only after stumbling badly right out of the blocks.

— 2 —

Max Thurman officially assumed the Southern Command on September 30, 1989.

On October 1, the incident that would grow into George Bush's first significant presidential embarrassment began with a contact fielded by SOUTHCOM's military intelligence from the wife of a PDF major whose best friend worked as a secretary in the SOUTHCOM Intelligence

Office. The wife said her husband and other PDF officers were planning to depose the General and wanted to have a conversation with an American "decision maker" immediately.

Instead of such a "decision maker," SOUTHCOM dispatched an officer from its G-2 and a CIA agent, who met with the major that evening. The major said a coup was planned for the next day and that, while the plotters wanted to avoid public identification with the Americans and planned only to retire the General and allow him to go free once they had seized power, they needed SOUTHCOM to provide some key assistance.

All the requests the major had in mind fit easily in the scheme of Sand Flea exercises that the United States had been staging for more than three months now. The plotters wanted three key roads blocked, to keep outlying troops known to be loyal to the General from rescuing the *comandancia,* the same for the exit from the Panamanian portion of Fort Amador in the Zone, and the coup also needed the gringo planes to circle over the Tocumén airfield to prevent it from being used to send the General reinforcements.

The two Americans told the major that they couldn't promise anything, wished him luck, and then reported back to the new commander.

From almost the first moment, Max Thurman was convinced that the major's coup was a phony. He had been told to expect that the General would test him soon upon his arrival, and Thurman thought this was that test. The General must be trying to lure Thurman into committing American troops only to leave Thurman enormously embarrassed when no coup materialized, thus scoring an armload of propaganda points for the General and his Panamanians. To Thurman, the whole thing smelled of a trap. Thurman's Intelligence people were also leery of the major, who had been known as a Noriega partisan, a key figure in thwarting the coup attempted the year before. The General was godfather to one of the major's children and had served as the major's best man at his wedding. On top of that, Max Thurman figured, what kind of coup maker sends his wife to her best friend who's a secretary when they want to make secret contact?

When Thurman reported the Intelligence agents' encounter with the PDF major in a 2:00 A.M., October 2, phone call to the new chairman of the Joint Chiefs — who'd been in his new job for even less time than Thurman had in his — Max Thurman assessed the major's approach as a concealed move by the General to make the new CinC look bad on his first day at SOUTHCOM. His suspicions were only reinforced when the

PDF major sent word shortly thereafter that the coup had been put off one more day, to October 3.

As things turned out, of course, Max Thurman's assessment was about as wrong as it could have been.

When deconstructing Thurman's complete absence of understanding, using the leverage afforded by hindsight, perhaps the most obvious explanation for his failure was that, despite being in country barely seventy-two hours on his first ever posting in Panama, despite not knowing the native language except for what a month of Department of Defense cramming could provide, and despite working unfamiliarity with even the operations of SOUTHCOM, much less those of the PDF, Maxwell Thurman did not seek the assistance of those on hand who had a better grasp.

First among them, of course, was *El Pocho Maldito,* Marc Cisneros. Thurman didn't even inform Cisneros what was going on until after briefing the new chairman on October 2, and then only to notify rather than to consult.

Later, Marc Cisneros's explanation for why was relatively simple. "First, Thurman saw me as Woerner's guy," Cisneros pointed out, "and he wanted to use people he was familiar with. Second, Thurman wasn't like Woerner, who always wanted input. This guy kept his own counsel and had a big ego. Thirdly, Thurman didn't trust Hispanics. I recognized that much right away."

When finally asked by Thurman to assess whether the major's coup was real or not, Cisneros urged his new boss not to worry about the fact the meeting had been arranged by the major's wife through a secretary. This was Panama, things worked differently here. Cisneros then observed that as part of the arrangements requested during the major's meeting with Intelligence, the major said he would be sending his family into SOUTHCOM ahead of time for protection. Cisneros told Thurman to keep an eye on that promise. These guys were Latins and they wouldn't send their families into American hands on a ruse. If the major's wife and kids showed up in the morning, Thurman could count the coup as a real deal.

And, with the coup rescheduled a day to October 3, Cisneros argued that SOUTHCOM had a ready means for dealing with it. A week before the new commander's arrival, under authority granted Cisneros as part of

Operation Sand Flea, Cisneros had already scheduled an "exercise" for the morning of October 3 and had notified the PDF accordingly. It was planned as the largest Sand Flea operation yet, putting a significant piece of the command's forces in a state of readiness. Cisneros argued to his new commander that the Sand Flea exercise would rattle the PDF's cage even if the coup were a fake. And if it weren't a fake, his troops could respond instantly, seal off the areas the plotters had requested, and the PDF might very well do the Americans' work for them with only a small contribution from SOUTHCOM.

But Thurman wasn't buying it. On the contrary, this remarkable "coincidence" of Cisneros's planning with the major's coup scheduling made Max Thurman suspicious that Marc Cisneros was operating in league with the Panamanians behind his back, for reasons of some imagined inter-Hispanic loyalty, though Thurman didn't reveal that feeling until after the coup had played itself out.

In the immediate moment, Max Thurman concluded that conducting troop movements would be playing into the General's plan to embarrass him upon his arrival. He then ordered Cisneros not to conduct any exercises at all.

Cisneros would spend much of October 2 arguing with Thurman's chief of operations about the prohibition on Sand Flea for October 3. He finally won permission to deploy an infantry force to block off the PDF inside Fort Amador, only the force had to be dressed in their workout clothes and engage in calisthenics to disguise their purpose, with their battle uniforms and weapons concealed in their trucks. Cisneros also managed to deploy some troops on his own authority on October 3, assembling on the side of the road at one of the choke points the plotters had requested be blocked, but not actually blocking it. Together, those two deployments amounted to the only American mobilization in advance of the coup.

Back at the White House on October 2, a meeting convened with the president at 9:30 A.M. to discuss the coup that had been scheduled to happen at 8:30, but when word of the coup's reschedule for the following day arrived, the meeting was canceled. Later in the day, Max Thurman checked in with Washington from down at SOUTHCOM and reported that he was even more convinced than ever that the whole thing was a hoax. So much so that no new meeting with the president on the possibility had been scheduled, and the secretary of defense was out of Washington when the Panama alarms went off.

And, when the PDF major's wife and children showed up at the SOUTHCOM gates seeking sanctuary on the morning of October 3, some two hours before the coup was meant to begin, no one at SOUTHCOM was expecting them and the military police almost turned the family away.

The United States Southern Command did not go on alert until almost 9:00 A.M. on October 3, when direct visual evidence made it impossible to ignore how badly the new commander had misread the situation. The SOUTHCOM command bunker was dug into Quarry Heights, overlooking the nearby *comandancia,* and the commencement of the major's coup was confirmed when American officers outside the bunker, observing with the naked eye, reported that a small arms firefight was raging below, inside the square block of PDF headquarters barracks and offices built around a central courtyard.

For the duration of the subsequent alert, Maxwell Thurman stationed himself in the windowless underground command center, known as the Tunnel, receiving reports and communicating with Washington. Unfortunately, since the Intelligence agents who had met with the major on the evening of October 1 had made no arrangements for contacting him when his coup was under way, Thurman's command was helpless to learn anything more directly.

Within an hour, however, the Americans did pick up evidence of the plotters' first serious mistake. At a little after 8:30, when the coup attacked the building housing the General's suite of personal offices, where the General had arrived a little before 8:00, the plotters failed to cut all the phone lines connecting the building to the outside world. So, while his besieged personal staff and security detail exchanged fire with the rebels around the courtyard, the General used the one phone line the plotters had missed to call his favorite mistress in Panama City and set her to the task of notifying his outlying allies and mounting a countercoup. Soon, a Boeing 727 belonging to the General took off from Tocumén airfield for Río Hato, where it loaded more than two hundred of the PDF's fiercest combat troops and then returned them to Tocumén, tracked all the way and back by American radar. The American embassy on Balboa Avenue also reported that another column from a Panama City battalion loyal to the General was rolling past it, heading for the *comandancia.*

Meanwhile, the General's defenders in the headquarters battle had run out of ammunition after close to two hours of skirmishing, and General

Manuel Antonio Noriega surrendered. The *comandante* remained in the plotters' custody for the next two hours, held under guard down in the *comandancia* courtyard for a while, and then in a bedroom in his office suite, which was, unbeknownst to his captors, the location of the one working phone connection in the building. When the door was closed, the General used the undiscovered phone to call his mistress again and check on the status of his rescue.

All the while, down in the courtyard, the major and the rest of the coup plotters were arguing over what to do with the General now that he was their prisoner. There was a faction who wanted to send him over to the Americans, but most backed the major's position that the General should be allowed to retire in Panama, a free man.

At some point in the process, the major interrupted the discussion to worry about possible counterattacks, so a delegation of two officers was dispatched over to Fort Clayton in the Zone to approach *El Pocho Maldito* and implore the Americans to get off their butts and block the access roads along which they expected the General's reinforcements to arrive. This delegation's request was the only direct contact between the coup and the American command.

The two rebel PDF officers were searched for weapons at the Fort Clayton gate and then brought straight to Marc Cisneros's office.

The encounter had a strange texture for Cisneros. Both the officers delegated to approach him had been hard-line backers of the General, heretofore known for their vehemence in public expressions of hatred for the gringos' hired Mexican. Now, however, there was little time for awkwardness at the turnaround.

The officers started by telling Cisneros that the coup had captured the General but that they weren't going to hand him over. Nonetheless, they wanted the Americans at least to cut the Pan American Highway so the General's troops in Río Hato couldn't drive down it to reclaim the *comandancia*.

Cisneros focused on the issue of the General first and asked again for the plotters to turn him over. Just drop him off in a truck and it would be their secret. Cisneros argued that the coup could announce Noriega had fled and sneak him over to SOUTHCOM. The Americans would figure out what to do from that point forward and the coup would be safe, assured that the General was out of circulation for good.

The PDF officers again refused, adamantly.

"They kept saying they wanted their General to retire in dignity," Cisneros explained. "I said, 'You're being stupid. He'll kill you if you fail.' But they wouldn't listen and kept saying 'We're not going to turn Noriega over to you.' I couldn't get them to budge."

So Marc Cisneros turned to the coup's request for assistance. He told the PDF officers that it wouldn't matter whether SOUTHCOM cut the Pan American or not. The troops from Río Hato had been ferried in by airplane to Tocumén field and were on their way to the *comandancia* at that very moment.

That news brought the two officers up short and, after a moment of pale silence, they asked Cisneros if they could use a private phone. Cisneros let them use his and left the room so they could talk.

When they summoned him back, it was apparent the negotiations were over. Cisneros offered both men asylum if they wanted it. One did. The other said he was going back and headed off toward the *comandancia,* where the small arms rattle was increasing and where, from outside Max Thurman's Tunnel on Quarry Heights, observers could distinguish the black berets of the Río Hato troops approaching the PDF headquarters still held by the coup.

In Washington, George Bush spent the morning holding short meetings every now and then to keep abreast of events.

The first of those, after the alarm had been sounded by SOUTHCOM and the White House had rounded up the secretary of defense, decided to do nothing and just see how things developed. At the time, Max Thurman was still insisting that the firing below his command center might well be part of a very elaborate ruse.

Then, once news of the meeting between Cisneros and the delegation reached Washington, another meeting was hurriedly summoned and the president ordered that Fort Amador be blocked, as Cisneros had already done with his disguised Sand Flea units, and that the Pan American Highway be blocked as well, to stop the troops from Río Hato, even though the Río Hato troops were already in Panama City. The president also asked to have SOUTHCOM demand a signed declaration of respect for democracy from the plotters.

Finally, at 1:30 P.M. Washington time, a full-fledged White House meeting was held. At this conclave, Bush ruled that SOUTHCOM could go over to the *comandancia* and take the General, but only if the coup plotters changed their mind and offered him first.

By then, unbeknownst to the White House, the black berets of the Río Hato troops had breached the coup's perimeter.

General Manuel Antonio Noriega later told his ghostwriter that once the two officers had departed the scene to talk to Cisneros about blocking the Pan American,

> something changed [inside the *comandancia*]. . . . [So, eventually] I spoke [up] in a loud voice . . . "You don't have control here," I said [to the rebels]. . . . "Reinforcements are moving in. . . . You might as well face reality. . . ."
>
> [Then] another captain came into the room, agitated. "Let's get out of here, let's take one of the trucks," he said. . . . They [then] started to force members of the general staff onto a nearby troop transport. . . . I found out later that this abortive act was part of a plan to imprison my senior staff . . . and then deliver . . . me separately to General Marc Cisneros. . . . I had to act quickly. I moved ahead of them and began giving orders. "Nobody's leaving here; get out of those trucks now . . ." I shouted, pushing them. "You don't have the capacity to rise up against this *Comandante,* not one of you!" I again shouted, looking around at all of them. "Not one of you has the balls to go against me." . . . I told [the major], speaking in an even soft tone to him, "You've lost it. . . ." [The major] knew I was right. . . . Eventually, [he] called me into the side room. . . . "Okay," he said, "let me go. I don't know where to go, but just let me go." I looked at him and remember feeling a mixture of pity and disgust. "Man, just get out of here," I said, waving him away.
>
> Within minutes, however, he was under arrest. . . . The tables had turned.

At this end point, the General and the major were in the courtyard, along with all the other conspiring officers the General's loyalist troops had been able to round up. The major was on his knees weeping and reportedly begged the General to let him go back to his wife. According to several published accounts, not including the General's, Noriega then took a pistol from one of his men, grabbed one of the plotters standing close by the major, and fired two rounds straight into the rebel officer's forehead as the major watched. The major began sobbing uncontrollably.

Then the General departed the retaken *comandancia* for his bunker at Fort Amador. He later claimed that he never saw the major again.

As it turned out, when George Bush convened his 1:30 meeting at the White House, the major's coup was already officially over.

According to later estimates, somewhere between thirty and one hundred soldiers had been wounded or killed in the fighting. The major's body was returned to his family several days later — the skull and both elbows broken, burn marks on his skin, as well as fatal bullet wounds in the head and chest. The simple accompanying explanation claimed that he had "died in combat."

— 3 —

The stateside reviews in the coup's aftermath were dismissive at best. *Newsweek* featured a photo of the General on its cover celebrating his close call with both fists raised in triumph — all of it headlined, "U.S. vs. Noriega: AMATEUR HOUR." "From the White House to the Pentagon," *Newsweek* panned, "the management of [the Panama] crisis smacked of inexperience and unpreparedness. . . . [This was] the Bush administration's turn to be tested by fire, and the first results are not comforting. . . . George Bush, it seemed, was halfway in and halfway out. As a result, he got the worst of both sides."

The bumbling continued even after the fact, when the president's press secretary asserted that the administration had never been informed about the plot ahead of time. "If we were," the press secretary insisted, "the President doesn't know about it . . . and the Secretary of Defense doesn't know about it." In fact, both, of course, did know about it and, when that was discovered within hours of the original denial, once again George Bush looked as if he had something to hide whenever the subject of General Manuel Antonio Noriega came up.

This all made for a very shaken White House, and the wires down to SOUTHCOM were burning for the rest of the week. Maxwell Thurman expected he would be summoned to Washington to answer for the situation, and he was right. What the new commander hadn't anticipated, however, was that he was ordered to bring Marc Cisneros with him. Thurman objected that there was no need to include his subordinate, but he was told specifically to bring Cisneros anyway. Now there were reports in the press that the plotters had actually offered Noriega to the United States and been refused. The president wanted to hear what Cisneros had to say on the subject, so Cisneros was coming along.

Thurman perceived this inclusion of his subordinate in the planned presidential briefing as a diminishment of his own standing and was visibly irritated. The inclusion also added fresh energy to his suspicions of the chicano general, and it was at this point that he brought those suspicions out in the open — in effect, questioning Cisneros's loyalty. When Thurman called his subordinate to let him know about the Washington orders, he immediately began grilling Cisneros on his connections to the coup.

Had Cisneros known about the coup before the Intelligence agents had met with the major?

Cisneros couldn't believe he was being asked such a question. Of course he hadn't. If he had, he would have told Thurman about it straightaway.

Had Cisneros been in secret contact with the Panamanians during any of this?

Again, Cisneros snapped, of course he hadn't. The only time he ever saw them was when the two showed up at Fort Clayton and all his contacts were immediately reported up the chain of command.

By this point, Marc Cisneros was, he remembered, "hot under the collar."

And he only got hotter when Thurman asked Marc if he would be willing to sign an affidavit certifying that what he had just told him was true.

Barely able to restrain himself, Cisneros said he'd sign whatever Thurman wanted, but if the general was looking for an explanation, he'd do better to remember that Thurman hadn't taken Cisneros's advice during any of the events in question. If Thurman had bothered to consult with him, it might not have ended up like this. Cisneros would certainly have known enough to recommend giving the major a radio so they could have contacted the plotters while the coup was going on. Had they done just that, they might have been shipping the General back to the States in handcuffs instead of flying north themselves to be called on the carpet.

After his exchange with Thurman was done, Marc Cisneros immediately called the army chief of staff in Washington.

He'd had it with his new commander, Cisneros told the chief of staff. The guy wouldn't listen and was "anti-Hispanic." Cisneros wasn't interested in working under those conditions. He told the chief he was going to request relief from his command and immediate transfer out of SOUTHCOM.

The chief told Cisneros to calm down and not to do anything until his trip to Washington. The two would talk about it when Marc was in town.

Over the course of their ride north to the District of Columbia in the SOUTHCOM commander's executive jet — first across the silver plate of the Caribbean in last light, then the dark mass of the North American continent — four-starred Max Thurman made sure two-starred Marc Cisneros understood what the subordinate's role in the upcoming briefing was to be. Thurman would be answering all the questions from the president or anybody else who was there, he explained, and only Thurman. Cisneros was along to talk about his dealings with the PDF rebels and only that. He wasn't there to address any other issue. And Thurman would tell him when he was to do so. Was that clear?

Cisneros responded that it was and played his role at the White House meeting as ordered. The conclave was held in one of the smaller presidential working rooms off the Oval Office. The secretaries of state and defense were both present.

Max Thurman explained to them that the coup had been "ill-conceived" at best, a kind of gang-who-couldn't-shoot-straight affair from start to finish. He also pointed out that these plotters' democratic credentials were questionable as well. In the coup's one radio announcement before being overtaken by events, the rebel officers had said they would continue to refuse to accept the results of the May 7 election, but would grant new "fair" elections. This Thurman noted, was significantly at odds with the president's own position that the May 7 winners be allowed to govern. The truth was, Thurman argued, these plotters hadn't deserved American support. They hadn't deserved it before the coup and they didn't deserve it afterward either.

The secretary of defense bolstered Thurman's interpretation by pointing out that great powers never just committed their forces when some unknown major said it was time. Great powers committed their forces when *they* thought it was time. And when they did, they made it stick.

At one point George Bush pointed out to the others in the room that he had no problem using military force, he just wanted to make sure it was going to improve the situation and not make it worse before he did so.

Eventually, Thurman turned to Cisneros for an explanation of his negotiations with the rebels at Fort Clayton. Cisneros told the president and his advisers about trying to convince the officers to surrender Noriega and how they'd refused. Cisneros pointed out if they'd ever said yes, he had been committed to grabbing the General first and sorting it out later. He had never had the chance.

Not long after that, the two generals left the presidential group to their deliberations — Thurman apparently feeling quite successful and Cisneros carrying a heavy dose of disgust at how the SOUTHCOM commander had been able to paper over the mess he'd made.

Marc Cisneros's only other appointment in the nation's capital was his session with the army chief of staff. He and the chief were on friendly terms, so Cisneros was direct with him about what had gone on.

"I told him the president had been ill-served on this one," Cisneros remembered. "Thurman had the best opportunity to grab Noriega anyone had ever had and he blew it. He was more interested in how he would look than he was about his mission and he wouldn't take any advice from me. And the reason for it was that the guy was simply anti-Hispanic. I also told the chief of staff again that I wanted to be relieved and get out of Panama."

The chief made some sympathetic noises in response to Cisneros's complaint, but he told Cisneros straight out that he couldn't let him leave SOUTHCOM. "I'm asking you to suck it up," he said, "for the good of the service." The chief explained that Cisneros was too important a cog in their machinery to replace at this particular moment.

Selecting his words with care, the army chief of staff allowed that there was just "too much about to happen" for such an adjustment, however Cisneros felt.

Too much about to happen?

The chief said he could not yet explain anything more, and after thirty years on the chain of command, Marc Cisneros knew better than to ask him to, so he left it at that.

Ten years later, of course, retrospect would made the explanation obvious.

The necessary impetus had been delivered. George Bush had reached the point of Enough Is Enough and Max Thurman was being sent back to the Isthmus under instructions to get Operation Blue Spoon up to battle speed and await further orders. The General's endgame was now in motion and the first significant military action by the United States of America since the end of the Vietnam War was barely ten weeks away.

Like the good soldier he was, Marc Cisneros sucked it up as the chief of staff had requested and flew south to report for duty with the posse now being mustered in the Canal Zone.

CHAPTER 8

ENDGAME

— 1 —

Hints of what was in the wings soon reached Miami as well.

About the time Marc Cisneros flew back to Panama, the United States Attorney's Office for the Southern District of Florida, apparently at the insistence of the Department of Justice in Washington, notified Kenny Kennedy that the office needed to get the Noriega case "in order." Kenny immediately notified Steve Grilli.

"I couldn't fuckin' believe it," Steve remembered. "It was like a bad dream. They wanted me to go back and do this again? I'd been away from it for nine months and my wounds still weren't healed. I was still surrounded by the wreckage of the first time around, you know what I mean? I still felt burnt by it, like it had made a mess out of my life. And nothin' had changed with Patti except maybe it had got worse. I was still away from the house far more than I was ever there, and when I was home I wasn't really there anyway. My head was somewhere else. The process of stayin' away had been learned by then. And for what? I still didn't have an answer to that question. But I'd become hardened and sort of protectionist about things by then. I looked at my career and I still felt like I'd been badly used. And now I figured I was gettin' set up to be used again. But I fuckin' went for it anyway. It was my case and I was still attached to it, even though the Christmas before I'd thought I for sure never wanted to get near it again."

Even rescued from hibernation, however, *United States v. Manuel Antonio Noriega* remained significantly less than a Drug Enforcement Administration priority that fall. On that front, nothing had changed. And Kenny Kennedy had long since given up trying to convince the agency otherwise. Steve made a pitch for more bodies to help him with this revival, but, Steve remembered, "Kenny was out of the game by this time. He'd been whipped. He didn't even bother to forward the request along before saying no."

"We ain't puttin' any more resources into it," Kennedy told Grilli, "because it ain't goin' nowhere."

As far as Kenny was concerned, the United States attorney was just trying to cover his bureaucratic ass, nothing more, probably because some guy in Washington asked some idle question about the status of the evidence. And, of course, Kenny already knew how DEA headquarters felt about the case.

As a result, the only agent on the General's tail that fall was still Steve Grilli, now paired with a junior assistant United States attorney, working in an otherwise empty task force office. Steve described himself at the time as having "escaped," but then been "recaptured." Nonetheless, his obsession about the General returned relatively quickly. He again found himself wanting to get the case right with a will that was almost involuntary and, again, perpetually anxious that he didn't have enough to make it stick, no matter how much evidence he already had.

And, unlike Kenny, Steve also thought something more must be going on besides just the United States attorney covering his bureaucratic ass in order for Justice to want this prosecution brought back up to speed.

When he asked the prosecutors directly why this sudden renewed interest, however, all he was told was the preparations were being made "just in case."

At first, Grilli wasn't even certain there was still a case left among the remains of the one they'd already made. Much of the evidence had been dispersed by that fall and much of the rest had gone at least a little stale. For reassurance that it was indeed possible to reassemble this thing, Steve and Kenny met Dick Gregorie for lunch, down at a marina restaurant in Coconut Grove, overlooking Biscayne Bay.

Dick was now trying lawsuits in civil practice, disconnected from the case entirely. During his first weeks after leaving the United States Attorney's Office, he'd received several phone calls from Floyd Carlton, looking for help with this or that, but all Dick could do was forward the messages to his former employers. And after Floyd figured out that Dick was in no position to help him, he stopped calling altogether. Until now, he'd heard nothing more about *United States v. Manuel Antonio Noriega* than whatever he read in the papers. Dick put up a satisfied front for this Coconut Grove reunion of their old team, but he was never quite happy defending corporate financial interests, despite the rewards. He was, however, far less driven, had developed a social life, and would soon be married.

That said, Dick was also ready to take the bit right back between his teeth when Steve and Kenny asked him whether he thought it was possible to get the Noriega RICO in shape to try.

Dick immediately wanted to know what was going on that they needed to ask?

Steve and Kenny told him they were "just wondering." People over their heads had been asking them that question and they needed to figure out an answer.

Gregorie's response that afternoon was quick and without doubt.

"Absolutely," he told them.

He then began making a verbal laundry list of things they would have to do to prepare for such an eventuality, while Grilli scribbled a few notes.

Dick also told his old team that if the United States attorney wanted him to come back should the Southern District actually get their hands on the General and needed Dick to try him, Dick was prepared to drop everything and do so in a hot minute.

But that, of course, was just talk. Dick Gregorie knew the chances of his being summoned in what he still assumed was the unlikely possibility of the General's arrest were either none or less than that. Dick's bridges were burned. So once he'd made his offer, he could only sigh and look out across the glitter of the bay, imagining for a moment the possibility of bringing the General to justice. Quite naturally, Dick felt a little bit left out.

Steve, on the other hand, departed their reunion lunch with a lot to do. Once committed to resuming the pursuit, he didn't hold back, working late in his task force cubbyhole while the Miami outside accelerated toward tourist season, the air balmy, the Atlantic lapping against the towering hulls of ocean liners leaving daily for swings through the tropics with perhaps even a stop at the Panama Canal.

Every now and then, however, Grilli leaned back in his chair, rolled his eyes, and shuddered a bit.

"Here we go again," he said to himself.

2

As for General Manuel Antonio Noriega, if he felt any trepidation about what might be in store, it was not worrisome enough to convince him to grab the best deal he could and save himself. That much was apparent in the outcome of a final informal negotiation with the State Department conducted in secret during October by the General's defense team of Ray Takiff and Frank Rubino.

According to Takiff, this final contact was initiated several days before the major's failed coup, when "the General called me and asked me to see if I could get his deal back." The "deal" to which the General referred was the one he'd rejected the year before. Takiff described the request as a feeler, as though the General wanted to find out what options were still available to him, rather than a desperate request from a man looking for a lifeboat.

When the request arose, however, Takiff advised his client that, for health reasons, Takiff would have to send his cocounsel Frank Rubino to Washington to handle the actual discussion in his stead. Ray had gone through a heart attack and his first open-heart surgery during the previous year and claimed he was under doctors' orders to reduce his exertions, but he told the General he would set the process in motion and immediately called the office of the undersecretary of state who had acted as chief negotiator the year before, making an appointment for Rubino to fly up and talk.

Ray Takiff's reasons for not going to Washington himself at that point were not, however, solely health related. The General's lead attorney also had a secret he kept hidden from his client and his cocounsel, and that secret had left him seriously compromised as a defense attorney. During August 1989, Takiff's career of shyster dealings had finally caught up with him, and after a secret two-and-a-half-year investigation, he was confronted by FBI agents saying they had him dead to rights on a handful of serious tax violations. The only option they offered Ray — besides a half million dollars in penalties, not to mention several felony counts carrying serious prison time — was going to work as the FBI's undercover operative in a sting operation pursuing corruption among the local judiciary. Ray Takiff sized up his situation and took the deal. Over the next year, wearing an FBI wire throughout, sleazy Ray Takiff distributed more than a quarter million dollars' worth of bribes to a half-dozen Miami judges, pretending to represent a big Colombian coke dealer looking for favorable judicial treatment of his organization's smuggling transgressions. All of the bribes were paid with marked FBI cash.

When Takiff's undercover role was finally disclosed during the General's trial, Takiff's former cocounsel, Frank Rubino, hauled Ray into court and charged him with having "served two masters at once."

That October, however, Takiff's role was still a secret and Rubino called Takiff from Washington to report on his meeting at State as a matter of course.

This last Washington conclave took place a week or so after the major's failed coup. Rubino had stayed in touch with State's lead negotiator on a sporadic basis since the 1988 negotiations, and even had Takiff not begged off, Rubino would likely have handled all the heavy lifting of the meeting anyway.

This time, Frank remembered, "I had the authority to elicit offers and negotiate possible options to then take to the General for him to listen to. When I got to State, [the lead negotiator] informed me that the secretary of state was in his office two floors up if we needed him, the attorney general was standing by in his, and even the president was available if need be — not to come over, but if we needed him on the phone. This was his way of telling me this was a real serious meeting."

The lead negotiator's "proposal," which Frank Rubino discussed with Takiff and then with the General and Takiff together, contained a lot of what had been offered in the spring of 1988, but not all: The General would honorably retire as *comandante,* with a suitable ceremony, which the secretary of state himself would attend. When the General resigned, the president would give a speech thanking him without any condemnation and the General would declare a new set of "free" elections. The ex-General would then depart to Europe to sit out the election, after which he could return to Panama but was banned from political activity. In exchange, the United States promised it would make no effort to seize any of the General's ill-gotten wealth or property, even in the United States, and the United States pledged it would make no effort to extradite the General from Panama or anywhere else outside the United States.

The Americans would not, however, drop the indictment. That would involve political suicide for George Bush and was unacceptable.

As far as Ray Takiff was concerned, the failure to kill the indictment was reason enough to reject the option, and he told the General so.

Some two years later, that advice on Takiff's part formed the heart of the "serving two masters" allegations against Takiff at Rubino's legal hearing, called in the middle of the General's trial, out of the presence of the jury. Rubino alleged that Takiff's involvement as a government informant on its Miami judicial corruption sting for the last six months he had remained as the General's counsel of record was more than sufficient grounds for a mistrial. And Rubino characterized the counsel Takiff did give during those six months as tainted by his desire to secure the approval of his FBI handlers. Takiff, for his part, denied ever being asked anything about the General by the FBI other than once, when a curious agent wanted "a piece of information," which Takiff claimed to have refused without hesitation. As for his argument against considering the deal offered that October, the General's onetime lead counsel claimed to have been against it on its merits, not because he thought it would please the FBI.

Frank Rubino, however, felt quite differently from Takiff when they consulted with the General on the subject of what the Americans were offering.

"I encouraged the General to take it," he remembered. "I said the United States is going to get you if it wants to. It can make your life miserable. I said, 'Trust me, General. I've been a lawyer for eighteen years dealing with the federal government. These people are serious. I don't know what they will do, but they will make Panama's life miserable. This isn't such a bad deal. Everybody has to retire sometime.'"

Despite such warnings, even Frank Rubino never imagined just how serious "these people" really were that October. "I thought it would snow in Panama before the United States ever invaded," Rubino later explained. "I thought the worst would be sanctions like before, only even tighter. I had no idea they'd go as far as they did. I'd never heard of any government ever doing that. It came out of nowhere as far as I was concerned."

Nor was Rubino alone in his attitude. Certainly there is no evidence that the possibility of imminent arrest was ever a factor in the General's consideration that October. After listening to his two gringo attorneys disagree, the General just told them, "I'll think about it," and left it at that. Then, over his remaining eleven weeks as a free man, he never raised the subject again. Not a yes, not a no, just blank air into November and on to December.

"The General had a tendency to try to solve problems by doing nothing," Rubino remembered. "And this was one of those instances where he thought he could just ignore things until they went away."

It would prove a failed approach, to say the least.

The closest General Manuel Antonio Noriega ever came to his own explanation for why he took such an approach was a two-sentence fragment in his ghostwritten memoir — giving the whole episode only passing mention and, not surprisingly, posturing as something of a Panamanian hero called to go down nobly with his native ship of state.

"I still could not accept being bought off by the Americans," the General claimed. "When that message became clear one final time, the invasion was the only option left to them."

At least the General got that very last part right. Whether he had figured it out yet or not when the fall of 1989 gave way to winter, Manuel Antonio Noriega's number was indeed up, and bargaining his way out of his endgame was no longer possible.

— 3 —

The actual decision to arrest General Manuel Antonio Noriega, *comandante* of the Panama Defense Force and "de facto ruler of Panama," was taken on December 17, 1989. It came after two straight days of incidents on the Isthmus in which one off-duty American officer was shot dead at a roadblock, another was arrested along with his wife and terrorized before being released, and a PDF policeman was shot and seriously wounded by an American officer on a Panama City street. Max Thurman and Marc Cisneros had long since revved SOUTHCOM up to battle speed, and a fight of some sort was in the air. Thurman himself had just left Washington for Panama that morning in order to deal with developments on the spot. He was eventually informed of the president's decision by secure phone from the Joint Chiefs.

The meeting at which that historic decision was taken would later be described in one account of the General's arrest as "pure Bush: an intimate gathering of trusted officials, a thorough briefing, complete with huge maps of Panama and the targets to be attacked . . . [all] designed to let the president sort through his options methodically."

George Bush, dressed in a blue blazer and gray slacks, convened the meeting at 2:00 P.M. He had returned from a trip to St. Martinique in the Caribbean for a visit with the prime minister of France late the previous evening and was given news of the latest dead American in Panama shortly after landing. Before the 2:00 P.M. meeting even convened the next afternoon, Bush had told his vice president that he was "going to do something about Noriega" today.

First, of course, it had to be talked through. And, though the General's arrest amounted to the only time in history this kind of action had been undertaken by the United States toward any foreign ruler, de facto or otherwise, there is no record of any discussion at all being devoted to this absence of precedent. That issue would simply be handed to the National Security Council's in-house lawyer the next day with instructions to concoct a legal justification for the move.

Instead, the meeting first devoted itself to assessing the possible reactions by other nations to an American move into Panama, or the absence of any such move, and reached agreement that a "strong response" to the General was now needed. This latest killing down there was too much for a Great Power to tolerate.

There were, it now seemed, three responses available to George Bush other than simply "wimping out":

The first would be to give the general one last chance to step down. The two high-ranking CIA executives who knew the General best were proposed as messengers to be sent south with an ultimatum to leave or face the consequences. It was argued that Noriega could be induced by someone he trusted to leave on short notice. "If the right person had been talking to him," one of those CIA executives later claimed, "the invasion, the bloodshed, and the expenditure of millions of dollars could have been averted." This, of course, was the same argument that had been being made since "The Blandon Plan" and it was rejected quickly this time around as simply too little, too late.

The second response available to Bush was to launch a "surgical strike" to snatch the General, but that option was even less viable now than it had been when rejected a year and a half earlier by the previous administration.

The final option was Operation Blue Spoon, the favored response of the new chairman of the Joint Chiefs. He called it a "hammerhead." And it was indeed that. As finally revised by Max Thurman, Blue Spoon was an overwhelming application of force that was meant to splatter the PDF in its tracks. Altogether, it involved some 22,000 troops, essentially doubling the size of SOUTHCOM's combat forces with reinforcements, many of which would be ferried from their Stateside postings on the day before the attack, in a pattern that was designed to confuse the PDF into thinking it was just one more Sand Flea "readiness" exercise. There was also an airborne assault, several "special operations" involving army Rangers, navy SEALS, and the top-secret Delta Force, and even a bombardment by the air force's new "Stealth" bombers.

The land assault, the chairman told the president, was divided into four separate task forces. The most significant of those, Task Force Bayonet, was commanded by Marc Cisneros and featured the reinforced 193rd Brigade's seizure of Panama City, assisted by a battalion of tanks on loan from the 82nd Airborne Division. Task Force Bayonet was expected to face the heaviest fighting as it worked its way through the narrow streets of Panama's largest city, but that, the chairman pointed out, was what they had trained for repeatedly over the last six months. The other task forces were to secure SOUTHCOM and the Canal, seize Tocumén field, and subdue Río Hato. The chairman of the Joint Chiefs expected the entire operation to have smashed the ten-thousand-man PDF, gained control of the Isthmus, and arrested General Manuel Antonio Noriega within no more than twenty-four hours. The ensuing clean-up might take as long as a month. Blue Spoon was now ready to go, awaiting simply a presidential order.

Indeed, the only change in the arrangement once the president had approved it was a new name. "Operation Blue Spoon" didn't cut it on the public relations front, so the operation was now retitled "Just Cause."

One of the president's first requests was for a projection from the chairman of how many casualties could be expected if Operation Just Cause went forward. The chairman estimated seventy American dead, some three times more than would actually be incurred.

The meeting at the White House continued to chew through the possibilities for a while, with George Bush's national security adviser playing devil's advocate with the chairman, but it seemed increasingly that the die was cast.

Finally, the president tied it all off. He told the gathering that he had thought it would come down to this, ever since the major's failed coup, and now it had.

"Let's do it," George Bush said.

At 4:00 P.M., the new chairman of the Joint Chiefs returned to the Pentagon and notified Max Thurman, in his command bunker down on Quarry Heights. The assault was scheduled to commence at 1:00 A.M. Panama City time, December 20, a little more than two days away.

In the meantime, Operation Just Cause remained an official secret, though there were several clues over those last forty-eight hours, which the right analysis might have used to surmise what was up.

Perhaps the most telling of those was, again, in the Southern District of Florida. There, on December 19, 1989, less than twelve hours before the posse was scheduled to strike, a CIA messenger suddenly delivered forty-five volumes of internal agency documents concerning the accused General Manuel Antonio Noriega to the United States Attorney's Office for the Southern District of Florida, a total of several cubic feet of paper.

The delivery represented the material Dick Gregorie had first requested a year and a half ago, only to be given a single letter file and told there was nothing more. Now, apparently concluding better late than never, the agency was "making good" on its original promise to cooperate in full.

Obviously, the General's endgame must have been coming to a head.

4

At the end of that same afternoon, about 6:00 P.M. Panama City time, the United States Joint Special Operations Command, the military unit assigned to track the General's movements, registered its last confirmed sighting prior to the Operation Just Cause assault. At that point, the General was at a house in Colón on the Caribbean end of the Canal, shortly after a military ceremony at the local PDF barracks. He had been in Colón for two days, having spent December 18 mediating a threatened local dockworkers' strike.

Joint Special Operations believed the General headed back toward Panama City from that house in Colón during the early evening of December 19 in a caravan of jeeps, Mercedes Benzes, and Toyota sedans. At one juncture in the highway, the caravan split into two halves, one fragment heading in the direction of Tocumén airfield; the other, including the General's preferred Mercedes with smoked windows, drove straight to the *comandancia,* where it was greeted with the military salutes reserved for the *comandante,* and a figure hustled from the Mercedes into the General's headquarters. Joint Special Operations, convinced that the General was using a double, discounted the scene at the *comandancia,* but had no idea where the other half of the General's caravan had gone.

Such deception, while thorough, was nothing special the General had put on for this occasion. Unpredictability and concealment were standard practices in his Israeli-designed personal security strategy. Other than this institutionalized wariness, however, the General later pointed out in his memoirs that he "had no idea what was [about] to come."

He had, however, received warnings. Both the Cubans and the Israelis had informed him over the previous two days that the Americans were up to something, though they didn't know exactly what. The PDF radar also tracked the planeloads of reinforcements landing at the Southern Command and, while in Colón, the *comandante* was notified that a wing of American transports, apparently full of paratroopers, had taken off from North Carolina on its way to Panama as well. The General took all these as indications of another set of "maneuvers" in the ongoing saga of Sand Flea — more gringo attempts to rattle his cage, nothing he hadn't seen before. Certainly General Manuel Antonio Noriega was in no mood to consider these incoming radar blips anything more serious.

"The atmosphere . . . was filled with Christmas cheer," the General remembered. "Panama is always ready for a party, but never more than during holiday time."

The General's own personal "party" that evening was at the Ceremi Recreation Center, an officers' "social club" and hotel on the grounds of Tocumén Air Base. He arrived there in a four-car caravan, riding in the backseat of a Toyota, wearing his general's uniform, with his civilian clothes in a valise. The General had come to the Ceremi to "unwind." In particular, there was a new young prostitute there whom one of his captains had highly recommended, and the General had scheduled the evening with her. He also, no doubt, drank at least some of his favorite Old Parr. The PDF wives who took refuge with SOUTHCOM during the major's coup had said the General was drinking very heavily during the summer and fall and only spent perhaps an hour a day when he wasn't at least a little loaded.

If he was still drinking heavily on this night, it did not keep him from moving quickly when he had to. According to prisoners later taken at the Ceremi, the General left there at approximately 1:07 A.M. on the dead run, his clothes in his hands, covered by little more than the red underwear which, according to the public message soon to be issued by the victorious Maxwell Thurman, the General wore "to ward off the evil eye."

Four minutes earlier, at approximately 1:03 A.M., four C-131 and three C-130 transport planes, having flown straight from Fort Bragg, North Carolina, had disgorged the 1st Battalion of the 75th Ranger Regiment of the 82nd Airborne Division over nearby Tocumén field, giving the General plenty of reason to run. Suddenly, the night sky was slashed with tracer rounds and fractured by the sounds of pitched battle. The General was in a private room with the prostitute at the time the fighting broke out, but didn't dally. Discarding his uniform in favor of civilian clothes he donned on the run, the General found his aides and drove off toward the airfield in the same small caravan in which he'd come.

After a short distance, however, the cars ran into a picket line manned by Company B, 1st Battalion, 75th Ranger Regiment. The paratroopers had stumbled over a PDF machine-gun nest early in their assault and lost several of their men, but, otherwise, they were busy securing Tocumén without significant opposition. Company B's task was to block the road system around the field and stop all Panamanian traffic.

The first vehicles to test that role included the Toyota with the General in its backseat. The Rangers fired warning shots, and when the caravan turned and fled, the American paratroopers were able to shoot out the tires of one of the vehicles, but not the one carrying the General.

That was the closest the American posse would come to arresting the fugitive Manuel Antonio Noriega for the next two weeks.

Within an hour or two of that encounter, the General had gone to ground with his entourage of some half dozen in the empty house of a government official who was on business in Peru. The house was located on higher ground, and from its windows the General watched the battle unfold as well as he was able. In the distance, the shantytown bordering the *comandancia* had begun to burn and, closer by, American gunships attacked a PDF outpost manned by a company known as "the Tigers." By 5:30 A.M., the Tigers had surrendered, their outpost reduced to a smoking hulk. Most of the Isthmus's phone exchanges were disrupted, so there was no way for the General to track exactly how the larger fight was going, but he figured it was likely not all that different than it had been for the Tigers, and he was right. By daybreak, SOUTHCOM's Max Thurman could report that two of Just Cause's three objectives were essentially in hand — his command had smashed the PDF and had the Isthmus in its grasp, though mopping up would continue throughout the next week.

What remained was to find the General, the reason they had come in the first place.

Which wasn't nearly as easy as the Americans had planned it to be. When the General wasn't captured by daybreak, Operation Just Cause began to cast a net for him. First to be searched were his offices and homes. At the former, of course, they found the General's voodoo altar with its special curses for Dick Gregorie and Steve Grilli. At his Panama City palace, they found lists of bank accounts in Switzerland and the Cayman Islands and three diplomatic passports. At his beach house, they found a maid and a watchman who showed the soldiers the General's bedroom. It was full of mirrors and porcelain figurines, mostly of the heads of young girls. The king-sized bed had what Special Operations would describe as "a Hindu love goddess" carved into its headboard. Not surprisingly, however, the General himself was nowhere to be found.

To further the search, an element of the elite Delta Force commandos was designated as the reaction team, pursuing all leads under the direct command of Max Thurman himself. Eventually they would conduct some forty such pursuits. The CinC SOUTHCOM also posted a $1 million reward.

In hiding, the General had moved on to the house of his civilian secretary, and his traveling party now included the secretary and two military aides, all dressed in casual civilian clothing. Part of the time they hid at the secretary's and part of the time they stayed at the luxurious villa of the General's silent partner in the gunrunning business, moving between the two in a dark blue Range Rover. That lasted until a worker from the home of the General's gunrunning partner, lured by the reward, provided a tip to Special Operations Command and the Delta Force pounced on the partner's villa. They found a steam bath, a wine cellar, six cars in the garage, and a huge satellite dish, but, again, no Noriega.

The General, now traveling with his favorite mistress, had fled a half hour earlier in a tiny helicopter designed to find fish for tuna fleets. The

General's two aides had fled separately in a green Mitsubishi sedan, and after a rendezvous with them, the General left his mistress behind and went on the lam for a little bit longer.

For a while, he hid in a graveyard, later explaining to his ghostwriter that "I was sure the Americans would be too scared to go in there at night." He also later claimed that he was looking for an opportunity to get out of Panama City and into the mountains, where he could mount a guerrilla campaign, but by Christmas Eve, he knew his realistic options had been reduced to finding asylum in an embassy, and that didn't look too good either. The embassies of Cuba, Nicaragua, and Libya — the most likely candidates — were all surrounded by American troops on the lookout for him. One embassy the Americans hadn't surrounded was the Vatican's, run by the papal nuncio. The nuncio was an enemy of long standing, whom the General disliked intensely, but the General dispatched an intermediary to approach the priest anyway. After the intermediary appealed to the Church's history of providing sanctuary and insisted the alternative would be that the General would go to the hills and prolong the fight, the nuncio agreed to provide asylum.

To bring the General out of hiding, a rendezvous at a Panama City Dairy Queen was arranged between a priest driving a Toyota with diplomatic plates and the General's party in the Mitsubishi. The General, dressed in Bermuda shorts, a T-shirt, and a baseball cap, and carrying a bundle wrapped in a blanket, jumped into the backseat of the papal Toyota. The car then sped toward the embassy.

The General's bundle, clutched tightly on his lap, contained an Uzi submachine gun and a hand grenade.

Unbeknownst to the General, the papal nuncio had tipped off Marc Cisneros to the General's move even before the fugitive arrived at his sanctuary. Cisneros immediately dispatched elements of his Task Force Bayonet in a race to surround the papal embassy and snatch the General before he reached diplomatic sanctuary, but they were too late. So the troops established a perimeter around the embassy and waited.

They remained in that position for the next nine days, including Christmas Day and New Year's Eve. In a futile attempt to hurry the General into surrendering, the Special Operations Command ordered its 4th Psychological Operations Group to the scene a couple days after

Christmas. The 4th Psy Ops set up huge loudspeakers and for the next three days and two nights played American rock 'n' roll music at top volume, featuring such oldies but goodies as "I Fought the Law and the Law Won" and "Workin' on a Chain Gang." The music was loud enough to shake the ground for blocks around. The cacophony was eventually shut down after the nuncio reported that the music seemed to have no effect on the General but it was driving everyone else inside crazy.

New Year's Day passed with no change in the standoff.

The General himself spent most of the time in the tiny room he'd been provided, silently pacing or lying on the bed, under which he'd hidden his Uzi. The rules of the asylum were that he could not use the phone, but the nuncio would deliver messages left for him.

One of those who called the nuncio once the new year had begun was the General's lead defense counsel in Miami, Ray Takiff. Under the pressure of his own secret compromise, the mouthpiece was within hours of officially resigning from the General's employ, but he made no mention of that in the message he asked the nuncio to deliver. "I told the General that there was absolutely no question in my mind that the whole reason for this war was to kill him," Takiff explained, "and that he had to find a way to end it and guarantee his own safety. I told him he was out of options, there was no place for him to go. I said he ought to surrender and go out of the place with dignity. We'd handle all the problems afterward in the United States as they occurred."

Though its legal propriety was later questioned, there is no evidence that Takiff's advice had any impact.

The message delivered by the nuncio to the General that had far more obvious weight in the General's thinking was from Marc Cisneros. The American battle commander was tired of things dragging along so, on January 2, 1990, now thirteen days since Operation Just Cause began, he told the nuncio to let the General know that while international law required his troops to respect the sanctuary offered in an embassy, there was no requirement that they keep the crowds of Panamanians that had formed beyond the soldiers' perimeter from entering the embassy and doing whatever they had a mind to.

At that moment, of course, the General in his room could hear shouting for his head and the like from out on the street.

The nuncio seized on that threat from *El Pocho Maldito* to belabor the General, insisting that he was going to end up being seized by a crowd and executed, like Mussolini had been in Italy. And this approach seemed to work.

> I was using my gray matter [trying] to come up with an escape plan, [the General recounted,] and I was analyzing the odds of coming out alive. Death was only to be an option in the line of fire.... [Never] did I even for an instant think of committing suicide.... [Instead] I... started to prepare myself mentally for what was likely to come. I knew I had a weapon to defend myself. The Uzi was my insurance, I thought, because if the mob or the Americans were going to come in, at least three or four would go with me before I was lynched.... I went up to my room [and discovered] someone had found [my Uzi] and delivered it to Marc Cisneros.... [As a consequence,] I was left to ponder what [the nuncio] had said. "Look at it as losing one battle," he said. "Accept that and prepare yourself for the legal battle ahead.... Your lawyers have been calling me and are awaiting you with optimism for [your] legal fight...."... My choice was capture by the Americans or face a long term future there in the Vatican embassy or, perhaps, an eventual attack by the Americans.

Around nightfall on January 3, 1990, General Manuel Antonio Noriega sent word through the nuncio that he was prepared to surrender. His terms were that he be allowed to do so in his general's uniform and that he would be treated under the rules of the Geneva conventions covering prisoners of war.

At approximately 9:30 P.M. Panama City time, the General was escorted in full military regalia through a receiving line inside the Vatican embassy that included the nuncio, who presented him with a Bible for his journey, and then out to the embassy gate, where American troops were waiting. They handcuffed him, walked him across the street to a helicopter, and he was flown over to one of SOUTHCOM's airstrips, where a C-130 was waiting to carry him to the Southern District of Florida.

Once in that transport's hold, the General was greeted by two agents from the Drug Enforcement Administration. They officially placed him under arrest.

"You have the right to remain silent," one of them began reciting to him. "Anything you say can and will be used against you in a court of law.

You have the right to an attorney and if you can't afford one, an attorney will be provided you. . . ."

— 5 —

When news of the General's surrender reached the DEA's Miami Divisional Office that night, Kenny Kennedy and Steve Grilli were at the Headquarters Club, "a bar around the corner from the office, where guys used to gather for a couple of pops and something to eat." Working late was pretty much a given for Steve. Things at his home in Deerfield Beach had now deteriorated to the point he was using what spare time he had to hunt for an apartment in which to set up separate housekeeping. In the meantime, he slept some nights at the office.

Almost everyone else who had been working late at the Miami office was at the Headquarters Club that evening as well. As the word about the General's arrest arrived, everyone's pagers went off at once.

This symphony of beeps was followed instantly by an impromptu celebration. Then the plan was passed along for most of the narcs to drive up to Homestead Air Force Base south of Miami where the General's C-130 was scheduled to land around 2:00 A.M. According to the strategy laid out to Kennedy on the phone, a DEA caravan bearing the prisoner would then return to Miami where the General would be booked into the Submarine under the courthouse annex.

Steve Grilli begged off the Homestead detail and returned to the office to put in several more hours of work instead. When it had been obvious the General's arrest was imminent, Steve had been offered the honor of flying to the Isthmus to take possession of the prisoner and bring him back to the United States, but he had turned the role down.

"It seemed frivolous to me," he explained. "There were a lot better things for me to do at the time besides showboating."

On top of that, the case itself was about to morph from a grand jury true bill, an evidentiary abstraction, to an actual docket number with a court date, at which time the case would undergo an overwhelming reality check in which a criminal court jury would have to be convinced of Grilli's allegations "beyond a reasonable doubt." And, of course, the pressure Grilli felt over the prospect was real.

Shortly after the invasion, the special agent in charge at the Miami station had made it clear to Grilli personally that, should the General be found not guilty, the verdict would easily amount to the greatest embarrassment in DEA history — enough, perhaps, to destroy the agency. And it would all be on Grilli's account. And he, Steve Grilli, would be remembered forever among the great fuckups of all time. The SAC would repeat the statement at regular intervals thereafter.

"I asked if it would all be on my account if the General was convicted as well," Steve remembered, "but he never answered me."

During the late evening of January 3, 1990, and early morning of January 4, Grilli was worried that if he used his time to go out to Homestead Air Force Base and watch the General get off a plane from Panama instead of on the case itself, he might be risking having to go out and watch him fly back the other direction a free man sometime down the line.

And that, of course, would have been the ultimate humiliation.

Kenny Kennedy, on the other hand, wouldn't have missed the trip out to Homestead for the world.

That night at least, the General's arrival felt like vindication to Kenny and he meant to enjoy it. Indeed, Kennedy's apparent revelry before even getting to Homestead was sufficient for the new first assistant United States attorney to complain that the DEA's ASAC had shown up there smelling like a tavern — though nothing ever came of the complaint.

The new United States attorney was out on the Homestead tarmac at 2:00 A.M. as well. So was one of the United States senators from Florida and a host of law-enforcement personnel, all hoping to get a look at the General in chains. The air base's perimeter was sealed, and the entire facility blacked out in a combat alert, except for the long string of blue lights marking the runway.

By the time the C-130 bearing the captured fugitive Manuel Antonio Noriega landed, the plans for dealing with the prisoner had changed somewhat, again for "security" reasons. Now, instead of a motorized police caravan on to Miami, the General would be transferred to an eight-seat passenger jet provided by the coast guard and flown the short hop into Miami International, then driven to the Submarine from there. The Homestead car caravan would return to Miami on the freeway as originally scheduled, acting as a decoy.

The ranking agent on the case, Kenny Kennedy, was given the honor of escorting the General from the C-130, across a stretch of dark tarmac to the coast guard jet, where he would hand him over to the agents inside. It was the kind of moment cops live for, Kenny remembered, when finally, eye-to-eye, the fox, like it or not, has to acknowledge that the hound has won, "just like in the fuckin' movies."

This moment, however, turned out to be something of an anticlimax by those standards.

As soon as he took custody of the prisoner, wearing his PDF uniform and handcuffs, Kenny was stunned at how small this living legend really was. In the dark, slightly hunched over at his circumstances, the General didn't look any larger than a junior high school underclassman. Nor did he project much of anything. Still in a state of shock at how far he had fallen, all the energy of his presence remained clenched inside himself.

Still, Kennedy would tell his wife afterward that there was "a sense of evil" about this prisoner. The General was carrying a Bible as he stepped out of the transport, and Kenny felt like asking Noriega if it burnt his fingers to touch the holy book. The only visceral aspect of the General that truly lived up to the advance billing was his physical ugliness. Even in the dark. "The guy had hellacious acne," Kennedy remembered, "I mean skin like a fuckin' horned toad."

That morning in the darkness, Kenny gripped the prisoner, Manuel Antonio Noriega, Miami Field Division arrest #56727, under his arm.

"This way, General," he said.

With that, the assistant special agent in charge walked the manacled former de facto ruler of Panama across the stretch of asphalt to the coast guard plane in silence and handed him over for his next flight.

Then the plane's hatch slammed shut and the captured General taxied off, already swallowed by the future no one had thought would ever catch up with him.

EPILOGUE

Kenny Kennedy, the only person whose involvement in *United States v. Manuel Antonio Noriega* lasted from the case's very beginning to its very end, finally retired from the Drug Enforcement Administration in August 1999, almost fourteen years since he'd first arrived in Miami as the hot new GS-15 assistant special agent in charge. At the time of his retirement he was still a GS-15 and still an ASAC. Kennedy now lives in south Florida, supported by his pension and income from his work with a security technology company and a private investigation firm, as well as teaching local courses in international drug-trafficking for the White House office for the War on Drugs.

Max Thurman, commander of the SOUTHCOM army that finally placed the General under arrest, retired from active duty within weeks of the completion of Operation Just Cause and died of leukemia, December 1, 1995.

Fred Woerner, the four-star commander whom Thurman relieved — and once the army's foremost Latin Americanist — retired from the service almost immediately after surrendering command in Panama. During the invasion, Woerner worked as CBS News' expert commentator on several television broadcasts and was full of praise for the job his successor had done. Woerner is now a tenured professor of international relations at Boston University, teaching courses on Latin America and United States' security, as well as serving as chairman of the American Battle Monuments Commission.

Marc Cisneros, *El Pocho Maldito,* SOUTHCOM's foremost battlefield commander, rotated out of Panama shortly after Operation Just Cause was completed and received a personal message from the new chairman of the Joint Chiefs, thanking him for having "sucked it up" for the good of the service, despite Thurman's prejudices against Hispanics. After tours as a two- and then three-star general at Fort Hood, Texas, Cisneros was considered for a fourth star and a return posting at the helm of SOUTHCOM, but was passed over in favor of a candidate with a closer relationship to the president. In 1996, Cisneros retired from the army and now lives in his native Texas.

SOUTHCOM itself vanished from the Isthmus a decade after the General's arrest. Under the terms of the Canal Treaties, the United States surrendered Fort Clayton, the final outpost of its ninety-six-year occupation of Panamanian territory, to the Republic of Panama on November 30, 1999. The Southern Command's functions are now divided between several Stateside military bases.

The government of the **Republic of Panama** was reconstituted after the American invasion under the administration of the opposition candidates from whom the 1989 election had been stolen. Elections were next held in 1994, when the party that had once been owned by the PDF finished first and returned to power. At the following elections, in 1998, the PDF's old party lost and was replaced by the first female chief executive in Panamanian history.

The **Panama Defense Force** was disbanded forever after its crushing defeat at the hands of Operation Just Cause and replaced by a national police force. The first leader of this new police force was the former PDF lieutenant colonel anointed by Elliott Abrams and Gabriel Lewis in 1988 as their best hope of prying the PDF away from Noriega. This former lieutenant colonel was soon relieved of his police command and briefly imprisoned after allegedly preparing a coup against the new civilian government.

Gabriel Lewis, the General's most significant exile antagonist, as well as Panama's principal negotiator of the Canal Treaties, master Washington lobbyist, and instigator in the *rabiblanco* uprising, served briefly as the reconstituted Republic of Panama's foreign minister some four years after the invasion, in the administration of the PDF's old political party. On December 19, 1996, at age sixty-eight, Lewis died from fibrosis of the lungs at a hospital in Denver, Colorado.

Jose Blandon, the General's once trusted political adviser, perpetrator of the failed "Blandon Plan," and star government witness during the spring of 1988, was expected to reprise the latter role in the fall of 1991, when the General was tried, but it didn't happen. Prior to the trial, the prosecution team began using Blandon to decipher tapes being made of the General's jailhouse telephone calls, in which the General often spoke in code, and Blandon secretly made copies of the tapes for himself, which he then leaked to the Cable News Network. When that impropriety was revealed, the ensuing uproar convinced the prosecution that Blandon couldn't be relied on as a witness, so he was never called to testify. After the prosecution's rejection, Blandon negotiated briefly with the defense about providing testimony for them, but nothing came of the talks. Eventually, Jose Blandon left American Witness Protection and returned to Panama where he resurfaced publicly as the host of a radio talk show.

Mike Harari, the "retired" Mossad agent whose role as the General's principal connection to the Israelis was first publicly revealed by Jose Blandon in his testimony before the Subcommittee on Terrorism, Narcotics and International Operations, was not captured in Operation Just Cause. Instead, tipped off by his American intelligence contacts, Harari fled Panama in an Israeli Air Force C-130 just six hours before the invasion commenced. Harari surfaced on Israeli television the day after the General was flown to the United States in manacles. "I have been the victim of a campaign of disinformation," he told an interviewer. "I am not, nor was I ever, Noriega's adviser. . . . Noriega is not my partner. I did not manage his business affairs. I did not manage or train his troops. I did not organize his security forces. . . . I am simply a private individual involved in business."

The **Senate Subcommittee on Terrorism, Narcotics, and International Operations**, which first recruited Jose Blandon and then provided him with his principal public forum, disbanded in 1989, following the issuance of a final report some six months prior to the American invasion of Panama. That 1989 document concluded that "the failure of U.S. officials to [yet] act [against General Manuel Antonio Noriega] was largely the result of the relationships [he] had developed with U.S. intelligence and law enforcement agencies in performing services for them on a variety of matters." In addition, the subcommittee claimed that "significant information essential to reaching a more complete understanding of the evolution of U.S. policy towards Noriega has been kept from the Congress by the Executive Branch." The subcommittee also asserted that "U.S. officials involved in Central America failed to address the drug issue for fear of jeopardizing the war in Nicaragua [where] there was substantial evidence of drug smuggling . . . on the part of individual Contras, Contra suppliers, Contra pilots, mercenaries who worked with the Contras, and Contra supporters."

Oliver North, the lieutenant colonel at the National Security Council who was always Bill Casey's devoted acolyte and often his cutout in various dealings with the General, resigned from the Marine Corps in May 1988 and then stood trial at the hands of the Iran-contra special prosecutor the following year, some six months before the General's arrest. North was convicted of aiding and abetting the Reagan administration's cover-up, destroying evidence, and accepting an illegal gratuity, and sentenced to 1,200 hours of community service. His convictions, however, were thrown out by the appeals court as violations of the congressional immunity agreement reached prior to his celebrated testimony before the select Iran-contra committee. In September 1991, all charges against North were finally dropped. Now — in his words —"exonerated," North was able to prosper financially from the proceeds of a bestselling book and his co-ownership of a Virginia security firm retailing bulletproof vests, as well as more than $10 million in public donations to his defense along the way. In 1994, the Republican Party selected the former marine as its nominee for the United States Senate in Virginia, a race he lost to the Democratic incumbent by a very slim margin. The following year, Ollie North became a radio talk show host for station WWRC, 980 AM, serving the greater Washington Beltway. The show's teaser bragged, "It's no lie — a shred of truth from Washington — your dial is set to true North."

Elliott Abrams, the boy wonder assistant secretary of state for inter-American affairs who twice changed his mind about the General before settling in as Noriega's most implacable foe inside the Reagan administration, was awarded the State Department's Distinguished Service Award by the secretary of state in August 1988. He also had to run the special prosecutor's gauntlet once he left government service, called to answer for the now infamous series of lies he told Congress over the course of the Nicawoggwha campaign. In October 1991, rather than stand trial for felony prevarication, Abrams finally pled guilty to two misdemeanor counts of withholding information from Congress and, on November 5, 1991, was sentenced to two years probation and community service, but never finished the sentence. On December 24, 1992, in the very last days of the George Bush presidency, Abrams and five others under sentence for their roles in the Iran-contra scandal received presidential pardons, because, President Bush explained, they "have already paid a price . . . grossly disproportionate to any misdeeds or errors of judgment they may have committed." Since this "exoneration," Abrams has moved around in the world of think tanks, serving as a fellow at the Hudson Institute, on the board of advisers of the Center for Security Policy, as a trustee at the Nicaraguan Resistance Education Foundation, and a member of the Council on Foreign Relations. In July 1996, Elliott Abrams was appointed to his current post as president of the Ethics and Public Policy Center.

Leon Kellner, the United States attorney for the Southern District of Florida whose backing was essential to the making of *United States v. Manuel Antonio Noriega* and who helped convince then Vice President George Bush to take a firm stand against cutting a deal with the General, returned to his private law practice in Washington, D.C., after resigning in Miami.

Ray Takiff, the General's lead counsel until his resignation on the day of the General's arrest, continued in his secret role as the undercover shill in a government sting of corrupt judges in Dade County until June 8, 1991, when the government filed charges against a half-dozen jurists and announced that Takiff had been secretly recording bribery sessions for the last year and a half. "On the tapes," the *Orlando Sentinel Tribune* reported, "[Takiff sounds like] a vulgar, bombastic, masterful liar who betrayed old and new friends during expensive dinners or clandestine meetings in parking lots. . . . [This role] was one in which Takiff excelled." After his service as government informant was over, Takiff returned to law practice, though banned in his plea agreement from doing so in Dade County and increasingly limited by his cardiac problems. After several more attacks, Takiff's heart eventually failed altogether and he died in the summer of 1998.

Frank Rubino, Ray Takiff's cocounsel who took over as lead attorney for the General's defense, surprised a lot of media observers with his adept, albeit unsuccessful, courtroom performance. The defense's subsequent appeals were nonetheless unsuccessful as well. Rubino's final courtroom appearance for the General came in December 1998, at a sentence reduction hearing before the original trial judge in the Miami federal courthouse annex. Among the witnesses Rubino called to testify on the General's behalf were the former ambassador to Panama and the CIA's former station chief there, the latter of whom went so far as to claim the General had received "a bad rap." Rubino urged the judge to reduce the General's original forty-year sentence to no more than fifteen, "for the good things he had done," claiming that it was "indisputable that General Noriega did furnish immeasurable help to the United States and was an asset to the United States." On March 4, 1999, the trial judge issued an order reducing the General's sentence to thirty years, citing the "disparity between the defendant's sentence and the sentences served by his coconspirators."

Danny Moritz, the DEA agent whose penetration of Floyd Carlton's smuggling conspiracy made *United States v. Manuel Antonio Noriega* possible, rotated through Cleveland, eventually did a tour at the Panama office after the invasion, and ended up in the DEA's local office for the District of Columbia, where he continues to serve.

Floyd Carlton, the General's old drinking buddy from Chiriqui and linchpin of Dick Gregorie's grand jury investigation, was paroled from the Federal Correctional Institution in Sandstone, Minnesota, to somewhere in south Florida. His wife, Maria, eventually left him for good and, after a lackluster performance on the stand at the General's trial, Floyd disappeared back into Witness Protection, where he continues to be maintained in a new identity by the United States Marshals Service.

The **Medellín Cartel**, with whom, thanks to the testimony of Floyd Carlton, the General was convicted of having conspired, has diminished as a factor in Colombian cocaine manufacturing and export over the last decade, supplanted by another cartel based in the city of Cali. Three of the

Medellín Cartel's six original members are now dead, all killed in shootouts of one sort or another with the Colombian police. Two others have reportedly "retired," and the remaining founder is being held in the high-security pavilion of the LaPicota prison in Bogatá, Colombia. The latter was recently quoted in the *New York Post* referring to the General as "that bandit." Though the cartel has been under indictment in the Southern District of Florida since 1984, none of the six founders has ever been extradited to the United States for trial.

The **Drug Enforcement Administration** changed its attitude toward *United States v. Manuel Antonio Noriega* almost instantly upon the General's arrest. Eventually, some forty agents were assigned to the investigation prior to the General's trial, and an internal history of the agency proudly described the case as "the most notorious drug trial in U.S. history." After the General's conviction, the agency changed its internal policies to require that any investigation of persons of political standing first be cleared by a committee of "supergrade" executives at DEA headquarters in Washington, thus ensuring that no case like the General's will ever be made again without the permission of the powers that be.

Dick Gregorie, the First Assistant United States Attorney who indicted both the cartel and the General, was never very comfortable in private practice. Once the General had been arrested, Gregorie made overtures to the U.S. Attorney's Office about coming back on as a special prosecutor for the case, but the U.S. attorney of the time instead issued written orders to his office that no one working on the Noriega prosecution was to have any contact whatsoever with the case's former prosecutor. Gregorie finally abandoned private practice in 1992, after the General's conviction, and secured a post with the Florida State Attorney's Office for Dade County. This turn as a state prosecutor led to an invitation from the next United States attorney to rejoin the staff for the Southern District of Florida as one of its elite senior prosecutors, where he remains today.

Steve Grilli, the DEA special agent who made *United States v. Manuel Antonio Noriega,* continued as its case agent through the General's trial and conviction. Afterward, Grilli was nominated for the prestigious Attorney General's Award for his leading role in the case. Much to Grilli's everlasting disgust, the honor was awarded instead to the Miami special agent in charge's personal choice for the award, the agent whom the SAC had selected to supervise the influx of DEA manpower to this investigation after the General's arrest. In 1995, in recognition of another international case that produced forty-one arrests, Grilli was promoted to GS-14 and transferred out of conspiracy investigations. Two years later, he was assigned to manage the DEA's Miami technical operations program, where he has been supervising the mechanics of the DEA's electronic intercept and surveillance operations. He and his wife Patti eventually divorced and both have since remarried. Steve plans to retire as soon as he becomes eligible in the year 2004 and doubts that he will ever be allowed to do another conspiracy case in the meantime. Grilli also expects to still be a GS-14 when he leaves the DEA.

General Manuel Antonio Noriega, once the de facto ruler of Panama, remains in Miami's Federal Correctional Institution off SW 137th Avenue out by the Metropolitan Zoo. Although one American secretary of state once estimated the General's wealth at $300 million, the United States government was never able to identify more than $20 million for purposes of confiscation. Noriega has reportedly become a born-again Christian during his imprisonment. In late September 1999, he was moved temporarily to the U.S. Medical Center for Federal Prisoners in Springfield, Missouri, for treatment of an illness his attorney, Frank Rubino, would only describe as "a bad flu." Whatever the ailment was, the General was returned to his Miami cell block for the tenth anniversary of his arrest and remains there today. With time off for good behavior, he is scheduled to be released in 2007, when, seventy-two years old, General Manuel Antonio Noriega will have been in American captivity for seventeen years, by far the longest such span for any prisoner of war in American history.

The War on Drugs continues to this day. According to a 1991 DEA estimate, the amount of cocaine being transshipped through the Republic of Panama and on to the United States — as well as the amount of illicit cash being hauled back the other way for laundering — equaled or exceeded pre-invasion levels within a year of the General's arrest, before his trial had even begun.

ACKNOWLEDGMENTS

The core of this book has been formed out of several dozen interviews with participants in and observers of these events, conducted during 1998, 1999, and 2000. In using quotes from those interviews, I have, in many cases, stitched together statements made to me by the same people at different times into single continuous quotations without, of course, altering their context or meaning.

For the original documents used in constructing this narrative, I have drawn heavily on the resources of the National Security Archive in Washington, D.C., the Congressional Information Service, and the published files of the Senate Subcommittee on Terrorism, Narcotics, and International Operations. That subcommittee's hearings and the joint hearings of the Senate Select Committee on Secret Military Assistance to Iran and the Nicaraguan Opposition and the House Select Committee to Investigate Covert Arms Transactions with Iran were also very helpful.

I was also greatly assisted by the work of a number of journalists who had explored this subject before I reached it. In particular, *Our Man in Panama* by John Dinges, *Panama* by Kevin Buckley, *Divorcing the Dictator* by Frederick Kempe, *The Case against the General* by Steve Albert, and *The Iran Contra Scandal* edited by Peter Kornbluh and Malcolm Byrne were invaluable in my research. As, of course, was *America's Prisoner* by Manuel Noriega and Peter Eisner. I also leaned heavily on the daily news coverage by the *New York Times* and *Washington Post* and the weekly coverage supplied by *Newsweek* and *Time,* as well as the reportage of a number of other publications.

In compiling and organizing this research a number of people assisted me with the legwork and drudgery accompanying any such project. My thanks to Aaron Padilla, Robert Zuber, Emma Brown, Jacqueline Pratt, Jesse Deeter, Peter Kornbluh, David Ramsey, Daniel Baum, and Elaine Harris. The necessary translation of documents into and out of Spanish was performed by Adele Negro and computer services were supplied by Peter Golitzen and Mark Kellor. I made extensive use of the Stanford University library system. As I traveled around the country collecting information, several generous souls provided me hospitality. My thanks to Alex Avery and Mike Jendrasak, Whit and Abby Fosburgh, Bill Forrester and Joan Anderman, Mr. and Mrs. John Train, and Helen Whitney. I was also blessed with a group of readers who reviewed my manuscripts and provided helpful advice: John Sullivan, Susan Abbott, Layton Borkan, Neil Reichline, Sim Van der Ryn, Elaine Hatfield, Dick Rapson, Cheri Forrester, Tom Nolan, and Elaine Harris. The legal review provided by Heather Kilpatrick and the copyediting of Mike Mattil were indispensable as well.

Perhaps the most thankless assistance afforded me was by Susan Abbott and Sophie Harris, who had to endure my often deranged presence while living with me through the throes of writing this book and all its attendant obsessions. Theirs was a sacrifice above and beyond the call of duty, for which I can only offer loving and abashed gratitude.

Finally, I owe a great debt to two wonderful women without whom this project would never have come to fruition. My agent, Kathy Robbins, held my hand as she has been doing for the better part of two decades and oversaw all the logistics, both financial and emotional, that made it possible for me to do the work required. And my publisher and editor, Sarah Crichton, provided the insight and guidance essential to making a narrative out of all this information and the encouragement, good will, and cheeriness that sustained me through the long months with no end in sight. I count myself very lucky to have them both in my life.

David Harris

INDEX